Wayne N. Outten is a member of the law firm of Lankenau Kovner & Bickford in New York City. His practice consists of general civil matters, including employment law, litigation, family law, and real estate. He is a member of numerous bar association and civil liberties committees concerning the rights of employees. Before entering private practice, he was an instructor at New York University School of Law and a law clerk for Senior United States District Judge Gus J. Solomon in Portland, Oregon. He is a graduate of New York University School of Law (J.D.) and of Drexel University (B.S.).

Noah A. Kinigstein attended Temple University Law School. He is a member of the New York bar and is in private practice in New York City where he specializes in workers' rights law. He has a monthly radio program on WBAI-Pacifica-FM on workers' rights.

Other Bantam Books in the series
Ask your bookseller for the books you have missed

QUANTITY PURCHASES

AN AMERICAN CIVIL LIBERTIES UNION HANDBOOK

THE RIGHTS OF EMPLOYEES

The Basic ACLU Guide to an Employee's Rights

Wayne N. Outten
with
Noah A. Kinigstein

General Editor of this series:
Norman Dorsen, President, ACLU

BANTAM BOOKS
TORONTO · NEW YORK · LONDON · SYDNEY

THE RIGHTS OF EMPLOYEES

*A Bantam Book / published by arrangement with
the American Civil Liberties Union*

Bantam edition / January 1984

ISBN 0-553-23656-3

Published simultaneously in the United States and Canada

*Bantam Books are published by Bantam Books, Inc. Its
trademark, consisting of the words "Bantam Books" and the
portrayal of a rooster, is Registered in U.S. Patent and Trademark Office and in other countries. Marca Registrada. Bantam Books, Inc., 666 Fifth Avenue, New York, New York
10103.*

PRINTED IN THE UNITED STATES OF AMERICA

O   0 9 8 7 6 5 4 3 2 1

Dedicated to
Ginny, Ross, and Sarah

Acknowledgments

A lot of people helped me with this book.

Noah A. Kinigstein and Paula Berg did a substantial amount of research and drafting on many chapters; without their help, this book would not have gotten done. Al Feliu did a fine job drafting the first three chapters. In addition, valuable contributions were made by the following persons on certain aspects of the book: Alexander P. Rosenberg, Gail Rosenblum, Philip Hoffman, Richard Adelman, Joel Giller, Steve Barrow, Josh Nessen, Peter Crispino, and Lisa Yee. Thanks to each of these people. For consistent support, I thank the firm of Lankenau Kovner & Bickford, and each of the attorneys and staff persons in it; special thanks to Mary Carlisle who typed many drafts of the manuscript with extraordinary cheerfulness.

Last, and most important, I thank my wife, Ginny, for her abiding support and encouragement throughout.

Wayne N. Outten

Contents

Preface

This guide sets forth your rights under the present law, and offers suggestions on how they can be protected. It is one of a continuing series of handbooks published in cooperation with the American Civil Liberties Union (ACLU).

Surrounding these publications is the hope that Americans, informed of their rights, will be encouraged to exercise them. Through their exercise, rights are given life. If they are rarely used, they may be forgotten and violations may become routine.

This guide offers no assurances that your rights will be respected. The laws may change and, in some of the subjects covered in these pages, they change quite rapidly. An effort has been made to note those parts of the law where movement is taking place, but it is not always possible to predict accurately when the law *will* change.

Even if the laws remain the same, their interpretations by courts and administrative officials often vary. In a federal system such as ours, there is a built-in problem of state and federal law, not to speak of the confusion between states. In addition, there are wide variations in the ways in which particular courts and administrative officials will interpret the same law at any given moment.

If you encounter what you consider to be a specific abuse of your rights, you should seek legal assistance. There are a number of agencies that may help you, among them, ACLU affiliate offices, but bear in mind that the ACLU is a limited-purpose organization. In many communities, there are federally funded legal service offices which provide assistance to persons who cannot afford the costs of legal representation. In general, the rights that the ACLU defends are freedom of inquiry and expression; due process of law; equal protection of the laws; and privacy. The authors in this series have discussed other rights (even though they sometimes fall outside ACLU's usual concern) in order to provide as much guidance as possible.

These books have been planned as guides for the people directly affected; therefore, the question and answer format. (In some areas there are more detailed works available for "experts.") These guides seek to raise the major issues and inform the nonspecialist of the basic law on the subject. The authors of these books are themselves specialists who understand the need for information at "street level."

If you encounter a specific legal problem in an area discussed in one of these handbooks, show the book to your attorney. Of course, he or she will not be able to rely exclusively on the handbook to provide you with adequate representation. But if your attorney hasn't had a great deal of experience in the specific area, the handbook can provide helpful suggestions on how to proceed.

Norman Dorsen, President
American Civil Liberties Union

The principal purpose of this handbook, as well as others in this series, is to inform individuals of their legal rights. The authors from time to time suggest what the law should be, but their personal views are not necessarily those of the ACLU. For the ACLU's position on the issues discussed in this handbook, the reader should write to Librarian, ACLU; 132 West 43rd Street, New York, NY 10036.

Introduction

This book is about your rights as an employee. About half the people in the United States work for someone else—for governments, large corporations, small businesses, institutions, individuals, etc. Yet most people know little about their employment rights. This book summarizes the most important of those rights.

The emphasis here is on private employees (that is, non-government employees). Another handbook in this series, *The Rights of Government Employees*, covers in detail rights that are peculiar to employees of federal, state, and local governments. Further, as referred to in appropriate places in this book, other handbooks in this series also discuss employment issues; those books are on racial minorities, women, older persons, union members, handicapped persons, gays, veterans, and privacy.

Part I covers the employment relationship generally. The first chapter provides a very brief overview of the historical, societal, and legal foundations of the relationship between employers and employees in the United States today. The next three chapters deal with the hiring process, discipline and discharge, and privacy in employment.

Part II discusses discrimination in employment. The first chapter of the part is on discrimination in general and covers matters that apply to more than one type of discrimination, such as complaint procedures, remedies, and affirmative action. Each of the remaining seven chapters discusses matters pertaining to a particular category of anti-discrimination laws: racial minorities, sex, religion, age, the handicapped, veterans, and sexual orientation.

Part III analyzes comprehensive laws that govern the employment relationship. The first chapter of the part covers labor-management relations, i.e., laws governing unions and collective bargaining. The next chapter discusses laws regulating occupational safety and health. The final chapter of the part covers matters affecting wages and hours; including, among other things, minimum wages, overtime, child labor, federal contractors, and payroll deductions.

Part IV addresses laws that provide a cushion for employees (and their families) who are no longer working due to retirement, disability, death, or involuntary unemployment. The chapters are on pensions, workers' compensation, social security, and unemployment insurance.

The laws discussed in this book are extensive and complex, and they often vary from state-to-state. For brevity and clarity, this book provides only an overview of your most significant rights. Some laws are not discussed at all, and many limitations and exceptions to laws are omitted. No attempt is made to discuss the laws of all the states. Also, the laws are constantly being changed and refined.

For these reasons, you should not base your actions solely on the contents of this book. Before you act, consult someone who can give you specific, current information about your situation; this may be, for example, a federal or state government official, a union representative, or an attorney experienced in the area.

Part I

The Employment Relationship

I

An Overview

The relationship between employers and employees in the United States today is the product of countless historical, societal, and legal factors that have made the relationship quite different from what it is in other countries, and quite different from what it was here fifty years—even ten years— ago. This chapter provides a brief overview of that relationship today, and some of the factors that have affected it. The subsequent chapters in this book discuss in detail specific questions you may have about your employment rights.

How is the employment relationship formed?

The employment relationship is contractual by nature, that is to say, it is an agreement between two people, or a person and an organization such as a government agency or corporation. The contract need not be written—it can be oral— nor need all the terms and conditions of employment be express. For example, one who accepts a position as a teacher may expect that he or she will be required to prepare lectures and grade exams. These terms will be implied even if they were not expressly agreed upon.

To be an employee, you must agree to perform a service for wages or other remuneration. A son's agreement to clean his room at the urging of his father fails to rise to the level of an employment agreement, but his agreement to work for a bank as a teller at the minimum wage would constitute an enforceable employment contract. The bank, by agreeing to pay the young man wages, becomes his employer and as such has the right to define and supervise his daily activities.

Would I be in a better position as an employee if my employment contract were in writing?

Probably. Employers are generally in a stronger position than their employees and have more options when difficult times arrive. When business is good, management has little difficulty meeting its obligations to its employees. When under pressure, however, management may try to modify earlier promises made to its workers, or may even renege on its obligations completely. If your employer fails to meet the terms of an enforceable employment contract, you may sue for breach of the contract. You are in a much better position if you can present to the court a written contract spelling out the terms violated. Otherwise, if the agreement was oral, it becomes a question of whom the court believes. For example, suppose you were told at a pre-employment interview that you are entitled to three weeks vacation a year, but you discover months later that you will be allowed only two weeks. Your employer would be hard-pressed to convince a court that the three weeks vacation it promised in writing was not enforceable.

Can I hold my employer to the terms of the employee personnel policy handbook handed to me when I began this job?

Traditionally, courts have said no, but that appears to be changing. The policies announced in an employee handbook are unilaterally established—employees rarely have any say as to their breadth or implementation. The essence of an enforceable contract is that the terms must be bargained for by the parties. In the past, courts, relying on this principle, have refused to hold employers to promises made in employee handbooks. The reasons given by those courts include: the policy was unilaterally promulgated; the handbook contained no specific reference to the employee, or to his or her particular job duties or compensation; and the employers' ability to alter the terms of the policies without consulting employees suggested that the terms were not contractual.

In recent years, however, courts have evidenced a greater willingness to require employers to abide by provisions appearing in employee handbooks. In a growing number of states, courts have concluded that certain significant provisions in an employee handbook—for example, a promise that employees will be discharged only for "just cause"—are a binding on the employer. These courts reason that the employer benefits from including these provisions in the handbook by creating a more favorable image of itself and by fostering good employee morale.

What if I have no oral employment contract and no employee handbook exists?

Then you are an employee solely at the will of your employer. Management can decide the terms and conditions of your employment and when your employment may be terminated, as long as it stays within the bounds of fair labor standards and anti-discrimination laws, which are discussed later in this book.

What difference does it make if I am a member of a union?

A great deal. Your rights against management are greatly enhanced by being a union member. As a single employee, your leverage against management is minimal. As part of a union, however, you surrender your rights to the entity—the union—and the collective rights of the members balance the authority of management, in theory, Federal law assures employees the right to organize and to bargain collectively with management through chosen representatives. These representatives sit down with management and periodically negotiate the terms of a collective bargaining agreement. That agreement is, in effect, a shared employment contract.

The rights and obligations appearing in it apply to all employees, union and non-union, working in that unit. When an employee has a dispute with management, he or she must raise the matter first with the union, which, if it feels the claim has merit, will pursue it through the grievance procedures established in the agreement. For example, most collective bargaining agreements establish a "just cause" standard for dismissal. If a dismissed employee challenges the discharge, the union may require that the employer demonstrate just cause for that action.

In contrast, non-union, private sector employees—the vast majority of U.S. workers—are for the most part subject to the unreviewable discretion of their employers when personnel decisions are involved.

Is it that way in other industrial nations?

No. All of the other major Western industrial countries, and many developing countries, provide all workers—union and non-union—with statutory protection against unjust dismissal. The only requirement is that the employee complete a probationary period, the length of which varies. A typical unjust dismissal law requires that the employer give advance notice for ordinary dismissals. Failure to do so may have severe consequences. For example, in Italy, failure to give adequate notice may result in the awarding of 12 months' pay to the dismissed employee, in addition to the normal termination allowance. Unjust dismissal laws also typically provide that disputes be resolved by a special tribunal or labor court established specifically for the purpose. Such tribunals are empowered to award money damages, and, in some countries (e.g., England), can order reinstatement of an unfairly dismissed employee.

At the core of each of these statutes is the requirement that the dismissal of any non-probationary employee be "fair" or not "socially unwarranted." The burden of demonstrating the fairness of the dismissal varies. For example, England and West Germany require an employer to prove the "fairness" or "reasonableness" of the dismissal. France, in contrast, places the burden on the employee to establish unfairness. If the dismissal is determined to be unfair, the employer is required to pay the employee damages based on the employee's salary, position, and years of service.

As stated before, the United States has no equivalent to an unjust dismissal law. Union members, if their collective bargaining agreement so provides, may be fired only if "just cause" exists. Civil servants and tenured employees have similar job security. All other employees, unless their employment contracts so provide, can be discharged without cause. Employees in the United States who are dismissed without cause generally are entitled to unemployment compensation, which partly offsets lost wages for a while (see Chapter 19).

Why do the rights of private employees in the United States differ so substantially from their counterparts in other Western industrial nations?

Employment law in Britain grew out of the medieval master-servant relationship, which in turn evolved from the status and class concepts inhering in the feudal lord-vassal relationship. Your rights and obligations were determined by the class into which you were born. Following the bubonic plague that killed one-quarter of Europe's population in the 14th century, the landed class sought to secure a class of servants to tend to their needs. Certain classes of individuals were required to accept employment, and the rule developed that the hiring of a servant was assumed to be a hiring for a year. This assured the master an employee's services for that period. In turn, the master agreed to dismiss the employee only for good cause, and to provide four months' notice before terminating the relationship at the end of the one-year period. Master-servant law was codified by Parliament by the enactment of the Statute of Labourers in 1562.

American courts at first abided by these doctrines, shorn of their medieval class-related basis. In particular, American courts treated a hiring for an indefinite period as an agreement to work for one year. By the end of the 19th century, however, employment for an indefinite period was treated as one purely at the will of the parties—either party could sever the relationship without penalty. Even the requirement that the employer give proper notice of a termination, which dated back centuries, was rejected.

Were constitutional principles the basis for this unique American approach?

Not really. The Constitution applies only to government interference with the rights enumerated in the Constitution and the Bill of Rights. The Constitution does not, for the most part, restrict private behavior, and the employment relationship, apart from government service, is inherently private. For example, under the First Amendment the police cannot prevent you from making a speech on a street corner in support of a presidential candidate, but your employer can prohibit the same speech if it is delivered on the shop floor. A private employer is not bound by the First Amendment when a speech is made on its property. An employer may even use, as the basis for a personnel decision, employee speech or activities that are unrelated to company matters and that take place off-hours away from company property.

In contrast, public employees may seek the protection of the Constitution if their employer, a governmental body, acts arbitrarily or in violation of a fundamental right. Any government personnel action or regulation must bear a rational

relationship to a legitimate governmental interest to be
sustained. For example, promotion decisions must be based
on job-related criteria and not extraneous matters. Further,
the decision to discharge a public employee may not be made
in an arbitrary or capricious manner. For example, habitual
tardiness is a permissible basis for discharge, while variant
taste in music is not. Public employees are also entitled to
notice of termination and a hearing on its validity. Private
employees may not demand any of these privileges of public
employment on the basis of the Constitution.

**What is the justification for this distinction between public
and private employment?**

Some commentators argue that this distinction denies private employees equal protection under the law. Nevertheless,
two basic arguments support the theory of the dual system, if
not its unequal results. First (and most likely to be heard
from private employers) is the traditional liberty of contract
argument: the free enterprise system depends on the inde-
pendence and diversity of its component parts, and restricting management's ability to decide, unencumbered by
government restrictions, what is in its best interest will dampen
the vitality of the free enterprise system. The second argument in support of distinguishing public and private employment is based on the proposition that our government was
established as one with limited powers: while the government
must act reasonably and with restraint toward its citizens,
neither the Founding Fathers nor later generations of Americans have sought to place the same overarching demand of
reasonableness and equity on citizens acting in a private
capacity.

Are there any indications that this may change?

There are signs of a general shift in attitudes. The view that
parties to an agreement should set its terms and conditions,
which underlies much of employment law, is tenable only
when the two parties are in relatively equal positions. If
parties are in substantially unequal positions, limitations may
have to be placed on the authority of the stronger party. For
example, Congress, state legislatures, and the courts have
restricted the conditions and terms retailers may impose on
consumers in the typical retail sale agreement. In much the
same way, our society has sought to limit employer preroga-

tives so as to minimize the abuses that may result from the unequal bargaining position of labor and management. For example, employers are required to pay minimum wages even though workers would accept less; employers are required to provide a safe workplace, though for generations employees toiled in sweatshops; employers are prohibited from acting in a discriminatory fashion, using race, sex, religion, etc., as a basis for employment decisions.

What prompted this change in attitude?

No single cause can be identified, but this movement toward greater employee rights is part of a larger movement toward greater individual rights generally. Two significant forces are at play here. First, Americans in general and employees as a class are more demanding and assertive than preceding generations, and are less willing to tolerate social inequities. A more educated citizenry—as ours has become—tends also to be more critical when expectations are not met. Some social commentators have argued that Americans have adopted a "psychology of entitlement"—the feeling that one has the right to what one deserves or needs—that underlies the demands for new and broader rights. Second, our government has been increasingly willing, since the New Deal, to take a more active role in regulating private activity that in some way violates public policy or accepted norms. These two forces have combined to make the demands for new rights and protections stronger and more frequent.

Will American workers demand a greater role in the exercise of corporate power?

For the most part, American workers have left to their employers the full authority to manage their organizations, without demanding a role for themselves in the process. Labor unions influence corporate behavior through the collective bargaining process, but that influence is indirect and is secondary to the basic economic concerns of the employees. In response to worker dissatisfaction and decreasing productivity, however, some companies have experimented with employee participation in corporate decision making, particularly in decisions that affect the nature of their employees' work. Among the formats tried are quality control circles, profit-sharing and participative management, employee ownership of enterprises, and quality-of-worklife programs.

Nonetheless, worker participation on the broad, corporate-wide or industry-wide scale practiced in Western Europe, particularly West Germany and Sweden, has yet to characterize American employment relations, and is not likely to do so in the near future. In Western Europe, employees often sit on the board of directors and participate as full partners in formulating company policies and activities. American experiments in cooperative decision making, where they exist, tend to be limited in the range of the issues covered and responsibilities shared, and in the breadth of employee participation.

What role does the law play in creating and protecting rights for employees?

The legislative branch and, to a lesser extent, the courts can impose on the parties to an employment agreement rights and obligations apart from those expressly agreed upon, and the courts and regulatory agencies are often empowered to oversee their implementation. The role of the law in employment relations has become more intrusive in five distinct areas: (1) providing economic protection to employees through minimum wage/maximum hours laws, pension plan oversight, etc.; (2) barring or restricting discrimination on the basis of race, sex, age, handicap, national origin, and in some states, on the basis of marital status, sexual preference, and other classifications; (3) seeking to ensure a safe and healthful workplace; (4) recognizing and protecting employee privacy rights; and (5) seeking to mandate fairness by, for example, recognizing the right to a hearing in discharge and disciplinary matters involving public employees, upholding the primacy of grievance procedures established under collective bargaining agreements, and requiring disclosure of the identity of toxic chemicals in the workplace.

The responsibility to establish new legal rights lies primarily with Congress and state legislatures when broad legislative mandates are appropriate, for example, in forbidding certain discriminatory practices. In contrast, courts must take the initiative when interpretation of the Constitution is required (e.g., in the case of public employees) or when the right to sue under the common law is involved. Enforcement of recognized rights is the role of administrative agencies and the courts. For example, an employee who is discriminated against for having sought an inspection of a worksite by a federal Occupational Safety and Health Administration inspec-

tor may seek the assistance of the administrative agency and
may have the agency's action or inaction reviewed by a court.
Similarly, an employee claiming that his or her employer has
not lived up to the terms of the employment contract may
seek redress in court.

How has the role of the law in the employment relationship changed in recent years?

Elected officials and judges generally are less willing today
to defer to the judgments of employers when a public interest
is involved. In resolving employment disputes in the past, an
employer's interest in running its business profitably and
efficiently and in retaining the best personnel available was
weighed against the employee's interest in being treated
fairly and within legal bounds, and in retaining the job. In
recent years courts have added the public interest to the
analysis, recognizing that the general public has a significant
interest in encouraging labor stability and peace. For example,
employment decisions based on activities outside the workplace
are receiving increased scrutiny from legal authorities.
Nonetheless, employer prerogatives remain significant, and
as long as recognized public policies are not violated, employers remain masters of their own businesses.

What role will the law play in coming years in redefining the rights and obligations of employers and employees?

The law continues to reflect—if not anticipate—changes in
attitudes and norms. Employers can expect further limitations on management's decisional autonomy—coming perhaps at a slower pace—but can also look forward to receiving
a more respectful hearing for their arguments in defense. For
example, the Supreme Court recently upheld an employer's
right to refuse a union request to divulge employee test
scores on the ground that to do so would violate privacy
interests. In turn, employees can anticipate increased concern for their rights in the workplace, but should also expect
prompt dismissal of frivolous or abusive claims.

Ultimately it is not the law, with its procedural roadblocks
and tedious pace, but the attitudes and approaches of people
toward the employment relationship that will most influence
policies, practices, and behavior in the workplace. The law
has imposed external obligations on the relationship between
employers and employees in response to changed societal

norms and the failure of employers to respond promptly enough to such changes. But the law is too cumbersome to govern day-to-day behavior. Instead, the law stands as a guide for behavior and as a haven for the mistreated. In the final analysis, the rights available to private employees will be determined by the vigor with which those rights are sought and by the receptivity of employers to their employees' concerns.

II

The Hiring Process

Getting a job is probably the most important subject in a book on employment rights. Without a job, many of the other subjects are academic. This chapter provides an overview of the hiring process; many of the topics are discussed in greater detail in subsequent chapters. For example, Chapter 4, "privacy," discusses employment issues that often occur at the hiring stage (such as polygraph tests and fingerprinting), and Chapters 5–12 cover discrimination in employment, including discrimination during the hiring process.

Can an employer refuse to hire for any reason?

No. Although employers have wide discretion in hiring, a hiring decision may not be intentionally discriminatory against a protected group of workers, nor may it be based on policies or practices having the effect of disproportionately excluding such protected workers from consideration.[1] Improper bases for hiring decisions under federal law include an applicant's race, color, religion, sex, national origin, and (under certain circumstances) age.[2] Companies doing a significant amount of business with the federal government may also be barred from discriminating against applicants on the basis of handicap.[3] In some states, it is unlawful to discriminate on the basis of an applicant's sexual orientation,[4] physical or mental disabilities,[5] arrest record,[6] political affiliation,[7] marital status,[8] color blindness,[9] unfavorable military discharge,[10] alien status,[11] or sickle-cell trait.[12] An employer is not required, however, to hire a minority or female applicant, for example, whenever the applicant's qualifications are equal to those of a white male applicant; the employer may choose among equally qualified applicants, so long as unlawful criteria are not used.[13]

What can a prospective employer ask on a job application form or at a job interview?

Prospective employers may ask almost anything without necessarily violating the law. If you choose not to answer a question that you find offensive, the prospective employer may, as a result, decide not to hire you. Nonetheless, pre-employment inquiries that directly or indirectly reveal your race, color, sex, age, religion, or national origin may be treated as strong evidence of unlawful discrimination if you do not get the job and you fall within a protected class.[14] As a result, employers are encouraged *not* to inquire into non-job-related matters such as age, citizenship, marital status, number of children, friends or relatives working for the company, arrest and conviction records, credit rating, terms of military discharge, and availability for work on weekends and holidays. The Equal Employment Opportunity Commission (EEOC), which has enforcement authority in this area, has determined that inquiries into otherwise improper areas are not unlawful if made in compliance with fair employment practice laws and approved by the government agencies having authority to administer those laws.[15]

Pre-employment inquiries are designed to select from an applicant pool those individuals who meet the job specifications for a vacant position and, to the extent possible, attempt to predict which applicants will become successful employees. Although information gathered at the pre-employment stage is used primarily to screen applicants, application forms and notes from job interviews are often retained and become part of an employee's personnel file. There is strong evidence that pre-employment inquiries have served in the past to limit or deny job opportunities for women, older workers, and members of minority groups.[16] For this reason, the EEOC has issued a "Guide to Pre-Employment Inquiries"[17] which seeks to limit the disproportionate impact that such non-job-related inquiries have on protected groups, by coaching employers on what may properly be asked of applicants. Similar publications are issued by state authorities.[18]

To withstand challenge, a pre-employment inquiry that excludes members of a protected class must be job-related and justifiable under a "business necessity" standard.[19] Courts strictly review claims of business necessity where discrimination has been shown to exist.[20] To be upheld, an inquiry, policy, or practice with a disparate impact on a protected class must be shown to be (1) necessary for the safe and efficient operation of the business; (2) effective in achieving this; and (3) the least discriminatory alternative available.[21] Employers choosing to perform a technical validation study can often demonstrate statistically that a pre-employment inquiry or selection procedure is job-related, even though it has a disparate effect on protected groups. If the employer does not perform such a study, it may be vulnerable in a suit alleging discriminatory practices.[22]

If you are a member of a minority group, a woman, or an older worker, and you believe you were denied a job because of an improper pre-employment inquiry, you may want to contact the EEOC or an equivalent state agency for advice on how to proceed.[23] If you are considering charging the employer with discrimination in court, you should first consider (1) whether you were qualified for the position sought; (2) whether that position went to someone less qualified or remained vacant for a period after your rejection; and (3) whether a legitimate, non-discriminatory reason existed for the denial of employment.

During a job interview, can I refuse to answer a question I think is improper or not "job-related"?

Yes, but it may cost you the job. If you are inclined to present a legal challenge to the question, you should answer truthfully; later, if you are denied the position because of your answer, you can have the improper question investigated. Some choose not to tell the truth under these circumstances, but an untrue answer to a pre-employment question may be sufficient grounds for later discipline or discharge.[24] It may be wise to inquire first into the relevance of the question and, before answering, express your opinion that the question may be illegal. If the employer insists on an answer, you must decide whether or not to comply based on your needs, the attractiveness of the job, the strength of your objection to the question, and the extent to which you feel your answer will be used in a discriminatory fashion.

Remember, though, the mere asking of an improper question does not in itself give you grounds to challenge a denial of employment; [25] either the employer must deny you the position for a discriminatory reason, or members of a protected class of which you are a member must be underrepresented in the employer's workforce without a legitimate business reason. Courts will assume, however, that all questions on an application form or in a pre-employment interview are relevant and had an impact on the hiring decision. After a bona fide charge of discrimination is lodged, the employer must articulate a legitimate, non-discriminatory reason for the hiring decision and must show that the hiring decision was not affected by the answers to the challenged questions.[26] Therefore, though an employer may ask "improper" questions, it invites problems by doing so.

Can you give some examples of proper and improper questions?

Sure. A prospective employer may not properly ask your race (unless given permission by a government agency as part of an affirmative action program), or the color of your skin, hair, or eyes, but it may ask about distinguishing physical characteristics for identification purposes.[27] An employer may ask your sex only when a bona fide occupational qualification ("BFOQ") exists.[28] The employer has the burden of demonstrating that a BFOQ exists and that all members of the excluded class are unable to satisfy the job requirements. For example, gender is a BFOQ for a job modeling bathing suits, but not for a job involving heavy physical labor.[29] An employer may not ask age or date of birth before hiring, but may require proof that you are not below the minimum legal working age.[30] (The Age Discrimination in Employment Act of 1967 bars discrimination against persons between 40 and 70 years of age.) Once hired, however, you may be required to supply proof of age. An employer may not discriminate on the basis of national origin; thus, an inquiry into your birthplace may be unlawful, if you were denied a job on that basis.[31] An employer can refuse to hire an alien, however, and may therefore ask whether you are a United States citizen.[32]

An employer may not ask about your religious beliefs or affiliations, but may inform you of normal work hours so as to avoid potential conflicts with religious obligations.[33] Nonetheless, employers must make "reasonable accommodations" for the religious practices of employees, unless undue hardship to the efficient running of the business can be shown.[34] In jurisdictions that prohibit job discrimination on the basis of marital status, employers may not ask your marital status, but they may ask whether you have outside commitments or responsibilities that may hinder your meeting work schedules. Also, an employer cannot require that you supply names and addresses of relatives, but may ask you for the names and addresses of any relatives already employed by that employer.[35]

Can an employer request that I submit a photograph with my job application?
Probably not. This practice could later be deemed unlawful if a disproportionate number of minority workers, women, or workers over 40 years of age are excluded from the employer's workforce. After hiring, you may be required to submit a photograph for identification purposes.

Must I give my Social Security number?
Yes. Nothing prohibits an employer or prospective employer from asking for or using your Social Security number at any time. On the other hand, no law requires that you disclose your Social Security number, except that *after* employment your employer must have it to provide tax and salary information to income tax authorities. In other words, before employment, you need not supply the number, but the prospective employer may not consider your job application as a result.

Can an employer ask about my credit rating?
Probably not. Because a larger percentage of non-whites than whites are below the poverty level, the EEOC has determined that rejecting applicants who have poor credit ratings produces disproportionate denial of jobs to non-whites. As a result, the EEOC has prohibited asking for information on credit ratings unless the employer can demonstrate a "business necessity."[36] For similar reasons, questions about your financial status (for example, ownership of a car or house, or prior bankruptcies or garnishments) violate the law if they are used in making an employment decision.[37]

Can an employer ask about arrests or convictions?
Sometimes. Questions about arrests and convictions raise two separate issues: discrimination against minority applicants, and considerations of privacy and fairness.

Discrimination

An employer's use of arrest and conviction records may have a discriminatory impact. Because minority group workers are statistically more likely to have criminal records than are whites, the use of such criteria tends to disqualify minority job applicants at a disproportionately high rate.

For that reason, an employer generally may not ask you about arrests, or use any information about arrests in making an employment decision.[38] The EEOC has determined that simply asking for such information unduly inhibits minority job applicants. Nonetheless, an employer may ask you about arrests if it can show that making an employment decision on the basis of arrest information is essential to the safe and efficient operation of the business. In one case, an employer withdrew a job offer for a sheet metal mechanic upon learning that the applicant had fourteen arrests, though no convictions; the court found the employer's action unlawful because it could show no business necessity for its practice.[39]

An employer generally may ask you about convictions. While *blanket* refusal to hire anyone with a conviction violates Title VII,[40] an employer may consider convictions in making *individual* hiring decisions. In doing so, the employer must be able to show that the conviction substantially detracts from your fitness to perform a particular job.[41] Factors to be considered in making this determination include the number of convictions, the nature of the offense or offenses, when they occurred, your age at the time, and the extent of your rehabilitation.[42] For example, a court found that an employer had not violated Title VII by firing a black hotel employee upon learning that the employee had been convicted of theft. The court held it permissible for the hotel to require that persons employed in positions involving access to the property of hotel guests must be "reasonably free" from convictions.[43]

Privacy and Fairness

The significance of an arrest that does not result in a conviction is questionable. Accordingly, several states—for example, California, Connecticut, Hawaii, Illinois, Maryland, Massachusetts, Michigan, Missouri, Minnesota, New York,

Ohio, Oregon, and Virginia[44]—restrict employer acquisition and storage of information about your prior arrests. Some of the statutes (e.g., New York and California) prohibit an employer from asking about or using any information about an arrest that did not result in a conviction. Some statutes require that you have taken action within a certain period of time to expunge the arrest record; in others, you need not take any action. Some statutes even authorize you to say that you have no arrest record in certain circumstances. Connecticut requires that any arrest record information be viewed only by the employer's personnel office. Michigan does not prohibit asking about arrests, but does require that such information be kept separate from other personnel records.

A few states even restrict the use of information about convictions. In New York, for example, an employer may ask about convictions, but may not penalize an ex-offender solely because of a conviction, unless (1) there is a direct relationship between the offense and the job sought, or (2) the applicant continues to pose an "unreasonable risk" to society.[45] A few states prohibit certain other kinds of inquiries: Maryland (psychiatric or psychological problems, unless they have direct bearing on fitness for the job); Massachusetts (treatment or institutionalization in a mental hospital); and Michigan (political associations or non-employment activities).[46]

Employers sometimes obtain information about applicants and employees from government sources. For example, criminal justice record systems that receive federal funds through the Law Enforcement Assistance Administration are permitted to disseminate conviction records to employers, though dissemination of arrest information is supposedly restricted.[47] Many states regulate storage of and access to criminal justice records, particularly regarding investigations and arrests.

Can a prospective employer require that I take a polygraph or psychological stress evaluator test?

In most states, yes. Polygraph and psychological stress evaluator examinations are used in the pre-employment screening process to check an applicant's honesty in answering questions, and to forecast the likelihood that the applicant will steal on the job, if hired.[48] The reliability of such tests is in serious doubt, and they raise serious privacy problems. For these reasons, about half of the states have either restricted the use of polygraphs[49] (and in a few instances, psychological stress evaluators)[50] in the employment context, or required that polygraph examiners be licensed.[51] For a more complete discussion of this subject, see Chapter 4.

Can I be required to give my height and weight on a job application form?

Not unless the employer can demonstrate that these factors are essential to the safe performance of the position being sought. For example, the Supreme Court ruled that Alabama's statute requiring that prison guards be at least five feet two inches tall and weigh at least 120 pounds was unlawful because the state failed to correlate this requirement with the strength needed to perform the job adequately.[52]

Can a potential employer ask about any handicaps I may have?

Sometimes. Most private employers can ask about mental or physical handicaps, can administer selection tests that screen out handicapped persons, and can decline to hire on the basis of handicap. There are two exceptions: (1) pursuant to the Rehabilitation Act of 1973,[53] an employer that has a contract with the federal government for more than $2500 or that receives federal financial assistance; and (2) an employer in a state having a law prohibiting discrimination on the basis of handicap. The rights of handicapped persons are discussed in greater detail in Chapter 10.

An employer subject to the Rehabilitation Act may "invite" you to reveal any handicap you may have. Compliance with this request is voluntary, however. The employer must indicate on the form or at the interview that employment opportunities will not be impaired by revealing any handicap, that the information will be kept confidential, and that the information is necessary to redress prior discrimination against the handicapped or to provide opportunities to the handicapped.[54]

If you are denied a position with an employer subject to the Rehabilitation Act because of a handicap, the employer must be able to demonstrate that "business necessity" and the safe performance of the job required the rejection. In general, such employers are required to make "reasonable accommodations" for your physical and mental limitations, unless to do so would "impose an undue hardship on the operation of its program.[55]

Can I be required to take a physical examination?

Yes. This is very often a standard part of the hiring process. Some employers require it before hiring, some after. If the position being sought is physically demanding, both you and the employer would want to know whether you are physically able to do the job. The employer should be careful, however, to ensure that the information gathered on you is used only in the hiring process and only to the extent that your ability to satisfy the job requirements is being assessed.[56] Pre-employment and post-employment physical examinations may also be used to establish a data base for conducting epidemiological studies and to establish a record of an employee's health for purposes of evaluating a subsequent workers' compensation claim.

Can genetic screening be used as a pre-employment test?

In most states yes, but that may change if it can be shown that such tests have a disproportionate impact on protected classes.[57] Only about one percent of the firms in the U.S. use genetic screening in the pre-employment stage, but it is predicted that this figure may rise to 16 percent in coming years.[58] Defenders of these tests contend that they help prevent occupational diseases by identifying workers who are unusually susceptible to certain occupational diseases. Those opposed argue that denying employment on the basis of genetic factors may have a disproportionate impact on selected racial and ethnic groups. The courts have yet to rule on these issues; when they do, the results will probably turn on whether the employer can demonstrate a BFOQ justifying such testing.

Do I get any preference if I am a veteran?

Yes, for jobs with companies that do significant business with the government. For a full discussion of preferences for veterans, see Chapter 11.

Can I be required to be a union member to get a job?

No. A "closed shop," in which only union members can be hired, is illegal. But you may be required to join a union soon after you start work. For a fuller discussion of when you may be required to join a union or to pay union dues, see Chapter 13.

Can I challenge an unfair pre-employment test?

Yes, if the test has the effect of discriminating on the basis of race, sex, national origin, or other proscribed grounds. An underlying aim of government efforts to eliminate employment discrimination is to reduce the influence of subjective factors on employment decisions; job applicants should be judged on their qualifications and not on unrelated criteria such as race, appearances, personal qualities, or beliefs. Pre-employment tests, if properly drafted and administered, can increase the likelihood that hiring decisions will be based on objective factors.

Unfortunately, some tests improperly screen out a disproportionate number of women and minority applicants. Such tests have been and are being successfully challenged in court when they are not job-related. For example, a test that favors candidates with a strong background in mathematics would be vulnerable if the presence of such a background is not job-related. On the other hand, tests that do not disproportionately exclude members of a protected class will survive legal challenge. If a pre-employment test has an adverse impact on a protected group, the employer may eliminate, modify, or replace the exam, or may seek to have it "validated" as prescribed by law. The validation process, done by professional testing services, is designed to review the test for its ability to predict and measure the job success of applicants.[59] (Test validation is discussed in Chapter 6.)

Are employment agencies bound by anti-discrimination laws?

Yes. Federal laws prohibiting discrimination on the basis of race, national origin, color, religion, and sex apply to every public or private employment agency that procures employees for an employer, or that provides job opportunities for applicants, if the relationship with the employer is ongoing, and if the employer has 15 or more employees and is in an industry affecting commerce.[60] Similar standards apply under the federal law against age discrimination, with some minor differences: one or more employers for whom employees are procured must be engaged in an industry affecting commerce and have 20 or more employees; federal government employment agencies are not covered; and agencies that help employees find jobs probably are not covered.[61]

Under what circumstances can an employment agency be found to have violated anti-discrimination laws?

An employment agency may be found to have engaged in unlawful activities if it discriminates against, fails to refer for employment, or otherwise classifies a person based on race, sex, color, religion, national origin, or age (when the person is between the ages of 40 and 70).[62] Also, agencies that deal with only one sex (unless sex is a BFOQ), or that provide information concerning the ages of prospective employees, may be found to have violated anti-discrimination laws.[63] Finally, an agency that seeks to satisfy a job order that it knows is illegal (for example, one requesting a young, white male for a particular position) shares responsibility for any illegal act that results from its referral of applicants.[64]

What restrictions are there on a potential employer's ability to check any reference I provide?

There are few legal restrictions on the ability of an employer to check references, or on the methods used. Often, a prospective employer will ask an applicant to sign a form authorizing the employer to request information on the applicant's employment and educational background. Many schools and prior employers will refuse to divulge such information without such a signed authorization. Employers may not, however, use references to gain information indirectly that the law bars them from receiving directly from the applicant. For example, a prospective employer may not seek information about an applicant's creditworthiness from a former employer if that inquiry would be improper on a job application form or in a pre-employment interview.

Can I do anything about bad references from former employers?

In general, prospective employers are entitled to contact an applicant's former employers to verify information given during the application process and to request any job-related information or opinions. Any reference that is not intentionally inaccurate or libelous is qualifiedly privileged and not subject to legal challenge. But if the reference is intentionally inaccurate and it injures your employment possibilities, you may have a remedy, if you can show that the statements made by the former employer constitute libel or slander.[65] Employees are seldom able to demonstrate that the former employer exceeded the bounds of the qualified privilege and rarely prevail in such legal challenges. Nonetheless, seven states (California, Connecticut, Indiana, Kansas, Missouri, Montana, and Nevada) specifically allow by statute suits against former employers who give intentionally inaccurate employment references.[66]

In general, how should I prepare to protect my rights during the hiring process?

First, try to find out as much as possible about the duties of the job for which you are applying and the skills needed to perform them successfully. This will permit you to spot improper, non-job-related inquiries more easily. Second, check the law in your state to see whether a prospective employer may request or require that you take a polygraph or voice stress evaluator exam as part of the hiring process (see Chapter 4). Finally, carefully assess your needs, how important the position is to you, and how far you would be willing to challenge questionable pre-employment inquiries and practices.

NOTES

1. *Griggs v. Duke Power Co.*, 401 U.S. 424 (1971).
2. 42 U.S.C. §§2000e *et seq.*; 29 U.S.C. §§621 *et seq.*
3. Vocational Rehabilitation Act of 1973, 29 U.S.C. §§701 *et seq.*
4. Wisc. Stat. Ann. §111.32(5).
5. For a complete listing of state laws *see* 8 Fair. Empl. Prac. Manual (BNA) 499:504. [Fair Empl. Prac. hereinafter cited as F.E.P.]
6. *E.g.*, 31 Conn. Gen. Stat. 557:31–511. For a complete listing of state laws, *see* 8 F.E.P. Manual (BNA) 499:502.
7. *E.g.*, Cal. Lab. Code §1102.
8. *E.g.*, N.H. Rev. Stat. Ann 31:354–A; N.Y. Exec. Law §296.
9. *E.g.*, Cal. Government Code art. 2, chap. 10, §19701, in 8A F.E.P. Manual (BNA) 453:836.
10. *E.g.*, Illinois Fair Employment Practices Commission, "Guidelines on Discrimination in Employment," art. VI, in 8A F.E.P. Manual (BNA) 453:2757.
11. *E.g.*, Mass. Gen. Laws. Ann. chap. 149, §19C.
12. *E.g.*, Fla. Stat. Ann. chap. 448, §075.
13. *Tex. Dept. of Community Affairs v. Burdine*, 450 U.S. 248 (1981).
14. *Albermarle Paper Co. v. Moody*, 422 U.S. 405 (1975).
15. "EEOC Guide to Pre-Employment Inquiries," 8 F.E.P. (BNA)

15. 443:65; 2 E.P.G. (CCH) ¶4120 at 2251–42 [hereinafter referred to *EEOC Guide*]. *See also EEOC Decision* No. 75-S-068, Nov. 14, 1974.
16. *EEOC Guide*, 8A F.E.P. Manual 443:65; 2 E.P.G. ¶4120 at 2251-42.
17. 8A F.E.P. Manual (BNA) 443:65; 2 E.P.G. (CCH) ¶4210 at 2251–42.
18. *E.g.*, Ohio Civil Rights Commission's "Guide for Application Forms and Interviews," in 8A F.E.P. Manual (BNA) 457:325
19. *Griggs v. Duke Power Co.*, *supra*.
20. *EEOC Guide*, 8A F.E.P. Manual (BNA) 443:65; 2 E.P.G. (CCH) ¶4120 at 2251–42.
21. *Chrisner v. Complete Auto Transit, Inc.*, 645 F. 2d 1251 (6th Cir. 1981).
22. *EEOC Guide*, 8A F.E.P. Manual (BNA) 443:65; 2 E.P.G. (CCH) ¶4120 at 2251–42.
23. For a listing of federal and state agencies that enforce fair employment practice laws, see F.E.P. (BNA) 451.201.
24. *Adams v. Tex. & Pacific Motor Transport Co.*, 408 F. Supp. 156 (D. La. 1975).
25. *EEOC Guide*, 8A F.E.P. (BNA) 443:65; 2 E.P.G. (CCH) ¶4120 at 2251–43.
26. *McDonnell Douglas Corp. v. Green*, 411 U.S. 792 (1973).
27. *E.g.*, Hawaii's Department of Labor and Industrial Relations, "Pre-employment Inquiry Guide," in 8A F.E.P. Manual (BNA) 453:2337 *et seq*.
28. *E.g.*, West Virginia's Human Rights Commission, "Pre-employment and Inquiry Guide," in 8A F.E.P. (BNA) 457:3075.
29. *Gunther v. Iowa State Men's Reformatory*, 612 F.2d 1079 (8th Cir.), *cert. denied*, 446 U.S. 966 (1980).
30. *Backus v. Baptist Medical Center*, 510 F. Supp. 1191 (E.D. Ark. 1981).
31. *E.g.*, New Jersey's Division on Civil Rights, "Pre-employment Inquiries," guide in 8A F.E.P. Manual (BNA) 455:2731.
32. *E.g.*, Missouri's Commission on Human Rights, "Guide for Pre-employment Inquiries," in 8A F.E.P. Manual (BNA) 455:5121.
33. *Espinoza v. Farah Mfg. Co., Inc.*, 414 U.S. 86 (1973).
34. 42 U.S.C. §2000e(j).
35. *Local 53 v. Volger*, 407 F.2d 1047 (5th Cir. 1969).
36. *EEOC Guide*, 8A F.E.P. Manual (BNA) 443:68; 2 E.P.G. (CCH) ¶4120 at 2251–44.
37. *Id*.
38. *See Gregory v. Litton Systems, Inc.*, 316 F. Supp. 401 (C.D. Cal. 1970), *aff'd as modified*, 472 F.2d 631 (9th Cir. 1972).
39. *Id*.
40. *Green v. Mo. Pacific Railroad Co.*, 523 F.2d 1290 (8th Cir. 1975).
41. *Id*.
42. *EEOC Guide*, 18A F.E.P. (BNA) Manual 443:67; 2 E.P.G. (CCH) ¶4120 at 2251–54.
43. *Richardson v. Hotel Corp. of America*, 332 F. Supp. 519 (E.D. La. 1971), *aff'd*, 486 F.2d 951 (5th Cir. 1972).

44. Cal. Lab. Code §§432.7 and 432.8; Conn. Gen. Stat. Ann. Appendix Pamphlet 1980; Hawaii Rev. Stat. 731–3.1; Ill. Rev. Stat. tit. 68 §2–104; Md. Ann. Code art. 27, §§292; Mass. Gen. Laws Ann. chap. 1513 §4, ¶9; Mich. Comp. Laws Ann. §423.501; Minn. Stat. Ann. §364.04; Mo. Ann. Stat. §610.100; N.Y. Exec. Law §296.16; Ohio Rev. Code Ann. tit. 21 §2151.358; Or. Rev. Stat. §652–750; and Va. Code §§19.2–392.4(a) and (c).

45. N.Y. Exec. Law §296.15.

46. Md. Ann. Code art. 100, §95A; Mass. Ann. Laws chap. 151B, §4; Mich. Comp. Law Ann. §§423.501 *et. seq.*

47. 42 U.S.C. §3771; 28 C.F.R. 1.

48. *See* ABA, *Labor and Employment Law*, 1982 Committee Reports, "Laws of Individual Rights in the Workplace," vol. II, p. 9.

49. For a complete list, *see* 8A F.E.P. (BNA) 499:505.

50. *E.g.*, Pa. Cons. Stat. 18:7507.

51. Ariz. Rev. Stat. §32–2701 (1981).

52. *Dothard v. Rawlinson*, 433 U.S. 321 (1977).

53. 29 U.S.C. §§701 *et seq.*

54. *Id.*

55. Department of Justice's "Guidelines on Non-discrimination on the Basis of Handicap in Federally Assisted Programs," in 8 F.E.P (BNA) 401:581 *et seq.*

56. *Batyko v. Pa. Liquor Control Board*, 450, F. Supp. 32 (W.D. Pa. 1978).

57. *See* Testimony of Joan Bertin, Hearings before Subcommittee on Investigations and Oversight, 97th Cong. 1st Sess., Oct. 14–15, 1981, "Genetic Screening and the Handling of High Risk Groups in the Workplace," pp. 179 *et. seq.*

58. *See* Statement of Gretchen S. Kolsrud, Ph.D., Mgr., Biological Applications Program, Office of Technology Assessment, 97th Cong. 1st Sess., June 22, 1982, "Use of Genetic Testing in the Workplace," p. 9.

59. *See generally* "EEOC Uniform Guidelines on Employee Selection Procedures," 29 C.F.R. §1607.

60. 42 U.S.C. §2000e. *See also* EEOC "Guidelines on Discrimination Based on Sex," 29 C.F.R. §1604.

61. *Dumas v. Town of Mount Vernon, Alabama*, 476 F. Supp. 866 (S.D. Ala. 1977). *aff'd* 612 F. ad 974 (5th Cir. 1980).

62. 42 U.S.C. §2000e-2(b).

63. 29 C.F.R. 1604.

64. *Id.* at §1604.6(b).

65. *Pirre v. Printing Developments, Inc.*, 468 F. Supp. 1028 (S.D. N.Y.), *aff'd*, 614 F.2d 1290 (2d Cir. 1979).

66. Cal. Lab. Code §1050, 1053, 1054; Conn. Gen. Stat. Ann. §31-51; Ind. Code §22–6–3–1 and 2; Kans. Stat. Ann. 44–808(3); Mo. Ann. Stat. §290.140; Mont. Rev. Code Ann. 39–2–801–804; and Nev. Rev. Stat. §§613.210 *et seq.*

III

Discipline and Discharge

Much of the friction between labor and management stems from discipline and discharge issues. In fact, the most frequent claims before labor arbitrators are discharge disputes; and next, disciplinary issues.[1] On an individual level, nothing is so disquieting to an employee as the apprehension of being laid off or fired, or the less severe but often no less traumatic threat of being disciplined, on either proper or improper grounds.

Historically, the relationship between management and its employees was outside the scope of the law. As a result, the conditions under which discipline and discharge issues were resolved depended on the type of employment relationship, (e.g., union or non-union setting, public or private sector, employment contract or none). The modern trend is to increase regulation and definition of the terms and conditions of the private employment relationship, and the rights and obligations of the parties. While the relationship between employers and employees is now more equitable, it has also notably increased in complexity.

This chapter considers discipline and discharge issues, with a particular focus on the increased recognition by the courts of an employee's right to challenge a wrongful discharge.

What limits my employer's ability to discipline or discharge me?

This depends on many factors:

Public (or governmental) employees are protected by a web of constitutional and statutory provisions, by civil service systems, and sometimes by union contracts. Generally, they cannot be disciplined or discharged without "good cause." For a full discussion of the good cause and due process protections of such employees, see *The Rights of Government Employees*, another handbook in this series.

As discussed in Chapter 1, private employees have few legal protections against discipline and discharge. Their possible protections fall into the following categories:

- anti-discrimination laws (federal and state prohibitions on discipline or discharge based on race, sex, religion, age, etc.);
- anti-retaliation laws (federal and state prohibitions on retaliation against employees for certain protected activities, such as union activity and reporting job safety violations);
- collective bargaining agreements (union contracts containing good cause and due process provisions—applicable to only about 25 percent of American workers);
- individual employment contracts (relatively rare, except for high-level employees);
- company policies (personnel manuals describing good cause or due process policies—occasionally enforceable);
- wrongful discharge cases (recent case law restraining employer actions that violate public policy).

Each of those categories is discussed in this book. Anti-discrimination laws are discussed in Chapters 5–12, and collective bargaining agreements are discussed in Chapter 13. The other categories are covered in this chapter.

Basically, if you do not fall under the protection of one of those categories, you cannot challenge discipline or discharge by your employer, even if you believe it is arbitrary, unreasonable, and unfair.

Why do I have such little protection against arbitrary actions?

The generally unlimited right of your employer to discipline or discharge you is rooted in the judicially established "employment-at-will" doctrine, the cornerstone of American employment law. Simply stated, this doctrine recognizes the authority of an employer to discipline or discharge with impunity an employee for any reason or for no reason at all.[2] The rationale for this century-old rule is that both parties to an employment contract should be able to terminate the relationship freely, thereby allowing each to gain the benefit of an unexpected opportunity or to escape an unsatisfactory work situation. In an earlier time, this belief flowed logically from the prevailing legal and economic notion of the time: freedom of contract. The Supreme Court viewed the situation in the following manner in the early 20th century:

> The right of a person to sell his labor upon such terms as he deems proper is . . . the same as the right of the purchaser of labor to prescribe the conditions upon which he will accept such labor from the person . . . [T]he employer and the employee have equality of right, and any legislation that disturbs that equality is an arbitrary interference with the liberty of contract.[3]

One generation's logic, however, may become another's fallacy. A major assumption underlying the at-will doctrine is that an employee would be able to move easily from one job to another—either voluntarily or by necessity—without suffering substantial injury as a result. Few today believe that employment can be lost without significant financial and emotional cost.[4] As a nation of wage earners, most Americans depend on their salary as their primary means of support. Continued employment is no longer merely desirable; it is essential. Society also has an interest in the continued employment of individual workers—first, in seeing that its citizens are self-sufficient, and second, in encouraging stable work relationships.

In time, society in general and the legal system in particular recognized that, as employers' authority over their workers grew, so did the opportunity to abuse the absolute right of discipline and discharge that they possessed. The first major intrusion on these acknowledged rights came in the 1930s with the enactment by Congress of the Railway Labor Act[5] and the National Labor Relations Act, which prohibited employer retaliation against workers who joined in union activity.[6] The Supreme Court rejected the employers' challenges to the constitutionality of those statutes.[7] The number of unions and unionized workers grew substantially in the following years. One of the first rights sought and gained by unionized employees through the collective bargaining process was the requirement that management have "just cause" for any disciplinary action taken against an employee.

Union employees today constitute about one-quarter of the American workforce. Most American workers—unlike employees in the rest of Western industrial society—have no generalized protection against unjust discipline or discharge.[8]

What legitimate interests does the at-will rule serve in modern society?

Employers argue that they need, and are entitled to, unbridled authority to hire and retain the best personnel they can find.[9] America's economic success is often traced to the free hand given to corporate management to conduct business in the way it sees fit. The less management prerogatives are restricted, it is argued, the more management is able to run efficient and profitable businesses. At the core of this theory is the at-will rule, allowing managers to place the best available employee in the most suitable position in the company. Employers often point to the inefficiencies of government bureaucracies as examples of the inevitable result of imposing limitations on an employer's right to discipline and discharge workers.

Few dispute that management flexibility is essential to the efficient running of a business, which in turn is essential to a healthy economy. Those who challenge the continued vitality of the at-will rule, however, contend that unfair or improper discipline or dismissal works counter to business success. A dismissal rooted in non-business-related considerations (such as an employee's race or age, or the rejection of a supervisor's sexual advances) may result not only in the loss of a valuable employee, but may seriously injure employee morale. Those who seek to limit an employer's authority to discipline or discharge employees cite with approval management's experience in Europe and in unionized settings in the United States to show that "just cause" discipline requirements and profitable business operations can coexist comfortably.[10]

Few on either side believe that an incompetent or unqualified employee must be kept on the job, and few contend that a discharge on improper discriminatory grounds should be condoned or permitted. Rather, the debate centers on what to do when no good business reason is given for a personnel action.[11] Employers would argue that, as long as the decision does not violate a clear legal prohibition, the decision is theirs alone to make. Defenders of the employees' position insist that a person should not be denied his or her livelihood unless the reason for the action is proper and performance-related.

Nevertheless, as discussed earlier, if the disciplinary action or discharge does not violate an anti-discrimination or anti-retaliation law, or the terms of an employment contract, there is generally no legal basis for challenging the action. Private employers are entitled to discipline or discharge non-union employees without having to offer a job-related reason, or any reason, for the action.

In recent years, Congress and state legislatures have pro-hibited and regulated employment decisions based on an applicant's or employee's race, color, national origin, sex, age, handicap, and in some states, political affiliation, sexual orientation, marital status, arrest record, or genetic trait.[12] Courts in an increasing number of jurisdictions have gone further and permitted employees to challenge dismissals that are found to violate a clear and significant public policy, or an implied or express term of employment agreement.[13] The first such court decision appeared in 1959, when a California court allowed an employee who was fired for refusing to perjure himself before a legislative committee to recover damages.[14] The court reasoned, "It would be obnoxious to the interests of the state and contrary to public policy and sound morality to allow an employer to discharge any employee, whether the employment be for a designated or unspecified duration, on the ground that the employee declined to com-mit perjury, an act specifically enjoined by statute."[15] It was not until the 1970s, however, that courts in other jurisdic-tions adopted this view and began recognizing wrongful, retaliatory, or abusive discharge suits brought by workers.

What is the theory behind a wrongful discharge action?

There are three basic types of wrongful discharge claims: a tort action claiming retaliatory discharge in violation of public policy; a breach of an express or implied contract; and a breach of the implied covenant of good faith and fair dealing.

Dismissals That Violate Public Policy

By far the most frequently heard challenge to the at-will rule, and the one with which employees have had the most success, is the claim that the discharge violated an express and significant public policy. In this type of suit, the em-ployee asks the court to recognize a narrow exception to the at-will rule, based on the facts of the particular case. If a court in your state is willing to make an exception under the right facts, you must demonstrate to the court that (1) you did something that the law encourages or protects, or you were adversely treated in a way the law forbids, and (2) your employer disciplined or discharged you in response to this behavior. Listed below are some examples of recent cases in which employees were permitted to bring such suits:

1. An employee, who was fired solely for having served on jury duty, was allowed to recover the damages incurred as a result of the unlawful dismissal. [16]

2. A court ruled that an employee could sue his former employer for wrongful discharge where the dismissal was prompted by the employee's attempt to get his company to comply with the state's food, drug, and cosmetics act. [17]

3. An employee was found to have been improperly dismissed for having filed a workers' compensation claim. [18]

4. The firing of an employee for refusing to participate in a price-fixing scheme in violation of the anti-trust laws was ruled unlawful. [19] The court in that case, the California Supreme Court, noted that .this trend in the case law of allowing employees to sue for wrongful discharge demonstrates "that the employer is not so absolute a sovereign of the job that there are not limits to his prerogative." [20]

5. A court looked to the state consumer credit protection act as a source of public policy in declaring unlawful the discharge of a bank employee for furnishing information to bank auditors regarding improperly overcharged accounts. [21] The court concluded that an employer's otherwise absolute right of discharge must be tempered "where the employer's motivation for the discharge contravenes some substantial public policy principle." [22]

Discharges have been held wrongful that were contrary to a clear mandate of public policy. What constitutes "public policy" in wrongful discharge cases, however, is uncertain and still being defined. Given the potential breadth of this concept, courts have been rather conservative in applying the term. For example, in a recent New Jersey Supreme Court case, [23] the director of medical research at a major pharmaceutical company refused to do research on an experimental drug that she felt contained a dangerously high level of saccharin. She argued that, as a professional, she was required by the Hippocratic oath not to continue work on the project. She was removed from the project and demoted; shortly thereafter, she resigned, claiming that the company's treatment of her constituted a constructive discharge. (Courts often treat resignations induced by improper management behavior as constructive discharges in ruling on the lawfulness or propriety of the personnel action.) The court ruled that an employee whose discharge violates a clear mandate of public policy may sue the employer for wrongful discharge. The court found support for its interpretation of public policy in "legislation; administrative rules, regulations or decision; and judicial decisions."[24] The court also noted that "[i]n certain instances, a professional code of ethics may contain an expression of public policy."[25] In that case, however, the court viewed the dispute as "a difference in medical opinions," and considered the employee's opinion to be based on her "personal morals" and not a clear mandate of public policy.[26] The court expressed its fear that "[c]haos would result if a single doctor engaged in research were allowed to determine, according to his or her individual conscience, whether a project should continue."[27]

If you think you have been disciplined or discharged in violation of a clear mandate of public policy and that this action was therefore "wrongful," ask yourself: (1) Is there a well-established basis for the public policy that you feel has been violated (for example, a law or judicial decision)? (2) Can you demonstrate that the adverse personnel decision you suffered was a direct result of this violation of public policy?

Breach of Express or Implied Contract

Today, courts are more willing to hold employers to their word and have begun to enforce written and oral promises to employees about job security and benefits. A few courts, most notably the Michigan Supreme Court and the New York Court of Appeals, have enforced statements made in a company personnel handbook and during the hiring process that workers would be dismissed only for "just cause."[28] In the past, courts dismissed employee suits that sought enforcement of such claims on the ground that the terms of the handbook or the oral statements were not bargained for and were therefore not part of the employment contract.[29] Courts are increasingly willing to find that management derives a benefit from making promises concerning job security and should be held to its promises.[30]

Implied Covenant of Good Faith and Fair Dealing

Generally, every contract contains an implied obligation of good faith and fair dealing that applies to both parties. Until recently, however, this obligation was never thought to apply to employment contracts, or to act as a limitation on an employer's right to discharge. Nonetheless, the highest courts in three states—California, Massachusetts and New Hampshire—have endorsed the view that each party to an employment contract may be obligated under certain circumstances to treat the other fairly and in good faith.

The Massachusetts Supreme Judicial Court found that this obligation existed in the employment contract of a salesman of 40 years' service who allegedly was dismissed so that his employer could avoid paying a substantial commission to him.[31] The California Supreme Court found the implied covenant of good faith and fair dealing to be violated in the summary dismissal of a long-term employee because the company failed to hold an impartial hearing, as it had promised in its personnel policies.[32] Finally, the New Hampshire Supreme Court ruled that the dismissal of a worker who refused the sexual advances of her superior was wrongful, and that a dismissal "motivated by bad faith or malice or based on retaliation is not in the best interest of the economic system or the public good and constitutes a breach of the employment contract."[33]

While the rationale of these cases has not yet been widely accepted or applied, it does present a potentially strong weapon for a court inclined to limit the perceived arbitrariness of employer personnel policies.[34]

Nevertheless, despite these developments, the at-will rule is still very much alive and continues to dominate the law of discipline and discharge. The cases described above are examples of narrow exceptions carved into the rule in a few states. In most states, courts still refuse even to listen to an employee's claim of wrongful discharge.

Do some companies provide due process mechanisms?

Yes. Collective bargaining agreements virtually always establish procedures for handling grievances. Interestingly, a growing number of companies are establishing grievance procedures for their non-union employees; many of those procedures mimic the systems established for union employees under collective bargaining agreements. Other policies established to resolve worker disputes include corporate "open-door" policies, which allow an employee to raise a work-related matter with any management person at any time, and the establishment of an ombudsman office in the company to receive and act on complaints from employees.

Two justifications are often cited for the unilateral creation of such procedures and policies for non-union employees by management. First, they aid management in discovering and resolving employee complaints at an early stage. Second, the existence of procedures and policies to resolve disputes in a non-union setting serve to inhibit an incipient or as yet unformulated union drive.

The nature and effectiveness of these procedures varies with the company and the personnel administering them. Among the actual and potential shortcomings of such non-union grievance procedures are lack of administrative and moral support for a single, inexperienced grievant; inadequate assurances of protection against reprisal; lack of a neutral third party to resolve the dispute finally; and the potential that they may come to displace informal dispute resolution policies already in place. Some of the potential benefits to employers are: employees have a clear and officially sanctioned place to take their problems; those in authority may become less arbitrary in their behavior toward employees and may feel the need to support their actions more carefully; and in general, these procedures may assist in establishing an atmosphere in which employees' views and problems are treated with more dignity and care. If an employee has a legal claim against his or her employer (for example, a race, sex, or age discrimination claim), the employee need not seek to resolve the claim through internal company procedures before going to court.

Are there other limitations on an employer's authority to discipline or discharge employees?

To summarize, the three basic limitations on the discretion of an employer to discipline and discharge are: (1) "just cause" requirements endemic to public sector employment and union membership; (2) statutory restrictions on employment related discrimination based on age, sex, race, national origin, handicap, or related categories, and on retaliation against employees for protected activity; and (3) judicially established limitations rooted in public policy or in a broad view of an employee's rights under an employment contract. Management's prerogatives have been further limited by a broadening of classes of individuals protected from employment discrimination by state law, typically through fair employment practice legislation enforced by state human rights agencies. Such state fair employment practice laws parallel federal law and, in some states, extend greater job security to applicants or employees discriminated against as a result of marital status, color blindness, genetic trait (such as sickle-cell anemia), unfavorable military discharge, sexual orientation, arrest history, or alien status. A number of states also bar employment discrimination based on political affiliation or the fulfillment of civic obligations, such as jury duty.[35]

Perhaps the newest development in this area has been the extension of job protection to whistleblowers, employees who report violations of laws or dangers to public health or safety to those in authority. Whistleblower protection has taken three forms. First, in a few notable cases, courts have recognized an exception to the at-will doctrine based on the belief that employer retaliation for the reporting of a violation of law or a danger to public health or safety by an employee violates public policy, and is prohibited. For example, the West Virginia Supreme Court of Appeals allowed a bank employee who was fired after telling bank auditors about improperly overcharged accounts to sue for wrongful dismissal.[36] Second, two states, Michigan and Connecticut, have enacted whistleblower protection acts that bar discrimination against employees who report violations of law to government bodies.[37] A handful of states have also enacted similar legislation, but restricted its coverage to state employees.[38] Finally, Congress and a growing number of states have attached to public safety, health, and environmental acts anti-reprisal provisions that prohibit retaliatory personnel actions against employees who report violations of those acts to appropriate authorities, or who pursue their rights under the acts.[39] For example, an employee who reports an imminently dangerous situation on the worksite to OSHA and requests an inspection is entitled to protection against any reprisal taken by the employer.[40]

Title VII of the Civil Rights Act of 1964, the centerpiece of employment discrimination law, provides protection against retaliation for having pursued rights under that law.[41] (For a list of federal anti-reprisal provisions, see Appendix 1.) Similarly, many state workers' compensation laws seek to alleviate the fear of filing a claim by assuring that no injury to a worker's employment will occur as a result.[42]

Perhaps the purest whistleblower-type anti-reprisal protection can be found in environmental protection statutes such as the Clean Air Act and Federal Water Pollution Control Act.[43] The type of claim sought to be protected there is one primarily in the public interest—for example, "My company is emitting poisonous gas into the air"—rather than one primarily in the employee's self-interest—"The factory roof may fall on my head."[44] In providing this protection, Congress and state legislatures are seeking to promote the purposes of the particular legislation, e.g., to safeguard our environment or otherwise promote public health or safety.

If you are a union member, management will almost certainly have to demonstrate "just cause" for any personnel action taken against you. Also, veterans who have received an honorable discharge and have returned to their former positions may not be discharged "without cause" for a period of a year following re-employment.[45] Employment contracts for a fixed term generally require "just cause" for dismissal as well.[46]

What constitutes "just cause"?

Over the years, some basic principles have emerged from the struggle of arbitrators to determine what constitutes "just cause."[47] First, the company rule or policy that you are accused of violating must be reasonably related to the safe and efficient operation of the company and must have been made known to you before your actions, unless the rule or policy is self-evident. Next, management must adequately and fairly investigate the charges made against you before disciplining or discharging you. You must also have been adequately warned beforehand of the consequences of breach of the rule or policy. Management's response must be corrective in nature, and not punitive, and must be reasonably responsive to the severity of the offense. Finally, the punishment must be consistent with prior practices and must not be discriminatorily or arbitrarily applied.

Employee offenses that are generally viewed as constituting "just cause" include: chronic absenteeism; violation of plant safety rules; inefficient or incompetent work performance; insubordination; disloyalty; dishonesty; disclosure of trade secrets; intoxication; gambling; gross negligence; fighting; and participating in an illegal strike. What constitutes "just cause" for discipline in a particular unionized employment setting is ultimately for an arbitrator to decide.

What is the difference between being laid off and being discharged?

Sometimes it is hard to distinguish the two, either because management has not clearly communicated its intention to the employee, or because management is unsure of the nature of the action it is taking. Simply put, a discharge is intended to be a permanent severing of the employment relationship, whereas a layoff is the temporary disruption of a still existing relationship. The focus is on the employer's intentions and actions. For example, if your company tells you on Friday not to come to work the next Monday due to a temporary slowdown in business, but states or implies that you will be recalled when business picks up, you have been laid off. On the other hand, if your company abolishes your position and takes other actions indicating that the relationship is permanently ended, you have been fired. Some employer actions that tend to indicate dismissal rather than layoff are: a cash settlement of accrued benefits, such as unused vacation or sick days; instructions to fellow employees or company security agents that you are not allowed back on company grounds; and an exit interview in which the basis of the discharge is discussed, and termination benefits are agreed upon. After a period of time, a layoff may be viewed as a discharge if reinstatement is no longer being considered.

The distinction between a firing and a layoff is not merely semantic, but may determine your rights upon release. For example, you might be entitled to severance pay under a collective bargaining agreement or employment contract only upon discharge. Further, the ability to file a discriminatory or retaliatory discharge suit under federal or state law may depend on whether you were fired or laid off. If your company tells you not to return to work for a while, you may want to press management to be more specific so you can better gauge your rights.

Am I entitled to advance notice before being laid off or fired?

In general, American workers are not entitled to notice before termination. Union members are in a slightly different position, however. A union worker who suffers a disciplinary discharge learns of management's displeasure well in advance of discharge under the progressive discipline procedures of collective bargaining, unless serious misconduct is the basis of the discharge. Unions have sought to negotiate notice periods before layoffs, but have as yet made little progress.

Company practices on giving notice differ substantially. Some companies terminate with little or no notice; others provide sufficient notice; some even keep soon-to-be-terminated employees on the payroll for a while to facilitate the search for further employment; and some provide a generous severance settlement to ease the financial burden caused by termination. You should know your company's policy about notice of termination before you actually *need* to know.

What are my rights if I am laid off or fired?

That depends, of course, on the particulars of your employment agreement. You should keep in mind some basic matters, however. You are generally entitled to unemployment insurance if you have been laid off or terminated for other than misconduct, and have worked long enough to qualify under the laws of your state.[48] You should explore with your employer immediately what termination benefits you are entitled to. For example, you should determine the amount of your accrued, unpaid wages and commissions, the number of unused vacation and sick days you have accumulated, and the amount of any severance pay owed you. You should ask about, and obtain in writing, the length of your coverage under your company's group hospital, surgical, dental, and life insurance plans, and information on the extent to which you can convert those plans into individual policies. If you are married and your spouse is employed, you should also determine whether you are covered under your spouse's company's insurance plans. Finally, you should read carefully the terms of the company's pension and profit-sharing plans; you are entitled to prompt and specific information on such benefits under federal law.[49]

If your company terminates you, it may conduct an "exit interview" to discuss the reasons for the action, and to answer any questions you may have. This is a ripe time to ask detailed questions about your rights upon termination. For example, in addition to learning what benefits are owed you, you may want to ask about the use of office staff and facilities while you seek new employment. You may also want to notify your employer that you will be requesting a service letter detailing the dates of employment and reasons for termination. Try to assess the type of reference your now ex-employer may make, and ask your employer to speak frankly about how your termination will be characterized in response to inquiries from potential employers.

What are exit agreements or releases and covenants not to sue?

In some instances, usually when management fears that you may bring a lawsuit, the company may ask you to sign a document stating that you will not sue your employer as a result of your termination, or that you will forgo any other potential claims against the company, in return for a guarantee of accrued benefits, and in some cases a cash settlement. Courts generally uphold the release of common law claims unless duress or fraud is involved. Courts are less willing to sustain the release of statutory claims, but will most likely do so if a full, or at least fair, settlement is made. The Supreme Court has sustained the waiver of an employee's Title VII claim where the waiver was voluntary and knowing.[50]

If your employer asks you to sign a release or a covenant not to sue following your notification of termination, you should seek the advice of your lawyer or of a union official before you sign.

What are my remedies in a wrongful discharge case?

If you win a wrongful discharge claim, you are entitled to compensatory damages (that is, back pay and lost benefits), and you may be reinstated to your former position, or an equivalent position within the company; the monetary damages award will be reduced by any income you earned in the period between your termination and the court judgment.

If your claim is that your company breached an employment contract with you (a contract claim), you may not be able to receive any additional damages. If you allege that your company violated public policy in discharging you (a tort claim), you may be able to recover additional damages, including punitive damages if the discharge was wanton and malicious. In addition to recovering damages from the company, you may be able to sue your supervisor if he or she had the authority to fire you and did so with the intent to injure you in a way that violates public policy.[51] You may also be able to sue for mental distress or pain and suffering, but such awards are rare.[52]

Where should I go to seek assistance in obtaining alternative employment?

You should first check with your unemployment insurance office to see how they may assist you in finding a new job. That office may be able to steer you to public or private employment agencies, or you may want to seek out those agencies on your own. Sometimes an employer will provide or help arrange job counseling or search services. You may ask at union recruiting halls whether the union knows of any employment opportunities. Of course, you may apply directly to potential employers. Perhaps the first, least expensive, and most sensible approach is to ask friends, relatives, and colleagues whether they know of any openings that you are qualified to fill.

NOTES

1. *Wall Street J.*, Aug. 31, 1981, p. 1.

2. *Payne v. Western & Atl. R.R.*, 81 Tenn. 507, 519–20 (1884), *overruled on other grounds Hutton v. Watters*, 132 Tenn. 527, 179 S.W. 134 (1915).

3. *Adair v. U.S.*, 208 U.S. 161, 174–75 (1908).

4. See Summers, "Individual Protection Against Unjust Dismissal: Time for a Statute," 62 Va. L. Rev. 481 (1976); "At-Will Employment and the Problem of Unjust Dismissal," 36 A.B.C. N.Y. Rec. 170 (April 1981).

5. 45 U.S.C. §§151–188.

6. 29 U.S.C. §158(a) (1).

7. *Texas & New Orleans Railroad Co. v. Brotherhood of Railway & Steamship Clerks*, 281 U.S. 548 (1930); *NLRB v. Jones & Laughlin Steel Corp.*, 301 U.S. 1, (1937).

8. See Peck, "Unjust Discharges from Employment: A Necessary Change in the Law," 40 Ohio State L.J. 1 (1979).

9. See, e.g., *Martin v. Platt*, 386 N.E.2d 1026 (Ind. App. 1979); *Geary v. U.S. Steel Corp.*, 456 Pa. 171, 319 A.2d 174 (1974).

10. *Peck, supra* note 8, at 46–49; *Summers, supra* note 4, at 508–19.

11. *Note,* "Defining Public Policy Torts in At-Will Dismissals," 34 Stan. L. Rev. 153, 170–72 (1981).

12. For a more complete discussion of these issues, *see* chaps. 5–12.

13. *See* note, Public Policy Limitations on the Retaliatory Discharge of At-Will Employees in the Private Sector," 14 U. of Cal., Davis 809, 820 (1981).

14. *Petermann v. International Bhd.*, 174 Cal. App. 2d 184, 344 P.2d 25 (1959).

15. *Id.* at 188–89, 344 P.2d at 27.

16. *Nees v. Hocks*, 272 Or. 210, 536 P.2d 512 (1975).

17. *Sheets v. Teddy's Frosted Foods, Inc.*, 179 Conn. 471, 427 A.2d 385 (1980).

18. *Frampton v. Central Indiana Gas Co.*, 260 Ind. 249, 297 N.E.2d 425 (1973); *Kelsay v. Motorola, Inc.*, 74 Ill.2d 172, 384 N.E.2d 353 (1978).

19. *Tameny v. Atlantic Richfield Co.*, 27 Cal.3d 167, 164 Cal. Rptr. 839 (1980).

20. *Id.* at 171, 164 Cal. Rptr. at 845.

21. *Harless v. First National Bank in Fairmont*, 246 S.E.2d 270 (W.Va. 1978).

22. *Id.* at 275.

23. *Pierce v. Ortho Pharmaceutical Corp.*, 84 N.J. 58, 417 A.2d 505 (1980).

24. *Id.* at 72, 417 A.2d at 512.

25. *Id.*

26. *Id.* at 75, 417 A.2d at 513.

27. *Id.* at 75, 417 A.2d at 514.

28. *Toussaint v. Blue Cross & Blue Shield of Mich.*, 408 Mich. 579, 292 N.W.2d 880 (1980); *Weiner v. McGraw-Hill, Inc.*, 57 N.Y. 2d 458, 457 N.Y.S. 2d 193 (Nov. 18, 1982). *Cleary v. American Airlines, Inc.*, 111 Cal. App. 3d 443, 168 Cal. Rptr. 722 (1980); *Chamberlain v. Bissell, Inc.*, 547 F. Supp. 1067, 1078 (W.D. Mich. 1982).

29. *Johnson v. National Beef Packing Co.*, 220 Kan. 52, 551 P.2d 779 (1976); *Shaw v. S. S. Kresge Co.*, 167 Ind. App. 1, 328 N.E.2d 775 (1975).

30. *See generally* DeGiuseppe, "The Effect of the Employment-At-Will Rule on Employee Rights to Job Security and Fringe Benefits," 10 Ford. Urban L.J. 1 (1981–82).

31. *Fortune v. National Cash Register Co.*, 373 Mass. 96, 364 N.E.2d 1251 (1977).

32. *Cleary v. American Airlines, Inc., supra* note 28.

33. *Monge v. Beebe Rubber Co.*, 114 N.H. 130, 133, 316 A.2d 549, 551 (1974). *Cf. Howard v. Dorr Woolen Co.*, 120 N.H. 295, 414 A.2d 1273 (1980).

34. *See* Comment, "Protecting at Will Employees Against Wrongful

Discharge: The Duty to Terminate Only in Good Faith," 93 Harv. L. Rev. 1816 (1980).

35. For a fuller discussion of these issues, *see* chaps. 2 and 4.

36. *Harless v. First National Bank in Fairmont*, 246 S.E.2d 270 (W.Va. 1978).

37. Mich. Stat. Ann. §§17.428.1–9; 1982 Conn. Pub. Acts 82–289.

38. Ind. Code Ann. §§4–15–10–1 *et seq*. (Burns 1981); Md. State Gov't Code Ann. §12G–K.

39. *See* Appendix 11.

40. Occupational Safety and Health Act of 1970, 29 U.S.C. §660(c) (1).

41. 42 U.S.C. §2000c–3(a).

42. *See, e.g.,* Conn. Gen. Stat. Ann. §31–379; Ill. Ann. Stat. chap. 48 §138.4(h).

43. Clean Air Act Amendments of 1977, 42 U.S.C. §7622(a); Federal Water Pollution Control Act of 1972, 33 U.S.C. §1367(a).

44. *Compare* Federal Water Pollution Control Act of 1972, 33 U.S.C. §1367(a), with Occupational Safety and Health Act of 1970, 29 U.S.C. §660(c)(1).

45. *See* chap. 11.

46. *See supra,* note 30, at 14–16.

47. *See Policy and Practice Series: Personnel Management* (BNA) 203:25–29.

48. For further discussion, *see* chap. 19.

49. For further discussion, *see* chap. 16.

50. *Alexander v. Gardner-Denver Co.,* 415 U.S. 36 (1974).

51. *Harless v. First National Bank in Fairmont*, 289 S.E.2d 692 (W.Va. 1982).

52. *Id.* at 702.

IV

Privacy

Broadly speaking, this chapter discusses your right to be let alone on the job, that is, to be free of unwarranted intrusions by your employer.

In recent years Americans in general, and employees in particular, have become increasingly concerned about intrusions into their private lives by government, credit institutions, employers, and others. This concern has been heightened by technological developments, such as computer processing of information. Many people wonder who knows what about them, why, what is being done with the information, and whether it is accurate. Many feel that much information about them is no one else's business and should not affect their jobs.

These concerns have generated various legal protections for employees' privacy; this chapter addresses those protections. Section A covers methods used by employers to gather information about employees and job applicants; this includes lie detector tests, fingerprinting, electronic surveillance, and searches and seizures. Section B deals with employers' maintaining and disseminating information about employees; this covers what personnel records can be collected, how they must be maintained, and who has access to them. Section C discusses matters of personal lifestyle, such as your personal appearance, marital status, and sexual preference. For further discussion on privacy issues, see the ACLU handbook *Your Rights to Privacy* by Trudy Hayden and Jack Novik.

No comprehensive law on employee privacy exists, but there is an uneven patchwork of federal and state laws.[1] The most significant statute is the Federal Privacy Act of 1974,[2] which provides some privacy protections for federal employees. For example, it requires federal agencies to (1) inform their employees of personnel records containing information about them, (2) permit those employees to examine, copy, and challenge that information, (3) maintain only accurate, relevant, and current information, and (4) limit access to that information by outsiders. Several states have similar acts pertaining to their public employees.

The Privacy Act also established the Privacy Protection Study Commission to investigate and make recommendations to Congress on regulation of privacy practices of private and government organizations, including employers. In its report in July 1977, the Commission recommended against extending the Privacy Act to cover private employees. Instead, it recommended that private employers implement voluntary guidelines in maintaining personnel records. The guidelines suggested by the Commission included protections comparable to those in the Privacy Act. Many large employers have in fact implemented such guidelines, and many others are considering privacy protections for employees.

The Commission did recommend that specific legislation be passed prohibiting polygraphs and strengthening disclosure provisions of the Federal Fair Credit Reporting Act. As discussed below, some states have passed statutes regulating polygraphs, and the credit disclosure provisions were strengthened.

A. Methods of Gathering Information

Must I take a "lie detector" test, if asked, to get or keep a job?

Yes, except in states that have statutes forbidding or restricting their use in employment.

Many employers ask or require employees and job applicants to submit to tests by polygraph ("lie detector") and other truth verification devices (such as the psychological stress evaluator or voice stress analyzer). Such tests may be used to screen job applicants, to examine current employees periodically, or to examine employees concerning a particular event, such as theft of company property. Sometimes a new employee is asked to sign a form agreeing to submit to such a test whenever the employer requests it.

These devices work on the principle that lying causes psychological conflict, which produces stress. Polygraph tests detect and record measurable physiological changes—blood pressure, rate of breathing, and electrical conductivity of skin—which, it is claimed, are produced by the stress of lying. Psychological stress evaluators (PSE), sometimes called voice stress analyzers, purport to detect and record fluctuations in your voice produced by stress. Unlike the polygraph, the PSE need not be connected to you; tests can be conducted without your knowledge (e.g., by hiding the machine or using it over the telephone).

The scientific reliability of such truth verification tests is in serious doubt. Two congressional committees that reviewed the available evidence were unconvinced of the accuracy, reliability, and validity of such tests.[3] An honest subject may exhibit physiological reactions caused by factors other than the stress of lying, such as illness, fatigue, anger, embarrassment, or even the test itself; on the other hand, a pathological liar, who has no fear of lying, may exhibit no physiological reactions. Also, the test examiner can affect the results, in terms of both the reactions produced (as by the manner and content of the questions) and the interpretation of those reactions. The results are affected by the examiner's biases, attitudes, and judgment. In light of these serious questions about reliability, the use of such tests in employment can be quite unfair to employees: jobs may be denied or lost, and careers may be ruined, by the result.

Aside from considerations of fairness, such tests are by their nature personally intrusive. By trying to reach into your mind and to read your thoughts and feelings, they invade your privacy and assault your personal dignity. In addition, the questions asked by polygraph examiners can delve into intimate personal matters that are none of the employer's business, such as illnesses, sexual preferences and activities, alcohol or drug use, religious and political beliefs, and prior misdeeds. Finally, use of a PSE test without your knowledge constitutes an unknown intrusion into your personal privacy.

These considerations of fairness and privacy have prompted many states to enact laws governing the use of truth verification tests in employment. These laws use a variety of approaches. Some states forbid such tests altogether; others permit them only if you volunteer to take them. Some states regulate what kinds of questions can be asked, and some license test examiners to require certain training. New laws are enacted every year. Following is a brief summary of state laws, as of 1982.

In many jurisdictions, you cannot be required to take a truth verification test. Three of those jurisdictions— District of Columbia, Massachusetts, and New Jersey[4]—prohibit the use of polygraphs in employment at all; in those states, such tests cannot be used for applicants or employees, even if you volunteer. Five other states—Alaska, Delaware, Maine, Minnesota, and Wisconsin—forbid employers to "require, request, or suggest, directly or indirectly," that you take such a test;[5] in those states, you presumably can volunteer to take a test. Ten other states—California, Connecticut, Hawaii, Idaho, Maryland, Michigan, Montana, Oregon, Pennsylvania, and Washington[6]—prohibit an employer from "requiring" a polygraph test as a condition of getting or keeping a job. In those states, an employer presumably can "suggest" that you take a test and you can take it voluntarily.

New York prohibits the use of PSE tests, but not polygraphs;[7] Pennsylvania and California permit employers to administer PSE tests only if the employer obtains your written consent first.[8] Several states—including Arizona, Illinois, New Mexico, and Virginia[9]—prohibit test examiners from asking about certain subjects such as religious and political beliefs and affiliations, opinions about or affiliation with unions, or sexual activities; many of those states also require licensing of test examiners. Some regulations focus on the use of the test results. In Nevada, for example, the results of a required polygraph test cannot be released without your consent.[10]

The statutes regulating truth verification tests sometimes except certain kinds of employees, typically law enforcement officials and persons having access to narcotics or dangerous drugs (e.g., pharmacists).[11] Generally, these state prohibitions pertain not only to employers, but also to employment agencies and test examiners.

What happens if I am asked or told to submit to a truth verification test?

The answer depends, of course, on what the law is in your state. If the employer's conduct is prohibited, you need not submit to the test, though in some states you may do so voluntarily. In those states, you cannot be discriminated against for refusal to take such a test or for filing a complaint about such a test.

Violation of these prohibitions is typically a misdemeanor, punishable by a small fine. You may therefore report a violation to the state prosecutor, though the laws are seldom enforced. None of the statutes specifically provides a private right of action for an aggrieved employee or job applicant. A federal court in New Jersey,[12] however, did grant an aggrieved employee money damages and ordered expungement of derogatory records resulting from an unlawful test.

Even if you are not in a state that prohibits the use of truth verification tests, some union contracts provide protection: such tests may be prohibited by contract; or your union may fight any discipline or discharge you suffer for refusing to take a test or for failing one, as not being "good cause"; or you may be entitled to have a union representative present during a test. Even in the absence of a contract, you can ask to have a representative or other witness present. Such contractual provisions would apply, of course, only to testing during the course of employment, and not to pre-employment testing.

If you take a test, you may not be entitled to access to the test results. You should ask about this and try to get a commitment from the employer; no law prevents the employer or examiner from sharing the results with you. Also, the employer or examiner will typically ask you to sign a waiver of any claims against them for any harm you may suffer as a result of the test.

If truth verification tests are permitted in your state and you are fired or disciplined for refusing to take a test or for failing one, you may have trouble getting unemployment benefits, even though you are otherwise eligible; your employer may assert that your discharge was for misconduct. But some states have rejected such assertions and allowed unemployment benefits.[13] (See Chapter 19, "Unemployment Insurance.")

Can I be required to take a psychological or personality test to get a job?

Yes. Employers sometimes require a job applicant to take a test or fill out a questionnaire to help them evaluate the applicant's personality, character, opinions, and attitudes. The employer may be seeking to weed out applicants with dishonest propensities, psychological problems, or undesirable personality traits. Such tests are inherently intrusive. Nevertheless, no law regulates their use on privacy grounds.

Such pre-employment tests are, however, subject to the general prohibition of tests that tend to discriminate on the basis of such grounds as race or sex. Any employment test that has such a discriminatory effect can be sustained only if the inquiries are job-related. This subject is discussed more fully in Chapters 2 and 6.

Can my employer use electronic surveillance?
Generally, yes.

The most important statute in this area is Title III of the federal Omnibus Crime Control and Safe Streets Act of 1968,[14] which prohibits all private individuals and organizations, including employers, from intercepting wire or oral communications of others. At first blush, this statute would seem to prohibit your employer from monitoring or recording your telephone conversations with others, or eavesdropping on your conversations with others, without your consent (or the consent of another party to the conversation). Nonetheless, this prohibition has been drastically narrowed in the employment context by what has been called the "extension phone exemption" to the statute. Under that exemption, your employer can, by listening on an extension, monitor your conversations on the employer's telephone system if the monitoring is done "in the ordinary course" of the employer's business. The boundaries of the exemption are still unclear, but the courts have generally favored the employer.[15] If your employer does violate Title III, you have a private right of action for actual and punitive damages, plus your costs and attorneys' fees. You do not have to prove malice or bad faith to recover.

Most states also have statutes restricting wiretaps and eavesdropping. Many of those statutes provide protections and remedies comparable to Title III.[16] In Pennsylvania, moreover, private wiretapping or eavesdropping is forbidden without the consent of *both* parties.[17]

Title III does not cover photographic surveillance, such as cameras to monitor your performance or honesty, though such surveillance can be quite intrusive and offensive. State laws provide no protection in this respect either, except that Connecticut prohibits employer use of sound or photographic equipment in "areas designated for health or personal comfort."[18]

Similarly, no federal or state law regulates the use of human agents, such as "spotters" posing as customers, except that California and Nevada prohibit discharge or discipline of an employee based on a spotter's report, unless the employee is afforded notice, hearing, and the right to confront the "accuser."[19]

Can my employer search me or my personal effects?

Generally, yes. Employers sometimes search employees or their personal effects (e.g., purses, desks, lockers) to obtain evidence of suspected theft, to prevent contraband (e.g., drugs) from getting onto company premises, and to deter theft. Generally, there is not much you can do about such searches. In fact, evidence obtained by such searches can be turned over to prosecutors and used against you in a criminal trial because the rule of criminal procedure excluding evidence from warrantless searches does not apply to nongovernmental actions.[20]

Nevertheless, you may have some protection. Your union contract may limit your employer's right to search; on-the-job searches are part of the "working conditions" that your union can seek to restrict. Further, your employer may be liable to you for any assault, battery, or false arrest committed against you. Thus, if your employer improperly detains you on suspicion of theft, you may have an action for false arrest.

Can I be required to submit to fingerprinting, tests, etc?

Usually, yes. Employers often ask job applicants and employees to submit to certain medical tests, and they sometimes request fingerprints, blood tests, chemical tests, and genetic tests. Such tests may be for identification, for background investigations, and for investigations of specific misconduct, such as theft or intoxication. Medical tests are sometimes used to ascertain an employee's qualifications for a job, such as fitness to do heavy work. Recently, some employers have begun using genetic testing to ascertain whether employees or prospective employees are particularly susceptible to certain occupational hazards, such as chemicals used on the job. These subjects are discussed in greater detail in Chapter 2, "The Hiring Process."

Generally, such tests are not regulated. In New York, however, most private employers cannot require you to be fingerprinted to get or keep a job; government employees and workers in certain industries are excluded from this protection.[21] California prohibits employers from requiring fingerprints or passing on your fingerprints to other employees to your detriment.[22]

Can an employer do a credit check on me?

Generally, yes. As discussed in Chapter 2, however, it has been ruled that denying you a job because of a poor credit rating may violate the anti-discrimination laws, because the percentage of non-whites with poor credit ratings is disproportionately greater than the percentage of whites.

In any event, if an employer does gather credit information on you, it must comply with the Federal Fair Credit Reporting Act.[23] Under that law, an employer that procures a "consumer investigative report" (i.e., a report based on personal interviews) must give you written notice that a report will be made concerning your character, general reputation, personal characteristics, and mode of living. Also, if you ask for it, the employer must tell you the nature and scope of the investigation. If you are denied a job, or otherwise adversely affected, on the basis of such a report, the employer must tell you of the adverse action and give you the name and address of the reporting agency. You then have the right to learn from that agency the nature and substance of the information, to have disputed information reinvestigated, and to have your version of the facts included in any subsequent reports. Many states have similar laws on fair credit reporting and investigation.

B. Maintaining and Disseminating Information

An employer typically acquires and retains a substantial amount of information about its employees. Some of that information is obviously necessary and relevant to the employer's legitimate business concerns. For example, an employer needs to know the job-related qualifications of applicants and needs to know about the abilities and performance of its employees. On the other hand, some information about employees is irrelevant to an employer's legitimate areas of concern; this includes, for example, information that can be the basis for unlawful discriminatory decisions, such as a person's race or religion. In addition, information kept by an employer should be accurate and current.

This section addresses your employer's accumulating,

maintaining, and distributing information about you. It also discusses the extent to which your employer can disclose information about you to people outside the company; this includes, for example, job references.

Are there limits on the types of information an employer can gather about me?

Not many. Generally, except for the following situations, your employer can gather and maintain whatever information it wants about you.

Employers are prohibited by law from discriminating against employees and job applicants on certain grounds, such as race, religion, and sex. Inquiries that tend to promote such discrimination may be unlawful, or at least provide evidence that the employer relied on unlawful considerations. For more on such inquiries, see the discussions in Chapter 2, "The Hiring Process," and in Part II, "Employment Discrimination."

In addition, some states prohibit questions about arrests, convictions, and other matters. These prohibitions pertain primarily to job applicants, as opposed to employees; this subject is therefore discussed in detail in Chapter 2. Notably, a unique Michigan statute prohibits employers from collecting information about off-duty political activities of employees.[24]

Many public employees have additional protections. The Federal Privacy Act of 1974,[25] which applies to employees of the federal government, requires government agencies to maintain in their records only such information as is "relevant and necessary to accomplish a [required] purpose of the agency . . ."; that Act also requires such records to be accurate, relevant, timely, and complete, and that such records be kept secure and confidential.[26] About a third of the states have similar laws that govern the records of public employees.[27] These protections do not extend to private employees.

Do I have a right to see my personnel file?

In most states, no. Employees of the federal government, and of states with statutes governing the records of public employees, typically have the right to see their files. Only seven states—California, Connecticut, Maine, Michigan, Oregon, Pennsylvania, and Wisconsin[28]—require that private employees have that right. Such statutes typically permit current and former employees to see and copy their files, but typically exclude from mandatory disclosure letters of reference and criminal investigative reports. In Connecticut and Michigan you may challenge material in your file, and you may limit the information your employer can release without your approval. In California a copy of your personnel file must be maintained at the place where you work.

In Connecticut, Ohio, and Wisconsin,[29] you also have the right to see your medical records. In Connecticut you can review and challenge any materials provided by a physician or psychologist. In Ohio an employer or physician must, upon your written request, let you see your medical records; a physician may, however, disclose the information to your doctor instead, if disclosing it to you would cause serious medical harm. An employer in Wisconsin can withhold any information that would be harmful to you, but can release such information to your physician. An employer in Maryland[30] cannot ask you about any physical, psychological, or psychiatric illnesses, disabilities, or handicaps that do not have a direct relationship to your fitness for the job in question.

Under regulations of the Occupational Safety and Health Administration, you (and your authorized representative) are entitled to access to certain medical and toxic records if you are exposed to toxic substances or harmful physical agents while working in general industry, the maritime field, or construction.[31] These records include your personal medical history and test results, and records of past and present exposure of you and other workers with similar duties and working conditions to toxic substances and harmful physical agents.

Are there limits on disclosure of information about me to people inside the company?

Generally, there are few restrictions on an employer's right to disseminate information about you within the company. The Federal Privacy Act, and similar state statutes applicable to public employees, limit disclosure of personnel information to officers and employees who "need to know" the information to do their job. Similarly, a few enlightened private employers have adopted privacy policies that limit disclosure to those who, in the course of business, need to know information about you.

In a few cases, the courts have limited the right of a union to obtain sensitive material from the employer about you. In

Detroit Edison Co. v. N.L.R.B.,[32] the union asked the employer for the scores of certain employees on psychological aptitude tests that were taken in connection with their applications for promotions. In refusing to require the employer to disclose this information, the court took official notice of the "sensitivity of any human being to disclosure of information that may be taken to bear on his or her basic competence. . . ."[33] It has been held that the Federal Privacy Act's ban on the disclosure of employees' records without their consent constitutes a defense to a union's request for certain sensitive employee data.[34]

Are there limits on disclosure of information about me to people outside the company?

Not many. Except for a few varied restrictions, your employer is free to disclose such information to outsiders.

As mentioned earlier, all federal employees and some state employees are protected against disclosure of personnel information to outsiders, unless the disclosure falls within certain authorized categories. Private employees and other public employees have no such statutory protection. The federal constitutional right to privacy offers limited protection because action by a government is a prerequisite for its application. In Connecticut and Michigan, however, employees can limit the information an employer can release from the file without authorization.[35] Similarly, employers in California are prohibited from releasing medical information about you without your express written approval; and if your employer violates that statute, you can sue for compensatory and punitive damages, plus litigation costs and attorneys' fees.[36] Sometimes, union contracts limit disclosure of personnel information.

In addition, the common law of torts provides limited protections. As discussed below all states recognize causes of action for defamation (i.e., libel and slander) and many states recognize causes of action for intentional infliction of emotional distress and for invasion of privacy. Generally, the employer's conduct must be quite outrageous in order for you to sustain a claim under either of these doctrines.

If your employer (or former employer) discloses information that is false and defamatory and that causes you serious injury, you may be able to assert a defamation claim. Proving your case may be very difficult, of course, particularly if the damaging information was conveyed orally. Furthermore, if the information was communicated to your prospective employer or creditor, it is generally covered by a "qualified privilege." The employer cannot be sued for defamation in that instance unless you can show "malice" (that is, ill will, culpable recklessness, or wanton disregard for your rights). This is usually very difficult to prove. Thus, if you learn that the employer is providing inaccurate information (e.g., in a job reference), you should try to show the employer how the information is inaccurate. If it does not change the disclosed information, at least you have helped establish a foundation for proving malice.

If you learn that inaccurate information (perhaps from a former employer) is in a credit report, you can challenge it by asking for a review under the federal or state fair credit reporting act. If the dispute is unresolved, you can go to court.

The most practical way to combat an inaccurate job reference is to give your own explanation of the facts to the prospective employer with whatever favorable references you can gather from co-workers or other employers.

The tort of invasion of privacy has been recognized in various forms in some states. The form most often applicable to employment is "public disclosure of private facts." Under that tort, you can sue your employer if it discloses to a large number of people (e.g., in a broadcast or news article) true but embarrassing private facts about you. For example, your personnel file may contain a substantial amount of "private facts" about your health, salary, and job performance. Generally, an employer's disclosure of such facts will not be to enough people to satisfy the "public disclosure" element of the tort.[37] In addition, as in defamation actions, employers are protected by a qualified privilege.[38] In one interesting case, a Michigan court held that an employer's disclosure of facts about an employee's health to his Army reserve officer satisfied the "public disclosure" requirement in that this information would be spread throughout the Army reserve office.[39] Generally, however, this element of the tort will be difficult to prove as employers rarely disclose this type information to enough persons.

The tort of "interference with prospective economic advantage" may be a basis for relief if a prospective employer decides not to hire you based on false statements or inappropriate facts disclosed to him by your former employer. Generally, to make out this cause of action you must demonstrate (1) a valid contractual relationship or business expectancy; (2) knowledge of the relationship or expectancy on the part of the former employer; (3) intentional interference, inducing or causing a breach or termination of the relationship or expectancy; and (4) resultant damage.[40]

In one unusual case, a court recognized a cause of action for negligent maintenance of personnel records.[41] In that case, the plaintiff alleged that his former employer negligently maintained and disclosed to a credit company inaccurate information about the circumstances of his termination of employment. The court held that the employer, in gratuitously supplying references, had a duty to supply accurate information.

C. Personal Lifestyle

This section addresses an assortment of issues pertaining to your employer's knowledge of or interference with your personal choice of lifestyle.

Can an employer inquire about my personal life?

Generally, yes. Private employers are subject to very few restrictions on the extent to which they can probe into your personal life. Basically, the law provides you little recourse if you feel your employer is too intrusive. But there are some limits.

As mentioned earlier, an employer may violate antidiscrimination laws by inquiring into certain areas of your life, such as your race, sex, and national origin; this is particularly true of your religious beliefs; see Part II, "Employment Discrimination." In addition, some states and local governments prohibit inquiry into other matters, such as marital status, and sexual preferences; see Chapter 2, "The Hiring Process," and Chapter 12, "Sexual Orientation." As discussed above, some states restrict information about any criminal activity on your part, a few states restrict information about any psychiatric treatment or problems, and a few states restrict the kinds of questions you can be asked during a truth verification test.

Can an employer require me to meet certain dress and grooming standards?

Generally, yes. For example, it is generally legal for your employer to prescribe how you wear your hair, whether you wear a beard or mustache, and how you dress.

Challenges to hair length, shaving, and dress code requirements have usually been brought as sex discrimination cases. Even in public employment, which is subject to much stricter standards than private employment, the courts have generally rejected arguments that such dress and grooming standards are illegal. For example, the U.S. Supreme Court found a rational connection between hair and shaving regulations for policemen and the public employer's needs, and upheld the regulations.[42] Because hair length is not an "immutable characteristic" or a fundamental right, it may be changed at will and is afforded less protection. The employer's regulation need only be reasonable under the circumstances.[43] An employee would have to show the employer's lack of good faith.

Although hair and weight regulations are generally lawful,[44] an employer's standards may be subject to greater scrutiny if certain protected groups of employees face more hardship in complying than other groups. For instance, if an employer prohibited Afro-style hairdos, black employees would be discriminated against in violation of the anti-discrimination law. Where weight standards are much more restrictive for female than for males, an employer would be unlawfully discriminating based on sex, unless it can justify the difference.[45] But the fact that only females are required to shave their legs (arguably an extra "hardship") was found not discriminatory when all employees were required to be neat and clean.[46] And where a black food clerk grew a beard to remedy a skin condition suffered almost exclusively by blacks, the court found that the employer's business necessity (employer was a food vendor) outweighed the slight discriminatory effect imposed by the no-beard regulation (the plaintiff was the only black ever to have been prejudiced).[47]

A First Amendment challenge to an air force regulation banning facial hair by a bearded Jewish rabbi was found to have merit by a district court.[48] First Amendment challenges to grooming regulations have been extremely limited. Other regulations were applied to the members of religious sects that prohibited shaving.[49]

NOTES

1. For a thorough survey and description of federal and state laws on privacy matters, including privacy in employment, see the "Compilation of State and Federal Privacy Laws" by Robert Ellis Smith, published by Privacy Journal, P.O. Box 8844, Washington, DC 20003, (203) 547–2865, which is periodically updated; price, $16.

2. 5 U.S.C. §§552a *et. seq.*

3. Subcommittee on Constitutional Rights, Senate Judiciary Committee, "Privacy, Polygraphs, and Employment" (Nov. 1974); House Committee on Government Operations, "The Use of Polygraphs and Similar Devices by Federal Agencies" (Jan. 1976).

4. D.C. Code §36–801; Mass Gen. Laws Ann. ch. 149, §19B; N.J.S.A. §2A:170–90.1.

5. Alas. Stat. §23.10.037; Del. Code tit. 19, §704; Me. Rev. Stat. Ann. ch. 87, L. 1979 §§7151, 7166, 7167; Minn. Stat. Ann. §181.75; and Wis. Stat . Ann. §111.326.

6. Cal. Lab. Code §432.2; Conn. Gen. Stat. Ann. §31–51g; Hawaii Rev. Stat. §378–21; Idaho Code §44–903; Md. Ann. Code art. 100, §95; Mich. Comp. Laws Ann. §338.1726; Mont. Rev. Codes Ann. §41–119; Or. Rev. Stat. §659.225; 18 Pa. Cons. Stat. Ann. §7321; and Wash. Rev. Code Ann. §49.44.120.

7. N.Y. Lab. Law art. 20-B, §§733 *et seq.*

8. 18 Pa. Cons. Stat. Ann. §7321; Cal. Lab. Code §432.2.

9. Ariz. Rev. Stat. §32.2701; Ill. Rev. Stat. chap. 38, §202; N.M. Stat. Ann. §67–31A–1; and Va. Code §§40.1–51.4:3 (1977).

10. Nev. Rev. Stat. tit. 54 §18.

11. *See, e.g.*, Alas. Stat. §23.10.037; Mass. Gen. Laws Ann. chap. 149 §19B; Mont. Rev. Codes Ann. §41–120; 18 Pa. Cons. Stat. Ann. §7321; Wash. Rev. Code Ann. §49.44.120.

12. *Humphrey v. First Nat'l State Bank,* Civ. Action No. 76–24 (D. N.J. 1977).

13. *E.g.,* Appeal Board, Unemployment Insurance Division, N.Y. State Department of Labor, no. 226,217, Sept. 8, 1976.

14. 18 U.S.C. §§2510–20.

15. *See Briggs v. American Air Filter Co., Inc.,* 630 F.2d 414 (5th Cir. 1980) (upheld monitoring on suspicion employee might be discussing business matters with competitor); *James v. Newspaper Agency Corp.,* 591 F.2d 579 (10th Cir. 1979) (upheld monitoring employees' handling of telephone transactions with public); *Simmons v. Southwestern Bell,* 452 F. Supp. 392 (W.D. Okla. 1978), *aff'd,* 611 F.2d 342 (10th Cir. 1979) (upheld monitoring to determine whether employees were making personal calls); *Jandak v. Village of Brookfield,* 520 F. Supp. 815 (N.D. Ill. 1981) (upheld police chief recording police officer's call to married woman with whom officer suspected of having affair). *But see U.S. v. Harpel,* 493 F.2d 346 (10th Cir. 1974) (extension phone exemption narrowly applied); *Awbrey v. Great*

Atlantic and Pacific Tea Co., 505 F. Supp. 604 (N.D. Ga. 1980) (employees' claims based on monitoring upheld; extension phone exemption not discussed).

16. *See, e.g.*, Fla. Stat. Ann. §934.01; Kan. Stat. §22–2514; Minn. Stat. Ann. §626A.01; Neb. Rev. Stat. §86–701; Nev. Rev. Stat. §200.610; N.H. Rev. Stat. Ann. §570–A:1; N.M. Stat. Ann. §40A–12–1; N.Y. Crim. Proc. Law §700.05; S.D. Comp. Laws Ann. §23–13A–1; Va. Code §19.2–61; Wisc. Stat. Ann. §968.27.

17. 18 Pa. Cons. Stat. Ann. §5701.

18. Conn. Gen. Stat. §31–48b(b).

19. Cal. Lab. Code §2930; Nev. Rev. Stat. §613.160.

20. *But see State v. Helfrich*, 600 P.2d 816 (1979) (Montana Supreme Court relied on Montana's constitutional privacy guarantee to exclude evidence obtained in a private search).

21. N.Y. Lab. Law §201–a.

22. Cal. Lab. Code §1051.

23. 15 U.S.C. §1681.

24. Mich. Comp. Laws Ann. §423.501.

25. 5 U.S.C. §552a.

26. 5 U.S.C. §522a(e)(1), (5), (10).

27. *See* Ark. Stat. Ann. §16–804; Cal. Civil Code §1798; Conn. Gen. Stat. Ann. §4–190; Ind. Code §4–1–6; Mass. Gen. Laws Ann. chap. 66A; Me. Rev. Stat. tit. 5 §554; Minn. Stat. Ann. §15.162; N.Y. Pub. Off. Laws §§91–99; Ohio Rev. Code §1347.01; Utah Code Ann. §63–50–1; and Va. Code §2.1–377; *see also* Ill. Ann. Stat. chap. 116, §43.5; Ky. Rev. Stat. Ann. §61.870; N.C. Gen. Stat. §§126–22, 153–A–98, 160A–168; N.Y. Pub. Off. Law §89; and Colo. Rev. Stat. §24–72–204(3) (a).

28. Cal. Lab. Code §1198.5; Conn. Gen. Stat. Ann. §31–1238(b); Me. Rev. Stat. tit. 26 §631; Mich. Comp. Laws Ann. §423.501; Or. Rev. Stat. §652.750; Pa. Stat. Ann. tit. 43 §1321; and Wis. Stat. Ann. §103.13.

29. Conn. Gen. Stat. Ann. §31–128c; Ohio Rev. Code Ann. §4113.23; Wis. Stat. Ann. §103.13.

30. Md. Ann. Code Art. 100, §95A.

31. 29 U.S.C. §655(b)(7).

32. 440 U.S. 301 (1979).

33. 440 U.S. at 318.

34. *See American Fed. of Gov't. Employees v. Defense General Supply Center*, 423 F. Supp. 481 (E.D. Va. 1976), *aff'd*, 573 F.2d 184 (4th Cir. 1978).

35. Conn. Gen. Stats. §31–128(f); Mich. Comp. Laws. Ann. §423.501.

36. Cal. Civil Code §56.

37. *See, e.g.*, *Beard v. Akzona, Inc.*, 517 F. Supp. 128 (E.D. Tenn. 1981).

38. *See Valencia v. Duval Corp.*, 132 Ariz. 348, 645 P.2d 1262 (1982).

39. *Beaumont v. Brown*, 401 Mich. 80, 257 N.W.2d 522 (1977).

40. *Mason v. Funderbuck*, 446 S.W.2d 543 (1969).

41. *Bulkin v. Western Kraft East, Inc.*, 422 F. Supp. 437 (E.D. Pa. 1976). *See also Quinones v. U.S.*, 492 F.2d 1269 (3d Cir. 1974).

42. *Kelley v. Johnson*, 425 U.S. 238 (1976).

43. *E.g., Tardiff v. Quinn*, 545 F.2d 761 (1st Cir. 1976); *Plancket v. N.H. Hospital*, 341 A.2d 267 (N.H. 1975); *Willingham v. Macon Tel. Publishing Co.*, 352 F. Supp. 1018 (M.D. Ga.), *rev'd and remand*, 482 F.2d 535 (5th Cir. 1973), *aff'd*, 507 F.2d 1084 (5th Cir. 1975) (en banc); *Barker v. Taft Broadcasting Co.*, 549 F.2d 400 (6th Cir. 1977).

44. *Gerdom v. Continental Airlines, Inc.*, 648 F.2d 1223 (9th Cir. 1976).

45. *Laffey v. Northwest Airlines*, 366 F. Supp. 763 (D.D.C. 1973), *vac'd and remand in part*, 642 F.2d 578 (D.C. Cir. 1976). *See Leonard v. National Airlines*, 434 F. Supp. 249 (S.D. Fla. 1973) and 434 F. Supp. 269 (1977) (Court upheld National's weight requirement though 30 percent of U.S. males but only 22 percent of U.S. females could meet National's regulations).

46. *Quist v. Young*, case no. FEP Sex 2361 (Conn. Commission on Human Rights, Jun. 30, 1975).

47. *Woods v. Safeway Stores*, 420 F. Supp. 35 (E.D. Va. 1976).

48. *Geller v. Secretary of Defense*, 423 F. Supp. 16 (D. D.C. 1976).

49. *Cupit v. Baton Rouge Police Dept.*, 277 454 (La. App. Ct. 1973); *Eastern Greyhound Lines, Inc. v. N.Y. State Div. of Human Rights*, 27 N.Y.2d 279 (1970).

Part II

Employment Discrimination

V

Discrimination in General

An employer "discriminates" whenever it treats one employee differently from another, but such different treatment is generally legal. Unless a private employee is protected by a union, an employer has almost unlimited discretion to play favorites. The employer may lawfully hire Yankee fans rather than equally qualified Oriole rooters; it may promote an inexperienced relative over a more competent person; it may pass over a person with an abrasive personality in favor of a less productive but passive person.

Nevertheless, a private employer's right to discriminate against employees has been curtailed in certain circumstances. Various federal and state statutes, as well as administrative regulations and local ordinances, forbid or restrict disparate treatment based on race, sex, religion, age, national origin, or handicap. In addition, discrimination is illegal in some jurisdictions on the basis of sexual preferences, marital status, arrest or conviction records, or other grounds.

The law of discrimination as it affects private employees is very complex. This and the following seven chapters outline some of the more significant rights and remedies under antidiscrimination laws. These laws are also discussed in other books in this series, e.g., *The Rights of Racial Minorities*, *The Rights of Women*, *The Rights of Gay People*, *The Rights of Older Persons*, *The Rights of Physically Handicapped People*, *The Rights of Veterans*, and *The Rights of Union Members*. You should consult the appropriate ACLU handbook for additional analysis. Furthermore, if you believe you have been discriminated against unlawfully, you should get in touch with an attorney, one of the organizations listed in Appendix 2, or your local Equal Employment Opportunity Commission office.

This chapter introduces you to the subject of discrimination in employment; it also covers procedures, remedies, and other matters that pertain to employment discrimination in general. In each of the seven chapters that follow, the law applicable to one kind of discrimination will be discussed. To thoroughly understand the law that applies to your situation, you should read this chapter, plus the chapter or chapters that pertain to you.

What laws prohibit employment discrimination?

The laws pertaining to discrimination in private employment are a complex web of federal and state constitutional provisions, statutes and regulations, and local ordinances. On the constitutional level, the Equal Protection Clause of the 14th Amendment to the U.S. Constitution prohibits the states from making laws that deny the equal protection of the laws to similarly situated persons. Most state constitutions also have equal protection clauses. The reach of the Equal Protection Clause in the area of employment discrimination is limited, however, because it has been held to prohibit only discriminatory actions taken by governments or parties acting under governmental authority. It does not apply to discrimination by private employers. The 13th Amendment to the U.S. Constitution prohibits slavery. While this clause does apply to private employers, it is limited as a weapon against discrimination because it has been narrowly interpreted to prohibit only the institution of slavery itself, and not the more subtle forms of discrimination that survived the abolition of slavery in the 19th century.

The most potent anti-discrimination law in the area of private employment is Title VII of the Civil Rights Act of 1964[1] ("Title VII"). This far-reaching statute prohibits discrimination in private employment on the basis of race, sex, religion, color, or national origin, with respect to compensation, terms, conditions, or privileges of employment. In addition, Title VII makes it illegal for an employer to discriminate against an employee in employment opportunities on the basis of these categories. It is also illegal for a labor organization to exclude from membership, limit, segregate, classify, fail to refer for employment, limit employment opportunities, or cause an employer to discriminate against an employee on the basis of race, sex, religion, color, or national origin.[2] Title VII is administered by the Equal Employment Opportunity Commission (EEOC), which is an agency of the federal government.[3] The EEOC is responsible for enforcing Title VII, and has the power to adjudicate and resolve charges of discrimination. A complaint under Title VII must be filed with the EEOC or a state human rights agency before it can be taken to court.

Two other federal laws pertain to racial discrimination by employers in the private sector. First, section 1981 of the Civil Rights Act of 1866[4] provides that all persons have the same rights to make contracts, to sue, and to receive the full and equal protection of the law in the area of private employment. This law has been read to prohibit intentional discrimination on the basis of race in private employment. Second, section 1983 of the Civil Rights Act of 1871[5] provides that every person acting under the color of state law can be liable for acts of racial discrimination. Essentially, this law is aimed at prohibiting employment discrimination by public officials and other persons somehow affiliated with the state. The courts have required that a person suing under section 1983 show that the defendant "intended" to discriminate against the employee.[6] As will be explained, this requirement poses considerable difficulty for plaintiffs suing under section 1983.

In 1965 President Johnson issued Executive Order 11246,[7] which requires that all federal contracts include an "equal opportunity clause." By signing a contract containing such a clause, the private contractor promises not to discriminate in hiring and to take affirmative action to eliminate discrimination. Additionally, firms that contract with the U.S. government for $50,000 or more, and have at least 50 employees, must file an affirmative action plan that sets forth specific steps for achieving equal employment.

Other federal laws limit certain employment discrimination on such grounds as age and handicap and provide special employment rights for veterans. These and other laws are discussed in the following seven chapters.

These federal laws are supplemented by state civil rights, human rights, and fair employment practices laws. All the states except Alabama, Arkansas, Georgia, Louisiana, Mississippi, South Carolina, Tennessee, Texas, and Virginia have such statutes. In many situations, the EEOC must defer to or cooperate with the agency created to enforce the state law.[8] In addition, many counties and cities have enacted similar laws. These may provide additional protection against particular kinds of discrimination.

What should I do if I believe I have been the victim of illegal discrimination?

You face many difficult decisions if you believe that you have been the victim of employment discrimination. In some cases the problem can be solved by simply bringing the matter to the attention of an appropriate person within your company. Since the enactment of Title VII, many private employers have grown more sensitive to the problem of discrimination and have established internal mechanisms to deal with discrimination complaints. Nonetheless, persons with discrimination claims often must seek help from governmental agencies and the courts to remedy completely the adverse effects of discrimination.

Unfortunately, because of the complexity of this area of the law and the backlog of cases filed with the EEOC, pursuing a discrimination claim through these channels is typically time-consuming and frustrating. You do not have to hire an attorney to bring an EEOC complaint, or even a lawsuit, against your employer. Nevertheless, because this area of the law is so complicated and is constantly changing, you should consult an attorney experienced in equal employment law. A list of some law offices that provide free or low-cost assistance to persons with discrimination claims is provided in Appendix 2.

Whether or not you retain an attorney, the first action you should take if you suspect that you have been a victim of discrimination is to keep a written record of all incidents and facts relating to your complaint. For instance, if the discrimination involves the hiring process, as soon as possible after the job interview you should prepare a summary of the comments and questions of the employer's representatives during your discussion with them. If you were subjected to discriminatory remarks, you should note the name of the person who made them, the precise words used, and the names of co-workers who heard the remarks and can be called as witnesses on your behalf. You should also observe and record the numbers of minorities and women employed by the company and their status. You should gather copies of any employer evaluations of your job performance, and you should record any informal comments by your supervisors. All records you make should show dates, times, and locations of incidents. To prevent discovery by supervisory personnel, you should not keep these records at work.

You should speak to any other employees in your company

who may have experienced discriminatory treatment from your employer. These employees may wish to participate in any action against the employer. A joint protest by employees is more likely to pressure an employer into making desired changes. In addition, workers engaged in any collective action to improve their working situation are protected against retaliation by their employer under the National Labor Relations Act, which prohibits retaliation against employees for their participation in "concerted activities for . . . mutual aid or protection."[9]

Before filing a formal charge you should determine whether you can achieve your immediate goals without taking action outside the company. Even if a lawsuit eventually succeeds, the emotional and financial expense may be greater than the relief the court awards you. Also, if you file a charge, you can expect to face a chilly work environment and, possibly, some form of retaliation. Therefore, you should try to inform your superiors of the substance of your charge and explore with them the internal measures that could be taken to solve the problem.

If your company is covered by E.O. 11246, you should direct your complaint to the EEO officer in your company. You should remember, however, that the EEO officer may not impartial, as he or she is an employee of your company. Therefore, when meeting with the officer, you have none of the procedural rights associated with a governmental hearing, such as the right to call witnesses or to be represented by an attorney. Your object during your discussions with the EEO officer should be to present the facts of your claim clearly and completely. Nevertheless, during these discussions, you should consider the EEO officer a representative of your employer and should not disclose information that you do not want passed along to your employer.

If your attempts at resolving your complaint internally fail, or if the time limit for filing a complaint is about to expire, you should file a formal complaint of employment discrimination. Generally, it is best to file a complaint under all of the laws that apply to your situation. For example, if you have been discriminated against on account of your race, you could file a complaint with a local agency or with the EEOC under Title VII, bring a court action under section 1981, and file a complaint under E.O. 11246. As the remedies under these laws are independent, you may pursue claims under these laws simultaneously.[10]

Does Title VII apply to all employers?

No. An employer must employ at least 15 employees to be covered by Title VII;[11] hence, if you work for a small employer, you may not be covered by Title VII. If your employer is too small to be covered by Title VII, however, a state civil rights law may protect you. For example, the New York State anti-discrimination law covers employers with as few as four employees.[12] Inasmuch as Title VII is by far the most pervasive anti-discrimination statute, the rest of this chapter deals mainly with that law.

How do I file a Title VII complaint?

Title VII requires that you file a formal charge of discrimination with the EEOC or a state or local fair employment agency before you can sue in federal court. If you do not file your complaint with a local agency, you must file your complaint with the EEOC within 180 days of the discriminatory act. If you do file with a local agency, you must still file with the EEOC within 300 days of the discriminatory act.[13] Filing a charge with your local agency will not protect your right to sue in federal court under Title VII; you must actually file with the EEOC within the 300 day period to protect that right.[14]

You should be aware that you may lose your right to sue if you miss these time limits. The Supreme Court has ruled that no extensions of the time will be granted merely because you pursued your discrimination complaint through contract grievance machinery,[15] through arbitration procedures,[16] or through a federal court action under section 1981.[17] Therefore, no matter how you choose to pursue your claim, make sure that you file a formal complaint within the time limits specified.

What can I do if more than 180 days have elapsed since I was discriminated against?

If the discriminatory practice occurred more than 180 days ago, your action may be time-barred, but you can still file your complaint if the discriminatory practice is "continuing." Continuing acts of discrimination are those actions of the employer that cause you to suffer discrimination repeatedly. For example, if an employer has set wages according to gender (an illegal practice), each paycheck constitutes another act of discrimination; the 180-day limitations period will begin to run anew with the receipt of each paycheck. If your suit is barred by the statute of limitations, other avenues may be available. For example, if the discrimination was on the basis of race, you may be able to bring a section 1981 or section 1983 action; these are discussed in the next chapter.

What is a discrimination charge?

The charge itself is simply a description of the employer's conduct that resulted in illegal discrimination. In filling out a charge form, whether with a local or state agency or with the EEOC, you should be careful to include *all* possible allegations of discriminatory conduct. Later proceedings will focus only on those issues that are related to the allegations stated in the charge.[18] Care must be taken to fill out the charge form accurately and completely, because inconsistencies between the charge and later testimony may be held against you. All persons or companies potentially responsible for the discriminatory practice should be named in the charge, because it is difficult to add additional defendants later in the lawsuit.

What does the EEOC do after a charge has been filed?

Tile VII requires that the EEOC must defer investigation of any discrimination complaint to the local human rights agency for a period of 60 days.[19] Thus, even if you do not file with your local agency, it will have the opportunity to handle your complaint.

Within ten days after receiving notice of the charge, the EEOC must notify your employer of the allegations of illegal conduct.[20] The EEOC or the local agency will then investigate the charge to determine whether there is "reasonable cause" to believe that the allegations are true. These investigations, carried out by personnel in EEOC offices, are supposed to last no longer than 120 days after the filing of the charge or after the 60-day local agency deferral period. Because of the backlog of cases filed with the EEOC, however, many investigations drag on for several years.

If the EEOC or the local agency finds "reasonable cause" to believe that your employer has violated Title VII, it will try "conciliation," i.e., to convince both sides to settle their differences informally. If no agreement can be reached, the EEOC can file a lawsuit in federal court against your employer to obtain relief for you.[21] The EEOC will be represented by its own attorneys at no cost to you. You can limit your role to that of a witness, or you may join the lawsuit as an "intervenor."

Can I bring a lawsuit in court without filing with the EEOC?

No. You may bring your own lawsuit in federal court under Title VII, but only after the EEOC has had an opportunity to examine your charge.[22] You must obtain a "right-to-sue" letter from the EEOC to initiate a private lawsuit. You have a right to obtain this letter 180 days after you file your charge with the EEOC,[23] regardless of whether the EEOC has taken any action on your complaint. EEOC regional offices may issue this letter before the expiration of 180 days, if requested.

If you wish to pursue your case privately, you must file suit in federal district court within 90 days after receipt of notice that the EEOC has dismissed the charge or receipt of the right-to-sue letter.[24] If you do not file within 90 days, you lose your right to sue under Title VII. As already stated, you may bring a private Title VII lawsuit in federal court without a lawyer. Because Title VII cases are usually too complex to be presented by non-lawyers, Title VII provides that a court may appoint an attorney for you if you need such help. Title VII also permits the court to allow the lawsuit to proceed without the usual payment of various court fees and security bonds,[25] and provides that the court can award attorneys' fees to the successful party.[26]

How do I pursue a claim against my employer if it has contracts with the federal government?

Complaints of discrimination that come under E.O. 11246 must be filed with the U.S. Department of Labor's Office of Federal Contract Compliance Programs (OFCCP) within 180 days of the violation.[27] OFCCP has full responsibility for the administration and enforcement of that executive order. In racial discrimination cases, however, OFCCP has restricted its role to reviewing the employment records of companies that have contracts with the federal government. Individual complaints filed with OFCCP are transferred to the EEOC for investigation and processing under Title VII. If E.O. 11246 applies, you should file a complaint with the OFCCP even if you plan to file a Title VII charge with EEOC, because your employer will be subject to losing its federal contracts if a violation is found.

What is a class action?

A class action is a lawsuit brought by one or more persons who are named in the complaint, and who bring the action on behalf of themselves and all others similarly situated. If certain procedural requirements are satisfied, the named plaintiffs in an employment discrimination class action may obtain relief for others who have suffered discrimination, even though those individuals have not filed claims of discrimination.

In a Title VII class action, only one person must go through the Title VII–EEOC charge processing before the whole class commences suit. The other class members need not file a charge or obtain a right-to-sue letter.[28] The class may not, however, include persons whose Title VII claims would have been time-barred when the class representative's charge was filed.[29]

Many lawsuits under Title VII have been class actions because claims of discrimination based on an inborn characteristic are particularly well suited for litigation in that form. Over the years, however, the courts have made it more difficult to fulfill the requirements for certification to proceed as a class action. In one case, a plaintiff who did not suffer *hiring* discrimination was not allowed to represent workers who did not suffer from that particular type of discrimination.[30]

What must I prove in a Title VII discrimination case?

The Supreme Court has ruled that a plaintiff suing under Title VII need not prove that the employer intended to discriminate. The knowledgeable employer will generally contend that a practice challenged as discriminatory was adopted solely for some legitimate business reason. Because Title VII is aimed at "the consequences of employment practices, not simply the motivation,"[31] an employer who has no intention to discriminate, but who engages in a practice that has a discriminatory effect, will be found to have violated Title VII.

In a case involving an individual employment decision, you must show that (1) you belong to a protected class (e.g., race or sex); (2) you applied for and were qualified for a job that the employer was seeking to fill; (3) despite these qualifications, you were denied the position; and (4) after the rejection, the employer continued to seek applications from people with qualifications like yours.[32] Upon proving these elements, you are said to have established a prima facie case of discrimination.

When an employment practice affects a large number of employees, statistics may play a major role in establishing the prima facie case. For example, an inference of discrimination can be raised by showing a significant statistical disparity between the proportion of protected group members in the employer's workforce as compared to their proportion in the general population within the geographical area from which the employer recruits employees.[33]

Upon your making out a prima facie case, whether on the basis of individual facts or statistics, the court will give your employer the opportunity to articulate some "legitimate, non-discriminatory reason" for its action.[34] This means that the employer must prove that the practice in question is rooted in legitimate business concerns. For example, if a pre-employment test is found to disqualify women disproportionately from a certain position, the employer must show that the characteristics valued by that test are truly necessary to perform the job.

If your employer demonstrates a legitimate business justification for the practice, you are given the opportunity to show that the practice is a pretext for discrimination.[35] Usually, this is demonstrated by showing that an alternative practice could have been used that would not have the effect of discriminating.

What remedies are available if I win a Title VII case?

Remedies authorized by Title VII are designed to place you in the financial and career position you would have been in had the discrimination not occurred. Remedies can take the form of an order to hire, reinstate, or promote you; an injunction forbidding continuation of the practice found to be discriminatory; or an award of back pay (i.e., the wages that you would have earned had the discrimination not occurred). Back-pay awards may also include interest, overtime, shift differentials, vacation and sick pay, and pension plan contributions.[36] Back pay is recoverable, however, for only the two years preceding the filing of the EEOC charge; and the court must reduce the amount of any back pay award by any amounts you earned or could reasonably have earned during the period.[37]

As previously stated, these Title VII remedies are available to the successful Title VII plaintiff even if actions brought under different laws result in sanctions against the employer. For example, an employer found to have discriminated in violation of E.O. 11246 and Title VII may not only be required to pay damages to the individual employees, but may also lose its right to be awarded future contracts with the federal government.[40]

Can a court require an employer to hire a certain number of employees from a certain group?

Yes. Title VII authorizes courts to order appropriate affirmative action to remedy past discrimination. Courts have ordered employers to hire and promote workers according to formulas that favor identified minority applicants. Such a formula might, for example, require hiring to proceed on an alternating black-white, one-for-one, basis until the percentage of minority workers reaches the percentage of minority group persons residing in the employer's locale.

Affirmative action in employment usually takes two forms. First, an affirmative action program may require that members of the protected class (typically, minorities and women) be actively recruited. This means that employers cannot rely on word-of-mouth recruitment, which tends to work to the disadvantage of these groups. Instead, employers must advertise in newspapers and other media read by persons in these groups, and must affirmatively seek applicants in the protected class. Second, an affirmative action program may require that employers set goals and timetables for hiring and promoting such employees into positions in which they are currently underrepresented. The goals and timetables are established as a means of ensuring that the employer is making progress toward achieving equal employment.

Affirmative action does not mean that a minority person who is not qualified for a job must be given that job. It means that qualified minority persons must be seriously recruited and considered for employment and promotion.

How far can an affirmative action plan go in remedying past discrimination?

Courts are hesitant to apply an affirmative action remedy. Title VII cautions against "preferential treatment,"[39] and the Supreme Court has warned that such formulas must strike a balance between the fair employment rights of victims of discrimination and the contractual rights of non-victim employees.[40] Most courts demand a clear showing of past discrimination before imposing quotas, though an intent to discriminate need not be shown.[41] Courts generally show an even greater reluctance to set quotas in the context of promotions, because such an order tends to conflict with the practice of promoting on the basis of seniority.[42]

In 1978, in *Regents of the University of California v. Bakke*,[43] the Supreme Court addressed the constitutionally of a voluntarily adopted race-conscious medical school admissions plan that set aside 16 percent of the places in each entering class for disadvantaged minority applicants. In a confusing 4-1-4 vote, the *Bakke* Court held this rigid numerical plan unlawful, but stated that any race-conscious plan that merely gave minority applicants extra points would be both lawful and constitutional. A year later, in *United Steelworkers of America v. Weber*,[44] the Supreme Court decided that a voluntarily adopted race-conscious affirmative action plan that set aside 50 percent of the openings in an on-the-job training program for minority workers was lawful under Title VII.

In *Weber*, the collective bargaining agreement between the United Steelworkers of America and the employer required that blacks comprise 50 percent of the employees selected for a program to train employees to become skilled craftworkers. The provision was adopted to reverse the company's pattern of racial discrimination, which had resulted in a gross underrepresentation of blacks in skilled job categories. In operation, the affirmative action plan allowed black applicants with less seniority than certain white applicants to be admitted to the training program.

The Supreme Court held that Title VII does not condemn private, voluntary, race-conscious affirmative action plans like the *Weber* plan. In addition, the Supreme Court held that this particular affirmative action plan was permissible under Title VII because it was designed to eliminate traditional patterns of conspicious racial segregation and because it did not require the discharge of white workers and their replacement with new black trainees.

In 1980, the Supreme Court held in *Fullilove v. Klutznick*,[45] that the minority business enterprise provision of the Public Works Employment Act of 1977,[46] which requires a "10 percent set-aside" of federal funds for minority businesses on public works projects, does not violate the equal protection clauses of the Fifth and 14th Amendments. That case, as well as other recent cases, indicates that the courts will allow a wide latitude for private employers in creating affirmative action plans to eliminate manifest racial imbalances in traditionally segregated job categories.

If I win a discrimination case, can I obtain attorneys' fees from the losing side?

As noted above, an employee involved in a discrimination case should try to obtain counsel, if possible. It is often difficult to retain an attorney, however, because discrimination suits are usually lengthy and may not involve much money. Title VII provides a partial remedy, granting the federal courts discretion to award attorneys' fees to the successful party.[47] Courts have generally awarded these fees to prevailing workers. Attorneys' fees are set according to the time and effort expended by the attorney, the difficulty of the issues, and the experience of the attorney. No fees are assessed for representation by the EEOC,[48] nor may legal services and non-profit organizations be compensated.[49] Fees have not been granted to employees' attorneys in cases brought under state law if the state law does not authorize payment.

Can I be punished for protesting discriminatory conditions?

No. Title VII prohibits discrimination against an employee "because he has opposed any practice made . . . unlawful . . . by [Title VII], or because he had made a charge, testified, assisted, or participated in any manner in an investigation, proceeding or hearing under [Title VII]."[50] Similarly, E.O. 11246 penalizes employers who do not prevent the intimidation or coercion of employees who aid in investigations of alleged discrimination by contractors.[51] These provisions clearly protect you from retaliation for filing a discrimination charge or for otherwise participating in formal proceedings. They also afford some protection against mistreatment or discharge in response to making an informal complaint. Certain forms of protest against discrimination are not protected by Title VII. To determine the limits of protected protest activity, a balance will be struck between the intention of the fair employment laws "to protect persons engaging reasonably in activities opposing . . . discrimination," and the right of employers to select and supervise personnel fairly.[52] For example, an employee who filed a discrimination charge with the EEOC was not protected from discharge by the anti-retaliation provision when his employer demonstrated that he had a long record of unexcused absences and that other employees with similar records of absenteeism had been discharged.[53]

In determining whether your employer's action amounts to illegal retaliation, a court can also ask whether you simply went "too far" in your on-the-job pursuit of a complaint.[54] One court stated that an action protesting discrimination is unreasonable and therefore outside Title VII if it is "calculated to inflict needless economic hardship upon the employer. . . ."[55] For example, an employer could properly fire a worker whose conduct went beyond legitimate complaints of alleged discrimination to the point of disclosing confidential information to newspaper reporters and circulating rumors that the company was in financial jeopardy.[56] An employee was protected from retaliation, however, for writing and circulating a petition that protested racial discrimination, and for organizing employees to assert their legal rights.[57] Finally, most courts will protect you against retaliation even if the underlying charge of discrimination is found to be without merit, if you had a reasonable belief that the opposed practice constituted illegal discrimination.[58]

NOTES

1. 42 U.S.C. §§2000e *et seq.*, as amended.
2. 42 U.S.C. §2000e–2(a)(1), (b).
3. 42 U.S.C. §2000e–4.
4. 42 U.S.C. §1981.
5. 42 U.S.C. §1983.
6. *Washington v. Davis*, 426 U.S. 229 (1976).
7. 30 F.R. 12319.
8. 42 U.S.C. §2000e–5(e).
9. 29 U.S.C. §§151 *et seq.*
10. *Johnson v. Railway Express Agency, Inc.*, 421 U.S. 454 (1975).
11. 42 U.S.C. §2000e(b).
12. N.Y. Exec. Law §292(5).
13. 42 U.S.C. §2000e–5(e).
14. 42 U.S.C. §2000e–5(e).
15. *Elec. Workers v. Robbins & Meyers, Inc.*, 429 U.S. 229 (1976).
16. *Alexander v. Gardner-Denver Co.*, 415 U.S. 36 (1974).
17. *Johnson v. Railway Express Agency, Inc., supra.*

18. *Jenkins v. Blue Cross Mutual Hosp. Ins., Inc.*, 538 F.2d 164 (7th Cir.), *cert. denied*, 429 U.S. 986 (1976).

19. 42 U.S.C. 2000e–5(c).

20. 42 U.S.C. §2000e–5(b),(e); 29 C.F.R. §1601.14.

21. 42 U.S.C. §2000e–5(b),(f)(1).

22. *Mohasco Corp. v. Silver*, 447 U.S. 807 (1980).

23. 29 C.F.R. §1601.28.

24. 42 U.S.C. §2000e–5(f)(1).

25. *Id*.

26. 42 U.S.C. §2000e–5(k).

27. 41 C.F.R. §60–1.21.

28. *Albemarle Paper Co. v. Moody*, 422 U.S. 405 (1975); *Hicks v. Crown Zellerbach Corp.*, 49 F.R.D. 184 (E.D. La. 1968).

29. *Wetzel v. Liberty Mutual Insurance Co.*, 508 F.2d 239 (3d Cir. 1975), *cert. denied*, 421 U.S. 1011 (1975).

30. *See, e.g., E. Tex. Motor Freight Systems Inc. v. Rodriguez*, 431 U.S. 395 (1977).

31. *Griggs v. Duke Power Co.*, 401 U.S. 424 (1971).

32. *McDonnell Douglas Corp. v. Green*, 411 U.S. 792 (1973).

33. *International Brotherhood of Teamsters v. U.S.* 431 U.S., 324 (1977).

34. *Board of Trustees of Keene State College v. Sweeney*, 439 U.S. 24 (1978).

35. *Tex. Dept. of Community Affairs v. Burdine*, 450 U.S. 248 (1981).

36. *See generally Albemarle Paper Co. v. Moody*, *supra* at 422.

37. 42 U.S.C. §2000e–5(g); *see Pettway v. American Cast Iron Pipe Co.*, 494 F.2d 211 (5th Cir. 1974).

40. 30 F.R. 1239.

39. 42 U.S.C. §2000e–2(j).

40. *International Brotherhood of Teamsters v. U.S.*, 431 U.S. 324 (1977).

41. *Erie Human Relations Commission v. Tullio*, 493 F.2d 371 (3d Cir. 1974).

42. *See Kirkland v. N.Y. State Department of Correctional Services*, 520 F.2d 420 (2d. Cir. 1975), *cert. denied*, 429 U.S. 823 (1976).

43. 438 U.S. 265 (1978).

44. 443 U.S. 193 (1979).

45. 448 U.S. 448 (1980).

46. 42 U.S.C. §6705(f)(2).

47. 42 U.S.C. §2000e–5(k).

48. 42 U.S.C. §2000e–5(k).

49. *EEOC v. Enterprise Assoc. Steamfitters Loc. No. 638*, 542 F.2d 579 (2d Cir. 1976), *cert. denied*, 430 U.S. 911 (1977).

50. 42 U.S.C. §2000e–3(a).

51. 41 C.F.R. §60–1.32 (1981).

52. *Hochstadt v. Worcester*, 545 F.2d 222 (1st Cir. 1976).

53. *Brown v. Ralston Purina Co.*, 557 F.2d 570 (6th Cir. 1977).

54. *Hochstadt*, *supra*.

55. *EEOC v. Kallir, Philips, Ross, Inc.*, 401 F. Supp. 66, 71 (S.D. N.Y.), *aff'd*, 559 F.2d 1203 (2d Cir.), *cert. denied*, 434 U.S. 920 (1977).

56. *Hochstadt, supra*.
57. EEOC no. 70–119, 10 FEP 811 (1969).
58. *Berg v. La Crosse Cooler Co.*, 548 F.2d 211 (7th Cir. 1980); *Sias v. City Demonstration Agency*, 588 F.2d 692 (9th Cir. 1978).

VI

Racial Minorities

What federal laws protect private employees from racial discrimination?

Many laws protect employees from discrimination on the basis of race.

On the federal level, the laws include the Civil Rights Act of 1866 (section 1981),[1] which was designed to implement the constitutional amendment abolishing slavery.[2] Section 1981 guarantees to all persons "the same right . . . to make and enforce contracts . . . as is enjoyed by white citizens.[3] Since 1975 the courts have recognized that this statute prohibits racial discrimination in private as well as public employment.[4]

Title VII of the Civil Rights Act of 1964,[5] furnishes the most comprehensive protection to the private sector worker, as it specifically outlaws racial discrimination in private employment. Title VII also prohibits discrimination on the basis of color or national origin. For the sake of simplicity, the discussion in this chapter focuses on race, though the principles and rules apply equally to color and national origin. For a full discussion of the procedures to be followed in filing a discrimination complaint under Title VII, see Chapter 5.

In addition to these federal statutes, some private employees are protected by Executive Order 11246, issued in 1965,[6] which is designed to promote equal employment opportunities for minority groups by requiring that any private employer having a contract with the federal government must agree not to discriminate on the basis of race. Such employers also may be required to take affirmative efforts to recruit and promote minority workers. The order is enforced by the Office of Federal Contract Compliance Programs (OFCCP) in the Department of Labor.[7]

In addition, every state except Alabama, Arkansas, Georgia,

Louisiana, Mississippi, South Carolina, Tennessee, Texas, and Virginia has enacted fair employment practice law that prohibits racial discrimination by private employers. Also, many cities have ordinances forbidding racial discrimination by local private employers or by municipal contractors or agencies. State and local fair employment laws often create agencies responsible for investigating complaints, granting relief, or instituting criminal proceedings. If such agencies meet federal standards, the EEOC will not act upon any discrimination charge that has not been previously examined at the local level.[8] Procedures for filing and processing charges are discussed in Chapter 5.

Many of the laws described above exempt certain categories of employers from the prohibition against racial discrimination. The most significant limitation is found in Title VII, which applies only to an employer of 15 or more employees that is engaged in interstate commerce (the transfer of goods and services between two or more states).[9]

What laws cover employers who are exempt from Title VII?

A person who suffers racial discrimination at the hands of an employer who is not subject to Title VII may nevertheless pursue a claim. Section 1981's prohibitions apply to all persons and to legal entities (such as corporations). Therefore, under that statute, an aggrieved employee can bring suit in federal court against *any* employer, no matter how large or small. Furthermore, in states and cities that have laws banning racial discrimination, an employee may also be able to file a charge or complaint against even a small or local employer, because state laws usually apply to small employers (e.g., as few as four employees) and there is no interstate commerce requirement. Finally, E.O. 11246 covers all federal contractors and subcontractors that have not been granted a specific exemption by the Secretary of Labor. In practice, such exemptions have rarely been granted to companies whose government business exceeds $10,000 annually. Most large employers hold sufficient government contracts to be subject also to the affirmative action requirements of E.O. 11246.

What racial groups are protected by the laws against racial discrimination?

Anti-discrimination laws protect all racial groups. Generally, such laws prohibit discrimination on the basis of color or national origin, as well as race. Not only black but Hispanic, Asian, and American Indian workers are protected. So are white workers.[10] Therefore, any employee who is a victim of racially discriminatory employment practices may assert a claim under these laws.

Many questions have been raised concerning the legality of affirmative action programs designed to increase the job opportunities of minority employees. Such programs range from increasing recruitment efforts in minority communities to establishing minority hiring goals and targets. Preferential minority hiring programs may appear to limit the employment options available to whites. Nevertheless, the Supreme Court has not ruled out the use of affirmative action programs in employment and has approved the establishment of a voluntary affirmative action program by an employer and union, even though there has not been a prior judicial finding of illegal discrimination.[11] For a fuller discussion of affirmative action, see Chapter 5.

What forms of employer conduct violate the prohibition against racial discrimination?

The federal and state fair employment laws prohibit all forms of overt racial discrimination. An employer may not pursue a "whites only" hiring policy or assign jobs or rates of pay on the basis of race. Less obvious forms of racial discrimination are illegal too. Practices that have the appearance of being even-handed may have a discriminatory effect. Accordingly, Title VII and many state fair employment laws prohibit employment policies that in practice operate to discriminate against racial groups, even if no discriminatory intent can be shown. Such discriminatory policies are legal only if the employer can prove an overriding business need for their use.[12]

For example, a high-school diploma requirement is illegal under all the anti-discrimination laws if it can be shown that the rule was instituted with the *intent* of favoring a particular racial group. If such a discriminatory purpose cannot be proved, the job requirement is nevertheless subject to attack under Title VII if the *effect* of the requirement is to discriminate against minority applicants. An employer can defend the diploma requirement, however, by showing that a high-school education is, in fact, required to perform the job properly.

The key to the business necessity defense is a showing that the job requirement in question is directly related to job performance in that an applicant who does not meet the requirement will be unable to perform the job successfully. An employer hiring an electrical engineer, for example, can legitimately require that an applicant hold a degree from a school of electrical engineering, because such a degree is considered a valid indicator of a skill related to the job. Courts have been suspicious, however, of diploma requirements not clearly related to job skills. The requirement of a 12th-grade education for applicants to all office and clerical jobs, for example, has been found to violate Title VII.[13]

It has also been declared unlawful for employers to deny jobs to minority applicants solely on the basis of arrests, convictions, or poor credit ratings. The EEOC has concluded that use of such criteria has a discriminatory impact because they tend to disqualify a disproportionate number of minority applicants. An employer must, therefore, show a business necessity for such a practice. This subject is discussed in greater detail in Chapter 2, "The Hiring Process."

What types of employee recruitment practices violate Title VII?

An employer whose workforce is predominantly white, and who relies on his employees for word-of-mouth recruiting, may be practicing a form of indirect racial discrimination. Such a policy has been found to be unlawful because it tends to perpetuate the racial composition of the existing workforce and limit the opportunities available to minority job seekers. While courts have recognized their inability to halt grapevine recruitment by a company's employees, they have ordered that specific job openings be advertised in media that reach the minority community, and that the company publicize that it is an equal opportunity employer.[14]

Courts have prohibited the use of several other recruitment policies. An employer may not have a policy of preferentially hiring the relatives of present employees if the workforce contains few minority workers.[15] Nor can an employer that owns two companies recruit workers for one company from the ranks of the second if the hiring policies of the second company discriminate against minorities.[16] Additionally, if an employer's present workforce is racially imbalanced, the employer may not recruit at only predominantly white educational institutions.[17]

Title VII also prohibits discrimination by private and public employment agencies. An employment agency may neither refuse to refer a person for employment nor classify applicants or job openings on the basis of race.[18]

Can an employer's use of tests during the hiring process violate Title VII?

Yes. Title VII explicitly approves the use of "ability tests" in the hiring process.[19] Nevertheless, such a test will be invalid if it operates to disqualify a disproportionately large number of minority applicants, unless the employer can demonstrate that "the test reliably predicts which applicants possess the reasonably necessary job skills and traits."[20]

The two most common methods of establishing that a test is job-related are called content validity and criterion-related validity. A test meets the content validity requirement if it directly measures a skill or knowledge necessary to perform the job. For example, a typing test is an appropriate examination for prospective typists. Criterion-related validity refers to the accuracy of a test in predicting an applicant's level of job performance. The employer must show that the test reliably identifies those applicants who will function successfully on the job. The use of a written aptitude test, for example, is suspect if, while it tends to screen out minority applicants, a significant number of those who pass the test failed to perform the job adequately. Such a result suggests that the test measures abilities irrelevant to job performance. The EEOC's Employment Selection Guidelines establish minimum standards for the validation of tests used for hiring or promotion.[21]

Does Title VII prohibit discrimination in working conditions?

Yes. The anti-discrimination laws afford some protection against on-the-job racial harassment, such as use of racial epithets, closer supervision of minority workers, and uneven application of disciplinary rules. Additionally, an employer must take reasonable steps to maintain an atmosphere free of racial intimidation and insults.[22]

If you contend that your work atmosphere is racially demeaning, you must be able to prove that management was aware, or should have been aware, of the offensive conduct, but failed to correct the situation.[23] In most cases, you should complain to your employer about the condition before initiating any legal action. Such a complaint will give your employer an opportunity to remedy the discriminatory working conditions, and may help establish that your employer had notice of the discriminatory practice. In any event, it is usually quite difficult to prove that any harassment was directed against an entire racial group, as opposed to being directed against an individual employee.[24]

An employer may not consider race in determining how to compensate employees. Therefore, the allocation of wages and hours (for example, the distribution of overtime or the assignment to graveyard shifts), workloads, and such benefits as vacations and bonuses must be made without regard to race.[25]

If an employer has practiced racial discrimination in the past, even an otherwise neutral policy may operate in a biased fashion. Any compensation plan based on an employer's job assignment policy is suspect if the underlying policy is discriminatory. For example, a company may properly compute retirement benefits based on past levels of compensation. But if the company previously paid lower wages to minority workers based on racially discriminatory job classifications, the apparently neutral retirement plan will operate illegally to lock in the effects of past discrimination.[26]

How do I prove that my employer's promotion practices discriminate on the basis of race?

An employer that does not discriminate in hiring policies may nevertheless discriminate in promotion practices. The first step in ascertaining whether this is happening is the most obvious: determine whether more minority workers are in lower-level positions than in higher-level positions of the company. A worker who presented statistics indicating that blacks were promoted at half the rate of white employees was held to have made a showing sufficient to prove illegal discrimination under Title VII, thereby shifting the burden to the employer to articulate a non-discriminatory business reason for the statistical disparity.[27]

The next step is to look for a particular practice that hampers the advancement of minority employees. For example, if blacks are concentrated in certain positions, it may be because they are denied equal access to training. A company's training programs, whether formal or informal, must be available equally to all employees. All personnel must receive adequate notice of such programs and of promotion opportunities.

Evaluations of employees that are used to determine promotions must meet the same standards that are applied to hiring practices. Test and degree requirements for a promotion must be job-related if they have a discriminatory impact.[28] Subjective evaluations of employee work performance are particularly suspect, as racial bias may influence such evaluations.

How can I prove that I was fired on the basis of my race?

An employer will often contend that an employee has been discharged for incompetence, insubordination, or other misconduct. A minority worker in such a situation should seek to determine whether similar behavior by white workers also resulted in termination. If whites were not terminated, the anti-discrimination laws may have been violated. For example, a trucking company could not legally discharge a black driver upon learning that his license had previously been suspended, when a white driver was not fired after the employer learned that he had lied on his job application about numerous traffic citations.[29]

The fair employment laws do not, however, prohibit an employer from discharging a worker for valid business reasons, as long as company policy is applied even-handedly. Therefore, a minority employee may be terminated or demoted for engaging in disruptive acts against his employer—even if those acts have been designed to protest the employer's racial policies—if whites were terminated for engaging in disruptive events of the same magnitude.[30]

Is a seniority system illegal if it perpetuates the effects of past discrimination?

No, unless the seniority system itself was created with the specific intent to discriminate. As previously explained, Title VII does not require the plaintiff to prove that the employer intended to discriminate; it is enough if the employment decision had a discriminatory effect. In the area of seniority systems, however, Title VII creates an exception to this rule. Section 703(h) states [31] that it—

. . . shall not be an unlawful employment practice for an employer to apply different standards of compensation, or different terms, conditions or privileges of employment pursuant to a bona fide seniority . . . system . . . *provided that such difference are not the result of an intention to discriminate because of race.*

In other words, even if a seniority system locks in the effect of past discrimination, it will not be found to violate Title VII, unless it was adopted because of its racially discriminatory impact.[32]

In a recent opinion, the U.S. Supreme Court reiterated the intent requirement and stated that a seniority system does not violate Title VII unless there is a finding of actual intent to discriminate on the part of those who negotiated or maintained the system. Furthermore, the Court held that a discriminatory motive cannot be inferred from anything less than a factual showing of actual motive.[33] Obviously, this standard for showing discrimination makes it extremely difficult to prove that a seniority system violates Title VII.

How do I bring a lawsuit for racial discrimination?

The procedures under Title VII are discussed in Chapter 5. The procedures under section 1981 are quite different.

Lawsuits under section 1981 are properly commenced directly in federal district court. The time period in which to file a claim is set by state statutes of limitations, not federal law.[34] Therefore, the length of time available to initiate such a suit varies from state to state and should be checked carefully.

A section 1981 claim is, for the most part, independent of a Title VII claim. Filing a Title VII claim does not alter the time limits for filing a section 1981 suit. Therefore, you should not wait for the EEOC to rule on a Title VII charge before filing a section 1981 lawsuit, because the section 1981 time period might expire during the course of the EEOC investigation.

In at least one situation, however, two discrimination claims may not be independently pursued. A U.S. court of appeals has ruled that a worker cannot bring a section 1981 claim after filing a claim with a state fair employment agency, losing at the agency level, and unsuccessfully appealing in the state courts. The court held that the state court case covered all the issues that would be litigated in a section 1981 suit.[35]

What must I prove in a section 1981 case?

After section 1981 was recognized as applying to private

acts of discrimination, courts assumed that the section 1981 standard of proof was the same as the Title VII standard.[36] In a recent decision, [37] however, the U.S. Supreme Court held that a plaintiff suing under section 1981 must demonstrate that the employer intended to discriminate. It is not enough to show that a certain employment practice has a disparate impact on a protected group.

What remedies are available under section 1981?

Remedies under section 1981 are broader than those under Title VII. For example, Title VII does not provide for punitive damages (which go beyond simple back-pay awards and are intended to punish the employer),[38] whereas section 1981 does allow this remedy.[39] Section 1981 also authorizes the issuance of a preliminary injunction to prevent an employer from continuing the disputed practice while the case is being litigated; no injunction can be issued in a Title VII case while a charge is being processed by an administrative agency. Additionally, a section 1981 back-pay award is not limited to two years, as is a Title VII award.[40] Also, under section 1981, a court can prescribe a formula for hiring and promotion designed to undo a pattern of discrimination.[41]

NOTES

1. 42 U.S.C. §1981.
2. U.S. Constitution, Amendment XIII.
3. 42 U.S.C. §1981.
4. *Johnson v. Railway Express Agency, Inc.*, 421 U.S. 454 (1975).
5. 42 U.S.C. §§2000e *et seq.*, as amended.
6. *See* 30 Fed. Reg. 12319 (1965), as amended by E.O. 11375 and 12086.
7. 41 C.F.R. §§60–1.1 *et seq.*
8. 42 U.S.C. §2000e–5(c).
9. 42 U.S.C. §2000e–(b).
10. *McDonald v. Santa Fe Trail Transportation Co.*, 427 U.S. 273 (1976); *Grasso v. Lutheran Medical Center*, N.Y.C. Comm. on Human Rts. (Oct. 18, 1982).
11. *See United Steelworkers of America v. Weber*, 443 U.S. 193 (1979).
12. *Griggs v. Duke Power Company*, 401 U.S. 424 (1971).
13. *Payne v. Travenol Laboratories, Inc.*, 416 F. Supp. 248 (N.D. Miss. 1976, *aff'd*, 565 F.2d 895 (5th Cir. 1978), *cert. denied*, 439 U.S. 835 (1978).
14. *U.S. v. Ga. Power Co.*, 474 F.2d 906 (5th Cir. 1973).

15. *McCoy v. Safeway Stores, Inc.*, 5 FEP 628 (D. D.C. 1973); *see also* EEOC Doc. no. 71–797, 3 FEP 266.
16. *EEOC v. N.Y. Times Broadcasting Co.*, 542 F.2d 356 (6th Cir. 1976).
17. *U.S. v. Ga. Power, supra.*
18. 42 U.S.C. §2000e–2(b).
19. 42 U.S.C. §2000e–2(h).
20. *U.S. v. Ga. Power Co., supra.*
21. 29 C.F.R. §1607.
22. *Rogers v. EEOC*, 454 F.2d 234 (5th Cir. 1971), *cert. denied*, 406 U.S. 957 (1972).
23. See *Love v. Pullman*, 569 F.2d 1074 (10th Cir. 1978).
24. *Watkins v. Scott Paper*, 530 F.2d 1159 (5th Cir. 1976), *cert. denied*, 429 U.S. 861 (1976).
25. *Newman v. Avco Paper*, 7 FEP 285 (M.D. Tenn. 1973).
26. *Kirkland v. N.Y. State Dept. of Correctional Services*, 520 F.2d 420 (2d Cir. 1975), *cert. denied*, 429 U.S. 823 (1976).
27. *Row v. General Motors Corp.*, 457 F.2d 348 (5th Cir. 1972).
28. See *Croker v. Boeing Co.*, 437 F. Supp. 1138 (E.D. Pa. 1977).
29. *Johnson v. Ryder Truck Lines*, 575 F.2d 471 (W.D.N.C. 1975), *cert. denied*, 440 U.S. 979 (1978).
30. *McDonnell Douglas Corp. v. Green*, 411 U.S. 792 (1973).
31. 42 U.S.C. §2000–2(h).
32. *American Tobacco Co. v. Patterson*, 634 F. ad 744 (4th Cir. 1980).
33. *Pullman-Standard v. Swint*, —— U.S. ——, 102 S.Ct. 1781 (1982).
34. *Johnson v. Railway Express Agency, Inc., supra.*
35. *Mitchell v. NBA*, 553 F.2d 265 (2d Cir. 1977).
36. *Carter v. Gallagher*, 452 F.2d 315 (8th Cir. 1971), *cert. denied*, 406 U.S. 950 (1972).
37. *General Building Contractors' Association v. Pennsylvania*, —— U.S. ——, 102 S.Ct. 3141 (1982).
38. See *Howard v. Lockheed-Ga. Co.*, 372 F. Supp. 854 (N.D. Ga. 1974).
39. See *Hernandez v. Erlenbusch*, 368 F. Supp. 752 (D. Or. 1973).
40. *Johnson v. Goodyear Tire & Rubber Co.*, 491 F.2d 1364 (5th Cir. 1974).
41. 42 U.S.C. §1988.

VII

Sex

Historically, women workers have been subject to many kinds of sex discrimination, ranging from receiving less pay for performing the same work as men to sexual harassment on the job. This chapter outlines some of the key laws that prohibit employment discrimination on the basis of sex. A more thorough discussion of sex discrimination in employment can be found in the updated ACLU Handbook *The Rights of Women* by Susan Deller Ross and Ann Barcher.

Discrimination in employment on the basis of sex was made illegal with the enactment of the Civil Rights Act of 1964.[1] The courts and the Equal Employment Opportunity Commission (EEOC) have applied that law expansively to remedy many types of unequal and unfair treatment of women on the job. For example, ten years ago sexual harassment was not considered "sex discrimination" at all; now it is considered to be illegal. If you believe you are being mistreated, you should check with the EEOC or an attorney to see whether you have any legal recourse.

What laws prohibit sex discrimination?

The most far-reaching law that protects private employees against sex discrimination is Title VII of the Civil Rights Act of 1964, as amended by the Pregnancy Discrimination Act of 1978.[2] Title VII outlaws discrimination based on sex. The only real defense is that gender is a bona fide occupational qualification (BFOQ) for the performance of a certain job,[3] but the courts have been quite strict in applying this defense.[4] In practice, the only types of jobs that have been protected by the BFOQ defense are jobs like wet nurse, model, and actor/actress.

Other important laws in the area of sex discrimination in

employment are the Equal Pay Act,[5] Executive Order 11246 as amended by E.O. 11375, the Age Discrimination in Employment Act,[6] and state sex discrimination laws. These laws will be discussed later in this chapter. Most courts have held that section 1981 of the Civil Rights Act of 1866 does not prohibit sex discrimination.[7]

May a company deny jobs, promotions, or overtime work to women because of state "protective" labor laws?

State "protective laws" were passed at the beginning of the 20th century to regulate the type of jobs in which women were allowed to work; the intent was to protect women from certain working conditions that, it was believed, would harm them. Such laws have been successfully challenged under Title VII.[8] The federal courts have rejected the claim that certain jobs could be performed only by men, and they have ordered employers to allow women to try out for such jobs.[9]

Are seniority rules illegal if their effect is to perpetuate past discrimination?

Your right to bid for a better job often depends on seniority (that is, the length of time with the company or in the job). Seniority also usually determines who will be laid off in times of slow business or recession. While seniority systems often operate to lock in the effects of past discrimination, the U.S. Supreme Court has held that, no matter what their impact, seniority systems do not violate Title VII unless the employer actually created the system for the purpose of discriminating.[10] A seniority system can be struck down under Title VII only if you can prove actual discriminatory motive on the part of your employer.

Can an employer use height or weight as a selection criterion?

No. The Supreme Court has specifically declared this practice illegal under Title VII.[11]

May an employer fire women who marry?

Men and women must be treated the same. Therefore, if an employer fires women who marry, it must also fire men who marry, or it has violated Title VII.[12] In some states, such a practice, even if applied equally to men and women, would violate state law prohibitions against discrimination on the basis of marital status.[13]

Are different retirement ages or benefits for men and women legal?

No. Both the Supreme Court and the EEOC[14] have taken the position that men and women must be treated equally with respect to retirement and all other benefits.

May an employer discriminate against me because I am pregnant?

No. In 1978 Congress amended Title VII to make it illegal to discriminate on the basis of pregnancy, childbirth, or any related medical condition (e.g., abortion). That law, referred to as the Pregnancy Discrimination Act,[15] makes clear that pregnant women who are able to and want to work must be treated like other workers. Also, women disabled by pregnancy, childbirth, or related medical conditions must be treated like other workers who are temporarily disabled by short-term medical disability.

The Pregnancy Discrimination Act prohibits an employer from refusing to hire or refusing to promote a woman because she is pregnant. An employer cannot fire a woman because of her pregnancy, or force her to take a leave of absence. When and if a medical leave becomes necessary, its length is to be determined by the woman and her doctor; the employer may not impose leave of a certain length on the woman. An employee must be permitted to continue working as long as she is physically able to perform the duties of her position and must be permitted to return to work as soon as she is able to do so in the same manner as other employees who are reinstated after taking a medical leave. With respect to any health or temporary disability plan available in connection with the employment, an employer must treat any disability associated with pregnancy the same as all other temporary medical disabilities. If the employer grants leaves of absence for medical disability, it must also grant maternity leaves. Moreover, a company medical plan must cover the pregnancies of employees' wives to the same extent it covers other medical expenses for dependents; providing less coverage for dependents' pregnancies constitutes illegal sex discrimination against male employees.[16]

What is sexual harassment?

Sexual harassment may be an unwelcome sexual advance, the request for a sexual favor, or any other verbal or physical conduct of a sexual nature that interferes with the employee's work or creates an uncomfortable working environment. Judicial recognition of sexual harassment as a form of discrimination violative of Title VII was slow to evolve. At present, however, the courts and the EEOC recognize sexual harassment as constituting an illegal discriminatory practice under Title VII.[17] In a recent federal case, the court held that the plaintiff was entitled to relief under Title VII because her supervisor's repeated advances, vulgarities, and sexual inquiries created a "hostile and demeaning" working environment.[18]

Is sexual harassment actionable if committed by a co-worker?

Generally the employer is liable for all acts of sexual harassment by a supervisor, even if the company is unaware of the practice. But if the harassment comes from a co-worker, customer, or client, the employer generally must be made aware of the harassment before it can be held liable for it. The rationale is that if an employer is aware that an employee is being sexually harassed and does not take steps to remedy the situation, it is, in effect, giving license to the person who is actually doing the harassment. Therefore, if you are being harassed by a co-worker, you should inform your employer so that it has the opportunity to remedy the problem; if your employer fails to do so, you may take legal action against it.

Must I suffer a loss in job status to be compensated for sexual harassment?

Until recently, a woman could recover under Title VII for sexual harassment on the job only if she lost some tangible benefits by refusing to yield to sexual advances. In a recent case, however, a court held that a woman could recover in such an instance even though her resistance to the harassment did not lead to her termination.[19] Under that decision, a plaintiff is entitled to be compensated for being victimized by the sexual harassment itself, and need not prove that she lost her job, had her salary cut, or suffered some other concrete loss of employment benefits.

What should I do if I believe I have been discriminated against on the basis of my sex?

You should consult the EEOC or an attorney to see whether you have any legal recourse. The procedures for filing a Title VII charge of sex discrimination are the same as the procedures for filing a charge of any other form of discrimination prohibited by Title VII. Those procedures are described in Chapter 5 and in the ACLU handbook on *The Rights of Women*.

What is the Equal Pay Act?

The Equal Pay Act makes it illegal for an employer to pay women less than men for the same work.[20] The guiding principle is "equal pay for equal work." This provision was added to the Fair Labor Standards Act (FLSA) in 1963.

To determine whether the Equal Pay Act has been violated, the courts first analyze the type of work performed by men and women. Only workers engaged in "substantially similar" work can be compared to determine inequalities in salary. The term "substantially similar" work means that the men and women work in the same establishment (i.e., the same physical space or location) and perform the same type of job requiring comparable "skill, effort, and responsibility."[21] In addition, the jobs must be equal in terms of working conditions, and the tasks of each job must be very similar.

The jobs compared need not be identical. Jobs may be compared despite insubstantial or minor differences in the skill, effort, or responsibilities required.[22] Jobs may not be compared, however, if they are substantially different. For example, the pay of a female bookkeeper can be compared to that of a male bookkeeper working on a different ledger, but cannot be compared to that of a male clerk. A comparison may be made when employees of one sex are doing work formerly done by employees of the opposite sex. For example, if male bank tellers are replaced by female bank tellers and the women are paid at a lower rate than the men, the equal pay provisions have been violated. But no comparison is possible when only men are employed in one job and only women are employed in a dissimilar job. Thus an employer cannot be found in violation of the equal pay standard because it pays telephone operators, all of whom are women, less than telephone repairmen, all of whom are men.

The equal pay requirement applies to virtually all forms of wages and benefits, including minimum wage, overtime pay, premium pay, and vacation and holiday pay, but excluding gifts, discretionary bonuses, maternity benefits, and expense reimbursement. An employer may not, for example, provide different life or health insurance coverage or different retirement or pension benefits based on sex; but there is no violation of the act when accrued benefits are unequal if the employer's contributions are equal, or when the employer's contributions are unequal if the accrued benefits are equal.[23] The equal pay requirements do not prohibit shift differentials, even if only one sex gets the higher pay; for example, if both men and women work on the same job during the day, but only men work on the job at night, a night-shift differential will be allowed. The FLSA specifically permits wage differentials that are attributable to bona fide seniority or merit systems or to incentive systems that reward productivity.[24] These systems need not be formal or written to qualify.

An employer may not correct an equal pay violation by reducing anyone's pay rate; rates can be equalized only by pay increases.[25] Thus a woman who is paid a lower rate than a man for the same work is entitled to have her pay raised to the man's level; the man's pay cannot be lowered to the woman's level. Also, the employer cannot remedy a violation by firing or transferring the higher-paid persons.[26]

The equal pay provisions apply to all private employees covered by the FLSA, except that employees who are completely exempt from the minimum wage laws (discussed in Chapter 15) are also exempt from the equal pay law; nonetheless, executives, administrators, professionals, and outside salesmen are not exempt from the equal pay law. Labor organizations are bound by the equal pay law, and may not cause or attempt to cause any employer to violate it. The equal pay requirement in the FLSA applies concurrently with other state and federal laws (such as Title VII) pertaining to sex discrimination in employment. In addition to Title VII, most states have equal pay laws. An employer must comply with any federal, state, or local law that establishes equal pay standards higher than those under the FLSA. On the other hand, compliance with any other applicable law does not excuse noncompliance with the equal pay law.

What if no men are doing the same work for more pay?

For years some courts took the position that in a wage discrimination claim under Title VII the plaintiff had to satisfy the Equal Pay Act requirement that a man be performing the same work for a higher wage. In a recent important decision, however, the Supreme Court held that women can sue under Title VII for sex discrimination in wages where the wages were initially set at a lower rate than for men, even if no men were performing the same work for more pay at the time of the suit.[27] That decision allows a woman to bring an action for equal pay even if no man is doing the same work for more money. In that decision, however, the Supreme Court rejected the "comparable worth" concept, under which a woman would have a claim if a man received a higher wage for performing a job of equal *value* to the company or community.

What should I do if I feel I'm not getting "equal pay for equal work"?

If you feel you are being discriminated against in violation of the Equal Pay Act, get in touch with your local EEOC office; responsibility for enforcing that law was transferred from the Department of Labor to the EEOC in 1979.

Upon receipt of a complaint under the Equal Pay Act, the EEOC will conduct an investigation. If a violation is found, the EEOC will try to collect the wages that are due and to persuade the employer to raise your wages. If a voluntary agreement between the employer and the EEOC cannot be reached, the EEOC may bring a lawsuit on your behalf to secure lost pay and to require that the employer change its policy.[28]

Unlike Title VII, the Equal Pay Act permits you to go directly to court without filing a charge with the EEOC; in that event, you should get an attorney. You must bring such an action within two years of the discrimination, or within three years if the discrimination was willful.

What can I recover if my action is successful?

You can be awarded up to two years of back pay, plus a similar amount as punitive damages to punish the employer for engaging in a discriminatory practice, plus attorneys' fees and court costs.[29]

What executive orders prohibit sex discrimination?

Executive Order 11246 forbids an employer that has a contract with the federal government to discriminate in employment. As originally issued, Executive Order 11246 applied only to race discrimination, but it was amended by E.O. 11375 to include a prohibition against sex discrimination. In an indirect way, these executive orders benefit private employees. Any company that has a contract with the government must sign a contract clause promising not to discriminate and promising to take "affirmative action" to ensure equal treatment for woman workers. The chief difference between Title VII and the Executive Order is that the Executive Order requires that all contractors subject to it must develop an affirmative action plan and file it with the government. E.O. 11246 is enforced entirely by the Office of Federal Contract Compliance Programs; you have no right to sue under E.O. 11246.

NOTES

 1. 42 U.S.C. §§2000e *et seq.*, as amended.
 2. *Id.*
 3. 42 U.S.C. §2000e–2(e).
 4. *Rosenfeld v. Southern Pacific Co.*, 444 F.2d 1219, 1225 (9th Cir. 1971).
 5. 29 U.S.C. §206(d)(1).
 6. 29 U.S.C. §§621 *et seq.*
 7. *E.g., Bobo v. ITT Continental Baking Co.*, 662 F.2d 340 (5th Cir. 1981).
 8. *E.g., Rosenfeld v. Southern Pacific Co.*, 444 F.2d 1219 (9th Cir. 1971).
 9. *See Rosenfeld v. Southern Pacific Co., supra; Kober v. Westinghouse Elec. Corp.*, 480 F.2d 240 (3d Cir. 1973); *Williams v. General Foods Corp.*, 492 F.2d 399 (7th Cir. 1974).
10. *Pullman-Standard v. Swint*, —— U.S. ——, 102 S.Ct. 1781 (1982).
11. *Dothard v. Rawlinson*, 433 U.S. 321 (1977).
12. *Sprogis v. United Airlines*, 444 F.2d 1194 (7th Cir.), *cert. denied*, 404 U.S. 991 (1971).
13. *See, e.g.*, N.Y. Exec. Law §291.
14. *Los Angeles v. Dept. of Water and Power Manhart*, 435 U.S. 702 (1978); 29 C.F.R. §1604.9(f).
15. 42 U.S.C. §2000e–(k).
16. *Newport News Shipbuilding & Dry Dock Co. v. EEOC*, —— U.S. ——, 51 U.S.L.W. 4829 (June 20, 1983).
17. 29 C.F.R. §1604.11.
18. *Henson v. City of Dundee*, 29 FEP Cases 787 (11th Cir. 1982).
19. *Bundy v. Jackson*, 641 F.2d 934 (D.C. Cir. 1981).
20. 29 U.S.C. §206(d)(1).
21. *Hodgson v. Corning Glass Works*, 474 F.2d 226 (2d Cir. 1973), *aff'd*, 417 U.S. 188.
22. *Id.*

23. Wage-Hours Opinion Letter no. 1117 (WH–70), Aug. 25, 1970.
24. 29 U.S.C. §206(d)(1).
25. *Id.*
26. *Hodgson v. Miller Brewing Co.*, 457 F.2d 221 (7th Cir. 1972).
27. *County of Washington, Ore. v. Gunther*, 452 U.S. 161 (1981).
28. 29 C.F.R. §1620.19.
29. 29 C.F.R. §1620.22.

VIII

Religion

Many immigrants to this country, including some of the first settlers, came to escape religious persecution and to live equally with others. Nevertheless, while the concept of religious freedom is deeply cherished in our country, religious prejudice has been present throughout our history, particularly in employment.

The First Amendment of the U.S. Constitution guarantees freedom of religion and prohibits the establishment of any official religion. Consequently, religious discrimination is forbidden in employment by federal, state, and local governments. But the First Amendment does not reach private employment.

Is religious discrimination illegal in private employment?

Yes. In Title VII of the Civil Rights Act of 1964, Congress specifically prohibited discrimination in private employment on the basis of religion. It is unlawful for an employer to refuse to hire, or to discharge, or to otherwise discriminate against anyone with respect to compensation, terms, conditions, or privileges of employment, because of the person's religion.[1] The term religion refers not only to religious beliefs, but also to religious observance and practice.

The most blatant form of religious discrimination in employment is intentional persecution, such as an employer refusing to hire you or firing you because of your religious heritage or beliefs. Such discrimination is clearly illegal and, fortunately, is relatively uncommon today. But religious discrimination often occurs in subtle or unintentional ways. For example, you may be asked to work on your sabbath; or a company dress code may preclude the wearing of a veil, which is required by your religious beliefs; or your religion may prohibit medical examinations that an employer requires. These employer actions may be illegal, because Title VII proscribes even actions that have the unintended effect of discrimination on the basis of religion. In these situations, the issue is whether your religious needs prevail over your employer's business needs.

Does my employer have to accommodate my religious beliefs?

Yes and no. Your employer must "reasonably accommodate" your religious observance, practice, and belief when they conflict with job-related duties. On the other hand, your employer need not make accommodations that would impose "undue hardship" on it. These two concepts of "reasonable accommodation" and "undue hardship" are set forth in Title VII itself, which states:

> The term "religion" includes all aspects of religious observance and practice, as well as belief, unless an employer demonstrates that he is unable to reasonably accommodate to an employee's or prospective employee's religious observance or practice without undue hardship on the conduct of the employer's business.[2]

The tension between these opposing concepts determines the extent to which your employer must make accommodations.

The leading case on this issue is *Trans World Airlines v. Hardison*,[3] in which the Supreme Court narrowly construed an employer's obligation to accommodate an employee's religious observance or practice. In that case, Hardison's religion required him to refrain from working on Saturday, its sabbath. As the result of a change of jobs, Hardison was assigned to work on Saturdays. He suggested various alternatives, but TWA and the union rejected them. TWA said the alternatives would increase its operating costs; for example, a replacement worker would be entitled to overtime pay on Saturdays. The union said that accommodating Hardison would violate the negotiated system under which Saturday work was assigned on the basis of seniority.

Hardison refused to work on Saturdays and was fired for insubordination. The court of appeals held that the discharge was illegal. The Supreme Court reversed, over a vigorous dissent, holding that TWA and the union did not have to accommodate Hardison's religious beliefs in the circumstances:

To require TWA to bear more than a de minimus cost in order to give Hardison Saturdays off is an undue hardship. Like abandonment of the seniority system, to require TWA to bear additional costs when no such costs are incurred to give other employees the days off that they want would involve unequal treatment of employees on the basis of their religion. By suggesting that TWA should incur certain costs in order to give Hardison Saturdays off the Court of Appeals would in effect require TWA to finance an additional Saturday off and then to choose the employee who will enjoy it on the basis of his religious beliefs. While incurring extra costs to secure a replacement for Hardison might remove the necessity of compelling another employee to work involuntarily in Hardison's place, it would not change the fact that the privilege of having Saturdays off would be allocated according to religious beliefs.

Under *Hardison*, therefore, your employer need not accommodate your religious beliefs if to do so would require incurring any significant cost, directly or indirectly.

After *Hardison*, the Equal Employment Opportunity Commission (EEOC) issued guidelines that incorporate and supplement the *Hardison* standards.[4] Those guidelines provide, for example, that in determining whether an accommodation would require more than a de minimus cost, and therefore constitute undue hardship, due consideration must be given to the identifiable cost in relation to the size and operating costs of the employer, and the number of employees who may actually need the accommodation.[5] Also, in assessing hardship, an employer may not assume that other employees with the same religious beliefs as the employee requesting an accommodation would need an accommodation too.[6]

Does Title VII apply to unusual religious and to individual beliefs?

Generally, yes. The phrase "religious belief" in Title VII has been given a broad definition. It is not confined to theistic concepts or to traditional beliefs, but includes ethical and moral beliefs that are sincerely held with the strength of traditional religious views.

A person can be deemed to have a religious belief even if no religious group espouses the belief, or even if the religious group to which the person professes to belong does not accept such a belief. On the other hand, a mere personal preference based on economic or social ideology does not constitute religious belief.[7] Membership in the United Klans of America has been held to be outside the protection of Title VII.[8]

Does Title VII apply to job applicants?

Yes. Under the guidelines of the EEOC, employers must accommodate the religious needs of job applicants, as well as employees. Thus, an employer may not schedule pre-selection tests during a period that conflicts with an applicant's religious practices. Furthermore, an employer, in asking about availability for work, cannot make any reference to religious practices, unless this is justified by business necessity.[9]

What should I do if I believe I am being discriminated against because of my religion?

You should promptly notify your employer (and your union, if you have one) of your religious views and of the need for accommodation.[10] Once notified, your employer is required to consider available accommodations. Although you are not required to propose acceptable accommodations to your employer,[11] it may be a good idea to do so.

If your employer does not make acceptable accommodations and you are discharged, or otherwise disciplined, for failure to comply with your employer's requirements, you may institute proceedings against your employer under Title VII; the procedures are discussed in Chapter 5.

To prevail in a Title VII religious discrimination case, you must plead and prove that (1) you had a bona fide belief that compliance with your employer's requirements was contrary to your religious beliefs, (2) you informed your employer of your views and of the need for accommodation, and (3) you were discharged, or otherwise disciplined, for failure to comply with the employment requirement.[12]

Can I collect unemployment compensation if I quit my job due to my religious beliefs?

Yes. In 1981, the Supreme Court held in *Thomas v. Review Board of the Indiana Employment Security Division*[13] that the First Amendment prohibits a state from denying you unemployment compensation when you have been forced to quit your job because of your religious beliefs. In that case, Thomas (a Jehovah's Witness) quit his job after he was transferred to a job making tank turrets, because making instruments of war violated his religious beliefs. The Court held, in effect, that his sincerely held religious beliefs must be deemed "good cause" for him to quit his job and that he could therefore collect unemployment compensation. For more on that case and on unemployment compensation, see Chapter 19.

NOTES

1. 42 U.S.C. §2000e–2(a)(1).
2. 42 U.S.C. §2000e(j).
3. 432 U.S. 63 (1977).
4. EEOC Guidelines on Discrimination Because of Religion, 29 C.F.R. Part 1605.
5. 29 C.F.R. §1605.2(e)(1).
6. 29 C.F.R. §1605.2(c)(1).
7. 29 C.F.R. §1605.1; *Edwards v. School Board*, 483 F. Supp. 620 (W.D. Va. 1980). *Cf. U.S. v. Seeger*, 380 U.S. 163 (1965); *Welsh v. U.S.*, 398 U.S. 333 (1970).
8. *Bellamy v. Mason's Stores, Inc.*, 368 F. Supp. 1025 (E.D. Va. 1973), *aff'd*, 508 F.2d 504 (4th Cir. 1974).
9. 29 C.F.R. §1605.3(b)(1).
10. 29 C.F.R. §1605.2(c); *Brown v. General Motors Corp.*, 601 F.2d 956 (8th Cir. 1979).
11. *Redmond v. GAF Corp.*, 574 F.2d 897 (7th Cir. 1978).
12. *Brown v. General Motors Corp.*, 601 F.2d 956 (8th Cir. 1979); *Anderson v. General Dynamics Convair Aerospace Div.*, 589 F.2d 397 (9th Cir. 1978); *Edwards v. School Board*, 483 F. Supp. 620 (W.D. Va. 1980).
13. 450 U.S. 707 (1981).

IX

Age

The most important federal statute regarding age discrimination is the Age Discrimination in Employment Act (ADEA),[1] enacted by Congress in 1967 and amended to extend its coverage in 1974 and again in 1978. It prohibits discrimination on the basis of age in such matters as hiring, promotion, terms and conditions of employment, referrals by employment agencies, and membership in labor unions. The ADEA also outlaws discriminatory employment advertising and retaliation against persons who have asserted their rights under the ADEA.[2]

The ADEA is currently the only federal law specifically banning age discrimination in private employment. Another federal statute, the Age Discrimination Act of 1975,[3] prohibits age discrimination in programs or activities receiving federal financial assistance. In addition to these federal laws, most states have laws against age discrimination; see Appendix 3 for a listing of states with such laws.

For additional discussion on age discrimination in employment, see the ACLU handbook *The Rights of Older Persons* by Robert N. Brown and others.*

Am I covered by the ADEA?

Probably yes, if you are between 40 and 70 years of age. Basically, in private employment,[4] the ADEA protects all persons who are at least 40 but less than 70[5] and who are either applicants for employment or employees of an employer covered by the ADEA,[6] except that certain high-level employees can be forced to retire at age 65 (discussed later). Persons under 40 or over 69 are not protected. If an em-

---

*Significant portions of this chapter are based on portions of that book.

ployer discriminates against a 50-year-old in favor of a 30- or 40-year-old, the ADEA would apply; but if the employer discriminates against a 35-year old in favor of a 25-year old, the ADEA would not apply.[7] In addition, the ADEA does not apply to age restrictions on entry into bona fide apprenticeship programs.[8]

Although the ADEA protects only persons between 40 and 70, persons under 40 or over 69 may still be protected under applicable state law. The ADEA specifically provides for deference to state age discrimination laws that are more inclusive in their protection.[9] Accordingly, an Alaskan law against age discrimination was upheld even though it contained no maximum age limit and thus went beyond the federal law.[10] On the other hand, when a state law, a local law, or a collective bargaining agreement is more *restrictive* than the ADEA, the federal law takes precedence.[11]

Who does the ADEA restrict?

The ADEA covers employers, employment agencies, and labor organizations.[12] It covers employers engaged in an industry affecting interstate commerce who have had 20 or more employees for each working day in each of 20 or more calendar weeks in the current or preceding calendar year. Employment agencies subject to the ADEA are those regularly undertaking to procure employees for an employer subject to the ADEA. The ADEA also covers, in effect, every labor organization with more than 25 members that is arguably connected with interstate commerce.

Can I ever be denied a job or fired if I am 40 to 70 years old?

Yes. An employer certainly does not have to hire you if you are not qualified for the job, and you can always be fired or otherwise disciplined for "good cause."[13] In fact, you can be turned down for a job or fired for any reason, so long as your age was not a factor in the decision.

Furthermore, discrimination on the basis of age is not illegal in certain other circumstances,[14] which will be further discussed later. For example, age discrimination is allowed where "age is a bona fide occupational qualification reasonably necessary to the normal operation of the particular business, or where the differentiation is based on reasonable factors other than age." Also, it is not unlawful to "observe the terms of a bona fide seniority system or any bona fide employee benefit plan such as retirement, pension, or insurance plan, which is not a subterfuge to evade the purposes of this Act, except that no such employee benefit plan shall excuse the failure to hire any individual, and no such seniority system or employee benefit plan shall require or permit the involuntary retirement of any individual" between the ages of 40 and 70.

Can my employer provide me with lower health benefits because of my age?

No. The Tax Equity and Fiscal Responsibility Act of 1982[15] amended the ADEA to require employers to provide employees between the ages of 65 and 69, and their dependents, the same health benefits provided younger employees.[16] That law went into effect on January 1, 1983.

Can I be forced to retire before 70?

Generally, no. The ADEA, as amended in 1978, prohibits mandatory retirement before age 70 for most employees. Your employer cannot force you to retire earlier; and no seniority system or employee benefit plan (e.g., retirement, pension, or insurance plan) can require you to retire earlier.[17] This does not, of course, prevent your employer from firing you for good cause,[18] and it does not preclude your employer from contending that the mandatory retirement age is a bona fide occupational qualification.[19] Also, the ADEA does permit mandatory retirement of an employee in an "executive or high policy-making" position who is 65 or older and who is entitled to total retirement benefits from the employer of $27,000 or more a year.[20]

It should be noted that the 1978 amendments prohibiting mandatory retirement before 70 are prospective only. Any retirement plan in effect before 1978 can still require retirement earlier, unless that requirement was a "subterfuge" to get around the ADEA.[21]

How do I prove age discrimination?

The easiest way to make out a case of age discrimination is to show that your employer explicitly relied on your age in making a decision.[22] For example, if an employer's personnel manual provided that no person under 21 or over 50 would be hired, and a 54-year-old applicant was rejected because of age, that would constitute a clear-cut case of age discrimination.[23] Even without evidence of overt discrimination, it may be possible to establish the employer's state of mind by showing instances of overt discrimination in similar circumstances. Such was the case where an employer told one discharged employee that the new owners of the firm were stressing youth, and later told the complainant that the new owners wanted younger and new people.[24]

Difficulties in proof arise when an aggrieved person lacks evidence of overt discriminatory behavior. The key questions are (1) how much and what sort of proof is needed to make out a prima facie case, and (2) what the effect is on the case of establishing a prima facie case. The law under the ADEA is not well settled on either of these issues, particularly the first.

1. There is general agreement that a plaintiff-employee must prove the elements of a prima facie case by a "preponderance of the evidence," which means that all the elements are more probably true than not.[25] Likewise, the courts agree that a plaintiff's failure to make out such a case results in summary dismissal, even before the defendant-employer's rebuttal. There is disagreement, however, on what precise elements must be shown to establish a prima facie case of age discrimination in instances of discharge.

Under the strictest view, you must initially show that you belong to the statutorily protected group (40-70 years old), were qualified for the job from which you were fired, and were replaced by a person *outside* the protected group (under 40 years of age).[26] Under a more lenient view, you must show only that, in addition to your being between 40 and 70 and qualified for the job, the replacement was a younger person, *even within the 40-to-70-year-old age group*.[27] The most liberal standard does not even refer to actual replacement; a prima facie case is established if, after discharge, your former position remained open and your employer continued to seek applications from younger persons with qualifications similar to yours.[28]

Given this split about the law, you should bring a claim of age discrimination upon discharge whenever you think you remain qualified for the job. Although it is helpful to be able to show replacement by a younger person (especially one under 40), this may not be an absolute requirement in making out your prima facie case; showing that your employer is considering other applicants "similarly qualified" to you may be enough.

2. Establishing a prima facie case does not necessarily mean that you will win. It merely avoids summary dismissal of the case and shifts the burden onto your employer to come forward with evidence. Your employer must then articulate a legitimate, non-discriminatory reason for your dismissal. Such reasons can include bona fide occupational qualification (discussed later), unsatisfactory job performance, declining health, or even failure to adjust to a new manager's style and zeal.[29] If the employer has articulated such a reason, the burden shifts onto you to prove that the reason advanced is a pretext for age discrimination. If you can show this by a preponderance of the evidence, you will prevail in the case.[30]

Can I prove age discrimination with statistics?

Cases dealing with racial and sex discrimination in employment under Title VII of the Civil Rights Act of 1964 provide support for the use of statistics in proving age discrimination by a particular employer.[31] Some question exists, however, whether the same sort of inferences can be drawn from age statistics as from data on other types of discrimination. Unlike race and gender, age is a progressive condition; this makes it more difficult to apply data and argues against wholesale adoption of case law under Title VII.[32] Nevertheless, because age discrimination is generally quite subtle, some courts seem to favor a broad-based inquiry that includes the use of statistical evidence.[33] Although statistical evidence alone might not make out a prima facie case, it has made a difference in a number of age discrimination situations. For example, evidence that a personnel reduction produced a drop of six years in average personnel age has been regarded as relevant,[34] as has evidence that, during the 18 months that a certain owner controlled a firm, the average age of district managers dropped by almost 13 years.[35] In another case, the court considered it important that, of 35 persons hired during a one-year period, none was over 40 and all but three were under 30.[36] In sum, you can use statistical evidence in an age discrimination case, though it is not as conclusive as in cases of race and sex discrimination.[37]

Can there be age discrimination even if age is not the only reason for the employer's conduct?

The issue frequently arises of the real reason for an

employer's action against an employee. If the only reason for the action was something other than age (such as the employee's chronic tardiness),[38] there is no case of age discrimination. If, on the other hand, age was the sole basis and the employer's stated reason is just a pretext, unlawful age discrimination is shown.

The more difficult situation is when age is one of several factors motivating the employer. To win, the employee need not prove that age was the sole consideration.[39] Rather, unlawful discrimination is shown if age was a *determining factor* in the employer's decision (that is, a factor that actually made a difference in the decision). Obviously, this leaves considerable room for judicial discretion.[40]

What about neutral employer actions that affect older workers disproportionately?

This is one of the most difficult issues in age discrimination law. Under Title VII, neutral practices with a disproportionate impact on protected minorities (race, sex, etc.) are not permitted without substantial justification.[41] This rule does not work easily in age cases, however, because the ADEA outlaws only *arbitrary* age discrimination. Practices that have an adverse effect on older workers may be quite logical from the perspective of employers.

If the criteria used by the employer accurately measure ability to do the job (such as health or physical fitness), the use of those criteria is lawful.[42] Nevertheless, if the criteria, though rational from an efficiency standpoint, are clearly contrary to the basic purposes of the ADEA, the courts tend to favor employees. Thus, courts have refused to (1) uphold discharges based upon lack of special electronics training that younger, less busy employees were more easily able to undertake,[43] (2) uphold denial of promotion due to the employee's impending mandatory retirement,[44] and (3) recognize the generalization that younger employees offer more promise or potential.[45]

On the other hand, some courts have accepted the "reasonableness" of employer actions based on the theory that older employees (with higher pay and more seniority) are more costly in terms of net productivity than younger ones doing the same work.[46] One court upheld an employer's rule that provided for mandatory retirement of employees over 55 whose efficiency (measured in dollars) was less than 75 percent of their salary.[47] Nonetheless, another court held that, where the economic savings are directly related to age (i.e., older employees tend to be higher paid), the discharge would be unlawful.[48] Even if such a labor-cost argument is accepted, it may still be possible to charge age discrimination in particular cases (e.g., if the employer refuses to offer an alternative job to the discharged employee, or even one at a lower salary).[49]

When is age a bona fide occupational qualification?

Under the ADEA, an employer who can show that age is "a bona fide occupational qualification [BFOQ] reasonably necessary to the normal operation of the particular business" can use an explicit age rule for hiring or discharge, depending on the claim established.[50] For a policy to constitute a BFOQ, your employer must show that "the job qualifications invoked to justify . . . [the] discrimination . . . [are] *reasonably necessary* to the essence of [the] business. . . ."[51] Additionally, an employer's refusal to place persons above a certain age in a certain job qualifies as a BFOQ only if the evidence shows that (1) all or substantially all persons above that age are unable to meet defendant's standards, *or* (2) there is no practical way to differentiate qualified from unqualified applicants among persons over the age cutoff.[52] Using this analysis, one court held that the County of Los Angeles' policy of not hiring persons over the age of 35 for deputy sheriff positions did *not* qualify as a BFOQ.[53] Similarly, a court ruled that a county's forced retirement of correction officers at age 60 was not a BFOQ because the county could not adduce sufficient facts to prove that a person's ability to perform the job was significantly affected by aging.[54]

Is any type of age-discriminatory "help-wanted" advertising permissible?

Generally not, unless age is a bona fide occupational qualification for the position or unless the controlling age discrimination law excludes the advertised job from its coverage.

What should I do if I believe I have been discriminated against because of age?

To ensure that all your rights are fully protected, you should take two actions immediately:

1. File a "charge" with the Equal Employment Opportu-

nity Commission alleging discrimination on account of age.
Local offices of the EEOC can advise you where the notice
should be sent.

2. If your home state (or state of employment) has an
agency authorized to deal with age discrimination, contact
that agency and file a formal complaint with it. You can get
advice on what agency to contact from local offices of the
EEOC, state departments of labor, or state employment services offices.

What should I include in the "charge" filed with the EEOC?

The basic purpose of the required charge is "to provide the
EEOC with sufficient information so that it may notify prospective defendants and to provide the Secretary of Labor
with an opportunity to eliminate the alleged unlawful practices through informal methods of conciliation." Thus, all that
is required is "the filing of a written statement which identifies the potential defendant and generally describes the action believed to be discriminatory.[55]

What are the time limits for filing a charge?

The charge should be filed within 180 days after the unlawful discriminatory practice occurred; if, however, the state
has an age discrimination law, and a complaint has been filed
with the appropriate state agency, the federal charge may be
filed within 300 days after the discrimination occurred, or
within 30 days after termination of the state administrative
proceeding, whichever is earlier.

You should not count on any time extensions. Some earlier
cases took the position that the time periods could not be
extended.[56] In amending the ADEA in 1978, Congress adopted
the view that the 180-day (or 300-day) filing requirements are
not "jurisdictional" and thus may be subject to "equitable
modification" in appropriate cases.[57] For example, in one case,[58]
a plaintiff who filed 36 days after the expiration of the 180-day
period was permitted to proceed. The court took into account
that the defendant-employer would not be prejudiced by the
delay and that the plaintiff, relying on unsound legal advice,
was not informed of the required filing time until after the
180-day filing period had expired. Similarly, an employer's
failure to post the required notice advising employees of their
rights under the ADEA,[59] may delay the start of the 180-day

statutory period until the victim knows or should know about those statutory rights.[60]

You cannot bring a lawsuit under the ADEA until the end of the 60-day waiting period after you filed your charge with the EEOC or the state agency.

Why do I have to wait before starting an age discrimination lawsuit?

The main purpose of the waiting period is to provide time to resolve the dispute by "conciliation, conference and persuasion," if possible. The waiting period also serves to avoid litigation, to alert the EEOC to potential cases of widespread importance, and to give timely notice to employers of pending discrimination charges against them.[61]

The ADEA and most state statutes make conciliation an absolute requirement: the EEOC or the appropriate state agency must try to settle the matter without litigation or other formal proceedings.[62] Most of the state statutes provide that all discussions during conciliation conferences are strictly confidential, though the ADEA has no such requirement.

What happens if the discrimination complaint cannot be settled by conciliation?

If conciliation fails, the next step is a formal adversary proceeding. The nature of these proceedings varies from state to state. There may be a hearing before the appropriate administrative agency;[63] or you may be able to sue directly in state court, bypassing the administrative process.[64] At state administrative hearings, the agency itself may present the case against your employer,[65] or you may do so on your own behalf.[66] The agency may also hear a presentation by the agency's legal staff, by you, or by both.[67] In some states, the agency's legal staff or the state attorney general may bring suit directly on your behalf, again bypassing the administrative process.[68]

As mentioned earlier, you can sue in federal court[69] 60 days after you filed the administrative complaint.[70] A federal lawsuit supersedes any pending state proceedings.[71] Also, the EEOC can bring a suit in its name on your behalf,[72] though such a suit forecloses any suit by private parties.[73]

Federal litigation is barred unless it is begun by filing a complaint in federal court within two years of the date of the discriminatory practice. If the discrimination was "willful," the period is three years.[74] Whichever limitations period is applicable, it is rarely extended.[75]

What are my remedies if I have been discriminated against because of my age?

In an age discrimination case under the ADEA, the court can "grant such legal or equitable relief as may be appropriate to effectuate the purposes of the legislation."[76] Those purposes are "to promote employment of older persons based on their ability rather than age" and "to prohibit arbitrary age discrimination in employment."[77] The courts may grant, among other relief, "judgments compelling employment, reinstatement or promotion, or enforcing the liability for" amounts owing as a result of violations of the ADEA, such as back pay for wrongfully discharged employees.[78] Declaratory judgments will generally not be issued unless justified by special circumstances.[79]

Remedies typically available under state age discrimination statutes include judgments requiring hiring, reinstatement, or promotions; restoration of or admission to labor union membership; back pay and benefits; and appropriate injunctive relief. The available remedies are discussed next.

Back Pay

If you were discriminated against on the basis of age, you should be "made whole" by being compensated for all wages and other monetary benefits lost as a result of the discrimination. You should be awarded all wages or salary that you would have received if hired (or not discharged) between the date of the discrimination and the date of the court judgment; you should also receive any other specific monetary benefits, such as increased pension benefits, that would have vested during that time. These amounts will be reduced by all earnings from other employment during that period.[80] The amount of pay you would have earned need not be proved with mathematical precision as long as a reasonable basis exists for the awarded amounts.[81]

If, before the end of the case, you are hired or rehired by the defendant-employer or you find a job that pays at least as much, a back-pay award may be limited to the period during which you actually remained out of work.[82] More generally, the back-pay award is reduced by:

- amounts actually earned on other jobs,[83] unless those earnings could have been earned even if you had been working for the defendant-employer (e.g., earnings from a part-time after-hours job);[84]
- severance pay arising from the discriminatory discharge—but not vacation pay, which is regarded as having been earned before the discriminatory discharge;[85]
- unemployment benefits received by the employee,[86] though this produces a windfall for the employer by shifting to the government part of the burden of financially compensating age discrimination victims.[87]

Hiring

In theory, the court can grant an injunction requiring an employer to hire an aggrieved party, but there are no reported cases of this under the ADEA. Courts have, however, issued injunctions against future discrimination; this may allow an aggrieved party to be hired if other hiring qualifications are met.[88]

Reinstatement

Employers have been ordered to reinstate dismissed persons to their original job (or one comparable to it) and to place reinstated employees on an accelerated training schedule to alleviate training obsolescence that they suffered as a result of age discrimination.[89] Reinstatement does not preclude a party from collecting other monetary damages, which may be ordered in addition to such an award.[90] A court generally will not order reinstatement if doing so would harm the parties and if other remedies would serve the purposes of the ADEA.[91]

Promotion

Courts have taken a position on promotions similar to that regarding hiring. Although an injunction could be granted requiring your employer to promote you to a position you would or might have received had there been no discrimination, it is more likely that an injunction forbidding future discrimination will be issued, as well as an award of monetary damages.[92] Under this approach you may be promoted when future vacancies arise, if other qualifications for promotion are met.

Other Damages

In addition to monetary losses, you may sustain other damages, such as pain and suffering from the humiliation of being fired. Some courts allow recovery for such pain and suffering;[93] others do not.[94] Courts that do not allow such recovery reason that the conciliation process, which is central to the ADEA's enforcement scheme, would be crippled by the potential for large uncertain awards; the possibility of recovering a large verdict for pain and suffering will make a claimant less likely to accept, in the administrative phase of the case, a settlement for only out-of-pocket loss.[95]

Fringe Benefits

Loss of fringe benefits is just as real and measurable as wage loss, and compensation should be awarded to make you whole. The courts have awarded a variety of lost fringe benefits, including employer pension plan contributions,[96] cost-of-living wage increases, bonuses, and group insurance premiums.[97] Like any damages, loss of fringe benefits must be established with reasonable certainty. Recovery will be denied if the earning of the benefits was only speculative (e.g., performance bonuses and contingently vesting pension benefits).[98]

Liquidated Damages

Liquidated damages—statutory double damages—are also available to victims of "willful violations" of the ADEA.[99] Awarding a full doubling of the proved wage loss, or less, is within the court's discretion.[100] For example, in one case the court awarded two-thirds of the net wage loss as liquidated damages.[101]

Injunctive Relief

In addition to reinstatement, hiring, and promotion, other injunctive relief is available under the ADEA, which grants the courts power to give any equitable relief that will "effectuate the purposes of this Act." The most significant injunctive remedies are prohibitory injunctions restraining further discriminatory acts, and mandatory injunctions requiring payment of awards for lost wages.[102]

NOTES

1. 29 U.S.C. §§621 *et seq*.
2. 29 U.S.C. §623(d) and (e).
3. 42 U.S.C. §§6101 *et seq*.
4. As enacted in 1967, the ADEA covered only private employers. In 1974, it was extended to cover federal, state, and local governmental employers.
5. 29 U.S.C. §631.
6. 29 C.F.R. §860.30.
7. 29 C.F.R. §860.91.
8. 29 C.F.R. §806.106.
9. 29 U.S.C. §633.
10. *Simpson v. Alas. State Commission for Human Rights*, 608 F.2d 1171 (9th Cir. 1979).
11. *Michael v. Majority of Board of Trustees of N.Y.C. Emp. Retirement System*, 80 A.D.2d 147, 437 N.Y.S.2d 977 (1st Dep't 1981) (ADEA overrides conflicting state law); *Johnson v. Mayor and City Council of Baltimore*, 515 F. Supp. 1287 (D. Md. 1981) (ADEA priority over city ordinance); *Levine v. Fairleigh Dickinson*, 646 F.2d 825 (3d Cir. 1981) (ADEA precedence over collective bargaining agreement).
12. 29 U.S.C. §630.
13. *See* 29 U.S.C. §623(f).
14. *Id*.
15. Pub. L. 97–248, 96 Stat. 324, Sept. 3, 1982.
16. *Id*., §116.
17. 29 U.S.C. §623(f).
18. *See Randlett v. Owen-Illinois, Inc*., 419 F. Supp. 103 (N.D. Tex. 1976); *cf. EEOC v. Home Insurance Co*., 27 FEP 1665 (2d Cir. 1982).
19. *Aaron v. Davis*, 414 F. Supp. 453 (E.D. Ark. 1976).
20. 29 U.S.C. §631(c).
21. *Carpenter v. Continental Trailways*, 635 F.2d 578 (6th Cir. 1980), *cert. denied*, 451 U.S. 986 (1980) (permitting retirement at 55;

Jensen v. Gulf Oil Refining & Marketing Co., 623 F.2d 406 (5th Cir. 1980) (allowing involuntary retirement at 51).

22. *Hodgson v. First Federal Sav. & Loan Ass'n*, 455 F.2d 818 (5th Cir. 1972) (interviewer's notes said "too old for teller").

23. *Hodgson v. Poole Truck Line, Inc.*, 4 FEP Cases 265 (S.D. Ala. 1972).

24. *Schultz v. Hickok Mfg. Co.*, 358 F. Supp. 1208 (N.D. Ga. 1973).

25. *Sutton v. Atlantic Richfield*, 646 F.2d 407 (9th Cir. 1981).

26. *Harpring v. Continental Oil Co.*, 628 F.2d 406 (5th Cir. 1980); *Houser v. Sears, Roebuck & Co.*, 627 F.2d 756 (5th Cir. 1980); *Johnson v. Mayor and City Council of Baltimore, supra; Carolan v. Central Freight Lines, Inc.*, 489 F. Supp. 941 (E.D. Tex. 1980).

27. *Moore v. Sears, Roebuck & Co.*, 464 F. Supp. 357 (N.D. Ga. 1979).

28. *Walter v. KFGO Radio*, 518 F. Supp. 1309 (D. N.D. 1981); *Eason v. National Highway Traffic Safety Administration*, 512 F. Supp. 1199 (D.D.C. 1981).

29. *Kerwood v. Mortgage Banker's Ass'n of America, Inc.*, 494 F. Supp. 1298 (D.D.C. 1980).

30. *Sutton v. Atlantic Richfield Co., supra; Eason v. National Highway Traffic Safety Administration, supra; Carolan v. Central Freight Lines, supra; Moore v. Sears, Roebuck & Co., supra; Tex. Dept. of Community Affairs v. Burdine*, 450 U.S. 248 (1981) (Supreme Court decision in Title VII sex discrimination case setting forth the same standards on burden of proof as outlined in lower-court age discrimination decisions).

31. *Hazlewood School District v. U.S.*, 43 U.S. 299 (1977).

32. *Williams v. City and County of San Francisco*, 483 F. Supp. 335 (N.D. Cal. 1979).

33. *Hall v. U.S.*, 436 F. Supp. 505 (D. Minn. 1977); *Surrisi v. Conwed Corp.*, 510 F.2d 1088 (8th Cir. 1975).

34. *Laugesen v. Anaconda Co.*, 510 F.2d 307 (6th Cir. 1975).

35. *Schultz v. Hickok Mfg. Co., supra.*

36. *Hodgson v. First Fed. Savings and Loan Assoc.*, 455 F.2d 818 (5th Cir. 1972).

37. *Moore v. Sears, Roebuck & Co., supra.*

38. *Brennan v. Reynolds & Co.*, 367 F. Supp. 440 (N.D. Ill. 1973).

39. Calille, "Three Developing Issues of the Federal Age Discrimination in Employment Act of 1967," 54 U. Det. J. Urb. L.

40. *EEOC v. Allegheny County*, 519 F. Supp. 1328 (W.D. Pa. 1981); *National Cash Register v. River*, 424 A.2d 660 (Del. Super. 1980); *Carpenter v. Continental Trailways*, 635 F.2d 578 (6th Cir. 1980), cert. denied, 451 U.S. 986 (1980); *Cleverly v. Western Elec. Co., Inc.*, 450 F. Supp. 507 (W.D. Mo. 1978), aff'd, 594 F.2d 638 (8th Cir. 1979); *Cunningham v. Central Beverage, Inc.*, 486 F. Supp. 59 (N.D. Tex. 1980).

41. *Griggs v. Duke Power Co.*, 401 U.S. 424 (1971).

42. 29 C.F.R. §860.103.

43. *Coates v. National Cash Register*, 433 F. Supp. 655 (W.D. Va. 1977).

44. *Marshall v. Board of Ed. of Salt Lake City*, 15 F.E.P. Cases 368 (D. Utah 1977).

45. *Hays v. Republic Steel Corp.*, 12 F.E.P. Cases 1640 (N.D. Alas. 1974), *modf'd on other grds*, 531 F.2d 1307 (5th Cir. 1976).

46. *E.g., Mastie v. Great Lakes Steel Corp.*, 424 F. Supp. 1299 (E.D. Mich. 1976).

47. *Donnelly v. Exxon Research & Eng'r. Co.*, 12 F.E.P. Cases 417 (D. N.J. 1974).

48. *Marshall v. Arlene Knitwear, Inc.*, 454 F. Supp. 715 (E.D.N.Y. 1978), *aff'd*, 608 F.2d 1369 (2d Cir. 1978).

49. *Surrisi v. Conwed Corp.*, *supra*.

50. 29 U.S.C. §623(f)(1).

51. *Usery v. Tamiami Trail Tours, Inc.*, 531 F.2d 224 (5th Cir. 1976).

52. *EEOC v. County of L.A.*, 27 FEP 904 (C.D. Cal. 1981); *Usery v. Tamiami Trail Tours, Inc.*, *supra* at p. 235–237.

53. *EEOC v. County of L.A.*, *supra*.

54. *EEOC v. County of Santa Barbara*, 27 FEP 1481 (9th Cir. 1981).

55. Conference Report to Accompany H.R. 5383, H. Rep. no. 95–950, 95th Cong., 2d Sess. 12 (1978) (dealing with 1978 amendments to the ADEA).

56. *Hiscott v. General Electric Co.*, 521 F.2d 632 (6th Cir. 1975); *Edwards v. Kaiser Aluminum & Chem. Sales Inc.*, 515 F.2d 1195 (5th Cir. 1975).

57. 29 U.S.C. §626(d).

58. *Dartt v. Shell Oil Co.*, 539 F.2d 1256 (10th Cir. 1976), *aff'd*, 434 U.S. 1089 (1977).

59. 29 U.S.C. §627.

60. *Charlier v. S. C. Johnson & Son*, 556 F.2d 761 (5th Cir. 1977); *Skoglund v. Singer Co.*, 403 F. Supp. 797 (D. N.H. 1975); *Bishop v. Jelleff Assoc., Inc.*, 398 F. Supp. 579 (D.D.C. 1974).

61. 29 U.S.C. §626(b), (d); *McCrickard v. Acme Visible Records, Inc.*, 409 F. Supp. 341 (W.D. Va. 1976).

62. Conciliation is a prerequisite to any later age discrimination suit by the EEOC under 29 U.S.C. §626(c). *Brennan v. Ace Hardware Corp.*, 495 F.2d 368 (8th Cir. 1974). Employer non-cooperation does not excuse failure to conciliate, since the Secretary may seek court orders compelling cooperation or issue subpoenas to aid an investigation. *Dunlop v. Resource Sciences Corp.*, 410 F. Supp. 836 (N.D. Okla. 1976). Under an occasional state statute, conciliation is optional rather than mandatory, *e.g.*, N.Y. Exec. Law §297–3a.

63. Conn. Gen. Stat. §31–127–132 (1977), 1973 Labor FEPs T31 chap. 563.

64. N.Y. Exec. Law §297–9.

65. Conn. Gen. Stat. §31–127.

66. Del. Code Ann. tit. 19, §712.

67. N.J.S.A. 10:5–6 (1976).

68. N.J.S.A. 10:5–14.1.
69. 29 U.S.C. §626(e).
70. 29 U.S.C. §626(c).
71. 29 U.S.C. §633(b).
72. 29 U.S.C. §626(b).
73. 29 U.S.C. §626(c).
74. 29 U.S.C. §633(a).
75. The statute is not tolled by pendency of administrative proceedings, *Unexcelled Chem. Corp. v. U.S.*, 345 U.S. 59 (1953), or by estoppel, *Shunney v. Fuller Co.*, 111 F. Supp. 543 (D.R.I. 1953) (employer misrepresentation of law).

    The 1978 amendments have changed these rules in one respect. Section 4(c) of the ADEA Amendments of 1978 amends §7(e), 29 U.S.C. §626(e), of the ADEA to provide for the tolling of the statute of limitations while the EEOC is attempting to secure compliance through conciliation under §7(b) of the ADEA, 29 U.S.C. §626(b). The statute may not be tolled, however, for more than one year. This special tolling provision is made applicable to the conciliation efforts required for actions by the EEOC under §7(b) of the ADEA, 29 U.S.C. §626(b), but not for the similar conciliation efforts supposed to occur during the 60-day waiting period before individual lawsuits under §7(d), 29 U.S.C. §626(d). *See* Conference Report to Accompany H.R. 5383, H. Rep. no. 95–950, 95th Cong., 2d Sess. 13 (1978).

76. 29 U.S.C. §626(b), (c).
77. 29 U.S.C. §621(b).
78. 29 U.S.C. §626(b), incorporating FLSA §16, 29 U.S.C. §226 (1970), except for subsection (a).
79. *Cavanaugh v. Texas Instruments, Inc.*, 440 F. Supp. 1124 (S.D. Tex. 1977).
80. *Monroe v. Penn-Dixie Cement Corp.*, 335 F. Supp. 231, 234–35 (N.D. Ga. 1971); *Brennan v. Ace Hardware Corp.*, 495 F.2d 368, 373 (8th Cir. 1974); *Morelock v. NCR Corp.*, 546 F.2d 682 (6th Cir. 1976); *Hodgson v. First Federal Sav. & Loan Ass'n*, 455 F.2d 818 (5th Cir. 1972); *Combes v. Griffin Television, Inc.*, 421 F. Supp. 841 (W.D. Okla. 1976); *Bishop v. Jelleff Assoc., Inc.*, 5 EPD §7995 (D.D.C. 1972); *Schultz v. Hickok Mfg. Co.*, supra; *Hodgson v. Sugar Cane Growers Coop.*, 346 F. Supp. 132 (S.D. Fla. 1973).
81. *Cf. Wirtz v. Turner*, 330 F.2d 11 (7th Cir. 1964); *Michigan Window Cleaning Co. v. Martino*, 173 F.2d 466 (6th Cir. 1949). These are Fair Labor Standards Act cases, but their applicability seems clear by virtue of §626(b) of the ADEA, 29 U.S.C. §626(b), as well as general damages law principles, *e.g.*, *Austin v. Rosecke*, 240 Minn. 562, 61 N.W.2d 249 (1953).
82. *Hodgson v. Poole Truck Line, Inc.*, supra.
83. *Brennan v. Ace Hardware Corp.*, supra.
84. *Laugesen v. Anaconda Co.*, supra.
85. *Id.*

86. *Bishop v. Jelleff Assoc. Inc.*, *supra*.

87. Richards, "Monetary Awards for Age Discrimination in Employment" 30 Ark. L. Rev. 305, 323; *Bang v. International Sisal Co.*, 212 Minn. 135, 4 N.W.2d 113 (1942) (action for breach of employment contract; unemployment benefits received by plaintiff do not mitigate damages).

88. *Hodgson v. Greyhound Lines, Inc.*, 354 F. Supp. 230 (N.D. Ill. 1973), *rev'd on other grounds*, 499 F.2d 859 (7th Cir. 1974), *cert. denied*, 419 U.S. 1122 (1974); *Hodgson v. First Federal Savings & Loan Ass'n*, *supra*.

89. *E.g.*, *Coates v. National Cash Register Co.*, 433 F. Supp. 655 (W.D. Va. 1977); *see also Houghton v. McDonnell-Douglas Corp.*, 553 F.2d 561 (8th Cir. 1977), *cert. denied*, 434 U.S. 966 (1977).

90. *Schultz v. Hickok Mfg. Co.*, *supra*.

91. *Combes v. Griffin Television, Inc.*, 421 F. Supp. 841, 846 (W.D. Okla. 1976).

92. *Marshall v. Board of Ed. of Salt Lake City*, 15 FEP Cases 368 (D. Utah 1977).

93. *Buchholz v. Symons Mfg. Co.*, 445 F. Supp. 706 (E.D. Wis. 1978); *Coates v. National Cash Register Co.*, *supra*; *Bertrand v. Orkin Exterminating Co.*, 419 F. Supp. 1123 (N.D. Ill. 1976); *Combes v. Griffin Television, Inc.*, *supra*; *Murphy v. American Motor Sales Corp.*, 410 F. Supp. 1403 (N.D. Ga. 1976).

94. *Dean v. American Security Ins. Co*, 559 F.2d 1036 (5th Cir. 1977), *cert. denied*, 434 U.S. 1066 (1978); *Rogers v. Exxon Research and Eng'r. Co.*, 550 F.2d 834 (3d Cir. 1977), *cert. denied*, 434 U.S. 1022 (1978); *Ellis v. Philippine Airlines*, 443 F. Supp. 251 (N.D. Cal. 1977); *Looney v. Commercial Union Assurance Co.*, 428 F. Supp. 533 (E.D. Mich. 1977); *Hannon v. Continental Nat'l Bank*, 427 F. Supp. 215 (D. Colo. 1977); *Platt v. Burroughs Corp.*, 424 F. Supp. 1329 (E.D. Pa. 1976).

95. *Rogers v. Exxon Research and Eng'r. Co.*, *supra*; *Dean v. American Security Ins. Co.*, *supra*; *see* Legislative History: H. Rep. No. 805, 90th Cong., 1st Sess. Reprinted in 1976–2 U.S. Code Cong. & Ad. News 2213, 2218.

96. *Monroe v. Penn Dixie Cement Corp.*, *supra*; *Bishop v. Jelleff Assoc. Inc.*, *supra*.

97. *Combes v. Griffin Television, Inc.*, *supra*.

98. *Monroe v. Penn-Dixie Cement Corp.*, *supra*; *Hodson v. Ideal Corrugated Box Co.*, 10 FEP Cases 744 (N.D. Va. 1974).

99. 29 U.S.C. §626(b), incorporating FLSA §16, 29 U.S.C. §216.

100. *Hays v. Republic Steel Corp.*, 531 F.2d 1307 (5th Cir. 1976).

101. *Combes v. Griffin Television, Inc.*, *supra*.

102. 29 U.S.C. §626(b) and (c). Federal district courts have jurisdiction to restrain violations of the ADEA, 29 U.S.C. §217.

X

The Handicapped

In 1970 the United States had about 10 million people with handicaps in the employable age group of 16 to 64; nearly half were unemployed. The gross disparity between the unemployment rates for non-handicapped and handicapped persons suggest that many handicapped people were victims of employment discrimination.

Until relatively recently, discrimination against the handicapped was legally sanctioned. But the handicapped have become a vocal interest group demanding their rightful place in society. In response to the demands and needs of the handicapped, Congress enacted the Rehabilitation Act of 1973,[1] which prohibits employment discrimination in the executive branch of the federal government and in federally supported institutions and programs.

This chapter deals with only the most significant laws and developments in the area of discrimination against the handicapped. Specifically, significant provisions of the Rehabilitation Act will be explained, along with some of the court decisions interpreting that law. If you are interested in a more detailed discussion of this subject, you should read *The Rights of Physically Handicapped People* by Kent Hull, another handbook in the ACLU series. If you are disabled and a veteran, you may be entitled to the additional protections of the Vietnam Era Veterans Readjustment Act of 1974.[2] For a discussion of that law, and other employment rights of veterans, see Chapter 11.

What employers does the Rehabilitation Act of 1973 cover?

Unfortunately, the laws outlawing discrimination against the handicapped are not as comprehensive as the laws aimed at eliminating discrimination on the basis of race, religion, sex, etc. Unlike Title VII of the Civil Rights Act of 1964,[3] the provisions of the Rehabilitation Act of 1973 do not apply directly to the private sector, but only to the federal government as an employer, to private employers who have substantial contracts with the federal government, and to employers who receive financial assistance from the federal government.

Three sections of the Rehabilitation Act offer employment protection to the handicapped:

1. Section 501[4] requires every department, agency, and instrumentality of the executive branch of the federal government to adopt an affirmative action plan for the hiring, placement, and promotion of handicapped persons. These plans must be updated every year and must be reviewed by an interagency committee designed to monitor the employment of handicapped persons within the federal government.

2. Section 503[5] requires that every contract in excess of $2500 entered into by a department or agency of the federal government must contain a clause requiring the contractor to take affirmative action in the employment of qualified handicapped persons. This section applies to any private employer who has such a contract with the federal government. In addition, any private employer who has a contract with the federal government for $50,000 or more, and who has 50 or more employees, must file a written affirmative action plan.[6]

Under the required affirmative action plans, contractors must review their employee selection procedures to ensure careful consideration of the job qualifications of handicapped applicants.[7] Employers must review their selection criteria to make sure that the stated job qualifications are necessary to perform the particular job.[8] Employers often establish job qualifications that handicapped people cannot meet, even though the qualifications are not necessary for the particular job. Such conduct, which may reflect indifference rather than design, effectively bars handicapped people from jobs. Section 503 is intended to prohibit employers from discriminating against handicapped people in this way.

3. Section 504[9] prohibits discrimination against handicapped persons under any program or activity receiving federal financial assistance, and under any program or activity conducted by the U.S. Postal Service or by any executive branch agency. This section is a direct ban on discrimination against handicapped persons, the violation of which triggers the same remedies and sanctions as afforded by Title VII of the Civil

Rights Acts of 1964. Remember, though, that this prohibition applies only to employers that receive financial assistance from the federal government.

How is the term "handicapped" defined under the Act?

The Rehabilitation Act applies to every person who has a physical *or mental* disability that affects his or her employability and who could benefit from vocational rehabilitation services.[10]

Is an employer required to make accommodations for my handicap?

Yes, if you are qualified for the job. The regulations under sections 503 and 504 state:

> A recipient [employer] may not deny any employment opportunity to a qualified handicapped employee or applicant if the basis for the denial is the need to make reasonable accommodations to the physical or mental limitations of the employee or applicant.[11]

In other words, the employer has a responsibility to reasonably accommodate the needs of the physically or mentally handicapped employee or applicant. An employer is not required, however, to make accommodations that would cause an "undue hardship" for the employer. The meaning of "undue hardship" is determined on a case-by-case basis. Thus it probably would not constitute an undue hardship for an employer to provide a different desk for an employee who is confined to a wheelchair, but it probably would be an undue hardship to require an employer to redesign a factory process to accommodate a handicapped employee.

Are there any restrictions on the testing of handicapped people in the selection of prospective employees?

Yes. Under the regulations, the employer cannot use selection tests that screen out or tend to screen out handicapped persons. The regulation approves tests that meet these two conditions:

1—The test score or other selection criterion, as used by the recipient, is shown to be job related for the positions in question; and

2—Alternative tests or criteria that do not screen out or tend to screen out as many handicapped persons are not shown by the Director to be available.[12]

In short, tests administered in selecting employees must test skills that are important for the job and must be fair and accurate in measuring the skills actually required to perform the job.

What do I do if I believe I have been discriminated against?

The procedure for making a complaint under the Rehabilitation Act depends upon which section of the Act covers the violation. If, for example, you are employed by the federal government and your agency violates section 501 by failing to engage in affirmative action hiring of handicapped persons, your only remedy is to complain to the Equal Employment Opportunity Commission; you cannot sue your employer directly. You must file your complaint with the EEOC within 180 days of the alleged violation. The EEOC will investigate the charge and try to resolve the matter. If it is unsuccessful at informal conciliation, the EEOC can sue and seek the same remedies as afforded by Title VII.[13]

If your employer contracts with the federal government and violates section 503, you must complain to the Department of Labor. You cannot sue your employer directly under section 503.[14] The Department of Labor will investigate your claim; if informal conciliation fails, the department can recommend that the Director of the Office of Federal Contract Compliance Programs bring a court action against your employer or discontinue payments on any outstanding contracts. Also, contractors found to have discriminated can be declared ineligible to receive future contract awards from the federal government.

Section 504, on the other hand, has been interpreted by most courts as conferring on private individuals the right to sue the employer directly.[15] Several courts have limited this private right of action, however, by holding that such an action cannot be maintained "unless a primary objective of the federal financial assistance [to the employer] is to provide employment."[16] In *Trageser v. Libbie Rehabilitation Center Inc.*, for example, the plaintiff brought an action under section 504; she was an employee of a private nursing home that received substantial income from Medicare, Medicaid, and other federal programs. Ms. Trageser was dismissed because of a visual impairment. The court held that she could not bring private action because the nursing home was primarily engaged in providing health care and was not a program whose primary purpose was employment. Other courts have not limited section 504's applicability in this manner.[17] Therefore, until the U.S. Supreme Court rules on this issue, your right to bring an action under section 504 depends on the law followed in the federal judicial circuit in which you live.

In any event, you should commence a section 504 action by filing a complaint with the agency that provides federal assistance to your employer. Although most courts have held that plaintiffs suing under section 504 are not required to exhaust administrative channels before filing a court action,[18] you may be able to resolve your problem through an administrative complaint and thus avoid the expense and time associated with litigation.

What remedies are available if I win a discrimination action?

The full range of Title VII remedies are available in discrimination actions brought under sections 501 and 504.[19] These remedies include back pay and possibly attorneys' fees. For a discussion of these remedies, see Chapter 5 on employment discrimination in general. The sanctions for violating section 503 are confined to loss of federal contracts and future ineligibility to receive federal contracts.

Can an employer pay me less than minimum wage because I am handicapped?

Yes. Under regulations promulgated under the Fair Labor Standards Act (which governs minimum wages), the Secretary of Labor may issue specific orders allowing the employment at less than the minimum wage of persons whose productive capacity is impaired by virtue of a physical or mental incapacity.[20] These regulations require, however, that such workers be paid not less than half the amount earned by workers who are not affected by a handicap.

Do any other federal laws apply to employment discrimination against the handicapped?

Yes. These laws, which are discussed in greater detail in

the ACLU handbook *The Rights of Physically Handicapped People*, include the following:

1. The Education for All Handicapped Children Act[21] provides federal assistance to each state for the education of all handicapped children in return for the state's assurance that it will actively seek out and employ qualified handicapped persons.

2. The Developmentally Disabled Assistance and Bill of Rights Act of 1975[22] provides for federal grants to aid the states in eliminating educational and architectural barriers to employing handicapped persons. In return, the states must promise to take affirmative action in the employment of qualified handicapped persons.

3. Section 402 of the Vietnam Era Veterans Readjustment Assistance Act of 1974[23] parallels the Rehabilitation Act. The law requires the executive branch to take affirmative action to employ disabled veterans. In addition, all federal contractors supplying personal property or nonprofessional services for $10,000 or more must have affirmative action plans for special disabled veterans and Vietnam era veterans. For further information on that law, see Chapter 11 and the ACLU handbook *The Rights of Veterans*.

Do states have laws prohibiting discrimination against the handicapped?

Yes. Many states have anti-discrimination statutes that protect the handicapped. These laws usually apply to most private employers, so they provide an important supplement to the narrow federal laws. Because the provisions of these state laws vary, you should check the law of your state.

NOTES

1. 29 U.S.C. §§701 *et seq.*
2. 38 U.S.C. §§2011 *et seq.*
3. 42 U.S.C. §§2000e *et seq.*
4. 29 U.S.C. §791.
5. 29 U.S.C. §793.
6. 41 C.F.R. §60–741.5(a).
7. 41 C.F.R. §60–741.6(a).
8. 41 C.F.R. §60–741.6(b).
9. 29 U.S.C. §794.
10. 29 U.S.C. §706(6).

11. 45 C.F.R. §84.12(d).

12. 45 C.F.R. §84.13(a).

13. 29 U.S.C. §794(a)(1).

14. 29 U.S.C. §793(b); *Davis v. United Airlines, Inc.*, 662 F.2d 120 (2d Cir. 1981), *cert. denied*, 102 S.C. 2045 (1982).

15. *Leary v. Crapsey*, 566 F.2d 863 (2d Cir. 1977); *Doe v. Calautti*, 592 F.2d 704 (3d Cir. 1979); *United Handicapped Federation v. Andre*, 558 F.2d 413 (8th Cir. 1977).

16. *Trageser v. Libbie Rehabilitation Center, Inc.*, 590 F.2d 87, 89 (4th Cir. 1978), *cert. denied*, 442 U.S. 947 (1978). *See also Scanlon v. Atascadero State Hospital*, 677 F.2d 1271 (9th Cir. 1982); *U.S. v. Cabrini Medical Center*, 639 F.2d 908 (2d Cir. 1981); *Carmi v. Metropolitan St. Louis Sewer District*, 620 F.2d 672 (8th Cir. 1980); *Simpson v. Reynolds Metals Co., Inc.*, 639 F.2d 1226 (7th Cir. 1980).

17. *See, e.g., Doe v. Colautti*, 454 F. Supp. 621, *aff'd*, 592 F.2d 704 (3d Cir. 1978).

18. *Pushkin v. Regents of Univ. of Colorado*, 658 F.2d 1372 (10th Cir. 1981); *Kling v. Los Angeles County*, 633 F.2d 876 (9th Cir. 1980).

19. 29 U.S.C. §794.

20. 29 C.F.R. §524.1(c)(1).

21. 20 U.S.C. §§1401 *et seq.*

22. 42 U.S.C. §§6001 *et seq.*

23. 38 U.S.C. §2012.

XI

Veterans

Upon leaving military service, veterans often encounter difficulties re-entering the civilian labor market. To ease this burden, Congress has enacted laws giving veterans various employment-related rights and benefits. These laws are discussed in this chapter. For discussion of other rights, see the ACLU handbook *The Rights of Veterans* by David F. Addlestone, Susan H. Hewman, and Frederic J. Gross.

As a veteran, you are generally entitled to job counseling, training, and placement services; to re-employment by your pre-service employer; and possibly to preferential treatment in getting a job. To qualify for these rights and benefits, you must be an "eligible" veteran; that is, you either (1) served on active duty in the military, naval, or air service for more than 180 days and were discharged or released with other than a dishonorable discharge, or (2) were released or discharged from active duty because of a service-connected disability.[1]

All eligible veterans are generally entitled to the rights and benefits described above. Depending on your classification as an eligible veteran (i.e., "Vietnam era" veteran, "disabled" veteran, or "special" disabled veteran), you may also be entitled to preferential treatment. You qualify as an eligible Vietnam era veteran (through December 31, 1991) if any portion of your active service as an eligible veteran was during the Vietnam era.[2] You qualify as a disabled veteran if you are entitled to receive compensation under laws administered by the Veterans Administration or were discharged or released from active duty because of a service-connected disability.[3] If you suffered a disability rated at 30 percent or more, you qualify as a special disabled veteran.[4]

Do I have a right to my old job when I am discharged from the service?

Yes. You must be restored to your previous position or to a position of equal status, seniority, and pay, if you are an eligible veteran who left a permanent job to perform military service. Additionally, once reinstated, you cannot be discharged without good cause for one year after re-employment. You are entitled to the protections of these provisions whether you enlisted or were drafted.[5]

To assert your statutory rights to re-employment, you need a certificate showing satisfactory completion of military service, and you *must re-apply* with your pre-service employer within 90 days after discharge from active training and service or from hospitalization that continued up to one year after discharge.

Can my length of total service affect my re-employment rights?

Yes. You are not entitled to re-employment rights if (1) you enlisted and your total service (other than in a reserve component) between June 24, 1948, and August 1, 1961, exceeded four years, or the total of any service performed by you after August 1, 1961, exceeded five years (unless involuntarily extended); or (2) you were drafted and your total active duty between June 24, 1948, and August 1, 1961, exceeded four years, or the total of any such active duty performed by you after August 1, 1961, exceeded four years (unless any additional period served was a result of your inability to obtain orders relieving you from active duty).[6]

Does my right to re-employment include retention of benefits offered by my pre-service employer?

Yes. In accordance with your employer's rules and procedures that were in effect when you entered the armed forces, you are entitled to be re-employed without loss of seniority and to participate in insurance or other benefits to the same extent as employees on leave of absence or furlough.[7]

Do I have re-employment rights as a member of the reserve or National Guard?

Yes. Ready reservists and National Guardsmen cannot be discriminated against because of their military obligations. Your employer cannot deny you your job or any promotion on that basis.[8]

You are entitled to all re-employment rights and benefits afforded by the statute if you are ordered to an initial period of active duty for training of at least 12 consecutive weeks. To assert these rights you must apply for re-employment within 31 days after (1) your release from active duty for training after satisfactory service, or (2) your discharge from hospitalization incident to such active duty for training, or within one year after your scheduled release from training, whichever is earlier. Once re-employed, you may not be discharged without cause for up to six months after reinstatement, but your re-employment rights will not entitle you to retention, preference, or displacement rights over any eligible veteran with a superior claim.[9]

At your request, you are entitled to be granted a leave of absence if ordered to an initial period of active duty for training or inactive duty training of less than 12 weeks. Upon your return to work, you are to be reinstated with the same status, pay, seniority, and vacation rights as you would have enjoyed without such absence. To assert these rights, upon your release or your discharge from hospitalization incident to such training you must report for work at the beginning of your next regularly scheduled work period following the last calendar day needed to return from your place of training or hospitalization to your place of employment (or within a reasonable time thereafter, if delayed due to reasons beyond your control), or within one year after your scheduled release, whichever is earlier. Failure to report for work as stated will subject you to your employer's disciplinary rules and regulations regarding absence from scheduled work.[10]

The U.S. Supreme Court held that the Vietnam Era Veteran's Readjustment Assistance Act of 1974 does *not* require an employer to provide preferential scheduling of work hours for an employee with military obligations if such scheduling accommodations are not made for other employees.[11] Furthermore, the Court held that the reservist was not entitled to all "incidents or advantages of employment," such as regular and overtime pay, received by other employees during the reservist's absence from work.

In addition to the federal laws that protect the re-employment rights of former reservists and members of the National Guard, more than half of the states have laws that afford additional re-employment protection and that prohibit discrimination.[12] You should check your state's law for additional rights and requirements.

Do I have any re-employment rights if I was rejected for military service?

Yes. If you enlisted or were inducted into military service but were subsequently rejected (e.g., for a physical impairment), your employer must treat your time away from work as a leave of absence. You are entitled to reinstatement upon reporting for work at the beginning of your next regularly scheduled work period following the last day needed to travel back from the place of pre-induction or other examination to the place of your employment, following your release or your discharge from hospitalization incident to such rejection or examination, or within one year after your scheduled release, whichever is earlier.[13]

If I receive an other-than-honorable discharge, am I entitled to re-employment rights?

Generally, no. To be entitled to re-employment rights you must have received a certificate evidencing your satisfactory completion of military service.[14] If, however, you successfully challenge and overturn an other-than-honorable discharge, you will be entitled to full re-employment rights.[15]

Do I have a right to re-employment as a conscientious objector?

Yes. You are entitled to re-employment rights and benefits if you are a conscientious objector. Your benefits will be denied only if you refused to perform military duty, wear the uniform, or obey lawful orders.[16]

Do I have re-employment rights if I am a disabled veteran?

Yes. As a former member of the armed services, National Guard, or reserve, your re-employment rights are protected if you sustain a disability that prevents you from performing your old job.[17] Under the statute, so long as you are qualified to perform the duties of any other position, you must be offered employment and, upon your request, be employed in a position that is equivalent to your former position in terms of status, seniority, and pay (or the nearest approximation thereof).

If I qualify for re-employment, can I still be denied my pre-service job?

Yes. An employer can contest your right to re-employment if circumstances existing at the time you applied for reinstatement have "so changed as to make it impossible or unreasonable" to re-employ you.[18]

Changed circumstances may arise where (1) all or a part of your pre-service employer's business has been sold, transferred, and reorganized, unless the nature of the business remains the same; or (2) a substantial decline in your pre-service employer's volume of business resulted in the elimination of positions to which you would have been transferred or advanced if employed continuously, as well as positions of like status, pay, and seniority; or (3) your pre-service job was abolished while you were serving in the military, and you are neither qualified (nor expected to qualify after reasonable training) for a similar position that may exist.[19]

Is it possible for me to waive my rights to re-employment?

Yes. You can waive your statutory rights, but only if the waiver is unequivocal and you understand what you are giving up. Nevertheless, you can be *assumed* to have waived your re-employment rights if, for example, you fail to apply for reinstatement within the statutory period, you refuse to accept your prior position, or you voluntarily quit a job after reinstatement. The courts have also found a valid waiver where a veteran voluntarily consented to final and binding arbitration on his re-employment rights, knowing that he could not contest the arbitrator's decision, and the arbitrator decided that he had no right to the position.[20]

What do I do if my re-employment rights have been violated?

You should contact the local field office of the Labor-Management Services Administration of the Department of Labor for information and assistance. You may also contact the national Office of Veterans Re-Employment Rights (OVRR) at:

U.S. Department of Labor
Labor-Management Services Administration
Office of Veterans Re-Employment Rights
200 Constitution Ave., NW, Rm. N5422
Washington, DC 20216
   (202) 523-6491

Once you make a claim, the OVRR and its field compliance officers will investigate all the facts about your military and employment history and attempt to resolve the dispute between you and your pre-service employer. (You may also pursue your claim through any grievance procedures provided for in your employer's collective bargaining agreement, but you are not required to do so.)[21] If your dispute is not resolved by the OVRR, the OVRR can refer your case to a United States attorney or comparable official in the judicial district in which your pre-service employer is located. If the United States attorney or other official is reasonably satisfied that you are entitled to the benefits you seek, you will be represented without costs or fees in any action instituted in federal court on your behalf.[22]

Can I be discriminated against by a prospective employer because I was given a less-than-honorable discharge?

Veterans discharged under less-than-honorable conditions frequently experience discrimination when applying for private employment. No federal law prohibits an employer from disqualifying a job applicant because he received an unsatisfactory discharge, even if the underlying reason for the discharge does not affect the person's ability to do the job.

Under certain circumstances, however, you may be able to prevent an employer from discriminating against you because of the character of your discharge. First, if a prospective employer has contracts in excess of $10,000 with the federal government, it may only consider that portion of your discharge papers and military record that relates to the specific job requirements of the position you've applied for.[23] Second, if you are a member of a minority group, you can challenge your disqualification on the ground that it constitutes illegal employment discrimination under Title VII of the Civil Rights Act of 1964. The EEOC and one federal court have held that, because members of minority groups are disproportionately given less-than-honorable discharges, the use of this criterion in the selection of employees has an illegal disparate impact upon minority group members.[24] Finally, some states have regulations that forbid a pre-employment inquiry into the character of a job applicant's military discharge. Generally, these regulations permit an employer to ask only about skills acquired during military service that are relevant to performance of the job. You should check your state's law in this regard.

Am I entitled to preferential treatment?

Under certain circumstances, eligible veterans are entitled to preferential treatment in job training and placement.

If you are an eligible disabled or Vietnam era veteran (or an eligible person requesting assistance, i.e., the spouse of any person who suffers from a total and permanent service-connected disability or who died of or from a service-connected disability), you can benefit from the Veterans Benefits law, which emphasizes the goal of promptly offering you job placement, development, or employment counseling services.[25] Eligible disabled veterans, especially of the Vietnam era, can benefit from an "outreach program" designed to provide jobs and job training opportunities.[26] In addition, both the federal government and private employers who contract with the federal government on jobs exceeding $10,000 must take affirmative steps to hire qualified disabled, Vietnam era, and special disabled veterans.[27]

As a Vietnam era veteran, you may be eligible for readjustment appointments (through September 30, 1984) and career conditional appointments with the federal government. Also, the federal government is required to have affirmative action plans in effect for the hiring, placement, and advancement of disabled veterans. As a qualified Vietnam era veteran or special disabled veteran you may receive preference for employment as veterans benefits counselors, claims examiners, and representatives in the outreach services programs.[28]

Private employers who contract with the federal government in excess of $10,000 are required to take affirmative steps to employ and advance in employment qualified Vietnam era and special disabled veterans. The employer is required to (1) file a statement with the Federal Office of Contract Compliance Programs giving the employment status of veterans under its employ; (2) consider the veteran's status a positive factor in decisions to hire, promote, or transfer the employee; and (3) list available positions with local employment service offices so that veterans may easily learn of job openings. If you believe a contractor of the United States has not complied with such affirmative requirements, you may file a complaint with the Secretary of Labor for investigation and appropriate action.[29]

NOTES

1. 38 U.S.C. §2011(4).
2. 38 U.S.C. §2011(2).
3. 38 U.S.C. §2011(1), (3).
4. 38 U.S.C. §2011(1).
5. 38 U.S.C. §2021.
6. 38 U.S.C. §2021(b)(1).
7. 38 U.S.C. §2024(a), (b)(1).
8. 38 U.S.C. §2021(b)(3); *see also Monroe v. Standard Oil Co.*, 452 U.S. 549 (1981).
9. 38 U.S.C. §2024(c).
10. 38 U.S.C. §2024(d).
11. *Monroe v. Standard Oil Co.*, *supra*.
12. These states are Ariz., Calif., Conn., Haw., Ill., Ind., Iowa, Ky., La., Maine, Maryland, Massachusetts, Michigan, Minnesota, Mo., Nebr., N.H., N.J., N.Y., N.D., Ohio, R.I., S.D., Tex., Vt., Wash., W.Va.
13. 38 U.S.C. §2024(e).
14. 38 U.S.C. §2021(a).
15. *Robertson v. Richmond*, 178 F. Supp. 734 (E.D. Va. 1959).
16. 38 U.S.C. §3103(a).
17. 38 U.S.C. §§2021(a)(A)(ii), 2024(d).
18. 38 U.S.C. §2021(a)(B).
19. Dep't of Labor, Veterans' Reemployment Rights Handbook 40 (1970); *see also* FRES, Job Discrimination §§7:21, 7:22 (Lawyers Co-Op. Publ. Co. 1976).
20. *Wright v. Ford Motor Co.*, 196 F. Supp. 538 (D. Mich. 1961).
21. *McKinney v. Mo.-Kans.-Tex. R. Co*, 357 U.S. 265 (1958).
22. 38 U.S.C. §2022.
23. 41 C.F.R. §60–250.6(b).
24. EEOC Dec. no. 74–25 (Sept. 10, 1973); *Dozier v. Chupka*, 395 F. Supp. 836 (E.D. Ohio 1975).
25. 338 U.S.C. §2007.
26. 38 U.S.C. §2003A.
27. 38 U.S.C. §§2012, 2014.
28. 38 U.S.C. §2014.
29. 38 U.S.C. §2012; *see generally* 41 C.F.R. §60–250.4.

XII

Sexual Orientation

This chapter discusses discrimination in private employment based on an employee's or job applicant's sexual orientation (also sometimes called sexual or affectional preference). No one knows how common such discrimination is. Gay people are largely an invisible minority. Most are not easily identifiable as gay, and choose not to declare themselves as gay. As a result, the extent and intensity of discrimination against them cannot be readily gauged.

It has been estimated that 10 percent of the adult male population is homosexual,[1] which suggests that there are many gay employees and job applicants. But there are relatively few known cases of discrimination by employers against gays. This is probably so because most employers are unaware of the employees' sexual orientations and because gay employees carefully avoid situations in which they might be found out. Furthermore, gays who are discriminated against are understandably reluctant to report the discrimination because they fear the exposure or embarrassment that might result, or because, as explained below, there is often no legal recourse.

Generally, governmental employers may not discriminate against employees on the basis of sexual orientation. Governments are subject to constitutional requirements that they act fairly and rationally toward all citizens, including employees. Private employers are not, however, subject to those constitutional strictures.

For a full discussion of the rights of gays in public employment—and in many other areas—see *The Rights of Gay People*, a recently revised book in this series. Also, you can contact the National Gay Task Force for useful booklets on employment of gays.[2]

Are federal anti-discrimination laws applicable to gays?

No. As discussed in preceding chapters, Title VII of the federal Civil Rights Act of 1964 forbids discrimination in employment on the basis of race, color, religion, national origin, or sex. Although many bills have been introduced in Congress to outlaw discrimination against gay people, none has passed. It has been consistently held that Title VII's prohibition of discrimination on the basis of sex does not reach sexual preference; the ban on sex discrimination is directed toward gender, not sexual practices and preferences.[3] Similarly, it has been held that Title VII does not reach discrimination against transsexuals or bisexuals[4] or against a male because he is effeminate.[5]

Are there any laws prohibiting discrimination against gays in private employment?

Yes, a few.[6] In 1981 Wisconsin passed a statute banning discrimination on the basis of sexual preference.[7] Such discrimination has been prohibited in two counties (Howard Co., MD, and San Mateo Co., CA) and in many municipalities: Alfred, NY; Amherst, MA; Ann Arbor, MI; Aspen, CO; Austin, TX; Bloomington, IN; Champaign, IL; Detroit, MI; East Lansing, MI; Hartford, CT; Iowa City, IA; Los Angeles, CA; Madison, WI; Marshall, MN; Minneapolis, MN; San Francisco, CA; Seattle, WA; Tucson, AZ; Urbana, IL; Washington, DC; and Yellow Springs, OH. In New York City, as in several other cities, private employers under contract with the city cannot discriminate against gays.

In one case,[8] the California Supreme Court held that a company's arbitrary exclusion of qualified gay people from employment opportunities violated the equal protection guarantee of the California state constitution, as well as certain state statutes. That ruling has limited applicability, however, because the employer was a public telephone company, and the court held that its activities were so intertwined with the state government and so important to the public welfare that it was quasi-governmental in character. It was this quasi-governmental character that made that employer subject to the constitutional strictures.

Are there any other protections for gay employees?

Not many. Some large corporations have established policies against discrimination on the basis of sexual orientation in hiring and advancement. At least 150 of the *Fortune* 500 companies have announced such policies,[9] including ABC, AT&T, Allied Chemical, Bank of America, Bethlehem Steel, CBS, Citicorp, IBM, Macy's, Mutual Life of New York, and NBC. A few state courts have held that promises made in employee handbooks or manuals are binding contractual obligations that can be enforced,[10] though other courts have held to the contrary.[11]

It is also possible, though not likely, that such discrimination may be forbidden by an applicable employment contract. A few unions—for example, the Screen Actors Guild (AFL-CIO) and the Wire Service Guild—have negotiated such provisions. If you are in a union, consult your union representative.

NOTES

1. *See* "Sexual Behavior in the Human Male," Alfred C. Kinsey et al., Saunders (1948); "Sexual Behavior in the Human Female," Alfred C. Kinsey et al., Saunders (1953).

2. NGTF, Suite 1601, 80 Fifth Ave., New York, NY 10011, (212) 741–5800. Booklets include "You and Your Job—A Gay Employee's Guide to Discrimination" and "Are There Gay People Working in My Business?—Answers to Employers' Questions."

3. *See DeSantis v. Pacific Telephone and Telegraph Co.*, 608 F.2d 327 (9th Cir. 1979). *Cf. Macauley v. Mass. Commission Against Discrimination*, 397 N.E.2d 670 (Mass. 1979) (Massachusetts statute prohibiting discrimination on basis of sex does not include sexual preference).

4. *Voyles v. Ralph K. Davies Medical Center*, 403 F. Supp. 456 (N.D. Cal. 1975), *aff'd without op.*, 570 F.2d 354 (9th Cir. 1976); *Holloway v. Arthur Andersen & Co.*, 566 F.2d 659 (9th Cir. 1977); *Powell v. Read's, Inc.*, 436 F. Supp. 369 (D. Md. 1977).

5. *Smith v. Liberty Mut. Ins. Co.*, 395 F. Supp. 1098 (N.D. Ga. 1975), *aff'd*, 569 F.2d 325 (5th Cir. 1978).

6. For a complete list, write the National Gay Task Force (see note 2) and ask for "Gay Rights in the United States and Canada."

7. Wisc. Stat. Ann. §111.32(5).

8. *Gay Law Students Assoc. v. Pacific Telephone & Telegraph Co.*, 595 P.2d 592, 156 Cal. Rptr. 14 (1979).

9. "The NGTF Corporate Survey" (1981) (survey of 850 major U.S. companies).

10. *E.g., Toussaint v. Blue Cross & Blue Shield of Michigan*, 408 Mich. 579, 292 N.W.2d 880 (1980); *Cleary v. American Airlines, Inc.*, 111

Cal. App. 3d 443, 168 Cal. Rptr. 722 (1980); *Weiner v. McGraw-Hill, Inc.*, 57 N.Y.2d 458, 457 N.Y.S.2d 193 (1982).

11. *E.g., Johnson v. National Beef Packing Co.*, 220 Kan. 52, 551 P.2d 779 (1976); *Shaw v. S.S. Kresge Co.*, 167 Ind. App. 1, 32F N.E.2d 775 (1975).

Part III

Labor Laws

XIII

Labor-Management Relations

During the 1930s labor unrest in the U.S. was widespread and often ended in violent confrontations between workers and employers. This ongoing battle caused severe disruptions in the flow of interstate commerce, and threatened to prevent the nation's recovery from the Great Depression.

In an effort to ameliorate the destructive economic side effects of the conflict between management and labor, Congress enacted the National Labor Relations Act (NLRA) in 1935 and has amended it several times since.[1] While recognizing that conflict between labor and management was unavoidable, the NLRA sought to limit and define the areas and rules of conflict by granting certain rights to all parties and by imposing certain restraints upon them.

Most significantly, the NLRA recognized the right of private employees to form and join unions, to bargain as a group with their employers, and to engage in collective action for their mutual advantage and protection.[2] The Act also prohibited employers from interfering with the formation or internal affairs of unions, making such interference an "unfair labor practice." Correspondingly, the NLRA, as amended, prohibited certain unfair labor practices by unions, thereby regulating the types of collective actions unions can take in seeking to achieve their goals. In addition, the NLRA created the National Labor Relations Board (NLRB) to promote and protect the ideals and interest embodied in the NLRA.[3] Among other things, the NLRB conducts representation elections and investigates and issues orders concerning charges of unfair labor practices.[4]

This chapter discusses the following issues of concern to private employees in the area of labor-management relations: certification or recognition of a union (section A); membership in a union (section B); contract negotiations and enforcement (section C); concerted employee activities (such as strikes, boycotts, and picketing) and employer counter-measures (section D); and other federal and state laws governing employer-employee relations (section E). This chapter does not discuss extensively union governance and other intra-union matters; those subjects are covered in the ACLU handbook *The Rights of Union Members*.

A. Certification or Recognition of a Union

How do private employees come to be represented by a union?

A union can become the exclusive bargaining agent for a group of employees either by gaining voluntary recognition from the employer or by winning an election conducted by the NLRB.

When can an employer voluntarily recognize a union?

An employer can voluntarily recognize a union as the exclusive bargaining representative for employees if the union has the support of a majority of the employees in the bargaining unit. Generally a union proves majority support by soliciting employees to sign cards stating their support for the union and then presenting these cards to the employer. If an employer recognizes a union that has only minority support, the employer will have violated section 8(a)(2)[5] of the Act, which prohibits employers from interfering in, dominating, or supporting any labor organization.[6] On the other hand, even if a union does have majority support, the employer can, absent certain unusual circumstances, decline to recognize the union and insist that the union proceed to an NLRB election.[7]

Must an employer remain neutral when two rival unions are seeking to represent employees?

It depends. When one of the rival unions is incumbent, the employer must bargain with the incumbent, even if the challenger has filed a petition with the NLRB. If the employer and the incumbent union reach agreement, they will sign a collective bargaining agreement. But if the challenger petitions the NLRB and wins the resulting election, the incumbent union is ousted and its agreement is voided. The employer must then bargain with the new union.[8]

When neither rival union is incumbent, the employer can recognize and bargain with one of them, if that union has majority support and if the other union has not filed a petition with the NLRB. If a petition has been filed, the employer may not recognize either union, and the bargaining representative will be determined by the election.[9]

Can a union solicit on company property and during working hours?

Under limited conditions, yes. A union may not solicit employees during actual work time because such activity interferes with the employer's legitimate interest in having employees work during the time that they are supposed to be working. An employer's ban on solicitation during actual work time is, therefore, presumptively valid.[10] Nevertheless, union representatives who are employees of the employer may solicit support on company property during non-work time during the working day, such as lunch and break periods. An employer may, however, ban *non-employee* union representatives from soliciting on company property if the union has available to it other adequate means of communication with the employees and if the employer applies the bar evenly to all non-employee solicitors.[11] Basically, this means that an employer must allow union organizers on company property if the union has pursued alternative methods of communication with employees and has found such methods totally inadequate.

How does a union gain recognition through an election?

The first step in the election procedure is the filing of a recognition petition with a Regional Office of the NLRB.[12] An election petition can be filed by an employee or group of employees, any individual or labor organization acting on behalf of employees, or an employer.

After a petition is filed, the NLRB will conduct an investigation of the petition to determine (1) whether enough employees in the bargaining unit (at least 30 percent) have signed cards expressing an interest in having the union be their bargaining representative[13]; (2) whether a question of representation actually exists; (3) whether the industry affects commerce (and is therefore within the jurisdiction of the NLRB); and (4) whether there is an appropriate bargaining unit (discussed later). .

When a petition is filed, the representative from the NLRB Regional Office will encourage the parties to agree to a "consent election." In a consent election the union and the employer reach an agreement on the election and attendant issues such as date, place, and bargaining unit. The advantage of a consent election is that the issues are resolved quickly, without resorting to a formal hearing.[14]

If the parties do not agree to a "consent election," a hearing officer in the Regional Office will conduct a formal hearing toward resolving preliminary questions such as jurisdiction and the appropriate bargaining unit.[15] After the hearing, the Regional Director will decide whether to dismiss the petition or to hold an election; in the latter instance, he will also define the appropriate bargaining unit.

The next step is determining who is eligible to vote in the election. An employee is eligible to vote if he or she holds a full-time or regular part-time job within the appropriate bargaining unit and is on the company payroll (1) at the end of the payroll period preceding the date the Regional Office orders the election, and (2) on the date of the election. Additionally, economic strikers (discussed later) and their permanent replacements are entitled to vote if the election is held within 12 months after the strike started.[17] Employees who are striking against an unfair labor practice are entitled to vote irrespective of the 12-month limitation;[18] replacements for such unfair labor practice strikers are not entitled to vote.[19] Employees who have been laid off and have a "reasonable expectation" of recall may vote.[20] Also, probationary employees, and employees on sick leave or leave of absence,[21] and regular part-time employees may vote.

What does the term "appropriate bargaining unit" mean?

An appropriate bargaining unit is a group of employees who, due to certain similar conditions of their employment, share a community of interest, and would therefore be appropriately represented in a single unit. While the Regional Director determines the appropriateness of the unit on a case-by-case basis, the NLRB has established broad guidelines to assist in this determination. The most important factors in determining an appropriate bargaining unit are the duties, skills, and working conditions of the employees; any history of collective bargaining; and the wishes of the employees; and to a limited degree, the extent of union organization among the employees.

The process of defining the appropriate bargaining unit is especially complex for multi-plant employers. In such situations, such additional factors as the extent of integration between plants, centralization of management and supervision, employee interchange, and the geographical location of the several plants will be considered.[22] Again, the key consideration is which workers have the same "community of interest."

Can the parties agree on to the appropriate bargaining unit?

Yes. The NLRB encourages parties to agree on the appropriate bargaining unit. In the interest of expeditious handling of representation cases, the NLRB will honor such agreements, even though including certain employees in the unit might be questioned if the matter were litigated, so long as not contrary to statute or strong NLRB policy.[23]

Are some employees excluded from bargaining units?

Yes. The following categories of employees are excludable from certain types of bargaining units:

Supervisors: Supervisors cannot be included in a bargaining unit because they are not employees covered by the NLRA.[24] A supervisor is defined in the NLRA as ". . . any individual having authority in the interest of the employer, to hire, transfer, suspend, lay-off, recall, promote, discharge, assign, reward or discipline other employees."[25] Thus there is no hard-and-fast line; each employee's status must be determined separately, with the employee's duties as the paramount consideration.

Managerial employees: The rationale for excluding managerial employees from a bargaining unit is obvious: their interests are with management. Whether certain employees are managerial employees depends on whether they actually perform the duties of management by formulating, determining, and effectuating the employer's policies, so that including them in the bargaining unit would create a conflict of interest.[26]

Professional employees: Professional employees may not be included in a collective bargaining unit with non-professional employees, unless a majority of the professional employees vote for inclusion in the unit.[27] In addition, professional em-

ployees already included in a mixed unit may request
severance; in other words, they cannot be kept in a mixed
unit against their will.[28] One of the reasons for special treatment of professional employees is the concern that their
needs will be overlooked by the more numerous non-
professionals in the unit. Professional employees are defined
in the NLRA as those engaged in work "predominantly
intellectual," involving "consistent exercise of discretion and
judgment" of such a character that the output cannot be
standardized, or "requiring knowledge of an advanced type in
a field of service or learning customarily acquired by a prolonged course of specialized intellectual instruction and study
in an institution of higher learning."[29]

Confidential employees: A confidential employee is defined
as one who assists or acts in a confidential capacity to a person
who determines, formulates, or effectuates management policies in the field of labor relations.[30] This includes secretaries
and clerks. Such employees may not be in a bargaining unit.

Temporary, seasonal, or casual workers: Such employees
are normally excluded because their interest in the job is not
considered sufficient to afford them the protections of the
NLRA. But if these employees can show a "sufficient community of interest with the year-round employees," they can be
included.[31]

Ex-employees: If laid-off employees have a reasonable expectation of being recalled, they can be included in a bargaining unit. On the other hand, employees discharged for cause
are excluded. A discharged employee can contest the discharge,
however, and cast a "challenged ballot" in the election, which
will not be counted until the unfair labor practice proceeding
has concluded in his favor.[32]

Guards: Guards may not be in the same unit with other
employees.[33] The rationale is that a guard's duty is to uphold
and protect the employer's regulations and property, and this
required allegiance to the employer could create a conflict of
interest if the union became embroiled in a labor dispute
with the employer.

**Is the union entitled to a list of the names and addresses
of employees in the unit who are eligible to vote?**

Yes. To ensure that the union has access to employees, the
NLRB in *Excelsior Underwear Inc.*[34] held:

Within 7 days after the Regional Director has approved a consent election agreement entered into by the parties . . . or after the Regional Director or the Board has directed an election . . . the employer must file with the Regional Director an election eligibility list, containing the names and addresses of all the eligible voters. The Regional Director, in turn, shall make this information available to all parties in the case. Failure to comply with this requirement shall be grounds for setting aside the election wherever proper objections are filed.

The *Excelsior* rule has been strictly applied, even if the failure to supply the list was inadvertent.[35] The NLRB is empowered to enforce this rule by a subpoena.[36]

When and where will the election be held?
The election is usually held between 25 and 40 days after the Regional Director has issued his decision. This is not a firm rule; it can be altered by the Regional Director when a delay would facilitate the election. In seasonal industries, for example, it may be necessary to wait until the workforce is more fully employed and at a peak.[37]

As a general rule, an election will be held on the employer's premises.[38] Regulations require that election notices be posted in conspicuous places and that they designate the time and place of the election.[39]

Are there rules governing the union campaign?
Yes. To ensure that employees have the opportunity to make a free and rational choice of a union, the NLRB has established standards to govern both union and employer behavior during the course of a unionization campaign. If evidence exists that employees were prevented from making a voluntary, informed choice, a new election will be ordered.[40]

Are misrepresentations or threats in election literature grounds for setting aside an election?
Not necessarily. Election campaign literature, not surprisingly, is often less than completely honest; but exaggerations, half-truths, name-calling, and minor misstatements are *not* grounds for setting aside an election, as long as these infractions do not reach the level of coercion, fraud, or trickery.[41]

Whether campaign literature reaches that level is determined on a case-by-case basis within the context of the campaign.[42]

Elections have been set aside when election literature or statements went beyond the usual standards of legitimate campaigning. Examples: employer characterized a union as "strike-happy";[43] employer said he didn't know how long he would be able to continue operating if the union was elected;[44] employer said that if the union won he would reduce everyone's wages to a minimum before negotiating for a collective bargaining agreement.[45]

What happens if the union or employer makes statements appealing to prejudice?

The mere mention of a racial or religious issue in order to appeal to prejudice is not a basis for overturning an election. On the other hand, if appeals to prejudice are so inflammatory as to prevent an employee from exercising free choice, then the election can be set aside.[46]

Can a union promise to waive initiation fees or dues if an employee signs a union card before an election?

A union's promise to waive initiation fees and dues for those employees who express support for it before the election constitutes improper interference with the election process; the employee, though not legally bound to vote for the union, will probably do so after openly expressing support.[47] But the election will stand when a union promises to waive initiation fees for *all* employees who join the union before a contract is signed without regard to who supported the union.[48]

Are there limitations on the making of speeches during an election campaign?

Yes. The NLRB will set aside an election when an employer or union makes a "captive audience" speech to employees during company time during the 24-hour period immediately preceding the election.[49] This rule is designed to allow employees time to reflect before making their choice concerning representation. In addition, though an employer may make derogatory remarks about the union or show an anti-union film,[50] the NLRA prohibits an employer from making speeches that contain threats of reprisal against employees who support the union. It has been held that such restrictions on speech during a certification election do not violate the First Amendment because the infringement on speech is outweighed by the employees' right to a free, fair, and informed election.[51]

Must the election be conducted by secret ballot?

Yes. All representation elections must be by secret ballot.[52] In addition, all handling of the ballots before, during, and after an election must be done by NLRB personnel.[53] The NLRB may require foreign language ballots if a large percentage of the unit members are foreign-speaking. For example, a court held that where one-third of the employees were Spanish-speaking, but no Spanish ballots were provided, the election process violated the minimum "laboratory conditions" standard; the election was set aside.[54]

Can the NLRB order recognition of a union without an election?

Yes, in limited situations. In addition to voluntary recognition and certification by an election, a union can become the bargaining representative for employees through an NLRB bargaining order. Such an order may be issued when an employer's unfair labor practices make it impossible to conduct a fair election. To order bargaining, two conditions must be met: (1) a majority of the employees have signed authorization cards stating that they want an election, and (2) the employer has committed serious and pervasive unfair labor practices. When both conditions are met, the NLRB can issue a bargaining order, if it finds that the possibility of conducting a fair election is slight, and the employees' interests (as expressed in the authorization cards) would be protected by issuing the bargaining order.[55]

How soon after an election can another election be held?

To lighten the heavy burden imposed on the NLRB by representation elections, to promote industrial stability, and to encourage sober thought by voting employees, Congress and the NLRB have created certain bars to the election process.

Section 9(c)(3) of the NLRA states: "No election shall be directed in any bargaining unit or any subdivision within which, in the preceding twelve-month period, a valid election shall have been held.[56] This "election bar" rule freezes the results of the election for a while, thereby promoting stability in the election process and preventing use of that process to harass employers. If a union has been certified, a petition for another election cannot be filed within 12 months of the certification. This "certification bar" gives the union some time to get organized.[57]

Finally, if a collective bargaining agreement is in effect, the "contract bar" rule bars any election for up to three years of the contract.[58] If the contract is for less than three years, an election is barred for the length of the contract. If the contract is for an unlimited duration, however, the contract bar rule does not apply.[59] The contract bar rule is subject to other exceptions that may permit an election before the contract has run.

B. Membership in a Union

This section briefly discusses issues of concern to individual union members about the internal workings of the union. These issues include dues, the obligations owed between a union and its members, and grievance and arbitration mechanisms. For a complete discussion of this area, see the ACLU handbook *The Rights of Union Members*.

Must I join the union if I'm hired by a unionized employer?

After a union has been certified as the exclusive bargaining agent for a unit, the union will generally seek to include a provision in the labor-management contract about the union status of employees newly hired into the unit. Such "union security clauses" help ensure that union strength will not be diminished through attrition and replacement.

Basically, there are three kinds of legal union security agreements: the union shop, the agency shop, and the "maintenance of membership" shop. The "closed shop," in which only members of the union can be hired, is illegal under the NLRA.[60]

If you are hired into a union shop, you must join the union after being on the job for a specified grace period, which cannot be shorter than 30 days.[61] You must remain a member of the union for the duration of any contract containing a union shop clause. Under the NLRA, you are not required, however, to become a full-fledged member of the union; it is enough if you pay your dues and fees.

If you are hired by an employer that has an agency shop

agreement with the union, you need not join the union, but after 30 days of employment you must pay the union for the services it renders to your unit as the bargaining agent. Usually, this payment is in the form of an initiation fee and monthly dues.

If you become an employee of an employer whose contract with the union contains a "maintenance of membership" provision, you are under no obligation to join the union or pay any fees. If you voluntarily join the union, however, you must continue to pay dues and fees for the duration of the contract.

In an "open shop" no union security agreement is in effect and you have no obligation to join a union or to remain a member if you do join. This arrangement is necessarily in effect in the "right to work" states.

How do I pay dues to the union?

You can pay the dues directly to the union; or the collective bargaining agreement may contain a "dues checkoff" clause under which your employer will automatically deduct the dues from your paycheck if you authorize this in writing. Dues checkoff provisions provide financial security to the union and lessen administration expenses.

Dues can be automatically deducted from your paycheck only if you voluntarily authorize such deduction. Also, even if you authorize such deduction, no other union fees may be deducted automatically, unless you explicitly authorize the deduction. You cannot be discriminated against for failing to elect a checkoff, nor may the union make the alternative to payment by checkoff unduly burdensome.

Can my dues be used to support candidates for political office?

Generally, no. Under the Federal Election Campaign Act of 1971,[62] a union cannot use your dues or assessments to make contributions or expenditures in connection with federal elections (primary or general) or federal conventions or caucuses. A union can, however, establish and administer a fund for such political purposes financed by voluntary donations, which must be kept in a separate segregrated fund. Union officials can solicit voluntary donations to the fund only under circumstances plainly indicating that the donations are for political purposes and that you may decline to contribute without fear of reprisal.[63] A union may not employ a "reverse checkoff" procedure under which donations to the political fund are automatically deducted from your wages and you must submit a written request for a refund if you do not want to contribute.[64]

The Federal Election Campaign Act does not pertain to non-federal elections or to other political activities by unions. As to those matters, public employees (under the First Amendment) and railway workers (under the Railway Labor Act) have additional protections. Such employees can demand a refund of that portion of their dues and assessments being used for political purposes.[65] Many unions have set up internal procedures to provide such refunds.

May an employer make contributions to a union?

No. Section 8(a)(2) of the NLRA makes it an unfair labor practice for an employer to "dominate or interfere with the formation or administration of any labor organization or contribute financial or other support to it.[66] The object of that provision is to maintain the union's autonomy and prevent employer manipulation of the union through financial contributions. It is not illegal, however, for an employer to "cooperate" with the union, unless such cooperation has the effect of "interfering" with the union.[67]

Must I include the union in trying to resolve a problem with my employer?

No, but you cannot exclude the union. Section 9(a) of the NLRA provides that an individual employee can meet directly with the employer as long as (1) the union is given notice and the opportunity to be present at the meeting, and (2) the grievance is not resolved in a manner that is inconsistent with the terms of the collective bargaining agreement.[68] Thus, if your dispute involves a subject covered by the union contract, any settlement agreement between you and your employer cannot place you in any better or worse position than your fellow workers.

Am I entitled to have a representative with me during an investigatory interview with management?

Generally, yes. You are entitled to have a union representative with you at an interview with your employer if you reasonably believe that the interview might result in disciplinary action against you.[69] If you are not in a union, you can have a co-worker with you.[70] Before the interview, you are entitled to know the nature of the matter being investigated and to consult with the person who will assist you at the interview.[71]

What do I do if I have a grievance against my employer?

If you cannot resolve the problem informally with your supervisor, you should follow the grievance procedure set forth in the collective bargaining agreement. These procedures vary greatly, but they typically begin with the filing of a written grievance. Then the supervisor and the union steward for your department will discuss the problem. If they cannot resolve it, higher-up representatives of the company and the union try. If a solution cannot be found at that level, the case can be taken to arbitration.[72]

What is arbitration?

Most collective bargaining contracts provide for some form of arbitration. In arbitration, the parties to the contract submit their dispute to an independent third party for resolution. For example, the parties may select an arbitrator to resolve a dispute about interpretation of a contract clause or about the propriety of one party's action. Through arbitration, the parties can resolve their differences without the filing of an unfair labor practice charge with the NLRB, without going to court, and without strikes or lockouts. Arbitration is faster, less expensive, and less formal than such procedures. The federal courts have the power to enforce arbitration clauses (that is, to force the parties to arbitrate) and to enforce the arbitrator's decision.[73] Federal law (not state law) governs any legal questions arising under such arbitration clauses in collective bargaining agreements subject to the NLRA.[74]

Are all disputes subject to arbitration?

Generally yes, but there are exceptions. In a series of cases called the Steelworkers' trilogy, the Supreme Court stressed that arbitration of disputes is an integral part of labor-management relations:

The collective agreement calls for the submission of grievances in the categories which it describes, irrespective of whether a Court may deem them to be meritorious. . . .

the function of the Court is very limited when the parties have agreed to submit all questions of contract interpretation to the arbitrator. It is confined to ascertaining whether the party seeking arbitration is making a claim which on its face is governed by the contract. Whether the moving party is right or wrong is a question of contract interpretation for the arbitrator.

The Courts, therefore, have no business weighing the merits of the grievance, considering whether there is equity in a particular claim or determining whether there is particular language in the written instrument which will support the claim. The agreement is to submit all grievances to arbitration, not merely those which the Court will deem meritorious. The processing of even frivolous claims may have therapeutic values of which those who are not of the plant environment may be quite unaware.[75]

This decision reflects the view that arbitration fosters industrial peace, which is a major aim of labor-management relations law.[76]

Is my union required to process my grievance?

As the employees' exclusive bargaining agent, the union has a duty to fairly represent those employees. This obligation of fairness and good faith extends to all union actions on the employees' behalf, such a negotiating and processing grievances.

Accordingly, your union cannot arbitrarily or discriminatorily fail to process a grievance and cannot process it in a perfunctory manner. The union must investigate your grievance, if investigation is needed, and must give you an opportunity to participate in resolving the grievance.[77] If the union treats a grievance improperly, you may have the basis for a lawsuit against the union and the employer.

C. Contract Negotiations and Enforcement

Sections 8(a)(5) and 8(b)(3) of the NLRA make it an unfair labor practice for employers and unions respectively to refuse to bargain collectively. Section 8(d) imposes a duty to bargain in good faith:

For the purposes of this section, to bargain collectively is the performance of the mutual obligation of the employer and the representative of the employees to meet at reasonable times and confer in good faith with respect to wages, hours, and other terms and conditions of employment, or the negotiation of an agreement, or any question arising thereunder, and the execution of a written contract incorporating any agreement reached if requested by either party, but such obligation does not compel either party to agree to a proposal or require the making of a concession.[78]

These provisions require the parties to meet and negotiate in good faith toward resolving their differences, on the assumption that this will foster the reaching of an ultimate agreement and will lessen the chances of a strike or other form of disruptive concerted activity.

Can an employer or union delay or condition bargaining?
No. An employer's or union's refusal to meet with the representative of the other party is a violation of the NLRA.[79] Further, neither party may engage in dilatory tactics that violate the requirement to meet at reasonable times. In deciding whether the timing of the meetings is unreasonable, the NLRB will look to a variety of factors. In one case, the NLRB held that a delay of one month between bargaining sessions was unduly long.[80] In addition, neither an employer nor a union can place unreasonable conditions on bargaining.[81]

Must an employer disclose information to the union?
Generally, yes. The employer must disclose to the union information that is necessary for the union to bargain effectively. This may include information about the employer's financial ability to pay wage increases:

Good-faith bargaining necessarily requires that claims made by either bargainer should be honest claims. This is true about an asserted inability to pay an increase in wages. If such an argument is important enough to present in the give and take of bargaining, it is important enough to require some sort of proof of accuracy. . . . . We agree with the Board that a refusal to attempt to substantiate a claim of inability to pay increased wages may support a finding of a failure to bargain in good faith.[82]

Nevertheless, an employer can refuse to disclose confidential information or trade secrets and can reject requests made for the purpose of harassment.[83]

May an employer communicate with employees during contract negotiations?

Yes. An employer may inform employees of the status of negotiations, of proposals made by either side, and of its version of a conflict. An employer may not, however, communicate with employees during negotiations for the purpose of coercing them or undermining the union.[84]

What subjects are discussed during negotiations?

Section 8(d) states that the parties involved in collective bargaining must confer "with respect to wages, hours, and other terms and conditions of employment."[85] These matters are referred to as "mandatory bargaining subjects." All other subjects, except prohibited bargaining subjects, are referred to as "permissive bargaining subjects." Basically, permissive subjects deal with the employer's relationship to third parties, the scope of the bargaining unit, and the union's relationship with its members. Parties are required to discuss only mandatory subjects; a party can refuse to discuss a permissive subject without committing an unfair labor practice.

With regard to a mandatory subject, either party may insist upon its position, and if necessary, support its insistence with a strike or lockout. For example, either party may insist upon a certain wage rate until an impasse has been reached; even without an impasse, a union can lawfully initiate a strike to pressure the employer to accede to its wage demand. A permissive subject, on the other hand, may not be the basis for bargaining to an impasse or for concerted action to pressure acceptance.

Mandatory subjects are "wages, hours, and other terms and conditions of employment." The term "wages" has been broadly construed. It includes not only rates of pay, but also "emoluments resulting from employment,"[86] increases or decreases in hourly rates, pay differentials on different shifts, overtime work, severance pay, and paid holidays and vacations.[87]

Bonuses are included if they are really remuneration for services performed rather than gratuitous gifts from the employer.[88]

The concept of "other terms and conditions of employment" encompasses both the employer-union relationship and the employer-employee relationship. Included in this category of mandatory subjects are plant safety rules; performance of bargaining unit work by a supervisor; seniority, promotion, and transfer; compulsory retirement provisions; layoffs; grievance procedures, arbitration, and no-strike clauses; and union security agreements.[89]

An employer's plan to "contract out" or subcontract work is a mandatory subject of bargaining, if unit employees will lose work as a result.[90] An employer's decision to relocate a factory can be a mandatory subject of bargaining, if the relocation decision could be affected by economic factors within the union's control. If, however, the relocation is coupled with complete discontinuation of a distinct segment of the employer's business, the decision falls within the area of "managerial prerogatives" and becomes only a permissive subject.[91] In sum, if the employer's decision is based on "economic reasons" or "business justifications" unrelated to the union, the employer can make its decision without consulting the union. Nevertheless, the employer is required to bargain with the union concerning the impact of its decision on bargaining unit employees.

Can an employer take unilateral actions during negotiations?

No, if it involves a mandatory bargaining subject, unless an impasse in negotiations has been reached. It is an unfair labor practice for an employer, during negotiations, to take any action regarding a mandatory subject without first consulting the union. For example, the employer cannot unilaterally change wages during negotiations prior to an impasse. The rationale for this rule is that, by undercutting the union as the bargaining representative, the employer is actually refusing to bargain, thereby hampering the collective bargaining process.[92]

An employer charged with taking an unlawful unilateral action can try to defend its action on four grounds: (1) the action concerned a permissive bargaining subject only; (2) the employer has bargained in good faith to an impasse; (3) the unilateral action was merely a continuation of past policies,

such as giving Christmas bonuses; or (4) the union waived its
right to bargain collectively on the subject at issue.

Can a union waive its right to bargain on certain subjects?

Yes. A union can waive its right to bargain on certain
subjects during the term of the contract in exchange for
concessions from the employer. The union may agree, for
example, not to raise new issues and demands during the
contract term, or not to challenge a unilateral action by the
employer regarding a mandatory bargaining subject. To be
effective, such a waiver must be made "clearly and unmis-
takably."[93] Thus, in authorizing the employer to take unilateral action on a mandatory subject, the areas of allowable
unilateral action must be specifically stated.[94]

What are the remedies if a party refuses to bargain or to sign a contract?

The extent and type of remedy depends on the circumstances of each case. Refusal to bargain in good faith is an
unfair labor practice under the NLRA.[95] Many factors affect
the determination of whether a party has engaged in good-
faith bargaining. This subjective determination must often be
based on inferences from the party's behavior, such as refusal
to offer any proposals or to make any concessions.[96] Simple
adamancy in support of a bargaining position is not bad-faith
bargaining, but making a "one firm and final offer" at the start
of negotiations probably is.[97]

As with all other unfair labor practices, the typical remedy
for a refusal to bargain in good faith is a cease-and-desist
order directing the party to stop engaging in the prohibited
conduct and to begin bargaining in good faith. Such a cease-
and-desist order is available to either the union or the
employer.[98]

Refusal to put into writing what has been agreed upon in
collective bargaining is also an unfair labor practice.[99] If a
party refuses to sign an already negotiated contract, the usual
remedy is an order directing the party to sign the contract
and granting back pay to the employees pursuant to the
terms of the contract.[100]

If employees are terminated by an illegal unilateral action
(i.e., the employer had a legal duty to bargain, but didn't),
the usual remedy is an order granting back pay from the date
of termination to the date an agreement is reached by the

arties or the parties bargain to good faith impasse. Economic ealities obviously affect the fashioning of remedies. For xample, if an employer unlawfully closed a plant and sold it, n order directing the employer to repurchase and reopen he plant would not be practical, and alternative remedies would be fashioned.

When can a contract be terminated or modified?

A party seeking termination or modification of a contract nust (1) serve written notice on the other party 60 days efore the proposed termination or modification, (2) offer to egotiate, (3) notify appropriate government mediation gencies, and (4) abide by the terms of the existing agreenent for 60 days without resorting to a strike or lockout.[101] These conditions require the parties to discuss their differnces and to try to resolve them. If employees engage in a trike during the 60-day notice period, they lose their status s employees under the NLRA and can be discharged by the mployer.

Must an employer negotiate about the terms of a contract during the term of the contract?

Generally, no. After a contract is signed, an employer has o obligation to negotiate any further *on the subjects covered n the contract*, with a few exceptions.

If the contract contains a "re-opener" clause (allowing negotition of contract provisions during the contract term), the mployer must bargain. On the other hand, if the contract as an integration or "zipper" clause (providing that all the erms are agreed upon and shall stand unchanged until the next contract), the union cannot seek to renegotiate during he contract term. Even if a contract has a re-opener clause as o the subjects covered in the contract, an employer may efuse to bargain about *permissive* bargaining subjects. In um, an employer may not refuse to bargain during the ontract term if (1) the subject was not previously negotiated, 2) the subject is a mandatory bargaining subject, and (3) the ontract contains no "zipper" clause.

Are there any types of provisions that may not be included n the contract?

Yes. The NLRA makes it an unfair labor practice for a ontract to contain a "hot cargo" clause, which requires the employer to cease handling or otherwise dealing with the products of, or to cease doing business with, another business enterprise.[102] Before enactment of that prohibition, unions often tried to help other unions by negotiating clauses in their contracts forbidding the employer from buying or handling the goods of another employer involved in a primary labor dispute with its own employees. This tactic exerted indirect pressure on the primary employer to settle its labor dispute. As with the prohibition on secondary boycotts (discussed later), the prohibition of hot cargo clauses was intended to contain the economic disruption caused by a labor dispute.

Clauses prohibiting the handling of another employer's product are legal, however, if the purpose is to prevent the loss of work for bargaining unit employees. In explanation, as one court has stated, the issue is—

> whether under all the surrounding circumstances, the union's objective was preservation of work for [the contracting employer's] employees or whether the agreements and boycott were tactically calculated to satisfy union objectives elsewhere. Were the latter the case . . . the boycotting employer would be a neutral bystander and the agreement or boycott would, within the intent of Congress, become secondary . . . the touchstone is whether the agreement or its maintenance is addressed to the labor relations of the contracting employer vis-a-vis his own employees or whether it seeks to benefit other than the boycotting employees to other employees of the primary employer.[103]

What happens when one employer acquires the business of another employer?

First, the acquiring employer is not bound by a collective bargaining agreement between the union and the predecessor employer, unless the acquiring employer assumes the agreement and the union consents to the assumption.[104] Second, the acquiring employer may be required to recognize and to bargain with the union representing the predecessor employer's workers, if there is "substantial continuity of identity in the business enterprise" before and after the change of ownership and a majority of the acquiring employer's workforce is composed of employees of the predecessor.[105] Third, the acquiring

ing employer is bound by an arbitration provision in the collective bargaining agreement of the predecessor if there is "substantial continuity of identity in the business enterprise" before and after the change of ownership and the acquiring employer hires a majority of the predecessor's bargaining unit employees.[106]

D. Concerted Activity

Section 7 of the NLRA guarantees private sector employees the right to engage in collective action for their mutual aid and protection. This collective action is generally referred to as "concerted activity." Over the years the NLRB and the courts have delineated the types of concerted activities that are protected by this provision.

Must employees be members of a union in order to engage in protected concerted activity?

No. Private employees need not have a union to be protected by the NLRA. Any group of employees can act in concert to better their employment situation as long as they do so in a manner that is recognized and acceptable under the NLRA. Examples of protected non-union collective action include:

- an employee's petition for a power of attorney to file back-pay claims for other employees;[108]
- a strike by all workers in a shop in support of a fellow worker's grievance, even though only the aggrieved worker had any immediate stake in the outcome;[109]
- a protest by employees over working conditions that they contend violate state law;[110]
- one employee protesting that an additional job was too onerous and threatening that a work crew would walk off the job if not relieved;[111]
- a strike in support of economic demands;[112]
- spontaneous temporary walkouts and work stoppages by employees in protest against excessive heat in a building.[113]

When private employees take concerted action in a manner acceptable under the NLRA, an employer commits an unfair labor practice if he retaliates by discharging them or otherwise discriminating against them.[114] In such a situation, affected employees may file an unfair labor practice charge with the NLRB, which could order reinstatement and back pay.

When can employees engage in protected concerted activity?

To be protected, the concerted activity must meet four conditions:[115]

- there must be a work-related complaint;
- the concerted activity must further some group interest;
- a specific remedy or result must be sought through such activity;
- the activity must not be unlawful or otherwise improper.

Any concerted activity that involves violence, assault, or trespass loses the protection of section 7;[116] this includes "sit-down" strikes in which employees physically occupy the employer's premises. Any activity that is "irresponsible" is also unprotected; this includes activities that risk harm to the employer's property, such as employees announcing a walk-out when leaving the plant that would result in costly damage to the employer.[117]

Furthermore, concerted activity that is normally protected can lose that status if it is conducted in an abusive or disloyal manner. Disloyal conduct is not protected even during a labor dispute and you can be dismissed for engaging in such conduct.[118] For example, if you go beyond the bounds of collective bargaining and outwardly attack your employer's product, you can be charged with disloyalty and your actions would not be protected.

Employees who are not represented by a union can strike with the protection of the NLRA. Employees who are represented by a union, however, are subject to restrictions on their right to strike. "Wildcat" strikes (i.e., strikes not sponsored by the union) are not protected by the NLRA on the theory that the union, which is elected to act in the employees' best interest, will choose when the bargaining unit as a whole will benefit from a strike. Further, union members cannot engage in most other forms of concerted activity, such as leafleting, without union authorization, if the disputed matter is within the union's jurisdiction. In this regard, the Supreme Court held that a group of black workers who held a press conference and leafleted to protest their employer's racially discriminatory practices were not protected by the NLRA; the employees had not gotten union approval, and a clause in the contract obligated the union to bargain about racial discrimination.[119]

A union may authorize a strike for "economic" reasons (i.e., to pressure the employer to accede to the union's bargaining demands when contract negotiations have reached an impasse), or to protest an unfair labor practice by the employer. Whether a strike is defined as an economic strike or an unfair labor practice strike is important because it determines the strikers' entitlement to reinstatement after the strike, as discussed later. An economic strike can be converted into an unfair labor practice strike if the employer commits an unfair labor practice during the strike and that unfair labor practice in fact prolongs the strike.

Can I be discharged for participating in a lawful strike?

No. Neither an economic striker nor an unfair labor practice striker can be discharged for engaging in a lawful strike. Under section 8(a) of the NLRA, an employee cannot be discharged because of union activity; upon proof that antiunion animus contributed to the discharge, the employer, to avoid liability, has the burden of proving by a preponderance of the evidence that the discharge would have taken place in the absence of the union activity.[120]

Am I entitled to reinstatement after the strike?

Although you have the right to strike under the NLRA, your employer has the right to hire replacements in order to continue doing business. Unfair labor practice strikers are entitled, upon proper application, to reinstatement, even if it requires the termination of replacements.[121]

Economic strikers face a different situation. Although they retain their status as employees, they can be permanently replaced. Economic strikers are, however, entitled to reinstatement as to replacements who were hired on a temporary basis or only for the duration of the strike.[122] In addition, economic strikers are entitled to reinstatement if their former positions become available. Economic strikers who are not reinstated are nevertheless entitled to be considered for employment on a non-discriminatory basis; that is, the employer cannot consider the former strikers' participation in the strike in making hiring decisions.

Am I entitled to back pay for the period of a strike?

No. Neither unfair labor practice strikers nor economic strikers are entitled to back pay for the time they were on strike. Nevertheless, if they request reinstatement, back pay will start to run five days after the request was made.[123]

Can my union call a strike if the contract contains a no-strike clause?

Generally, no. A no-strike provision in a collective bargaining agreement is usually given in exchange for the right to submit disputes to compulsory arbitration; in fact, when an agreement contains a compulsory arbitration clause, a no-strike restriction is generally implied by law as to arbitrable matters, unless the agreement specifically preserves the union's right to strike over such matters.[124] If a union strikes in violation of a no-strike restriction, the employer can obtain a court order enjoining the strike. If the injunction is violated, the employees and the union can be held in contempt of court.

Five requirements must be met before a court will enjoin a strike:[125]

1. There must be a contract between the union and the employer.
2. The contract must contain an express or implied no-strike clause.
3. The contract must contain a provision requiring final and binding arbitration.
4. The dispute that caused the strike must be subject to resolution by arbitration.
5. The employer must agree to submit the dispute to arbitration.

Notwithstanding a no-strike clause, workers can walk out in response to unsafe working conditions; section 502 of the Taft-Hartley Act provides that a good faith walkout due to *abnormally* dangerous conditions is not a "strike" under the NLRA.[126]

Can an employer "lock out" employees?

Yes. The Supreme Court has upheld employer lockouts in certain circumstances. An employer can take actions that "serve legitimate business interests in some significant fashion, even though the act committed may tend to discourage union membership. . . . [U]se of the lockout does not carry with it any necessary implication that the employer acted to discourage union membership or otherwise discriminate against union members as such."[127] Thus, if an employer locks out employees for a valid business reason, and not because of anti-union animus, the action is protected.

Am I protected if I participate in a slowdown?

No. A work slowdown is an impermissible form of concerted activity.[128] An employee who is collecting full pay has a duty to perform job duties in full. A slowdown can result in a discharge.

Am I protected if I refuse to cross a picket line?

You are protected if you honor your own union's picket line at your employer's plant.[129] The courts are split, however, on whether you are protected if you refuse to cross a picket line at your workplace that was set up by a union that does not represent you.

Another set of rules applies to your refusal to cross a picket line at another employer's plant. If your union's contract contains a provision authorizing you to honor pickets at another employer, you are protected; if your contract prohibits this, you are subject to discipline. If your contract is silent on the issue, the NLRB has held that your employer may not discharge or discipline you in reprisal, but may permanently replace you in order to preserve the efficient operation of its business.[130]

When can I picket my employer?

Since the 1940s the U.S. Supreme Court has considered peaceful picketing in the context of a labor dispute to be "speech," entitled to the protection of the First Amendment to the Constitution.[131] Nonetheless, recognizing that picketing can induce action and result in coercion, the Supreme Court has sustained state laws that limit picketing in order to promote legitimate and substantial local interests.[132] For example, a state may prohibit picketing that is violent, that constitutes a trespass, that would cause traffic problems, or that would block public access to sidewalks or streets.

Picketing is protected by the NLRA and the Constitution if it is peaceful and is in support of legitimate objectives. You may legitimately picket your employer during an economic strike or an unfair labor practice strike. You may also picket your employer if the picketing is "informational" in nature; information picketing is aimed at informing the public of certain conditions that exist at the workplace. Examples of protected informational picketing include publicizing that your employer's wages, hours, or other conditions fall below area labor standards or that your employer uses non-union labor.

You may *not* picket if the purpose is organizational or "recognitional" (i.e., to force your employer to recognize a union) if (1) the employer has recognized a union, and questions concerning representation are inappropriate (i.e., the contract bar period is in effect), (2) an election has been held within the last 12 months (i.e., an election bar is in effect), or (3) the picketing is conducted for more than 30 days and a petition for a representative election has not been filed.[133]

After a picketing union files a petition, the employer can request an expedited election. As stated by the NLRB,[134] the purpose of the expedited election procedure is "to shield aggrieved employers and employees from the adverse effects of prolonged recognition or organization picketing." An expedited election is conducted without a formal hearing. The Regional Office will announce the appropriate bargaining unit and order an election immediately.[135] To initiate the expedited election procedure, the employer must file an unfair labor practice charge; if no charge is filed, the picketing can continue while the petition is pending and during the election period. If recognitional picketing is conducted in violation of the NLRA, the union has committed an unfair labor practice and its picketing may be enjoined.

When may I picket another employer in support of a strike against my employer?

The NLRA prohibits boycotts (i.e., strikes or any other form of concerted activity) against a neutral employer for the purpose of pressuring that neutral employer to force your employer to settle with your union. This type of illegal activity is called a "secondary boycott." An example may prove helpful. Suppose there is a labor dispute at Company A, and the employees have gone out on strike. To speed up negotiations and put pressure on Company A to settle, the union from Company A might go to Company B, which uses the products produced by Company A, and set up a picket line.

The employees in Company B might, for example, honor the picket line and stop the operation of Company B, thereby putting economic pressure on Company A by decreasing demand for its products. This economic pressure may force Company A to settle with its union. Such concerted activity—putting pressure on a neutral employer in order to pressure the primary employer to settle—is illegal; such activity is counter-productive to the peaceful resolution of labor disputes.[136]

The secondary boycott prohibition relates only to an employer not involved with the primary labor dispute. If a secondary employer (Company B in the example) is actually doing work for the primary employer (Company A) in order to offset the effects of the strike against the primary employer, then the activity, such as picketing, is not prohibited.[137] This rule, known as the "ally doctrine," protects employees when they engage in concerted activity against an employer who is aligned with their employer, with whom they are involved in a labor dispute.

If primary employees induce other primary employees on their job site to engage in concerted activities against the primary employer, this is not secondary activity and is protected. In addition, if an employer owns more than one plant or has an "alter ego," then concerted activity can take place on the sites of the other plants as well. As one court said:[138] "In determining whether an employer is in fact neutral in a labor dispute, the courts have considered such factors as the extent to which a corporation is defacto under the control of another corporation, the extent of common ownership of the two employers, the integration of the business operations of the employers, and the dependence of one employer on the other employer for a substantial portion of its business."

Can a union lawfully picket premises occupied by both the primary employer and a neutral employer?

Generally, yes. The NLRB has held that picketing is allowed wherever primary employees are working.[139] Nevertheless, to protect the interests of the owner of a neutral site at which primary employees are working, such picketing is limited to:

- times when primary employees are on the neutral employer's premises;

- times when the primary employer is engaged in its normal business on the premises;
- places reasonably close to the premises;
- picketing that clearly discloses that the dispute is with the primary employer.[140]

Are there any limitations on the secondary boycott prohibitions?

Yes. A union is allowed to picket stores that sell the product of a struck employer. Although the NLRA states that it is illegal to "threaten, coerce, or restrain any person engaged in commerce,"[141] the Supreme Court has interpreted this section to allow picketing directed at consumers.[142]

Another limitation on the secondary boycott prohibition is the publicity provision of the NLRA, which expressly protects publicity used to advise the public of a labor dispute.[143] That provision protects "publicity, other than picketing for the purpose of truthfully advising the public (including consumers and members of a labor organization), that a product is produced by an employer with whom the labor organization has a primary dispute and is distributed by another employer." Nevertheless, if the publicity has the effect of inducing secondary employees not to perform services or handle the goods of the primary employer, it is impermissible.

E. Federal and State Labor Laws

Most areas of labor-management relations are subject to exclusive federal control, because of the need to keep the channels of interstate commerce open and the need for national uniformity. Nevertheless, states are free to enact labor laws that deal with areas not covered by the federal labor laws or that are designed to promote substantial state interests. Accordingly, most states have labor laws and have a state labor relations board to promote those laws. This section briefly discusses the coverage of and relationship between federal and state labor laws.

Are all employees covered by the NLRA?

No. As mentioned earlier in this chapter in the context of bargaining units, some employees are not covered by the NLRA. These[144] include agricultural laborers; domestic servants;

persons employed by a parent or spouse; independent contractors; supervisors; persons employed by an employer subject to the Railway Labor Act; and persons employed by someone who is not an "employer" as defined by the NLRA (e.g., public employees). Also, managerial employees (i.e., those who help formulate and effectuate management policies)[145] are not covered by the NLRA. For example, the Supreme Court held that professors at a university were not covered by the NLRA because they were intimately involved in constructing the curriculum and managing different aspects of the university community.[146]

Does the NLRA apply to all labor-management problems?

No, but it applies to most. Generally, the NLRA preempts any state regulation of labor activity that is arguably or potentially subject to the NLRA. The NLRB has exclusive jurisdiction if the employer involved is engaged in interstate or foreign commerce and the labor activity in question is arguably protected or arguably prohibited by the NLRA.[147] The interstate or foreign commerce requirement is very broadly construed; virtually any impact on such commerce suffices.

What types of activities do state labor relations laws regulate?

About 20 states have "right to work" laws, which restrict or forbid union security agreements. Also, about half the states have laws restricting the issuance of labor injunctions to stop a strike or other form of concerted activity. As previously stated, states are free to regulate unprotected activity (such as violence) and conduct that touches interests deeply rooted in local responsibility (such as the protection of the health and safety of state citizens).

NOTES

1. 29 U.S.C. §§151 *et seq.*
2. 29 U.S.C. §157.
3. *NLRB v. Nash-Finch Co.*, 404 U.S. 138 (1971).
4. 29 U.S.C. §160.
5. 29 U.S.C. §158(a)(2).
6. *International Ladies' Garment Workers v. NLRB*, 366 U.S. 731 (1961).

7. *Linden Lumber Division, Summer & Co. v. NLRB*, 419 U.S. 301, 87 LRRM 3236 (1974).
8. *RCA Dell Caribe, Inc.*, 262 NLRB no. 116, 110 LRRM 1369 (1982).
9. *Bruckner Nursing Home*, 262 NLRB no. 115, 110 LRRM 1374 (1982).
10. *Essex Int'l, Inc.*, 211 NLRB 112 (1974).
11. *NLRB v. Babcock & Wilcox Co.*, 351 U.S. 105 (1956).
12. 29 U.S.C. §159(c)(1).
13. 29 U.S.C. §159(c)(1), (2).
14. 29 C.F.R. §101.19.
15. 29 C.F.R. §101.20.
16. *H&K Mfg. Co.*, 180 NLRB 247 (1969).
17. 29 U.S.C. §159(a)(3).
18. *Kellburn Mfg. Co.*, 45 NLRB 322, 11 LRRM 142 (1942).
19. *Tampa Sand & Material Co.*, 137 NLRB 1549, 50 LRRM 1438 (1962).
20. *Rish Equip. Co.*, 150 NLRB 1185, 58 LRRM 1274 (1965).
21. *NLRB v. Atkinson Dredging Co.*, 329 F.2d 158 (4th Cir.), *cert. denied*, 377 U.S. 965 (1964).
22. *Continental Baking Co.*, 99 NLRB 777 (1952).
23. *Stop 127, Inc.*, 172 NLRB 289 (1968); 29 C.F.R. §101.19(a)(1).
24. 29 U.S.C. §152(3).
25. 29 U.S.C. §152(11).
26. *NLRB v. Bell Aerospace Co. Div. of Textron, Inc.*, 416 U.S. 267, (1974).
27. *Leedon v. Kyne*, 358 U.S. 184 (1958).
28. *S. S. White Dental Mfg.*, 109 NLRB 117 (1954).
29. 29 U.S.C. §152(12).
30. *B. F. Goodrich*, 115 NLRB 722 (1956); *NLRB v. Hendricks Cty. Rural Electric Membership Corp.*, 454 U.S. 170 (1981), 108 LRRM 3105 (1981).
31. *California Vegetable Concentrates, Inc.*, 137 NLRB 1779 (1962); *Richman Bros. Co.*, 157 NLRB 1666 (1966), *aff'd*, 387 F.2d 809 (7th Cir. 1967).
32. *Hunt Heater Corp.*, 113 NLRB 167 (1955).
33. 29 U.S.C. §159(b).
34. 156 NLRB 1236, 1239 (1966).
35. *Pacific Gamble-Robinson Co. v. NLRB*, 186 F.2d 106 (6th Cir. 1950).
36. *NLRB v. Wyman Gordon Co.*, 394 U.S. 759 (1969).
37. *General Electric Co.*, 106 NLRB 364 (1953).
38. NLRB Casehandling Manual, CCH ¶11302.2 (1976).
39. 29 C.F.R. §101(19)(a)(1).
40. *General Shoe Corp.*, 77 NLRB 124, 21 LRRM 1337 (1948).
41. *General Knit of California, Inc.*, 239 NLRB no. 101 (1978).
42. *Midland National Life Ins. Co.*, 263 NLRB no. 24, 110 LRRM 1489 (1982).

43. *NLRB v. Gissel*, 395 U.S. 75, *reh. denied*, 396 U.S. 869 (1969).
44. *Parke*, 219 NLRB 546 (1975).
45. *Ferroxcub Corp.*, 166 NLRB 63 (1967).
46. *See Southern Car & Mfg. Co.*, 106 NLRB 144 (1953).
47. *Savair Manufacturing Co.*, 414 U.S. 270 (1973).
48. *Lawrence Security, Inc.*, 210 NLRB 1048 (1974).
49. *Peerless Plywood Co.*, 107 NLRB 427 (1953).
50. *Litho Press of San Antonio*, 86 LRRM 1471 (1974).
51. *Bausch & Lomb, Inc. v. NLRB*, 451 F.2d 873 (2d Cir. 1971).
52. 29 U.S.C. §159(a)(1) (1976).
53. NLRB Casehandling Manual, CCH §11306 (1976).
54. *Marriott In Flite Service Div. of Marriott Corp. v. NLRB*, 417 F.2d 563 (5th Cir. 1969), *cert. denied*, 397 U.S. 920 (1970).
55. *NLRB v. Gissel Packing Co.*, 395 U.S. 575 (1969), *reh. denied*, 396 U.S. 869 (1969).
56. 29 U.S.C. §159(c)(3).
57. *Brooks v. NLRB*, 348 U.S. 96 (1954).
58. *General Cable Corp.*, 139 NLRB 1123 (1962).
59. *Pacific Coast Ass'n of Pulp and Paper Mfgs.*, 121 NLRB 990 (1958).
60. 29 U.S.C. §158(a)(3).
61. *Id*.
62. 2 U.S.C. §431.
63. *Pipefitters Local 562 v. U.S.*, 407 U.S. 385, 80 LRRM 2773 (1972).
64. *Federal Election Comm. v. NEA*, 457 F.Supp. 1102 (D. D.C. 1978).
65. *Abood v. Detroit Bd. of Education*, 431 U.S. 209 (1977) (public employees); *Railway Clerks v. Allen*, 373 U.S. 113 (1963) (railway workers).
66. 29 U.S.C. §158(a)(2).
67. *Chicago Rawhide Mfg. v. NLRB*, 221 F.2d 165 (7th Cir. 1955).
68. 29 U.S.C. §159(a).
69. *NLRB v. Weingarten, Inc.*, 88 LRRM 2689 (1975); *ILGWU v. Quality Mfg.*, 420 U.S. 276, 88 LRRM 2698 (1975).
70. *Materials Research Corp.*, 110 LRRM 1401 (1982).
71. *Pacific Tel. & Tel. Co.*, 110 LRRM 1411 (1982); *Amax*, 94 LRRM 1177 (1977).
72. Clarence M. Updegraff, *Arbitration and Labor Relations*, B.N.A., 1970, p. 137.
73. 29 U.S.C. §185.
74. *Textile Workers Union v. Lincoln Mills*, 353 U.S. 448 (1957).
75. *Steelworkers v. American Mfg. Co.*, 363 U.S. 564, 567–568 (1960).
76. *Steelworkers v. Warriors Gulf Nav. Co.*, 363 U.S. 574 (1960).
77. *Newport News Ship Building Co.*, 236 NLRB 197 (1978); *Figueroa de Arroyo v. Sindicato de Trabajadores Packinghouse*, 425 F.2d 281 (1st Cir.), *cert. denied*, 400 U.S. 877 (1970).
78. 29 U.S.C. §158(d).
79. *NLRB v. Lettie Lee, Inc.*, 140 F.2d 243 (9th Cir. 1944).

80. *B. F. Diamond Constr. Co.*, 163 NLRB 161 (1967), *enf'd*, 410 F.2d 462 (5th Cir. 1969), *cert. denied*, 396 U.S. 835 (1969).

81. *S & M Mfg. Co.*, 165 NLRB 663 (1967).

82. *NLRB v. Truitt Mfg. Co.*, 351 U.S. 149, 152–53 (1956).

83. *NLRB v. Robert S. Abbott Pub. Co.*, 331 F.2d 209 (7th Cir. 1964).

84. *Procter and Gamble Mfg. Co.*, 160 NLRB 334 (1966).

85. 29 U.S.C. §158(d).

86. *W.W. Cross & Co. v. NLRB*, 174 NLRB 875 (1st Cir. 1949).

87. *Smith Cabinet Mfg. Co.*, 147 NLRB 15606 (1964); *Tom Johnson Inc.*, 154 NLRB F.2d 342 (9th Cir. 1967); *Singer Mfg. Co. v. NLRB*, 119 F.2d 131 (7th Cir. 1942), *cert. denied*, 313 U.S. 595 (1942).

88. *Gas Mach. Co.*, 221 NLRB No. 129 (1975); *Czas Publishing Co.*, 205 NLRB 958 (1973).

89. *NLRB v. Gulf Power Co.*, 384 F.2d 822 (5th Cir. 1967); *Crown Coach Corp.*, 155 NLRB 625 (1965); *NLRB v. Katz*, 369 U.S. 736 (1962); *Inland Steel Co. v. NLRB*, 170 F.2d 247 (7th Cir. 1948), *cert. denied*, 336 U.S. 960 (1949); *U.S. Gypsum Co.*, 94 NLRB 112 modified, 206 F.2d 410 (5th Cir. 1953), *cert. denied*, 347 U.S. 912 (1954); *NLRB v. Boss Mfg. Co.*, 118 F.2d 187 (7th Cir. 1941).

90. *Fibreboard Paper Products Corp. v. NLRB*, 379 U.S. 203 (1964).

91. *NLRB v. Transmarine Naval Corp.*, 380 F.2d 933 (9th Cir. 1967).

92. *NLRB v. Crompton-Highland*, 337 U.S. 217 (1949).

93. *Beacon Piece Dyeing & Finishing Co.*, 121 NLRB 953 (1958).

94. *Leroy Machine Co.*, 147 NLRB 1431 (1964).

95. 29 U.S.C. §158(a)(5).

96. *Reed and Prince Mfg. Co.*, 205 F.2d 131 (1st Cir. 1953) *cert. denied*, 346 U.S. 887 (1953).

97. *Chevron Oil Co. v. NLRB*, 442 F.2d 1067 (5th Cir. 1971); *NLRB v. General Electric Co.*, 150 NLRB 192 (1964), *enf'd*, 418 F.2d 736 (2d Cir. 1969), *cert. denied*, 397 U.S. 965 (1970).

98. 29 U.S.C. §160(c).

99. 29 U.S.C. §158(a)(5), (d); *H.J. Heinz Co. v. NLRB*, 311 U.S. 514 (1941).

100. *NLRB v. Strong*, 393 U.S. 57 (1969).

101. 29 U.S.C. §158(d).

102. 29 U.S.C. §158(e).

103. *National Woodwork Mfgs. Ass'n v. NLRB*, 386 U.S. 612, 644 (1967).

104. *NLRB v. Burns Int'l Security Services, Inc.* 406 U.S. 272, 80 LRRM 2225 (1972).

105. *Id.*

106. *Howard Johnson Co. v. Detroit Loc. Jt. Exec. Bd.*, 417 U.S. 249 (1974).

107. *McGuire v. Humble Oil Ref. Co.*, 355 F.2d 352 (2d Cir. 1966), *cert. denied*, 384 U.S. 988 (1966).

108. *Salt River Valley Water Users Assoc. v. NLRB*, 206 F.2d 325 (9th Cir. 1953).

109. *NLRB v. Peter Cailler Kohler Swiss Chocolates Co.*, 130 F.2d 503 (2d Cir. 1942).
110. *Morrison-Knudsen Co. v. NLRB*, 358 F.2d. 411 (9th Cir. 1966).
111. *Bob's Casing Crews Inc. v. NLRB*, 485 F.2d 1301 (5th Cir. 1972).
112. *NLRB v. U.S. Cold Storage Corp.*, 203 F.2d 924 (5th Cir. 1953), *cert. denied*, 346 U.S. 818 (1953).
113. *NLRB v. Southern Silks Mills Inc.*, 209 F.2d 155 (6th Cir. 1953), *reh'g. denied*, 347 U.S. 976 (1954).
114. 29 U.S.C. §158(a)(1).
115. *Shelly & Anderson Furniture Mfg. Co. v. NLRB*, 497 F.2d 1200 (9th Cir. 1974).
116. *Milk Wagon Drivers Local 753 v. Meadowmoor Drivers, Inc.*, 312 U.S. 297 (1941).
117. *North Elec. Mfg. Co.*, 84 NLRB 136 (1949).
118. *NLRB v. IBEW Local 1229*, 346 U.S. 469 (1953).
119. *Emporium Capwell Co. v. Western Addition Community Organization*, 420 U.S. 50 (1975).
120. 29 U.S.C. §158 (a) (1), (3); NLRB v. Transportation Management Corp., —— U.S. ——, 51 U.S.L.W. 4761 (6/15/83).
121. *Mastro Plastics Corp. v. NLRB*, 350 U.S. 270 (1965).
122. *NLRB v. Mackay Radio & Tel. Co.*, 304 U.S. 333 (1938); *Pioneer Flour Mills v. NLRB*, 427 F.2d 983 (5th Cir. 1970).
123. *D'Armijene, Inc.*, 148 NLRB 2 (1964), *modified*, 353 F.2d 406 (2d Cir. 1965).
124. *Local 174, Teamsters v. Lucas Flour Co.*, 369 U.S. 95 (1962).
125. *Boys Market Inc. v. Retail Clerks Loc. 770*, 398 U.S. 235 (1970).
126. 29 U.S.C. §143; *Gateway Coal Co. v. United Mine Workers*, 414 U.S. 368, 85 LRRM 2049 (1974).
127. *American Ship Building Co. v. NLRB*, 380 U.S. 300, 311–312 (1965).
128. *Elk Lumber Co.*, 26 LRRM 1493 (1950).
129. *NLRB v. West Coast Casket Co. Inc.*, 205 F.2d 902 (9th Cir. 1953).
130. *Teamster, Chauffeurs, etc. v. NLRB (Redwing Carriers, Inc.)*, 325 F.2d 1011 (D.C. Cir. 1963), *cert. denied*, 377 U.S. 905 (1964).
131. *Thornhill v. Alabama*, 310 U.S. 88 (1940).
132. *American Radio Ass'n v. Mobile S.S. Ass'n*, 419 U.S. 215 (1974).
133. 29 U.S.C. §§158(b)(7).
134. *Int'l Hod Carriers Bldg. Etc., Local 840*, 135 NLRB 1153, 1158 (1962).
135. 29 U.S.C. §158(b)(7)(C).
136. *Parks v. Atlantic Printing Pressmen & Assistants Union*, 243 F.2d 284 (5th Cir. 1957), *cert. denied*, 354 U.S. 937 (1957).
137. *National Woodwork Mfrs. Assn. v. NLRB*, 386 U.S. 612 (1967).
138. *NLRB v. Local 810 Steel Fabricators*, 460 F.2d 1, 5 (2d Cir. 1972), *cert. denied*, 409 U.S. 1041 (1972).
139. *Sailors Union of the Pacific, (Moore Dry Dock Co.)*, 92 NLRB 574 (1950).

140. *Id.* at 549.
141. 29 U.S.C. §158(b)(4)(ii).
142. *NLRB v. Fruit and Vegetable Products*, 377 U.S. 58 (1964).
143. 29 U.S.C. §158(b)(7)(C).
144. 29 U.S.C. §152(3).
145. *NLRB v. Bell Aerospace Co. Div. of Textron, Inc.*, 416 U.S. 267 (1974).
146. *NLRB v. Yeshiva University*, 444 U.S. 672 (1980).
147. *San Diego Bldg. Trades Council v. Garmon*, 359 U.S. 236, 43 LRRM 2838 (1959); *see Teamsters, Local 20 v. Morton*, 377 U.S. 252, 56 LRRM 2225 (1964).

XIV

Occupational Safety and Health

You are entitled to a safe and healthy workplace. Your rights regarding safety and health at work are described in this chapter. Knowing and using these rights could save you and your fellow employees from injury or death.

Job-related injuries and illnesses cause incalculable human suffering and impose a substantial burden on the nation's commerce in the form of lost production and wages, medical expenses, and workers' and disability compensation. To address this problem, Congress passed the Occupational Safety and Health Act of 1970[1] to assure so far as possible safe and healthful working conditions for every working man and woman in the nation and to preserve our human resources.[2]

To achieve this purpose, the Act was designed, among other things, to:[3]

encourage employers and employees to reduce hazards in the workplace and to implement new or improve existing safety and health programs;

establish "separate but dependent responsibilities and rights" for employers and employees to achieve better safety and health conditions;

develop and effectively enforce mandatory job safety and health standards;

encourage the states to assume the fullest responsibility for establishing and administering their own occupational safety and health programs, which must be "at least as effective" as the federal program. The Occupational Safety and Health Administration was created within the Department of Labor to administer the Act.

The Act imposes many responsibilities on employees and

175

the Occupational Safety and Health Administration (OSHA) and grants employees many rights and protections. It encourages employers and employees to work together to eliminate safety and health hazards.

OSHA is responsible for promulgating safety standards for workplaces. To enforce its standards and regulations, OSHA can conduct workplace inspections. If it finds a health or safety violation, it can require your employer to correct the hazard within a fixed time period, and possibly pay a fine.

You and your fellow employees are often in the best position to discover and identify hazardous practices and conditions and to evaluate and monitor the remedies. The Act therefore provides that you (or your representative) have the right to complain to your employer or OSHA about workplace hazards, to participate in discussions about hazards and remedies, to check whether your employer is correcting any hazard within the deadline set by OSHA, to appeal any such deadline that you think is too lenient, and to participate in any hearing or proceeding that concerns a workplace hazard. Furthermore, it is against the law for your employer to punish you in any way for exercising any of these rights.

What does the Act require my employer to do?

The "general duty" clause of the Act provides that every employer "shall furnish to each of his employees employment and a place of employment which are free from recognized hazards that are causing or are likely to cause death or serious physical harm to his employees."[4] Among the general duties of your employer are:

- examining workplace conditions to make sure that they conform to applicable safety and health standards;
- assuring that employees have and use safe tools and equipment (including personal protective equipment) and that such equipment is properly maintained;[5]
- removing potential hazards, or using color codes, labels, or signs to warn employees of them;[6]
- providing medical examinations when required by OSHA standards.[7]

In addition, every employer must be familiar with and comply with any specific OSHA standards, rules, and regulations that apply to the employer's business.[8] These OSHA standards may require specific working conditions, or the adoption or use of specific practices, means, methods, or processes reasonably necessary or appropriate to protect workers on the job. Even if no specific standards apply, the employer is bound by the general duty clause.

What information must an employer supply to employees?

An employer must inform its employees about OSHA and about any safety and health matters concerning the workplace. The employer must make copies of the Act and relevant OSHA rules and regulations available to employees on request. An employer also must post certain materials at a prominent location in the workplace. These include the following:

1. *The job safety and health protection* poster informing employees of their rights and responsibilities under the Act. If the state operates an OSHA-approved job safety and health program, the state's equivalent poster and/or the OSHA poster may be required.

The employer also must notify employees that they can get assistance and information about workplace safety, including copies of the Act and of specific safety and health standards, from the employer or the nearest office of the Department of Labor.[9]

2. *Summaries of petitions for variances from standards or recordkeeping procedures:* Under the Act, an employer may apply to OSHA for a variance from a standard or regulation if the employer lacks the means to readily comply, or if they can prove that their facilities or methods of operation provide employee protection that is at least as effective as that required by OSHA.[10] If an employer submits a variance application, it must certify that a copy of it has been given to the employee's authorized representative, and that a summary of the application has been posted where notices are normally posted. In addition, the employees must also be informed that they have the right to request a hearing on the employer's application. Similar procedures apply when an employer files for a record-keeping variance.

3. *A copy of any OSHA citation* for violation of a standard must be posted immediately at or near each place where the alleged violation occurred.[11] The citation must remain posted for three days or until the violation is abated, whichever is longer.[12]

Furthermore, if an employer contests a citation, the time set for abatement of the violation, or the proposed penalty by filing a "notice of contest,"[13] the employer must give a copy of that notice to the employees' authorized representative. If any or all of the affected employees are not represented by such a representative, a copy of the notice must be posted in a prominent location at the workplace, or else served personally upon each non-union employee.

Posted copies of the notice must inform employees that they have the right to participate in Review Commission procedures and that they must identify themselves to the Commission or hearing examiner before or at the beginning of the hearing. The employer and any employee have the right to participate in the hearing, and they do not have to be represented by attorneys.

4. *Summary of occupational injuries and illnesses:* This annual summary must be posted within one month of the close of the year, and remain posted for at least 30 days.[14]

Occasionally, OSHA standards, or the research activities of the National Institute for Occupational Safety and Health (NIOSH), require an employer to measure and record employee exposure to potentially harmful substances.[15] Employees have the right (in person or through an authorized representative) to be present during the measurements and to examine the records kept of the results. Each employee or former employee has the right to see his or her own examination records and must be told by the employer if the exposure to hazardous substances has exceeded the levels set by standards. The employee also must be told what corrective measures, if any, are being taken.[16]

Where are notices posted?

OSHA regulations require the employer to post notices in a conspicuous place or a place where notices to employees are customarily posted.[17] These regulations are strictly enforced. An employer's keeping of the poster or OSHA forms at the main office,[18] a home office,[19] a construction shack,[20] a trailer,[21] a desk drawer,[22] and at a general contractor's shack[23] have all been declared a violation when those areas were an unreasonable distance from the job site. An "unreasonable distance" can range from 50 feet[24] to 30 miles.[25] There is no violation if every person to whom the employer owes an obligation of posting is afforded a full opportunity to see the posted notice. Thus posting at the location from which all employees are dispatched each day,[26] inside a construction trailer entered by all employees,[27] at the base of operations of the employer,[28] or at the main office of the employer where all the employees report daily,[29] all comply with the Act.

The employer also has a duty to make sure that the posted notices are not altered, defaced, or covered by other material.[30] Posting on the back of a men's-room door, with the poster being partly blocked by clothing hung in front of it, was a violation.[31] It is, however, permissible to post notices inside the lids of employees' toolboxes, as long as they are clearly visible.[32]

Merely showing the OSHA poster to employees at the worksite does not fulfill the duty to display.[33] On the other hand, an employer who orally explained the contents of the notice of employee rights and responsibilities to non-English-speaking employees, while committing a technical violation by not posting the notice, did satisfy the purpose of posting by regularly holding oral discussions on safety.[34]

Regulations on the posting of citations are also strictly enforced. The requirement that the citation be posted immediately upon receipt was violated when the employer failed to post it until the third working day after receiving it.[35] The citation itself must be posted; posting a slip of paper at various locations in lieu of the citation violates the Act.[36] Finally, posting a copy of the complaint on the employer's bulletin board is not equivalent to posting a notice of contest under the Act and thus is a violation.[37]

What should I do if there are hazards or violations in my workplace?

If you detect or even suspect imminent danger, you should tell your employer or supervisor immediately. If your employer does not eliminate the danger promptly, you or your representative should contact the nearest OSHA office. If an OSHA inspector finds that an imminent danger exists, and your employer still fails to correct it, OSHA can seek an injunctive order from a federal court to require the employer to correct the violation.[38]

If the hazard or violation does not pose an imminent danger, you should discuss it with other workers, your union representative, or a plant safety committee, and ask your employer to correct the problem. If necessary, you can ask OSHA to make an inspection. Any request to OSHA for an inspection should identify the workplace location, detail the hazard or condition, and include your name, address, and telephone number. Although your employer has the right to see a copy of the complaint if an inspection results, your identity will be withheld if you so request.[39]

The OSHA area director will review the information presented and determine whether there is a reasonable basis for your complaint. OSHA has recently established guidelines for determining whether a workplace will be inspected.[40] Under those guidelines, an inspection will be conducted only when a complaint indicates that a violation threatening "physical harm or imminent danger" exists. If OSHA decides not to inspect your workplace, it must notify you of this decision, and if requested, review its decision.[41]

Can I walk off the job if I think I am in danger?

Generally, no. Under OSHA regulations and case law, you generally have no right to walk off the job because of potentially unsafe conditions in the workplace.[42] The reasons given are that (1) an employer ordinarily will correct a hazardous condition once it is brought to his attention, and (2) even if the employer fails to correct the condition or denies the hazard, you can request an OSHA inspection,[43] or call upon other public agencies that have safety and health responsibilities. Thus, your employer ordinarily would not violate the Act by disciplining you for refusing to perform normal job activities because of alleged safety or health hazards.[44]

You may, however, walk off the job in certain exceptional circumstances rather than subject yourself to a real danger of death or serious injury arising from a hazardous condition in the workplace. OSHA regulations[45] provide that an employee who refuses in good faith to expose himself to a dangerous condition will be protected against subsequent discrimination if all of the following are true:

1. The danger was so grave that a reasonable person in the same situation would conclude that there is a real danger of death or serious physical injury.

2. The employee had no reasonable alternative.

3. The danger was so imminent that there was insufficient time to eliminate the danger through normal enforcement procedures.

4. The employee, if it was possible, asked the employer to eliminate the danger and the employer failed to do so.

You and your fellow workers may have the right, under section 7 of the National Labor Relations Act (NLRA)[46] to engage in protest, including work stoppages, over what you believe to be unsafe or unhealthy working conditions. Under the NLRA, which is discussed more fully in Chapter 13, employees may engage in concerted activity for their mutual aid and protection; these rights supplement your rights under OSHA. Thus, employees who walk out to protest unsafe working conditions may not be discriminated against for that concerted activity; this protection has been broadly applied to a walkout by *several* employees, and the Supreme Court will decide during its 1983–84 Term whether it applies to a walkout by a single employee.[47]

What happens at an inspection?

To enforce its standards and regulations, OSHA is authorized under the Act to conduct workplace inspections.[48] Every establishment covered by the Act is subject to inspection by OSHA compliance officers. Among other things, these officers are authorized to question any employer or employee privately. You should cooperate with an officer who inquires about safety and health conditions in the workplace. Information you provide to OSHA can help make sure that all violations are uncovered, that any penalties are appropriate, and that the time for correcting any violations is no longer than necessary.

Although most inspections are conducted without advance notice, OSHA may in special circumstances give up to 24 hours' notice to the employer. In this case the employer must notify your authorized representative, or arrange for OSHA to do so.

Your representative is usually given the opportunity, along with an employer representative, to accompany the officer during the inspection. If you are represented by a union, the union will ordinarily designate who will accompany the compliance officer. In the absence of a union, the employee members of a plant safety committee will designate the employee representative. If no union or plant safety committee is present, the employee representative may be selected by the employees themselves, but not by the compliance officer or the employer. Although the Act does not require an employee representative on each inspection, the compliance officer must consult with a reasonable number of employees concerning safety and health matters in the workplace. An employer is not required to pay employees for the time spent on these "walkaround" inspections, though many employers and unions do compensate employees for that time.[49]

During an inspection, the compliance officer may inspect required records of deaths, injuries, and illness and may check to see if the annual summary of occupational injuries and illness has been posted. He may also check on whether the OSHA workplace poster is prominently displayed, and may examine any required records of employee exposure to toxic substances.

Employees are consulted during the inspection tour. The compliance officer may stop and question workers, in private if necessary, about safety and health conditions in their workplaces.[50] Employees have the right before or during an inspection to bring to the compliance officer's attention any condition they believe to be a violation of a standard.[51] Each employee is protected under the Act from any discrimination against him or her for exercising these rights.[52]

After the inspection tour, the OSHA compliance officer holds a "closing conference" with the employer. At that conference the compliance officer discusses what he has found and identifies the apparent violations for which a citation may be issued or recommended. The employer may describe what safety and health precautions have been taken in the past, and how much time will be needed to correct current alleged violations.

You (or your representative) have the right to a closing conference with the compliance officer, usually jointly with the employer. You can describe the violations that you think exist, what you think should be done to correct them, and how long you think it should take. You can also provide facts to help the compliance officer determine your employer's "good faith." For example, unless you bring it up, OSHA may not know that the employer has ignored earlier requests to correct a hazard, that a hazard has already caused an accident or illness, or that your employer has previously showed awareness of the hazard by fixing the same problem in another part of the workplace.

What happens after an inspection?

The OSHA area director reviews the results of the inspection and issues citations for any employer violations that were found. The citations describe the hazards, any penalties your employer must pay, and the timetable for correcting the hazards.[53]

There is no prescribed penalty for any particular violation. The amount of any penalty depends on the circumstances, such as how hazardous the condition is, the employer's "good faith" in trying to prevent or fix the hazard, the employer's history of previous violations, and the size of the business. In setting the timetable, OSHA takes into account practical problems, such as how soon parts can be obtained or installed, and whether workers may be exposed to danger if correction is delayed.

If an imminent danger is found at the workplace, the compliance officer will ask the employer to abate the hazard voluntarily and to remove endangered employees from the area. If the employer fails to do this or if the OSHA compliance officer believes that practices or conditions exist in the workplace that present a danger of death or serious physical harm immediately or before the danger can be eliminated through other enforcement procedures, the compliance officer will recommend that immediate injunctive relief be sought.[54] The compliance officer will notify the employees at the affected workplace that he believes such conditions exist and that he is requesting injunctive relief. If OSHA arbitrarily or capriciously declines to bring court action, the affected employees may petition the federal district court to compel it to do so.[55] Such action can produce a temporary restraining order (immediate shutdown) of the operation or section of the workplace in which the imminent danger exists.

What happens if a citation is issued?

You have a role to play in checking to be sure your employer corrects hazards on time. A citation must be prominently posted at or near each place that a violation occurred. It must remain posted for 3 workdays (not counting Saturdays, Sundays, or federal holidays) or until the hazard is corrected, whichever is later. A copy of all citations will be provided by OSHA to a workers' representative. Make sure the citation remains posted until the violation is corrected. The law requires it to be there as a constant reminder to workers whose health and safety may be affected by the hazard.

If the violation involves hazards that cannot be eliminated immediately, your employer must give OSHA a written plan for "abatement," including a schedule for correcting the hazards. As part of the plan your employer may be required to submit regular progress reports to OSHA. Ask your employer for copies. If your employer does not provide them, ask OSHA to do so. Study them carefully, and make sure they are accurate.

OSHA requires your employer to seek ways to "fix the workplace, not the worker." In other words, your employer must try to redesign the workplace or work procedures to eliminate the hazard at its source. As a last resort or while these controls are being implemented, your employer must provide personal protective equipment, such as respirators, to reduce exposure to danger. If personal protective equipment is required while these controls are implemented, make sure it is being used and maintained properly.

Make sure that the violation is corrected by the established deadline. OSHA cannot always make a follow-up inspection to see if the hazard has been removed. Your employer's failure to meet the deadline may result in increased penalties, possibly including a new citation for a willful or repeated violation.

Work with your employer to be sure that workplace changes really remove the hazard. If, for example, new equipment installed to control noise has not in fact significantly reduced noise levels, the violation may be continuing. Insist that the corrective measures be maintained. If a new machine guard is removed, or a special ventilation system is installed but not used, the violation may not have been corrected.

If your employer fails to meet his or her obligations and ignores your complaints, contact the nearest OSHA area office. OSHA will ask your employer to comply with the original citation and abatement plan and, if necessary, may make a follow-up inspection.

Can I challenge the amount of time OSHA allows my employer to correct a hazard?

Yes. To do so, notify the OSHA area director in writing within 15 working days after the citation is posted that you intend to contest the "abatement period."

Your letter does not have to explain why you are filing a contest. Simply state that you think the abatement period is unreasonable, and clearly identify the employer, citation, and workplace involved. Your contest will be decided by the Occupational Safety and Health Review Commission in much the same way as an employer's contest.

Within 10 calendar days after receiving your notice, OSHA's lawyer must file a statement with the Commission telling why the abatement period is reasonable. You then have 10 calendar days to tell why it is unreasonable.

An employer's contesting OSHA's abatement deadline delays that deadline, but contesting by employees does not. If you contest the abatement period, your employer may participate in the case by notifying the Commission.

What can I do if my employer tries to get a citation withdrawn or overruled?

You (or your representative) have a right to oppose such an effort.

Your employer can request an "informal conference" to discuss citations with the OSHA area director. As a result of that conference, OSHA may withdraw citations, change the proposed penalties, or give your employer more time to correct the hazards.

The OSHA area director must inform you (or your representative) of the informal conference, and encourage your participation. If subjects of a "delicate nature" are brought up by either the employer or employee representative, separate discussions may be held. In any case, OSHA may not withdraw or change a citation without first obtaining the opinion of the employee representative.

You (or your representative) can also request an informal conference with the area director if you want to bring information to OSHA's attention, or if you believe OSHA has made mistakes in its inspection or citation.

In addition to requesting an informal conference, your employer may, within 15 working days after receiving a copy of the citation, notify the OSHA area director in writing that the citations, proposed penalties, abatement deadlines, or any combination of these will be challenged. This "contest" by your employer is forwarded to the Occupational Safety and Health Review Commission, an independent agency which is not part of the U.S. Department of Labor. The Commission has the power to uphold, change, or overrule any action OSHA has taken. It is made up of three commissioners, and employs "administrative law judges" to hear cases. Your employer will not be legally required to comply with any contested part of a citation until the Commission issues a final ruling on your employer's contest.

It is OSHA's responsibility to oppose your employer's contest, but you (or your representative) have a right to participate as well. By participating, you may be able to:

• make sure OSHA and the Commission have all the facts about hazards at your workplace and your employer's health and safety record;
• guarantee that workers are able to present their views through their own representative;
• influence settlements reached between OSHA and your employer;
• tell the Commission if you think OSHA should be asking for stronger fines or shorter abatement periods, or should have considered a violation as "serious" rather than "other," or "willful" instead of "serious."

Your employer must post notices and inform your union representative, if there is one, that a contest has been filed and that the affected workers and their representatives have a right to participate in the case.

How do I participate if my employer contests a citation?

At any time before a hearing is held by a Review Commission judge, you (or your representative) can send a letter to the Commission saying that you intend to participate in the proceedings. (Only in special cases will the Commission grant a request to participate that is filed after the hearing begins.) If you belong to a union, you must be represented by your union. Your letter does not have to include the arguments you will make during the case. It should simply say you intend to participate and should identify the employer, workplace, and citation involved. Include the "docket number" for the case, if you know it. Ask the Commission to send you copies of its rules, and read them carefully.

In the legal terms used by the Commission, you will become a "party" to the case. You will have "elected" to have "party status." As a party to the case, you have the right to:

- receive copies of all papers filed with the Commission by any of the other parties, such as your employer and OSHA;
- participate in settlement negotiations;
- cross-examine witnesses presented by your employer, OSHA, or other parties to the case;
- present witnesses and evidence at the hearing before the Commission judge;
- object to evidence other parties wish to introduce;
- give the Commission judge your views;
- ask the full Commission to review the Commission judge's decision;
- appeal the Commission's final decision to a federal Court of Appeals.

Papers related to a case should be sent to:
    Executive Secretary
    Occupational Safety and Health Review Commission
    1825 K St., NW
    Washington, DC 20006

After an administrative law judge has been assigned to the case, all papers should be sent to him or her.

Within 20 days after the employer contests OSHA's actions, OSHA must file a written "complaint" with the Commission, explaining the citation, the proposed penalty, and the abatement period. Your employer must file a written answer within 15 days after receiving a copy of that complaint. The employer is considered to have admitted any charges not specifically denied in the answer. If you are a party to the case, you will receive copies of both the complaint and the answer. You do not have to comment on them unless you choose to.

After these steps have been taken, the parties in the case may exchange information in various ways. If the case is not settled, a hearing will be held before the administrative judge, who will issue a decision.

Can I be fired for complaining about unsafe working conditions?

No. Under section 11(c)[56] of the Act you cannot be punished or discriminated against for exercising such rights as:

- complaining to your employer, your union, OSHA, or any other government agency about job safety or health hazards;

- filing safety or health grievances;
- participating in workplace committees or union activities concerning job safety or health;
- participating in OSHA inspections, including talking with a compliance officer;
- instituting or causing to be instituted any proceeding regarding job safety or health;
- testifying or otherwise participating in any proceeding regarding job safety or health.

Your employer cannot discriminate against you in any way for exercising these or other safety and health rights. Such unlawful discrimination includes firing, demotion, taking away seniority or benefits you have earned, transferring you to an undesirable job or shift, or threatening or harassing you. In addition, it may be unlawful to start treating you differently from the way you were treated before or differently from other employees because you exercised your rights. (Examples include suddenly punishing you for leaving work early, when you had done so before without being punished; or singling you out for punishment though others are doing the same thing.)

What should I do if I have been discriminated against for exercising my rights?

If you believe you have been punished for exercising your safety and health rights, you should contact the nearest OSHA office immediately. Generally, your complaint must be filed within 30 days of the time you find out you have been punished improperly.[57] Your union representative can file your complaint for you. You do not have to fill out any forms—just supply the OSHA staff with the facts.

If OSHA determines that you have been discriminated against for exercising a right under the Act, it will ask your employer to restore your job, earnings, and benefits. If necessary, OSHA can bring an action in a federal court against your employer. The relief sought may include, when appropriate, rehiring or reinstating you to your former position, with back pay. In any case, OSHA will notify you of its decision within 90 days after you file the complaint.[58]

It should be stressed that your exercise of rights under the Act does not make you immune from discharge or discipline for legitimate reasons, or from adverse action based on non-prohibited considerations.[59] In one district court case,[60] the court found that the employer was justified in firing the employee, irrespective of a safety complaint filed by the employee with OSHA, because the employee was not fired for filing the safety complaint. In its decision, the court stated that—

it is not for this court to second guess or look over the shoulder of an employer insofar as the discharge of an employee is concerned. Management can discharge an employee for good cause, bad cause, or no cause. It has, in the operation of business affairs, complete freedom in the discharge of an employee with one specific qualification insofar as this case is concerned—it may not discharge an employee [for exercising a right protected by the Act].[61]

To establish a violation of OSHA's anti-discrimination section, your engagement in protected activity must be a "substantial reason" for your discharge or other adverse action. Under the regulations, "if protected activity was a substantial reason for the action, or if the discharge would not have taken place 'but for' engagement in protected activity, [the anti-discrimination section] has been violated."[62]

The above standard was applied in a case in which two employees claimed that a substantial reason for their discharge was the safety complaints they had filed with OSHA.[63] The employer, on the other hand, said he fired the employees because of an accident in which they were involved and because of their poor-quality work. The court carefully examined the facts and found that the employees could not have been fired because of the accident, because they were not involved in it. The court further found that dissatisfaction with the employees' work was not sufficiently established, noting that management had never reprimanded them for unsatisfactory work; on the contrary, the employees had been given increased responsibilities.

The court next turned to the question of how much back pay the employees should get. The employer argued that, even if the two employees had not been discharged, it was doubtful that they would have remained with him for long; therefore, he should not have to pay them for the entire time of their discharge. The court disagreed and held that such uncertainty does not preclude an order to reimburse workers for lost wages, lost benefits, and travel expenses in search of new employment. It has also been held that an employee who is unlawfully discharged is entitled to back pay from the date of his discharge to the date of the judgment.[64]

Retaliation by an employer can take forms other than dismissal. In one case, the court held that the employer violated the Act by refusing to permit the union's representative to enter the employer's premises for monthly safety meetings, contrary to past practices and in retaliation for the union's filing of safety complaints with OSHA.[65]

Can I complain to OSHA without my employer finding out?

Yes. If you request confidentiality, the Act prohibits OSHA from disclosing your name to your employer. The names of persons who give statements to OSHA investigators have also been determined to be exempt from disclosure under the Freedom of Information Act.[66] Also, OSHA's refusal to disclose the name of an employee with whom a compliance officer spoke during an inspection of the employer's plant has been held proper in light of the public's interest in the efficient enforcement of the Act and the informer's right to be protected against possible retaliation, notwithstanding the employer's need to prepare for trial.[67] In that case, the employer had been given a copy of the complaint with the employee's name deleted. The court held that the complaint alone gave the employer sufficient information to allow the employer to prepare for trial.

What happens if I have been exposed to toxic substances on my job?

Regulations promulgated under section 6(b) of the Act establish maximum levels of various toxic substances to which you can be exposed.[68] In promulgating those regulations, OSHA is not required to balance costs and benefits; it can force employers to value the health of employees over the costs of making the workplace safe with respect to toxic substances.[69] These regulations also require that you be removed from exposure to certain toxic substances when a medical examination reveals that your health has been impaired by the exposure.

Depending upon the type of substance involved, the regulations may or may not require that you be transferred rather than dismissed from your job. For example, the regulations require that an employee who works with vinyl chloride be removed from his job if his health has been adversely affected; there is no requirement, however, that the employer retain the employee.[70] On the other hand, an employee whose blood level of lead is found to be above a specified level must be removed from exposure; and he must be retained at the same earning rate, seniority, and benefit level for up to 18 months, and upon return must be restored to his original job status.[71]

If a medical examination reveals that your health has been adversely affected because of exposure to toxic substances at work, you should check with the nearest office of OSHA for applicable regulations. Additionally, the regulations give you a right to see records of exposure and medical records in the possession of your employer.[72]

Some states go further than the OSHA regulations by requiring employers to inform employees regarding all toxic substances found in the workplace (without regard to the level of exposure) and the toxic effects of such substances.[73] An employer that violates that obligation can be subjected to civil and criminal penalties.

Can I sue my employer for violating the Act?

No, not directly. The Act does not create any private right of action for an employee to recover damages for personal injuries alleged to have resulted from a violation of the Act.[74] Your rights under the Act can be enforced only through OSHA. On the other hand, the Act does not diminish any other rights you have. The Act itself states that nothing in it "shall be construed to supersede or in any manner affect any workmen's compensation law or to enlarge or diminish or affect in any other manner the common law or statutory rights, duties, or liabilities of employers and employees under any law with respect to injuries, diseases, or death of employees arising out of, or in the course of, employment."[75]

Even though you do not have a cause of action for an OSHA violation, you may be able, in certain circumstances, to use the violation of an OSHA health or safety standard to prove an employer's negligence in an action for personal injuries.[76]

Are all employees covered by the Act?

In general, the Act covers all employers and their employees in the 50 states, the District of Columbia, Puerto Rico, the Canal Zone, and all other territories under federal government jurisdiction.[77]

As defined by the Act, an employer is any "person engaged in a business affecting [interstate] commerce who has employees, but does not include the United States or any State or political subdivision of a State."[78] Therefore, the Act covers employers and employees in such varied fields as agriculture, law and medicine, charity and disaster relief, construction,[79] longshoring,[80] organized labor, private education, and religious groups[81] to the extent that they employ workers for secular purposes. Coverage under the Act does not depend on the number of employees on the payroll.

In addition, officers and part owners of businesses and corporations are covered by the Act if they perform work along with the regular employees[82] (e.g., a vice-president of a construction company who also works with a shovel in excavation).[83] An employer's family members who are engaged in construction activities on the employer's behalf are also covered,[84] as are merchant seamen engaged in offshore construction and ship repair.[85] But employees working on an offshore mobile drilling unit on the high seas are not covered.[86]

The following are *not* covered under the Act:

- work by self-employed persons;
- family-owned and -operated farms;[87]
- workplaces already protected by other federal agencies under other federal statutes, though OSHA regulations will apply to those areas in which the agency has not promulgated any regulations;[88]
- state and local governments in their roles as employers. (The Act provides, however, that any state seeking OSHA approval for its occupational safety and health program must cover its own state and local government workers at least as effectively as private employees are covered.)[89]

What is the effect of the Act on other federal job safety laws?

Already existing safety and health standards promulgated under certain federal statutes were incorporated into the Act.[90] The affected statutes were:

- the Walsh-Healey Act;[91]
- the McNamara-O'Hara Service Contract Act;[92]
- the Construction Safety Act of 1969;[93]
- the Longshoremen's and Harbor Workers' Compensation Act;[94]
- the National Foundation on Arts and Humanities Act of 1965.[95]

The Occupational Safety and Health Act provides that safety and health standards promulgated under these earlier laws are superseded on the effective date of corresponding OSHA standards that have been determined by the Secretary of Labor to be more effective.[96] Standards issued under these earlier laws and in effect on or after the effective date of the Act are to be considered as OSHA standards, as well as standards issued under the earlier statutes.[97]

The Federal Coal Mine Health and Safety Act[98] and the Federal Metal and Nonmetallic Mine Safety Act[99] were not superseded by the Act, although the Secretary of Labor is mandated by the Act to recommend legislation to avoid unnecessary duplication and to achieve coordination between OSHA and other federal laws.[100] Those acts are almost exactly like OSHA in scope and effect. The Federal Coal Mine Health and Safety Act applies only to coal and ingot mines, whereas the Federal Metal and Nonmetallic Mine Safety Act applies to all mines.

What is the relationship of the Act to state job safety and health laws?

State laws on occupational safety or health govern in all cases in which OSHA has not promulgated standards.[101] If the Act does not cover the area, then the state law applies.

The Act requires OSHA to encourage the states to develop and operate their own job safety and health programs.[102] These programs must be at least as effective as the federal programs.[103] As a result, the Act and the standards promulgated under it are, in effect, minimum standards with which the states must comply.

You should find out if your state has submitted a plan for OSHA approval and, if so, become familiar with it. State safety and health standards under approved plans must guarantee employee rights as much as OSHA does.[104]

Summary of Employee's Rights

As an employee, you have the right to:

- review copies of any OSHA standards, rules, regulations, and requirements that the employer should have available at the workplace;
- request information from your employer on safety and health hazards in the area, precautions that may be taken, and procedures to be followed if an employee is involved in an accident or exposed to toxic substances;
- request (in writing) the OSHA area director to conduct an inspection if you believe hazardous conditions or violation of standards exist in your workplace;
- have your name withheld from your employer, upon request to OSHA, if you file a written, signed complaint;
- be advised of OSHA actions regarding your complaint and have an informal review, if requested, of any decision not to make an inspection or not to issue a citation;
- file a complaint to OSHA within 30 days if you believe you have been discriminated against, discharged, demoted, or otherwise penalized because of asserting an employee right under the Act, and be notified by OSHA of its determination within 90 days of filing;
- have the authorized employee representative where you work accompany the OSHA compliance officer during the inspection tour;
- respond to questions from the OSHA compliance officer, especially if there is no authorized employee representative accompanying the compliance officer;
- observe any monitoring or measuring of hazardous materials and have the right of access to records on those materials, as specified under the Act;
- request a closing discussion with the compliance officer following an inspection;
- submit a written request to the National Institute for Occupational Safety and Health (NIOSH) for information on whether any substance in your workplace has potential toxic effects in the concentration being used, and have your name withheld from your employer if you so request;
- object to the abatement period set in the citation issued to your employer by writing to the OSHA area director within 15 working days of the issuance of the citation;

- be notified by your employer if he or she applies for a variance from an OSHA standard, testify at a variance hearing, and appeal the final decision if you disagree with it;
- submit information or comment to OSHA on the issuance, modification, or revocation of OSHA standards, and request a public hearing.

NOTES

1. 29 U.S.C. §§651–78 (1976). All section (§) references in this chapter are to this Act, unless otherwise indicated.
2. §651(b).
3. §§651(b) and 667(c)(2).
4. §654(a)(1).
5. 29 C.F.R. §1926.300.
6. *Id.* §1926.200.
7. *Id.* §1926.23.
8. §654(a)(2).
9. 29 C.F.R. §1903.2(a)(1), (a)(2).
10. §655(d).
11. §658(b); 29 C.F.R. §1903.16(a).
12. 29 C.F.R. §1903.16(b).
13. §659(b).
14. §657(c)(1).
15. §655(b)(7), (c)(3); as of May 1980, NIOSH became part of the Dept. of Health and Human Services.
16. *Id.*
17. 29 C.F.R. §1903.2(a)(1).
18. *Warner Bros., Inc.* Rev. Comm. J. no. 76–4233, 5 BNA OSHC 1575 (1977); *Kesler and Sons Construction Co.*, Rev. Comm. J. no. 306, 3 BNA OSHC 1589 (1975).
19. *San Juan Construction Co., Inc.*, Rev. Comm. J. no. 9662, 3 BNA OSHC 144 (1975).
20. *Gem Paving Co., Inc.*, Rev. Comm. J. no. 9577, 3 BNA OSHC 1773 (1975).
21. *Par Construction Co., Inc.*, Rev. Comm. J. no. 11092, 4 BNA OSHC 17779 (1976).
22. *Cash-Way Building Supply*, Rev. Comm. J. no. 5487, 2 BNA OSHC 3314 (1975).
23. *San Jose Crane and Rigging, Inc.*, Rev. Comm. J. no. 1740, 1 BNA OSHC 3069 (1973).
24. *Gem Paving Co.*, *supra* n.43.
25. *Kesler and Sons*, *supra* n.40.
26. *Allen Co.*, 14 OSAHRC 481, 2 BNA OSHC 1460 (1974).
27. *Eduplay, Inc.*, Rev. Comm. J. no. 4808, 1 BNA OSHC 3293 (1974).

28. *Armor Elevator Co., Inc.*, Rev. Comm. J. no. 20007, 1 BNA OSHC 3170 (1973).

29. *B&W Pool Construction Co.*, 9 OSAHRC 130, 2 BNA OSHC 3037 (1974); *Enterprise Roofing & Sheet Metal Co.*, Rev. Comm. J. no. 12395, 3 BNA OSHC (1975).

30. 29 C.F.R. §1903.2(a)(1).

31. *Crushed Toast Co.*, Rev. Comm. J. no. 16042, 5 BNA OSHC 1360 (1977).

32. *Western Steel Erectors, Inc.*, Rev. Comm. J. no. 10556, 3 BNA OSHC 1466 (1975).

33. *Kinney Steel*, Rev. Comm. J. no. 11050, 3 BNA OSHC 1453 (1975).

34. *Belau Transfer and Terminal Co.*, Rev. Comm. J. no. 76–4631, 6 BNA OSHC 1592 (1978).

35. *C&H Erection Co.*, Rev. Comm. J. no. 3226, 3 BNA OSHC 1293 (1975).

36. *Monkiewicz, Inc.*, Rev. Comm. J. no. 3001, 1 BNA OSHC 3259 (1973).

37. *Hamilton Metal Products, Inc.*, Rev. Comm. J. no. 458, 1 BNA OSHC 1025 (1972).

38. §657(f)(1) (1976); 29 C.F.R. §1903.11(a) (1981).

39. *Id*.

40. *See* OSHA Instruction CPL 2.12 B, Feb. 1, 1982.

41. 29 U.S.C. §657(f)(1) (1976).

42. *Id*. §1977.12(b)(1).

43. §657(f).

44. 29 C.F.R. §1977.12(b) (1981).

45. *Id*. §1977.12(b)(2). These regulations were upheld by the Supreme Court in *Whirlpool Corp. v. Marshall*, 445 U.S. 1 (1980).

46. §§151 *et seq*.

47. *NLRB v. Tamara Foods, Inc.*, 692 F.2d 1171 (8th Cir. 1982), *cert. denied*, —— U.S. —— (5/16/83); *City Disposal Systems, Inc. v. NLRB*, 683 F.2d 1005 (6th Cir. 1982), *cert. granted*, —— U.S. —— (3/28/83). *See also NLRB v. Interboro Contractors, Inc.*, 388 F.2d 495 (2d Cir. 1967).

48. §§657 *et seq.*; 29 C.F.R. §§1903.8 *et seq*.

49. In *Chamber of Commerce v. OSHA*, 636 F.2d 464 (D.C. Cir. 1980), the OSHA regulation (29 C.F.R. §1977.21) that required walkaround pay was invalidated.

50. 29 C.F.R. §1903.10.

51. §657(f)(2) (1976); 29 C.F.R. §1903.11.

52. §660 (c)(1).

53. §658(a).

54. §659(a), (b), (c); 29 C.F.R. §1903.13.

55. §662(c), (d).

56. §660(c).

57. §660(c)(2).

58. §660(c)(2), (3).

59. 29 C.F.R. §1977.6(a).

60. *Dunlop v. Bechtel Power Corp.* (D.C. La.), 6 BNA OSHC 1605 (1977); *see also Marshall v. Granite Groves*, (D.D.C.), 5 BNA OSHC 1935 (1977).

61. *Id.*

62. *Marshall v. P&Z Co., Inc.*, 6 BNA OSHC 1587 (D.D.C. 1978); 29 C.F.R. §1977.6(b).

63. *Marshall v. P&Z Co., Inc.*, *supra.*

64. *Dunlop v. Trumbull Asphalt Co., Inc.* (E.D. Mo.), 4 BNA OSHC 1847 (1976).

65. *Marshall v. Kennedy Tubular Products*, (D.D.C.), 6 BNA OSHC 1320 (1978).

66. *T.V. Tower, Inc. v. Marshall*, 444 F. Supp. 1233 (D.D.C. 1978).

67. *Stephenson Enterprises, Inc. v. Marshall & OSHRC*, 578 F.2d 1021 (5th Cir. 1978).

68. 29 C.F.R. §§1910 *et seq.* (1981).

69. *American Textile Mfrs. Institute, Inc. v. Donovan*, 452 U.S. 490 (1981).

70. *Id.* §1910.1017(k)(5).

71. *Id.* §1910.1025(k).

72. *Id.* §1910.20.

73. *See, e.g.,* N.Y. Lab. Law §§875 *et seq.*

74. *Jeter v. St. Regis Paper Co.*, 507 F.2d 973 (5th Cir. 1975); *Byrd v. Fieldcrest Mills, Inc.*, 496 F.2d 1323 (4th Cir. 1974); *Russell v. Bartley*, 494 F.2d 334 (6th Cir. 1974).

75. §653(b)(4).

76. *See Melerine v. Avondale Shipyards, Inc.*, 659 F.2d 706 (5th Cir. 1981).

77. §653(a).

78. §652(5).

79. 29 C.F.R. §1975.4(b).

80. *Id.* §1918.

81. *Id.* §1975.4(c)(1).

82. *Colwell Excavating Co.*, Rev. Comm. J. no. 13920, 5 BNA OSHC 1984 (1977); *Miller Construction Co.*, 14 OSAHRC 145, 2 BNA OSHC 3282 (1974); *Baker Roofing and Sheet Metal Co.*, Rev. Comm. J. no. 12721, 4 BNA OSHC 1418 (1976); *Mangus Firearms*, Rev. Comm. J. no. 9342, 3 BNA OSHC 1214 (1975); *Kement and Son Construction, Inc.*, 8 OSAHRC 276, 2 BNA OSHC 3002 (1974); *Ellenville Handleworks, Inc.*, Rev. Comm. J. no. 1960, 1 BNA OSHC 3121 (1973); *Kensington Electric Products Co., Inc.*, Rev. Comm. J. no. 1424, 1 BNA OSHC 3095 (1973).

83. *D&H Pump Service, Inc.*, Rev. Comm. J. no. 16246, 5 BNA OSHC 1485 (1977).

84. *Clauson Plastering Co.*, Rev. Comm. J. no. 76–2669, 5 BNA OSHC 1760 (1977).

85. *Petrolane Offshore Construction Services, Inc.*, Rev. Comm. J. no. 391, 3 BNA OSHC 1156 (1977).

86. *Clary v. Ocean Drilling and Exploration Co.*, 609 F.2d 1120 (5th Cir. 1980).
87. 29 C.F.R. §1975.4(b)(2).
88. §653(b)(1).
89. §667(c)(6).
90. §653(b)(2).
91. 41 U.S.C. §§35 *et seq.*
92. 41 U.S.C. §§351 *et seq.*
93. 40 U.S.C. §333 (1976).
94. 33 U.S.C. §941 (1976).
95. 20 U.S.C. §§951 *et seq.*
96. §653(b)(2).
97. *Id.*
98. 30 U.S.C. §§801 *et seq.*
99. *Id.* §§721 *et seq.*
100. §653(b)(2).
101. §667(a).
102. §651(11).
103. §667(c)(2).
104. §667(c)(6).

XV

Wages and Hours

Chapter 13, "Labor-Management Relations," discussed laws governing the bargaining process between employers and employees over the terms and conditions of employment. This chapter, on wage-and-hour laws, covers laws that place certain limitations on the terms and conditions of employment that employers and employees may legally adopt. These laws set minimum standards for wages, overtime, child labor, and equal pay for equal work.

The most important wage-and-hour law is the federal Fair Labor Standards Act (FLSA).[1] This comprehensive statute applies to all enterprises and industries involving interstate or foreign commerce. It requires that employees covered by the law be paid a minimum hourly wage, and time and a half for overtime hours. It sets rules on child labor and requires equal pay for equal work. The FLSA and related state laws are discussed in section A of this chapter.

Section B covers other federal wage-and-hour laws that set special standards for persons employed under public works contracts and under government supply and service contracts. These are the Davis-Bacon Act,[2] which determines wage rates for federally financed or assisted construction; the Walsh-Healey (Public Contracts) Act[3] and the McNamara-O'Hara Service Contract Act,[4] which determine wage rates for contracts to provide supplies and services to the federal government; and the Contract Work Hours and Safety Standards Act,[5] which sets overtime standards for federal contracts. Section B also discusses the Migrant and Seasonal Agricultural Protection Act,[6] which protects migrant farm workers.

Section C covers federal and state laws that affect your take-home pay, such as laws on garnishment, bankruptcy, and tax deductions.

Some laws affecting wages are discussed elsewhere in this book. For example, prohibitions against wage discrimination on the basis of race, sex, religion, age, and other factors are covered in Chapters 5–12, and laws pertaining to collective bargaining on wages are discussed in Chapter 13.

Note: The laws discussed in this chapter are very detailed. For brevity and clarity, this chapter provides only an overview of the laws—many limited rules, special provisions, and exceptions are necessarily omitted. You should consult the appropriate agency for more specific information.

A. The Fair Labor Standards Act

The Fair Labor Standards Act (FLSA)—popularly known as the Federal Wage and Hour Law—is the overall federal wage-hour law regulating private employment.* It was enacted in 1938, and amended several times since, to create labor conditions assuring a minimum standard of living necessary for the health, efficiency, and general well-being of employees, and to eradicate the burdens on commerce caused by substandard labor conditions.[7]

The FLSA is administered and enforced by the Wage and Hour Division of the U.S. Department of Labor.[8] The Division has ten regional offices and hundreds of district offices throughout the country to monitor compliance with FLSA requirements. (See Appendix 4 for a list of the ten regional offices.) More detailed information about the FLSA and other federal laws administered by the Wage and Hour Division is available from your local wage-and-hour office. Also, employers having employees subject to the FLSA must display a poster informing the employees of their FLSA rights and where they can get more information.

What does the FLSA provide?
Under the basic wage standards of the FLSA, a covered, non-exempt employee is entitled to (1) a prescribed minimum wage[9] and (2) overtime pay at not less than one and a

---

*A 1974 amendment to FLSA extended the minimum wage and overtime pay coverage of the FLSA to federal, state, and local public employees. Public employment is outside the scope of this book, but is the subject of another book in this series: *The Rights of Government Employees*.

half times the employees' regular rate after 40 hours of work in the week.[10] The FLSA also sets rules for child labor, including age limitations and the kind of work children are allowed to do.[11] In addition, the Equal Pay Act,[12] which is part of the FLSA, requires equal pay for equal work without regard to the employee's sex. All of these provisions are discussed in detail later.

The FLSA does *not* require the following: vacation, holiday, or sick pay; rest periods, holidays off, sick days, or vacations; premium pay for weekend or holiday work; severance pay; fringe benefits; or a limit on hours of work for employees 16 years of age or older. These are matters for agreement between the employer and the employees, or their authorized representatives.

Does the FLSA apply to all private employees?

No. First, the FLSA covers only employees whose work somehow affects interstate or foreign commerce.[13] Second, some employees "covered" by the FLSA are "exempt" from the minimum wage, overtime pay, equal pay, or child labor provisions; these exemptions are discussed later in connection with the appropriate provisions.

In short, the FLSA covers (1) employees who are personally engaged in activity affecting interstate or foreign commerce, and (2) all employees of certain "covered" enterprises engaged in activity affecting interstate or foreign commerce. In the first category, you are covered if you are personally engaged in interstate or foreign commerce (for example, communication and transportation workers), or in the production of goods for transportation in such commerce (for example, employees who handle, ship, or receive goods moving in interstate commerce). In the second category, even if your particular job has no relation to interstate or foreign commerce, you are covered if you work for a "covered" enterprise[14] (for example, your employer manufactures goods to be shipped out of your state, or sells goods shipped into your state).

For an enterprise to be "covered" it must have more than one employee either (1) engaged in interstate or foreign commerce, (2) producing goods for transportation in such commerce, or (3) handling, selling, or otherwise working on goods or materials that already have been moved in or produced for such commerce.[15] This is the only prerequisite for the following types of enterprises: laundry and dry-cleaning business; construction or reconstruction business; and hospitals, nursing homes, and schools. All other enterprises must, in addition, meet a dollar standard to be covered. A retail and service establishment is covered if its annual gross volume of business is not less than $362,500.[16] Any other type of business, including an agricultural business, is covered if its annual gross volume of business is not less than $250,000.[17] Retail excise taxes are excluded from these dollar volume standards. Any establishment having as its only regular employees the owner or members of the owner's immediate family is not covered.[18]

Even if an employee is not covered by the FLSA, or is exempted under some FLSA provision (as discussed later), he may be entitled to similar rights under a state wage-and-hour law. The FLSA and other federal wage-and-hour laws have not completely pre-empted state regulation in the area of fair labor standards. For example, employers engaged in purely intrastate commerce are beyond the jurisdiction of federal fair labor laws, but remain subject to state laws and regulations. In addition, states may enact labor standards laws that apply to employers that are covered by the federal laws, as long as the state standards are consistent with federal standards. If a particular industry is subject to both federal and state law, employers in that industry must abide by both sets of standards. Basically, this means that the employer subject to both federal and state regulations must comply with whichever requirements are more stringent. Thus if a state's minimum wage is higher than the federal standard, the employer must pay the higher state rate.

When and how must my employer pay me?

A covered employee must, of course, be paid for all hours worked in a workweek.[19] But the payroll period need not coincide with the workweek. The FLSA places no restrictions on the length of the payroll period, which can be weekly, bi-weekly, semi-monthly, or monthly. Some states, however, have laws limiting the length of the payroll period; these laws typically require payment at least every two weeks or semi-monthly. In computing the pay due during a particular payroll period, the beginning day of the workweek may not be changed for purposes of evading the FLSA's overtime requirements.

The FLSA does not specify acceptable forms of wage payment. Every state does specify acceptable forms—most require payment in cash or by negotiable check.

For which hours must I be paid?

Under the FLSA, you are entitled to be paid for all "hours worked."[20] This includes the time you must be on duty, on the employer's premises, or at any prescribed place of work. It also includes any additional time you are "suffered or permitted" to work, whether or not requested to do so. As discussed more fully below, hours worked can include time spent in idleness and in incidental activities, as well as in productive work.[21]

Am I entitled to be paid for holidays, sick days, or vacations?

No, unless your employer has agreed to pay for such absences. Many states have laws requiring that you be given time off on certain designated holidays (such as the Fourth of July), but those laws do not require that you be paid for those days. The FLSA does *not* require your employer to pay you for absence due to holidays, vacations, illness, or similar causes.[22] And the FLSA does not require an employer to include such absences as part of straight-time hours in determining whether overtime pay is due.[23]

Of course, many employers do pay for such absences. They sometimes are required to do so by employment contracts or collective bargaining agreements. They sometimes do so voluntarily as a matter of policy. If your employer has such a policy, this pay may be considered part of your contract of employment, and your employer may be liable to you for breach of contract if it fails to abide by the policy.[24] If your employer does pay for such absences, these absences may be considered part of straight time, and this pay may be ignored when computing your regular pay rate for overtime pay purposes (discussed later).[25]

Am I entitled to be paid for absences due to voting or jury duty?

Although no federal law requires that you be given time off to vote with pay, twenty-nine states have enacted statutes with this requirement.[26] Typically, the state law will specify the maximum amount of time off that must be granted and will provide that such time off is to be granted without loss of pay.[27] Many of those laws contain penalties that can be assessed against an employer who refuses to grant voting-time privileges or who penalizes employees for exercising such privileges.

Twenty-six states have laws that require your employer to give you time off for jury duty. Those statutes prohibit your employer discriminating against you because you have taken time off to serve on a jury. Nevertheless, only the laws of Alabama, Hawaii, Massachusetts, Nebraska, and Tennessee require that your employer continue to pay you while you are on jury duty.[28]

Am I entitled to be paid for incidental activities, such as maintaining equipment or changing my clothes?

Maybe. Difficult questions arise on the compensability of time spent by an employee on activities incidental to his principal duties. Such incidental activities may include setting machinery for work, supplying the workbench, changing clothes and washing, waiting for work, rest periods, meal periods, civic and charitable activities, and traveling to and from work. Compensability depends on the particular facts of each case.[29]

Time spent on incidental activities that are an integral part of the principal duties is compensable.[30] For such integral activities, it does not matter when they are performed (before, during, or after the workday) or whether any contrary contract, custom, or practice exists. Thus, setting machinery for work and supplying the workbench are compensable activities. On the other hand, time spent changing clothes and washing, even though an integral part of the duties, can be made non-compensable by a union contract, or by custom or practice under such a contract.[31]

Time spent on incidental activities that are not an integral part of the principal duties is compensable when performed during the workday if the time spent is for the employer's benefit; controlled by the employer so the employee cannot use it for his own purposes; "suffered or permitted" by the employer; or at the employer's request.[32] Thus compensation is due for short rest periods and coffee breaks, for being on call on or near the employer's premises, or for doing charitable work at the employer's request. You are not entitled to pay for meal periods during which you are completely relieved of work, though you are entitled to pay for such periods if you do any work then or if you are "on call."

Time spent on incidental activities that are not an integral part of the principal duties is not compensable when performed before or after the principal duties are done. The only exception is when such activities are made compensable by a contract between the employer and the employee or his union, or by the employer's custom or practice.[33] Thus, traveling to and from work and waiting in a time-clock or paycheck line are not compensable in the absence of a contrary contract, custom, or practice.

How is my wage determined?

Since January 1, 1981, the minimum wage under the FLSA has been $3.35 per hour. Of course, Congress may change the minimum rate at any time. In addition, a state law setting a higher minimum wage prevails over the federal rate. Except as discussed later, this rate applies to all covered employees (including agricultural workers), without regard to whether coverage is on an individual or enterprise basis.

Usually any compensation to be received beyond the minimum wage arises either from a private agreement between the employee and employer or from a collective bargaining agreement between the employer and the union representing the employee. In the absence of such an express agreement, the law will assume that the employer promised to pay for work performed and will require the employer to pay for the reasonable value of services rendered. The reasonable value of services rendered is based on such factors as the nature of the work, the customary rate of pay, and the amount of time.

Can my employer reduce my wages for tips I receive?

Sometimes. Your employer may consider tips as part of your wages if you customarily and regularly receive more than $30 a month in tips.[34] But such a tip credit cannot exceed 40 percent of the minimum wage. If your employer elects to use the tip credit, he must tell you in advance[35] and must be able to show that you receive at least the minimum wage when direct wages and the tip credit are combined. Also, you are entitled to keep all of your tips, except to the extent that you participate in a tip-pooling arrangement with other employees who customarily and regularly receive tips.[36]

Can my employer consider the value of room, board, meals, etc., as part of my wages?

Usually. Your employer can meet the minimum wage standard by adding together the money paid as wages and the value of certain goods or services given to you.[37] The proper amount is determined by the Wage and Hours Administration.

Generally, your employer may not deduct the value of anything provided to you that is necessary to or an incident of the work itself. For example, if your employer sends you on a business trip, the cost of your transportation cannot be deducted as "wages" for the purposes of meeting the minimum wage requirement. On the other hand, if your employer provides you with transportation to and from work during non-work time, the value of the transportation can be deducted, even if this causes your cash wages to fall below the minimum.[38] Similarly, the value of tools needed to perform your job may not be deducted, nor may the costs of laundering a required uniform.[39] The value of an employer-furnished automobile that is indispensable to the performance of your job cannot be deducted from wages, even if you use the car for non-work purposes.[40] Your employer may, however, deduct the value of furnished meals, housing, or merchandise from the company store, if these items are for your primary benefit and are independent from the requirements of your job; on the other hand, discounts on merchandise you bought from your employer may not be deducted.

Can my employer lower my wages?

Sometimes. If you do not have a contract (personally or through a union) with your employer, your employer can lower your future wages and benefits. Your wages and benefits cannot be lowered retroactively, cannot be lowered below the minimum wage, and cannot be lowered because of illegal discrimination (see Chapters 5–12) or in retaliation for certain lawful acts on your part (see Chapter 3).

If your wages and benefits are established in a collective bargaining agreement, any effort to reduce them would be a violation of that agreement, and you should consult your union representative; a grievance may be filed. If your wages and benefits are fixed in a contract directly between you and your employer, any attempt to reduce them would be a breach of contract. If you cannot resolve the problem with your employer, you could sue for that breach.

These considerations also apply to a promised bonus. If your employer promised to pay you a bonus and you performed the services required to earn the bonus, your employer's failure to pay it would be a breach of the contract or the collective bargaining agreement.

Are all covered employees entitled to the minimum wage?

No. The FLSA and the regulations of the Wage and Hour Division set forth numerous partial and complete exemptions from the minimum wage law. These exemptions are specific and narrowly defined, with exacting terms and conditions. The following examples are illustrative only. Detailed information is available from your local wage-and-hour office.

The following employees are partly exempt from the minimum wage and may be paid sub-minimum wages: learners; apprentices; handicapped workers; messengers; and full-time students working in retail or service establishments, in agriculture, in institutions of higher education, and for schools.[41] Subminimum wages may be paid to such employees only after the employer has obtained specific authorization from the Wage and Hour Administration.[42] In Puerto Rico, the Virgin Islands, and American Samoa, industry wage orders may set wage rates below the minimum wage.[43]

In addition, the following employees are completely exempt from the minimum wage provisions of the FLSA:[44]

- executives, administrators, or professionals (including academic administrative personnel or teachers in elementary or secondary schools);
- outside salesmen;
- casual babysitters or companions to ill or aged persons;
- seamen on non-American vessels;
- employees of certain small retail and service establishments selling primarily intrastate;
- employees of certain small retail establishments that make most of the goods they sell on the premises (e.g., bakeries);
- employees of amusement and recreational establishments having seasonal peaks;
- agricultural employees who are migrant laborers, members of the employer's immediate family, minors working as harvesters on a farm with their parents, or "cowboys" (working on the range producing livestock); and agricultural workers who work for an employer that used no more than

500 man-days of agricultural labor during any quarter of the preceding year;
- employees engaged in the fishing industry (including off-shore processing of seafood);
- employees of weekly, semi-weekly, and daily newspapers of less than 4000 circulation, most of which is in the county of publication or contiguous counties;
- switchboard operators of independently owned public telephone companies having no more than 750 stations;
- employees engaged in delivering newspapers to consumers;
- homeworkers making evergreen wreaths;
- certain overseas employment.

Many of these employees may nevertheless be covered by state minimum wage laws. Although state laws vary widely, some generalizations can be made. About 80 percent of the states have laws that either establish a statutory minimum wage or authorize the creation of wage boards to establish minimum wages on an industry-by-industry basis. Generally, state minimum wage rates are lower than or equal to the federal standard, though Alaska and Connecticut have a higher minimum wage. Employers must pay the highest applicable wage rate. Forty states have established minimum wage rates for employees working under state public works contracts. Forty-one states exempt employers who employ handicapped workers from minimum wage rate requirements for those workers.

When am I entitled to overtime pay, and how much?

The basic rule is that you are entitled to overtime pay after 40 hours of work in the workweek, and the overtime pay rate must be at least one and a half times the regular pay rate.[45]

The workweek is defined as a period of 168 hours during seven consecutive 24-hour periods.[46] The employer may begin the workweek on any day of the week and at any hour of the day. Each workweek stands alone: no averaging of two or more workweeks is allowed. Hospitals or nursing homes are an exception to this averaging prohibition;[47] these employers may adopt, by agreement with the employees, a 14-day overtime period in lieu of the usual 7-day workweek, if the employees are paid at least time and a half their regular pay rate for hours worked over 8 in a day or 80 in a 14-day work period.[48] Other exceptions are seamen on American vessels, and police and firefighters.[49]

The FLSA does not require overtime pay for working more than a certain number of hours in a day; it does not require premium pay for working on a Saturday, Sunday, or holiday, and it does not require premium pay for pre-shift, post-shift, or night work.[50] You may, of course, be entitled to such premium pay under an employment contract or a collective bargaining agreement. The FLSA only requires extra pay for weekly overtime hours—generally, those hours in excess of 40 in a week.

How is overtime pay computed?

The method of computation depends on whether you are paid on an hourly, piecework, or salary basis. Under each method, the first step is determining your regular hourly pay rate.[51] Basically, this regular rate is your total weekly pay less statutory exclusions (see below), divided by the total weekly hours worked for which you were paid. The following kinds of payments are excluded when computing your regular rate: expense reimbursements; gifts; Christmas and discretionary bonuses; pay for absences due to holidays, vacations, illness, voting, jury service, weather conditions, or a sick family member; profit-sharing, savings plan, and welfare plan payments; and premium pay for hours worked in excess of normal daily or weekly standards, or on holidays or normal days off.[52] Generally, the kind of premium pay just mentioned not only can be excluded in computing regular pay, but also can be credited by your employer against overtime pay required by the FLSA.[53] Premium pay for hazardous work, for undesirable working conditions, and for undesirable working hours cannot be excluded from regular pay or credited against overtime pay.[54]

If you are paid by the hour, the computation is simple: for each hour over 40 that you worked in the workweek, your employer must pay at least one and a half times the regular hourly rate. Assume, for example, that you are paid $5 an hour and worked 45 hours in a workweek. For the first 40 hours, you would be entitled to $5 an hour times 40 hours, or $200. For each hour over 40, your hourly rate would be 1½ times $5, or $7.50; and your overtime pay would be $7.50 an hour times 5 hours, or $37.50. Your total pay for the week would be $200 plus $37.50, or $237.50.

If you are paid on a piecework basis, your regular pay rate is determined by dividing your total weekly earnings by the total number of hours you worked that week.[55] For each hour over 40 worked in that week, you are entitled to overtime pay of at least one-half the regular rate, in addition to your full piecework earnings.[56] Suppose, for example, that you produced enough units to earn $180 during a 45-hour week. The regular pay rate for that week would be $180, divided by 45, or $4. You would be entitled to overtime pay of $2 (half the regular rate) for each of the 5 overtime hours, or $10. Your total pay for the week would be $180 plus $10, or $190. ·

If it is agreed to before the work is performed, another way to pay pieceworkers for overtime is to pay one and a half times the piece rate for each piece produced during overtime hours. The piece rate used in this overtime computation must be the one actually paid during straight time and must be enough to yield the minimum wage for each straight-time hour.[57]

If you are paid a salary for a specified number of hours each week, your regular pay rate is determined simply by dividing your salary by the specified number of hours. If, however, you are paid a salary for an unspecified or varying number of hours each week, the regular pay rate is determined by dividing your salary by the number of hours actually worked each week.[58] For each hour over 40 worked in a workweek, you are entitled to one-half the regular rate, in addition to the salary.[59] Assume, for example, that your hours of work vary each week and that you are paid $300 a week for whatever hours you actually work. If you worked 50 hours in a workweek, the regular pay rate for that week would be $300 divided by 50 hours, or $6 an hour. For each of the 10 overtime hours, you would be entitled to $3 an hour (one-half the regular rate), for a total of $30 in overtime pay. Your total pay for the week would be $300 plus $30, or $330.

If you are paid a salary on other than a weekly basis, your weekly pay must be determined before computing the regular rate and overtime. If the salary is for a half month, your weekly pay is determined by multiplying your salary by 24 (the number of pay periods in a year) and then dividing the product by 52 (the weeks in a year). Similarly, for a monthly salary, multiply by 12, and divide the product by 52.[60]

Are all covered employees entitled to overtime pay?

No. As with minimum wage requirements, many catego-

ries of employees are partly or completely exempt from overtime pay requirements. Like the minimum wage exemptions
discussed earlier, overtime pay exemptions are specific and
narrowly defined. The exemptions described below are illus-
trations only; more detailed information is available from your
local wage-and-hour office.

All employees who are completely exempt from the minimum wage provisions of the FLSA are also completely exempt from its overtime pay provisions. The following *additional*
employees are completely exempt from overtime pay provisions:[61]

* agricultural employees generally;
* employees engaged in the local transportation of fruits or
  vegetables, or of harvest workers;
* live-in household employees;
* taxicab drivers;
* drivers and drivers' helpers on local deliveries when paid
  on the basis of trip rates;
* firefighters and law enforcement personnel working for small
  agencies (less than five such employees);
* employees of federally regulated motor carriers, railroads,
  express companies, water carriers, and air carriers;
* salesmen, partsmen, or mechanics employed by automobile,
  truck, or farm implement dealers; and salesmen employed
  by trailer, boat, or aircraft dealers;
* seamen;
* employees of motion picture theaters;
* outside buyers of poultry and dairy products;
* certain employees who process maple syrup;
* employees of non-profit agricultural irrigation systems;
* employees of country elevators with less than six employees;
* forestry or logging employees for an employer with less
  than nine such employees;
* certain resident houseparents at non-profit educational
  institutions;
* announcers, news editors, and chief engineers of radio and
  television stations in small communities.

Under a partial exemption, the employee is entitled to
overtime pay under a standard different from the normal
standard of time and half for hours in excess of 40 in a
workweek. For example, hospital and nursing home employ-

ees are entitled to overtime at time and a half on the basis of a 14-day period rather than the usual 7-day workweek, if the employee agrees to the arrangement and receives overtime for hours in excess of 8 daily and 80 during the period. The following categories of employees are partly exempt from overtime pay provisions:[62]

- commission employees at retail or service establishments;
- hospital and nursing home employees;
- employees of certain wholesale petroleum distributors;
- employees working under certain collective bargaining agreements;
- employees who gin cotton, make sugar or syrup, or process or handle leaf tobacco; and cotton or sugar service employees;
- employees of private concessionaries in national parks, forests, and wildlife refuges.

Can my employer pay me less than a person of the opposite sex for the same work?

No. The Equal Pay Act of 1963 added to the FLSA a requirement of equal pay for equal work regardless of sex.[60] An employer must give equal pay and benefits to men and women employed in the same establishment on jobs that require "equal skill, effort, and responsibility" and that are "performed under similar working conditions."[63] The application of the Equal Pay Law is discussed in detail in Chapter 7 on sex discrimination.

Can children work?

Yes, under certain conditions. The FLSA contains provisions regulating the ages at which children can work and the hours they can work.[64] A few other federal laws have special provisions regarding child labor, and most states have laws regulating child labor. Many of those state laws require that a child be a certain age before being allowed to work in certain industries, particularly hazardous industries, and many of them have provisions governing such matters as schooling and rest periods that must be followed when children are employed. An employer must abide by highest child labor standards that are applicable to it.

These provisions are designed to protect the educational opportunities of children and to prohibit their employment in jobs and under conditions detrimental to their health or well-being.[65]

In what circumstances can a child work?

Whether a child can work depends on numerous factors, including the child's age, the kind of work involved, who the employer is, and when the work is performed. The only exemptions from the child labor provisions of the FLSA are newspaper delivery; performing in radio, television, movie, or theatrical productions; working for parents in a non-hazardous, non-manufacturing, non-mining job; and making evergreen wreaths at home.[66] The FLSA regulations on child labor differ for non-farm and farm work, generally being laxer for farm work.

Non-farm work: A person 18 years of age or older can do any job, whether hazardous or not, for unlimited hours.[67] A 16- or 17-year-old can do any non-hazardous job for unlimited hours.[68] Lists of non-farm jobs deemed too hazardous for anyone under 18 are available from your local wage-and-hour office.

A 14- or 15-year old can work outside of school hours in a non-hazardous, non-manufacturing, non-mining job under certain conditions.[69] The child can work no more than 3 hours on a school day, 18 hours in a school week, 8 hours on a non-school day, or 40 hours in a non-school week.[70] The child may not begin work before 7 a.m. or end work after 7 p.m., except from June 1 through Labor Day, when work must end by 9 p.m.[71]

Farm work: A person 16 years of age or older can do any farm job, whether hazardous or not, for unlimited hours. A 14- or 15-year-old can do any non-hazardous farm job outside of school hours;[72] lists of farm jobs deemed too hazardous for anyone under 16 are available from your local wage-and-hour office.

A 12- or 13-year-old can work in a non-hazardous farm job outside of school hours either with parental consent or on the same farm as a parent or guardian.[73] A child under 12 can work only outside of school hours on a farm owned or operated by a parent or guardian, or with the parents' written consent in a non-hazardous job on a farm exempt from minimum wage requirements.[74] Under limited circumstances prescribed by the Secretary of Labor, a 10- or 11-year-old can hand-harvest short season crops, outside of school hours and for no more than 8 weeks between June 1 and October 15, for a local employer who has received approval from the Secretary of Labor.[75]

A child of any age can work at even a hazardous job for a parent or guardian on a farm owned or operated by that parent or guardian.[76]

What should I do if I think my wage-hour rights have been violated?

Probably your best initial course of action would be to contact your local wage-and-hour office, which can provide you with free information and advice. Furthermore, an FLSA compliance officer may investigate your complaint to determine whether your employer's practices comply with FLSA. These compliance offices have broad powers to enter the employer's premises to inspect and copy records and to question employees and employers.[77] Even in the absence of an employee complaint, FLSA compliance officers investigate employers by periodically inspecting employer records, by spot-checking suspected violators, and by reinspecting past violators.

If an FLSA official finds a violation, several things may happen. Generally, the official will try to bring the employer into voluntary compliance with the law by recommending changes in employment practices and by inducing the employer to pay any back wages due to employees.[78] The Wage-Hour Division may supervise payment of these back wages.

If the employer does not voluntarily comply with the FLSA, the Secretary of Labor may sue for back pay and an equal amount of liquidated damages.[79] The Secretary also may sue for an injunction to restrain an employer from future violations of the law, including the unlawful failure to pay proper minimum wage, overtime, and equal pay compensation.[80] The Secretary can bring a lawsuit for back pay, or an injunction suit, or both, without employee consent.[81]

As an employee, you may file a private lawsuit for back pay and an equal amount as liquidated damages, plus attorneys' fees and court costs.[82] In such a private suit, the court may deny or reduce the liquidated damages if your employer acted in good faith.[83] You may not sue, however, if you have been paid back wages under the supervision of the Wage-Hour Division or if the Secretary has already filed a suit to recover the wages.[84]

An FLSA wage suit, whether brought by the Secretary of Labor or by an employee, must be started within two years of a non-willful violation, or within three years for a willful violation.[85] The two- or three-year period begins when the wages become due and the employer fails to pay them.[86]

In addition to the above sanctions, an employer who willfully violates the FLSA can be criminally prosecuted and fined up to $10,000 for a first conviction.[87] A second conviction can result in a six-month prison term in addition to the fine. Criminal prosecutions may be brought any time within five years after the violation.[88] An employer who violates the child labor provisions is subject to a $1000 civil penalty for each violation.[89]

It is illegal for an employer to fire or otherwise discriminate against an employee for filing a complaint, or for instituting, or causing to be instituted, any proceeding under or related to the FLSA, or for participating in any proceeding under or related to the FLSA.[90]

B. Other Federal Wage-Hour Laws

This section briefly discusses the federal laws regulating the wages and hours of employees working under public works contracts, government supply and service contracts, and contracts for federally financed and assisted projects. These laws exhibit considerable interlocking with each other and with the FLSA. The result is a complex patchwork of coverage, with some overlapping coverage and some anomalous gaps in coverage. Generally these laws and the FLSA are supplementary, not mutually exclusive. Thus an employer may be subject to one or more of these wage-and-hour laws and still be subject to all FLSA requirements. These laws and regulations are under review by the federal government, so some changes may be forthcoming.

This section also covers special provisions pertaining to migrant farm workers.

What are the wage-and-hour laws for employees under a public works contract?

The Davis-Bacon Act,[91] enacted in 1931, guarantees minimum wages and fringe benefits for laborers and mechanics employed by contractors or subcontractors on federal contracts for more than $2000 to construct, alter, or repair public buildings or public works.

Employees under such a public contract must be paid at

least the wage rate found by the Secretary of Labor to be prevailing for corresponding workers employed on similar projects in the locale in which the work is to be performed. The Act was passed to protect employees from substandard earnings by fixing minimum wages and benefits; it also protects local union workers from being displaced or undercut by non-union workers willing to work for less.

Employees under a public contract must be paid not only the prevailing wage rates, but also the prevailing fringe benefits—or equally valuable fringe benefits, or supplemental wages equivalent to the value of those benefits. Thus, any fringe benefit prevailing in the area must be matched, including medical or hospital care; pensions; life, disability, sickness, and accident insurance; vacation and holiday pay; unemployment benefits; and training programs. When an employee receives supplemental wages in lieu of fringe benefits, those supplements are excluded from the base pay rate used for overtime pay purposes.

The Contract Work Hours and Safety Standards Act,[92] enacted in 1962, requires among other things that all laborers and mechanics covered by the Davis-Bacon Act receive overtime pay of at least one and a half times the basic rate of pay for hours in excess of 8 per day or 40 per week.[93]

Another law affecting public contract employees is the Copeland Act, commonly known as the "Kickback" or "Anti-Kickback" Act,[94] enacted in 1934. To evade the scale of wages imposed on public contracts, some employers were inducing employees to kick back to the employer part of their pay. The Copeland Act made such kickbacks a crime punishable by a $5000 fine, five years in prison, or both. It pertains to all employees (not just laborers and mechanics) on all public contracts and on all federally financed or assisted construction projects.

The Miller Act[95] requires the prime contractor on a public contract exceeding $2000 to furnish a bond protecting the payment of wages to all workers, not only laborers and mechanics, on the project. An employee who is not paid within 90 days after finishing work on a project can sue directly on these bonds. Also, trustees of an employees' health and welfare fund can recover delinquent employer contributions under these bonds. The government can waive these bonds on certain foreign, "cost-plus," or military projects.

If an employer violates the law covering employment under a public contract, the government may terminate the contract, withhold payment on the contract in order to pay the workers, and blacklist the employer. In addition, if the withheld payments are insufficient to pay the amounts owed to the laborers and mechanics as minimum wages, the workers can sue the contractors and their sureties (which are required by the Miller Act) directly for recovery.

What are the wage-and-hour laws for employees under contracts for federally financed or assisted projects?

Contracts for projects that are wholly or partly financed or assisted by federal money are covered by the Contract Work Hours and Safety Standards Act (regarding overtime) and by the Copeland ("Anti-Kickback") Act; but such contracts are not automatically covered by the Davis-Bacon Act (regarding prevailing wage rates) or the Service Contract Act (to be discussed later). As a result, dozens of statutes pertaining to specific federally financed or assisted projects contain provisions extending the Davis-Bacon wage standards to laborers and mechanics employed on such projects. These statutes include the Federal-Aid Highway Act of 1956, the Area Redevelopment Act, the Federal Airport Act, the Equal Opportunity Act of 1964, and statutes for construction of hospitals, schools, and community facilities.[96] In addition, the National Foundation on the Arts and Humanities Act of 1965[97] effectively extends the Davis-Bacon Act provisions not only to laborers and mechanics, but also to professionals retained under programs financed under that Act by the National Foundation on the Arts and the Humanities, or any of its subdivisions or agents.

What are the wage-and-hour laws for employees under government supply contracts?

The Walsh-Healey Act[98] (also known as the Public Contracts Act), enacted in 1936, provides that all employees (except executives, administrators, professionals, and office, custodial, and maintenance employees) who work under a contract to supply the federal government with materials, supplies, articles, or equipment for more than $10,000 are protected by minimum wage and overtime pay requirements, and by safety and health standards. This Act was designed to use the leverage of the government's immense purchasing power to raise labor standards.

Under the Walsh-Healey Act, the Secretary of Labor fixes specific minimum hourly rates for particular industries and a general minimum hourly rate for all other industries. These minimum rates are fixed on the basis of prevailing minimum rates in the industry or in similar industries. This Act also provides that employees under a government supply contract must receive overtime pay of at least one and a half times the basic rate of pay for hours in excess of 8 per day or 40 per week. Unlike the Davis-Bacon Act and the Service Contract Act (discussed below), the Walsh-Healey Act provides no right to prevailing fringe benefits.

In addition to the minimum wage and overtime pay standards, the Walsh-Healey Act prohibits the employment of children under 16 and of convict labor under the contract and requires safe and sanitary working conditions.[99]

If an employer violates the Walsh-Healey Act, the government can cancel the contract and blacklist the employer. Unlike the FLSA, the Walsh-Healey Act does not authorize employees' suits for recovery of unpaid compensation, liquidated damages, or attorneys' fees, but it does provide for collection by the federal government of unpaid compensation for the benefit of employees.

What are the wage-and-hour laws for employees under government service contracts?

The Service Contract Act (SCA), sometimes called the McNamara-O'Hara Act,[100] was enacted in 1965 and amended in 1972. It requires payment of minimum wages and fringe benefits to employees who work under a contract with the federal government when the principal purpose of the contract is to furnish services through service employees; the SCA also requires safe and sanitary working conditions under such contracts. Regardless of the contract amount, all service and non-service employees under the contract must be paid at least the minimum wage specified by the FLSA. If the contract amount exceeds $2500, the service employees must be paid minimum wages and fringe benefits at rates determined by the Secretary of Labor to be the prevailing rates and benefits for such employees in the locality where the services are performed; if the employees under the contract are covered by a collective bargaining agreement, the Secretary must take into account in making his determination the agreement's wages and fringe benefits. As under the Davis-

Bacon Act, the fringe benefits obligation may be fulfilled by any combination of fringe benefits or supplemental cash wages equal to the value of the standard fringe benefits.

The SCA itself does not provide for overtime pay. But the service employees covered by the SCA may be entitled to overtime pay under other federal laws, including the Contract Work Hours and Safety Standards Act (for laborers and mechanics), the Walsh-Healey Act (for employees of supply contractors), and the FLSA (for employees who are covered and not exempt under this general law).

The Service Contract Act is supplemented by two special FLSA provisions. One sets minimum wage requirements for all workers employed in establishments that provide linen supply services to the federal government and requires that such workers receive equal pay for equal work.[101] The other statute[102] extends the same minimum wage and equal pay standards to employees under federal service contracts who are not covered by the Service Contract Act.

What protections exist for farm workers?

On January 14, 1983, the Migrant and Seasonal Agricultural Worker Protection Act (MSPA) was signed into law, repealing and replacing the Farm Labor Contractor Registration Act of 1963. MSPA is designed to protect migrant and seasonal agricultural workers, producers of agricultural products, and the general public from abuse by "irresponsible" farm labor contractors. A farm labor contractor is someone paid to recruit, solicit, hire, furnish or transport migrant or seasonal agricultural workers (excluding members of his immediate family) for farm work. A migrant agricultural worker is someone who is employed in agricultural employment of a seasonal or other temporary nature and who is required to be away from his permanent home overnight; a seasonal agricultural worker is someone who is employed in agricultural employment of a seasonal or other temporary nature and who is not required to be away from his permanent home overnight when employed in certain field work or in certain related canning or processing operations. Labor unions are explicitly exempt from the Act.

MSPA requires a farm labor contractor and a farm labor contractor employee to obtain a certificate of registration from the Secretary of Labor, and to comply with all provisions of MSPA. Administration and enforcement of the MSPA is handled by the Wage and Hour Division of the U.S. Labor Department.

To qualify for a certificate of registration, an applicant must file an affidavit stating his permanent place of residence and his conduct and method of operation as a farm labor contractor; a set of fingerprints; a statement identifying all vehicles to be used for transporting migrant workers and all property to be used for their housing, together with proof that the property conforms with federal and state safety and health standards; and a designation of the Secretary as agent for service of process in any action against the farm labor contractor if he has left the jurisdiction in which the action is commenced or is otherwise unavailable. A certificate will not be issued to a person who has done any of the following: made false statements in his application; failed to comply with the Act or any regulation under the Act; failed to perform agreements entered into or to comply with the terms of any working arrangements made with migrant workers, without justification; recruited or employed, or assisted another in recruiting or employing, illegal aliens; or been convicted of any crime involving gambling or the sale of alcoholic beverages incident to his activities as a farm labor contractor; or been convicted of robbery, extortion, bribery, or the like.

After a certificate has been issued, each farm labor contractor and each farm labor contractor employee is required to carry his certificate at all times when engaged in farm labor contracting activities, and to display his certificate upon request. The farm labor contractor is required to give workers each pay period detailed information, in the workers' own language, concerning wages and deductions. MSPA also governs housing controlled by farm labor contractors for farm workers and requires such contractors to fulfill other obligations designed to protect the interests of farm workers. If a farm labor contractor is found to have knowingly violated MSPA, he can be liable for civil damages of $500 per plaintiff per violation and for criminal fines (not to exceed $1,000 for a first offense or $10,000 for any subsequent offenses) and penalties.

If you are aggrieved by the violation of any provision of the Act, you can sue in federal court; you need not exhaust the administrative remedies provided by the FLCRA. The court has discretion to appoint an attorney for you. If the contractor is found to have intentionally violated the Act, the court may award damages up to the amount of your actual damages, or $500 for each violation (with a $500,000 limit in class actions), and may grant equitable relief.

Retaliation for filing a complaint or for instituting any proceeding under the Act is prohibited. If you believe that you have been discriminated against, you can file a complaint with the Secretary of Labor about it. Any attempted waiver of your rights against a farm labor contractor is void.

C. Other Laws Affecting Wages and Hours

Your wages and hours are also directly and indirectly affected by other federal and state laws.[104] The amount of your take home pay can be substantially affected by such things as tax deductions and wage garnishments. Some of the laws that may affect your paycheck are discussed in this final section on wages and hours.

What can my employer deduct from my gross pay?

Virtually all employers are required to withhold federal and state income taxes and social security taxes from your wages. The amount of the income tax deducted from your wage depends upon your marital status, the number of exemptions you claim, and your income bracket. In addition, as of January 1, 1982, 6.7 percent of your wages must be deducted from your salary as social security tax. Your employer must contribute an equal percentage of your earnings to your social security account and cannot deduct his share of social security taxes from your salary.[105]

Although most employers are required to pay for unemployment insurance, only Alabama, Alaska, and New Jersey allow an employer to deduct such unemployment insurance contributions from your wages.[106] If you do not live in one of those three states, and your employer is deducting for unemployment compensation, your employer may be violating your state's wage-and-hour law. No state allows deductions for workers' compensation.

Almost all states have statutes protecting your wages from unauthorized deductions. For example, Connecticut prohibits an employer from withholding wages unless a law requires it or you authorize it in writing.[107] Also, some states expressly limit an employer's right to deduct from or otherwise adjust your salary because of defective workmanship or lost or stolen property.[108]

Your employer may not take a deduction from your wages

to satisfy a debt you owe your employer. Like any other creditor, your employer must obtain a court order authorizing such a deduction, and the garnishment has to comply with the Federal Wage Garnishment Law, which is discussed later.[109] Of course, you may voluntarily assign a portion of your wages and authorize your employer to make a deduction for this purpose. Voluntary wage assignments are covered next.

May I assign my wages?

Generally, yes. An assignment is a voluntary agreement whereby you give your rights to something to another; for example, you may assign part of your wages to a person to whom you owe a debt. Or you may assign a certain amount of your wages to your union for dues, or to an employment agency as payment for getting you your job. Upon receiving notice of an assignment, your employer must deduct the assigned sum from your wages and pay it directly to your creditor.

Most states have laws that restrict the assignment of wages. For example, Minnesota forbids an assignment of the future wages of a married person without the written consent of the spouse.[110] Tennessee imposes a limit of 10 percent on the amount of your wages that can be assigned as security for a loan.[111] In New York, you cannot assign any part of your wages if you earn less than $85 per week.[112] If you are asked to assign part of your wages to a third party, you should check the provisions of your state law to see whether the assignment is allowed.

Am I entitled to unpaid wages if I am terminated?

Yes. All states except Alabama, Florida, Georgia, Mississippi, Ohio, and Tennessee specifically require that an employee who is discharged must be paid any unpaid wages very shortly after termination, usually the next business day. If an employee dies and is owed wages or other remuneration, most states specifically require that the employer pay these moneys to the employee's estate. If your employer fails to pay you accrued wages upon termination, you should contact the Wage and Hour Division of the U.S. Department of Labor.

Am I entitled to payment for accrued fringe benefits upon termination of my employment?

Generally, your employer is not required to pay you for

unpaid fringe benefits (such as vacation, holidays, sick days, etc.) when your employment ends; but a strong argument can be made that such benefits are a form of deferred wages for services and that payment should be on a pro rata basis. Frequently, however, such a provision will be part of a union employment contract or a voluntarily adopted employer policy. In recognition of this, many states have enacted laws requiring an employer to pay a terminated employee accrued fringe benefits within a certain period if the employer has such a policy or if the union contract contains such a clause.

Am I entitled to severance pay if I am terminated?

Only if required by contract. Severance pay is a sum of money, in addition to unpaid wages, that is paid to an employee upon involuntary termination of employment or upon retirement. Severance pay is not required by any federal or state laws or regulations. Thus you are not entitled to it unless your employer has agreed to pay it either as part of your individual employment agreement or as part of your union contract. When paid, severance pay often consists of continuing salary payments for a specified period after discharge.

What happens if my employer goes bankrupt and I am owed wages?

When a company goes bankrupt, the company's employees are typically among those who compete for payment from the remaining assets of the company. The Bankruptcy Code of 1978[113] establishes a priority list of those persons who seek the repayment of debt incurred by the bankrupt company.[114]

Under the Code, employees' claims for wages, salaries, and commissions (including vacation, severance, and sick-leave pay) are given a very high priority. The purpose of this provision is to protect those who are dependent upon their wages and who, upon losing their jobs, especially need legal protection.[115] This high priority applies only to compensation earned within 90 days before the date your employer filed for bankruptcy, or within 90 days before your employer ceased doing business, whichever occurred first. Also, only the first $2000 of wages owed to you is entitled to priority; additional amounts are general unsecured claims against the bankrupt's assets. As a practical matter, you probably won't have to do anything to exercise your rights. The bankruptcy judge handling your employer's case will simply order your employer to comply with the priorities established under the Code. Some states make officers or major shareholders of corporate employers personally liable for unpaid wages.[116]

Finally, your state may have a special provision to protect the employees of a partnership that goes bankrupt. For example, in New York, the wages of an employee of a partnership must be paid before any other claim is paid.[117] Additionally, partners are personally liable for the debts of the partnership, so a judgment for unpaid wages can be enforced against the personal assets of any of the partners.

Can my wages be garnisheed?

Yes. "Garnishment" occurs when a court orders your employer to withhold a portion of your earnings for the payment of your debts. Usually, to get a garnishment order from a court, your creditor must prove that you, in fact, owe the money and that you have failed to make payments on the debt.

Federal and state laws restrict the garnishment of wages. The Federal Wage Garnishment Law[118] (FWGL) limits the amount of your wages that may be garnisheed and prohibits your being discharged on the ground that your wages are subject to a garnishment order. The FWGL states that a garnishment may not exceed 25 percent of your disposable earnings for the workweek, or the amount by which disposable earnings for a workweek exceed 30 times the federal minimum hourly wage (which is $3.35 as of January 2, 1981), whichever is less.[119] Thus, if your disposable earnings are less than $134 per week, only the amount over $100 may be garnisheed. The FWGL defines "disposable earnings" as the income that remains after deductions required by law (such as federal, state, and local income taxes and social security taxes) are made. Deductions that are not mandated by law (such as for union dues and health insurance) are included in "disposable earnings" for purposes of garnishment.

The FWGL also contains a special provision for the garnishment of wages for the payment of child support and alimony. Under these sections, 50 percent of your disposable earnings can be garnisheed for child support or alimony if you are also supporting another person; if you are not responsible for the support of another, up to 60 percent of your earnings may be garnisheed.

In addition to the Federal Wage Garnishment Law, many

states have laws that impose further restrictions on the garnishment of wages. Many of these laws establish a maximum percentage of your wages that can be garnisheed. For example, in New York your salary cannot be garnisheed unless you earn more than $85 per week, and 90 percent of your weekly salary is exempt.[120] If the state rule on garnishment is stricter than the federal rule, the state rule governs.[121]

The IRS is entitled to levy against your wages to collect unpaid taxes. The Federal Wage Garnishment Law limitations on the amount of your earnings that can be garnisheed do *not* apply to a garnishment to pay back taxes.[122]

NOTES

1. 29 U.S.C. §§201 *et seq.*
2. 40 U.S.C. §§276a *et seq.*
3. 41 U.S.C. §§35 *et seq.*
4. 41 U.S.C. §§351 *et seq.*
5. 40 U.S.C. §§327 *et seq.*
6. 29 U.S.C. §§1801 *et seq.*
7. 29 U.S.C. §202.
8. 29 U.S.C. §204(a).
9. 29 U.S.C. §206.
10. 29 U.S.C. §207(a)(1).
11. 29 U.S.C. §212.
12. 29 U.S.C. §206(d).
13. 29 U.S.C. §202.
14. 29 U.S.C. §203(s).
15. 29 U.S.C. §203(r).
16. 29 U.S.C. §203(s)(2).
17. 29 U.S.C. §203(s)(1).
18. 29 U.S.C. §203(e)(3).
19. 29 U.S.C. §206.
20. *Id.*
21. 29 U.S.C. §203(o).
22. *Boll v. Federal Reserve Bank of St. Louis*, 365 F. Supp. 637 (E.D. Mo. 1973), *aff'd*, 497 F.2d 335 (8th Cir. 1974).
23. Wage and Hour Field Operation Handbook ¶32d03C.
24. *See, e.g., Olson v. Rock Island Bank*, 339 N.E.2d 39 (Ill. App. Ct. 1975).
25. 29 C.F.R. §778.216.
26. The following states have laws requiring that employees be given a specified amount of time off to vote: Ala., Ariz., Ark., Cal., Colo., Ga., Hawaii, Ill., Ind., Iowa, Kan., Kty., Md., Mass., Minn., Mo., Neb., Nev., N.M., N.Y, Ohio, Okla., S.D., Tenn., Tex., Utah, W.Va., Wis., Wyo.

27. The following states prohibit employers from deducting pay for time spent voting: Ala., Ariz., Ark., Cal., Colo., Hawaii, Iowa, Kan., Md., Minn., Mo., Neb., Nev., N.M., N.Y., Ohio, Okla., S.D., Tenn., Tex., Wyo.

28. Ala. Stat. §12–16–8; Hawaii Stat. §95–26; Mass. Stat. §234a–37; Neb. Stat. §25–1640; Tenn. Stat. §22–4–108.

29. 29 C.F.R. §790.7(b).

30. *Steiner v. Mitchell*, 350 U.S. 247 (1956); *Mitchell v. King Packing Co.*, 350 U.S. 260, *reh'g. denied*, 350 U.S. 983 (1956).

31. 29 U.S.C. §203(o). *See Hoover v. Wyandotte Chemicals Corp.*, 455 F.2d 387 (5th Cir. 1972), *reh'g. denied*, 409 U.S. 847 (1972); *Nardone v. General Motors, Inc.*, 207 F. Supp. 336 (D.N.J. 1962).

32. 29 C.F.R. §785.7; *Tennessee Coal, Iron & Railroad Co. v. Muscoda Local No. 123*, 321 U.S. 590 (1944).

33. 29 U.S.C. §254. This is part of the Portal-to-Portal Act of 1947, which amended the FLSA in relation to compensation for incidental activities. *See* 29 C.F.R. part 790.

34. 29 U.S.C. §203(m).

35. 29 U.S.C. §203(m)(1).

36. 29 U.S.C. §203(m)(2).

37. 29 U.S.C. §203(m).

38. 29 C.F.R. §531.32(a).

39. *Schultz v. Hinojosa*, 432 F.2d 259 (5th Cir. 1970).

40. *Brennan v. Modern Chevrolet Co.*, 363 F. Supp. 327 (N.D. Tex. 1973), *aff'd*, 491 F.2d 1271 (5th Cir. 1974).

41. *See Donovan v. Miller Properties, Inc.*, 547 F. Supp. 785 (M.D.L.A. 1982).

42. 29 U.S.C. §§213(a)(7) and 214.

43. 29 U.S.C. §206(a)(2) and (3).

44. *See* 29 U.S.C. §213(a) and (d).

45. 29 U.S.C. §207(a)(1).

46. 29 C.F.R. §778.105.

47. 29 C.F.R. §778.601(a).

48. 29 C.F.R. §778.601(d).

49. 29 U.S.C. §§213(b)(20) and 207(k).

50. 29 C.F.R. §778.102.

51. *Masters v. Maryland Management Co.*, 493 F.2d 1329 (4th Cir. 1974).

52. 29 U.S.C. §207(e).

53. 29 U.S.C. §207(h).

54. 29 U.S.C. §207(e)(6).

55. 29 C.F.R. §778.111(a).

56. *Walling v. Alaska Pacific Consol. Mining Co.*, 152 F.2d 812 (9th Cir. 1945), *cert. denied*, 327 U.S. 803 (1945).

57. 29 U.S.C. §207(g).

58. 29 C.F.R. §778.114.

59. *Id.*
60. *General Electric Co. v. Porter*, 208 F.2d 805 (9th Cir. 1953), *cert. denied*, 347 U.S. 951 (1954).
61. *See* 29 U.S.C. §213(b).
62. 29 U.S.C. §206(d).
63. 29 U.S.C. §206(d)(1).
64. 29 U.S.C. §212.
65. *Lenroot v. Western Union Tel. Co.*, 52 F. Supp. 142 (S.D.N.Y. 1943), *aff'd*, 141 F.2d 400 (2d Cir. 1944), *rev'd on other grounds*, 323 U.S. 490 (1944).
66. 29 U.S.C. §213.
67. 29 U.S.C. §203(1).
68. *Id.*
69. 29 U.S.C. §203(1)(1).
70. 29 C.F.R. §570.119.
71. *Id.*
72. 29 U.S.C. §203(1).
73. 29 U.S.C. §213(c)(1).
74. 29 U.S.C. §213(c)(1)(A).
75. 29 U.S.C. §213(c)(4)(A).
76. 29 U.S.C. §213(c)(2).
77. 29 U.S.C. §211(a).
78. Wage and Hours Field Operations Handbook §53c14(a).
79. 29 U.S.C. §216(b), (c).
80. *Id.*
81. *Id.*
82. *Id.*
83. 29 U.S.C. §258.
84. 29 U.S.C. §216(b).
85. 29 U.S.C. §255(a).
86. 29 C.F.R. §790.21.
87. 29 U.S.C. §216(a).
88. *Id.*
89. *Id.*
90. 29 U.S.C. §215(a)(3).
91. 40 U.S.C. §§276a *et seq.*
92. 40 U.S.C. §§327 *et seq.*
93. 40 U.S.C. §328.
94. 40 U.S.C. §§276b and 276c.
95. 40 U.S.C. §§270a *et seq.*
96. *See* 29 C.F.R. §5.1.
97. 20 U.S.C. §954(j).
98. 41 U.S.C. §§35 *et seq.*
99. 41 U.S.C. §35(d), (e).
100. 41 U.S.C. §§351 *et seq.*
101. 29 U.S.C. §213(e)(2).
102. 29 U.S.C. §213(e)(1).
103. 29 U.S.C. §§1801 *et seq.*

104. For a thorough discussion of state fair labor standards laws on a state-by-state basis, see BNA, *Labor Policy and Practice, Wages and Hours*.
105. 29 C.F.R. §531.38.
106. Ala. Code §25–4–54; Alaska Stat. §23.20.165; N.J.S.A. §43:21–7.
107. Conn. Stat. §31–71e.
108. *E.g.*, Wis. Stat. §§103.455, 134.57.
109. *Sears, Roebuck & Co. v. A.T. & G. Co., Inc.*, 66 Mich. App. 359, 239 N.W.2d 614 (1976).
110. Minn. Stat. §1810.07.
111. Tenn. Stat. §45–2119.
112. N.Y. Labor Law §48–6.
113. 11 U.S.C. §§101 *et seq*.
114. 11 U.S.C. §507.
115. *Re Bauer Co.*, 3 B.C.D. 1147 (S.D. Ohio 1977).
116. *See, e.g.*, N.Y.B.C.L. §630.
117. N.Y. Partnership Law §71–a.
118. 15 U.S.C. §§1671 *et seq*.
119. 15 U.S.C. §1673(a).
120. N.Y.C.P.L.R. §§5231(b) and 5205(d).
121. 15 U.S.C. §1677(1).
122. 15 U.S.C. §1673(b)(1)(C).

Part IV

Income Substitutes

XVI

Pensions

If you are covered by a pension plan, you should know certain facts about your pension. Your plans for retirement probably depend largely on the income you can expect from your pension and social security benefits. It's important to know what these benefits will be and what you must do to qualify for them, so you can plan intelligently for your retirement years. Just because you are covered by a pension plan does not mean that you will automatically get a pension—you must meet the requirements of your plan. If you don't know what your plan requires, you may fail to qualify for benefits.

This chapter explains some aspects of pension plans generally so you can better understand your own plan. It does not cover every aspect of every plan. Pension plans vary greatly, and it's important to understand the provisions of your particular plan. As explained more fully later, you are entitled to a summary of your plan's provisions and to periodic reports on your rights under the plan. If you do not understand any provision of the plan or how it applies to you, ask your plan administrator, union representative, or employer to explain it to you.

The federal government publishes several very useful free booklets on pensions; these are described in Appendix 5. These booklets and other information are available at area offices of the U.S. Labor-Management Services Administration, which are listed in Appendix 6. Another useful reference is the ACLU handbook *The Rights of Older Persons* by Robert N. Brown, et al.*

---

*A significant portion of this chapter is based on the "private pensions" chapter of that handbook.

Does the law guarantee me a pension?

No. An employer is not required to establish a pension plan or to continue a plan once it has been established. Nonetheless, more than 40 million private employees—about half of the private workforce—work for employers with pension plans. In addition, as explained later, federal income tax laws now encourage employees to establish "individual retirement accounts," which are like personal pension plans.

What is a pension?

The term "pension" describes an agreement or program under which an employer, an employee, a union, or all of these contribute money to a fund during an employee's working years to provide income for the employee upon retirement or disability. The term really involves three separate ideas: a pension plan, a pension fund or trust, and a pension benefit. A pension plan is the agreement or program established by the employer, employee, or union. A pension fund or trust is the collection of money contributed by these parties held for the benefit of employees under the pension plan. And a pension benefit is the money from the pension fund that is paid, usually monthly, to the employee after retirement or disability. In this chapter we use the term "pension" loosely, sometimes referring to pension benefits, sometimes to all three concepts—plans, funds, and benefits.

To understand your rights under your pension plan, you must first understand what kind of plan you have.

What kinds of pension plans are there?

If the amount of pension benefits you will receive when you retire is determined in advance but the amount of money contributed to the fund varies, your plan is a *defined benefit* plan. Each year, the employer contributes the amount needed, based on your age and the amount already in the fund, to provide the defined benefit.

If contributions to the fund are fixed but the actual benefit amount is not known, your plan is a *defined contribution* plan. Under defined contribution plans, also known as individual account plans, the plan administrator maintains a separate account for each participant. Each year, the employer contributes to each participant's account based on the employee's annual earnings or based on the employer's profits. The income earned from investing these contributions accumulates

free of income tax and is credited to your account. Your
retirement benefits are based on the amount of money in
your account at retirement.

Additional terms that apply to pension plans are set forth in
note 1.

What laws govern pension plans?

Although an employer does not have to set up a pension
plan, any plan that is established must meet certain minimum
standards to qualify for favorable tax treatment. These standards stem from the tax laws and the Employee Retirement
Income Security Act (ERISA), enacted in September 1974,
which applies to pre-existing and new plans. The purpose of
ERISA is to protect the interests of workers who participate
in pension plans, and their beneficiaries. This purpose is
promoted by provisions attempting to assure: that workers
are not required to satisfy unreasonable age and service requirements before becoming eligible for pension plan participation (through the participation provisions); that persons
who work for a specified minimum period under a pension
plan are assured of at least some pension at retirement age
(through the vesting, benefit accrual, and breach-in-service
provisions); that enough money is contributed each year to
pay the pension benefits when they are due (through the
funding provisions); that plan funds are handled prudently
(through the fiduciary provisions); that employees and their
beneficiaries know their rights and obligations under the
plans (through the reporting and disclosure provisions); that
spouses of pensioners are given better protection (through
the joint and survivor provisions); that the benefits of workers
in certain defined-benefit pension plans are protected if a
plan terminates (through the plan termination insurance
provisions); and that the tax laws relevant to pensions are more
equitable (through amendments to the Internal Revenue Code).

ERISA provides a complex set of guidelines that all private
sector qualified pension plans must follow. It provides significant protections for employees who retire or become disabled
after the effective date of the Act. ERISA is not retroactive,
however, so it does nothing for employees who retired or
became disabled before the Act went into effect. And because
of a number of omissions and exceptions in the Act, some
significant problems remain, even for those retiring or becom-

ing disabled after ERISA went into effect. The balance of this chapter discusses ERISA in more detail.

In addition to ERISA, a number of other laws regulate private pensions. These include the Labor Management Relations Act, the Age Discrimination in Employment Act of 1967, the Securities Act of 1933, the Securities Exchange Act of 1934, the Civil Rights Act of 1964, and the Internal Revenue Code.

How can I find out about my plan?

You cannot enforce your rights in your plan unless you know what those rights are. ERISA therefore includes detailed reporting and disclosure requirements.

Plan administrators—the people who run plans—must tell you the most important facts you need to know about your plan, in writing and free of charge. They must also let you look at plan documents and buy copies of them at reasonable cost if you ask.

What information am I entitled to?

A plan description (Form EBS–1) must be filed each year with the Department of Labor, giving information on what the plan provides and how it operates. In addition, the plan administrator must provide each plan participant or beneficiary with a "summary plan description," which must be written in a manner that can be understood by the average plan participant and that accurately and comprehensively advises participants and beneficiaries of their rights and obligations.

The description must include the names and addresses of the administrator and trustees of the plan. It must outline the requirements for participation, benefit accrual, and vesting, as well as conditions that will result in forfeiture of benefits. And it must include the procedure to be followed in presenting claims for benefits, and remedies available when claims are denied.

In addition, the plan administrators are required to file various reports with the Department of Labor. These include, in addition to copies of all documents that must be furnished to you, a plan description giving information on what the plan provides and how it operates; an annual report containing financial statements and schedules of the plan; and terminal plans for winding up their affairs.

The information that must be disclosed to participants and beneficiaries falls into four categories: (1) information that the administrator of the plan must furnish automatically; (2) information that must be furnished free within 30 days of written request; (3) information that must be furnished within 30 days of written request and payment of a reasonable charge; and (4) information that must be made available at the principal office of the administrator and other places. The information that must be supplied in each category is as follows:

1. The administrator must furnish automatically to each paticipant and to each beneficiary receiving benefits:

- the summary plan description, within 90 days after a person becomes a participant or beneficiary, or within 120 days after the plan was initiated;
- a summary of any change in the plan description or a summary of a material change in the terms of the plan, within 210 days after the end of the plan year in which the change is adopted;
- an updated summary plan description every five years integrating all amendments if there have been any; and, if no amendments have been adopted, another summary plan description every ten years;
- a summary of the annual report, within nine months after the end of the plan year;
- a statement of total benefits earned, and the percentage of such benefits that are vested, upon termination of employment or a one-year break in service;
- a statement upon termination of employment of the nature, form, and amount of deferred vested benefits;
- if a claim for benefits is denied, a written explanation;
- a written explanation before the annuity starting date of the terms and conditions of any joint and survivor annuity and the effect of electing against such an option.

2. The administrator must furnish to any pension plan participant or beneficiary, within 30 days of written request, a statement of total benefits accrued and whether those benefits are vested. If benefits have not yet vested, the statement must indicate the earliest date on which the accrued benefits will become vested. This statement need not be furnished more than once in a 12-month period.

3. The administrator must furnish to any participant or

beneficiary, within 30 days of written request and payment of a reasonable charge, the latest updated summary plan description; the plan description; the latest annual report; the documents under which the plan was established or is operated; and any terminal reports.

4. The administrator must make available to any participant or beneficiary at the principal office of the administrator and other places the plan description; the latest annual report; and the documents under which the plan was established or is operated, such as the collective bargaining agreement or trust agreement.

The Internal Revenue Service furnishes to the Social Security Administration information on deferred vested benefits of plan participants who have terminated employment during a plan year before retirement. The Social Security Administration keeps this information to provide to employees and their beneficiaries upon request, or automatically when they apply for Social Security benefits.

In addition to the foregoing, the public may inspect and copy all plan documents filed with the Department of Labor and many documents filed with the Treasury Department.

Am I automatically entitled to participate in the pension plan where I work?

No. You are a "participant" in a plan when you become a member of the plan. Before ERISA, pension plans often excluded large groups of employees, especially part-time employees, from participation. ERISA set certain minimum standards for participation. Now employees of a certain age who work a certain number of hours per year must be allowed to participate in the pension plan where they work. When you become eligible to participate in a pension plan, you begin to accumulate, or accrue, credits toward your pension.

Generally, you must be allowed to participate if you are at least 25 years old and have completed one year of service with the employer that sponsors the plan. If the plan provides full and immediate vesting (which will be discussed later), you must be allowed to participate if you are 25 and have at least three years of service. Once these minimum age and service requirements are met, participation must begin at the start of the next plan year or six months after meeting the requirements, whichever is earlier.

For purposes of participation and vesting (discussed below), a "year of service" is defined as a 12-month period that begins when you start work and during which you have at least 1000 hours of service.[2] Generally, "hours of service" include the hours you are actually on the job, plus other hours for which your employer is required to pay you (for example, vacation, holiday, disability, illness, layoff, jury duty, military leave, or leave of absence); but an employer need not credit more than 501 hours of service to you for any continuous period during which you did no work.[3]

Generally, you may not be excluded from participation because you are too old. If, however, your plan is a defined-benefit plan (that is, the amount you will receive upon retirement is set in advance), you can be barred from participation if you begin work within five years of the plan's normal retirement age.

These requirements are the minimum permitted by law. Your employer can have more generous rules, such as allowing you to participate as soon as you are hired.

What is benefit accrual?

Once you have satisfied the requirements for participation in a pension plan, you begin to accumulate or accrue credits that will determine the amount of your pension. Normally, the size of the pension is based largely on the number of years of service you have after becoming a participant in the plan. Under ERISA, if you have worked at least 1000 hours during a year, you must be credited as having accrued at least some benefits that year. An employer is permitted by ERISA to require you to work more than 1000 hours to obtain credit for a full year of accrued benefits, but credit for at least a partial year of accrued benefits must be given if you work at least 1000 hours.

The "accrued benefit" is the benefit that you have earned to a particular point in time.[4] Benefit accrual is the process of accumulating pension credits or, in the case of a defined contribution plan, accumulating funds in your individual pension account. Normally, you start accruing benefits as soon as you become a participant in a pension plan, though ERISA allows defined-benefit plans to delay the process of benefit accrual until you have worked two years in a row for the employer.

What is vesting?

Although you accrue retirement benefits while participating in a pension plan, you are not entitled to receive those benefits unless they are vested. Accruing benefits over long periods means little if you can lose those benefits. Before ERISA, an employee could work for decades, be fired one day before retirement, and forfeit all pension credits earned over the years. Through its vesting provisions, ERISA assures employees who work for a specified minimum period under a pension plan that they will receive at least some pension at retirement.[5]

Under ERISA, "vesting" has to do with when you acquire a legal right to receive your accrued benefits at retirement. Your accrued benefits are "vested" when you are given a non-forfeitable right to receive the benefits at retirement, even if you should leave your job before retirement age. Usually, if you leave your job before retirement, your accrued benefits based on employer contributions become vested only if you have worked for a specific period of time. Individuals employed under a pension plan at the time of "normal retirement" under the plan must be fully vested in their accrued benefits.[6] Accrued benefits derived from your own contributions are fully vested immediately.[7]

ERISA permits vested benefits derived from *employer* contributions to be contingent upon your living until retirement.[8] In other words, the plan may provide that your vested right to accrued benefits based on your employer's contributions ends if you die before retirement; this does not apply, however, if you are eligible for a joint and survivor annuity and a survivor annuity is in fact payable. Also, this condition does not apply to the accrued benefits derived from your own contributions, if any. These benefits must be payable to your beneficiary if a survivor annuity is not payable.[9]

Vesting is different from benefit accrual, as can be seen from the following example. Joe Smith began working for Ford Motor Company when he was 30 years old. After working at Ford full time for five years, he quit his job and went to work for General Motors. Because Joe worked more than 1000 hours per year while at Ford, and because he was over 25 years old when he went to work there, he was a participant in Ford's pension plan after his first year; and he has four years of accrued pension benefits. Nevertheless he may never receive these benefits; as discussed below, a company could require an employee to be employed for ten years before his benefits vest. An employee who leaves before his benefits vest will never receive them. On the other hand, if Joe stayed at Ford for ten years, at least some of his benefits would vest; he would receive them even though he quit working at Ford long before retirement age.

How does vesting work?

As previously mentioned, a pension plan must provide full and immediate vesting of benefits derived from your contributions, if any. Employer contributions must vest at least as fast as required by one of the following three schedules:

- cliff vesting: full (100 percent) vesting after 10 years of service (with no vesting prior to completion of 10 years of service);[10]
- graded vesting (5 to 15 years): 25 percent vesting after 5 years of service, plus 5 percent for each additional year of service up to 10 years (50 percent vesting after 10 years), plus an additional 10 percent for each year thereafter (100 percent vesting after 15 years of service);[11]
- "rule of 45" (based on age and service): 50 percent vesting for an employee with at least 5 years of service when his age and years of service add up to 45, plus 10 percent for each year thereafter.[12]

Under each of these schedules, you must be at least 50 percent vested after 10 years of service and 100 percent vested after 15 years, regardless of age. "Class-year" plans (profit-sharing, stock bonus, and money purchase plans in which each year's contributions vest separately) must provide for 100 percent vesting not later than the end of the fifth plan year following the year for which the contributions are made. Keogh plans (discussed later) must vest 100 percent immediately.

For vesting purposes, the definition of a year of service is basically the same as for participation purposes. The general rule is that all years of service in which at least 1000 hours are worked are to be counted. As a result, plans may no longer disregard long periods of service because short breaks have occurred, but must recognize the aggregate of all years of service. There are some exceptions, however, and it is important to note that years of service before the enactment of ERISA may not count.

Cliff Vesting

The ten-year, 100 percent vesting schedule is the one most employers use. Under this schedule, the plan must provide a 100 percent vested pension at retirement to an employee who has at least 10 years of service. In other words, under this schedule if you quit after 9 years, you will receive no pension. But if you quit after 10 years, you will receive a pension based on your 9 years of service as a plan participant. If the plan is a defined-benefit plan paying $5 per month for each year of service, at retirement you will receive a pension of $45 per month. If you continue working for your employer after 10 years, you will have a vested right to receive a pension based on all the years you participated in your employer's plan. So if you work an additional 10 years, your pension will be $95 per month.

Note that you would receive a pension of $45 (not $50) after 10 years and $95 (rather than $100) after 20 years. This is because all years of service are counted for vesting purposes, but only years of participation are counted for benefit accrual purposes, that is, for determining the amount of benefits that will be paid. Since you normally will not be a plan participant until you have worked for a year, years of participation will differ from years of service.

The ten-year, 100 percent vesting option provides the employee who works ten full years greater protection than other minimum standards, since the employee will be fully vested at the end of 10 years of service. Considering that the average employee covered by a private pension plan has been on the job less than 10 years, vesting that does not begin until 10 years of service offers little or no protection for large numbers of employees.

Graded Vesting

Under graded vesting, at least 25 percent of your accrued benefits from employer contributions must be vested after 5 years of service. An additional 5 percent must be vested for each of the next 5 years of service; and another 10 percent must be vested for each year of the third 5-year period. At 15 years, you are fully vested. The operation of this schedule can be seen from the following table:

Nonforfeitable Years of Service	("Vested") percentage
5	25
6	30
7	35
8	40
9	45
10	50
11	60
12	70
13	80
14	90
15 or more	100

To illustrate the way graded vesting works, assume that you work for a company with a defined-benefit plan paying $5 per month at retirement for each year of service. If you worked for 15 years, your pension would be fully vested and you would receive $70 per month at retirement (100 percent × $5 × 14 years). If you left after only 5 years, you would receive a pension at retirement (whereas under 10-year, 100 percent vesting you would not), but your pension would be only 25 percent vested and would be only $5 per month (25 percent × $5 × 4 years). (Again remember that the first year of service is counted for vesting but not for accrual purposes.)

The benefits of the graded option are that it guarantees employees at least partial vested rights after only 5 years of service and that it promises to increase substantially the number of employees with vested rights. On the other hand, the protection afforded participants by graded vesting is questionable for an employee who changes jobs often, because the total benefits received may be very small.

Rule of 45 Vesting

Under the "rule of 45," an employee with 5 years of service must be at least 50 percent vested when the sum of his age and years of service totals 45. For each additional year, the employee's vested percentage is increased by 10 percent so that, not later than 5 years after meeting the threshold "45" requirement, the participant is 100 percent vested. The option further provides that the participant who has completed at least 10 years of service regardless of age must be 50 percent vested in accrued benefits at the end of the 10 years and must be vested in an additional 10 percent for each of the next 5 years of service. The following table may clarify the way this schedule works:

If years of service equal or exceed	And age + service equals or exceeds	Or if years of service regardless of age equal	Then the non-forfeitable percentage is
5	45	10	50
6	47	11	60
7	49	12	70
8	51	13	80
9	53	14	90
10	55	15	100

An example also may help. You begin work at age 32 and become a participant at 33. At 39, you become 50 percent vested in accrued benefits because the sum of age (39) and years of service (7) equals or exceeds 45; at age 44, you are 100 percent vested. If the plan is a defined-benefit plan paying $5 per month at retirement for each year of service, you would receive a pension at retirement of $55 per month (100 percent × $5 × 11 years) if you quit when you were 44 after working 12 years. If you quit at 39 after 7 years of work, you would receive a pension at retirement of $15 per month (50 percent × $5 × 6 years).

This schedule has some disadvantages. Because age is directly related to plan costs under the "rule of 45," this rule may encourage the employer to consider age when hiring. The optimum plan entry age from the employee's perspective is age 35 or older, because the employee will be 50 percent vested after only 5 years of service. From the employer's standpoint, however, the optimum age is 26 and below, because members of this age group need a full 10 years of service to become 50 percent vested.

What is a break in service?

A break in service can have serious consequences for your pension. Before ERISA it was not uncommon for a participant to lose all pension credits earned because of an absence from work. This can still happen, but the circumstances under which it can happen are somewhat more limited. ERISA has laid down rules governing what constitutes a break in service and the effect of such a break on benefit accrual and vesting.

Most pension plans have break-in-service rules. Those that do may have more liberal rules than ERISA requires as a minimum standard, but they may not be more strict.

ERISA requires your employer to at least partly credit you with benefits accrued during each year in which you work more than 1000 hours. If you work between 500 and 1000 hours during a year, the employer need not give you credit for accruing benefits, but the employer cannot declare that a break in service has occurred. Only if you have worked 500 or fewer hours during the year can your employer declare that a break in service has occurred, thus potentially affecting credit for benefits accrued in past years.

ERISA also protects you by limiting the adverse effects of a break in service. It does this by requiring that pension plans give employees credit for years of work before a break in service in most situations. The effect of a break in service depends on (1) the type of plan, (2) the vesting status of your accrued benefits, and (3) the number of years of break compared with the number of years of service counted for purposes of vesting before the break. In any event, a plan can require that you complete a year of service before taking into account years of service before the break.

If your benefits earned before the break are *fully vested*, the pre- and post-break service must be added for all purposes. For *non-vested* and *partly vested* benefits, the rules on vesting vary, depending on the type of plan and the length of the break.

ERISA does not permit defined-benefit plans (other than those funded solely by insurance contracts) to provide that employees with totally non-vested benefits who incur a break in service lose credits for pre-break service until the number of years of break equals the number of years of the pre-break service. Participants in such plans who have any percentage of vesting must have their pre- and post-break service added for all purposes, regardless of the number of years of break.

The rules are more complicated and less generous for participants in defined-contribution plans and plans funded solely by individual insurance contracts. If you participate in one of these plans, it is very important that you understand the rules. ERISA permits those plans to provide that if you have a break in service the vesting percentage in benefits earned before the break is not increased as a result of post-break service. In other words, such plans may provide that non-vested accrued benefits are permanently forfeited upon a break in service. (And, remember, you can incur a break in service without terminating your employment.)

If the benefits are totally *non-vested* and the number of years of your break equals or exceeds the number of years of the pre-break service that are counted toward vesting, your pre- and post-break service need not be added; in such cases, pre-break service may be disregarded even for purposes of vesting the post-break benefit accrual.

This is confusing, so an illustration may help. Say you participate in a defined-contribution plan that vests accrued benefits 100 percent after ten years, with no vesting before ten years. If you incur a break in service after eight years of credit toward vesting, you are totally non-vested and the plan may provide that you forfeit all the benefits you earned (your account balance) during those eight years. If you later return (within seven years) and work for two years (ten years total service), the plan must count your pre-break service toward the vesting of the benefits you earned after your return to employment under the plan, but it may provide that you forfeit all the benefits you earned during the eight years before the break. In this case, two years after your return to employment under the plan, you would be 100 percent vested in only the benefits you earned during the two years after your return. If you return eight or more years after the break, your pre- and post-break service need not be added because your number of years of break equaled or exceeded your pre-break service credited for vesting.

In the case of *partly vested* benefits in defined contribution plans and plans funded solely by individual insurance contracts, if you incur a break in service and then return to employment covered by the plan, the plan is permitted to provide that the pre- and post-break service are added only for the purpose of vesting benefits accrued after the return to employment. The result is that those partly vested benefits earned before the break remain frozen at that partial vesting. To illustrate: A defined contribution plan may provide that a participant who has accrued $1000 of benefits and is 25 percent vested in that accrued benefit ($250) before a break in service forfeits the non-vested portion ($750) upon the break. Upon a return to employment under the plan, the benefits accrued before the break remain frozen at that vesting level ($250), though the pre-break service will count toward the vesting of benefits earned after the return to employment under the plan.

Inasmuch as a break in service can have very serious consequences, you should carefully examine your plan's "hour of service," "year of service," and "break in service" rules so that you do not inadvertently and unnecessarily forfeit pension benefits you've earned. Remember, these are minimum standards only. Plans can be more liberal and generous, and some are.

Will years of service accumulate while working for one employer be lost if the business is acquired by a new employer?

No. ERISA requires that all years of service with the "employer or employers maintaining the plan" must be counted. Thus, when a new employer continues an old plan—in the case of a merger, for example—years of service from the previous employer's period of control must be counted.

When do pension payments begin?

If you are a participant in a pension plan, payment of your benefits must begin (unless you elect a later date) as of the sixtieth day after the close of the plan year in which the *latest* of the following events occurs:[13] (1) you reach age 65 or you reach the normal retirement age specified under your plan, if it is earlier than 65; (2) you complete ten years of participation in the plan; and (3) you terminate your service with the employer.

If your plan permits you to elect early retirement after a stated age, or number of years of service, or combination of age and service, then you are entitled to receive your vested benefits (reduced to an actuarial equivalent) after you reach the early retirement age.[14]

How do I file a claim to receive a pension?

ERISA requires that all plan participants be given a plan summary that explains the procedure to be followed by anyone filing a claim. ERISA also requires that an appeal procedure be established, including the following provisions:[15]

1. The plan must entitle you to written notice of the decision on your claim for benefits.

2. If your claim is denied, the specific reasons for the denial must be stated.

3. This decision must be made within a reasonable time. If no decision is reached within a reasonable time, your claim will be treated as if denied, and you can proceed to appeal.

4. Appeals under ERISA are to be in writing.

5. You have 60 days, from notice that your claim was denied, in which to file your appeal.

6. A decision is to be reached on your appeal within 60 days of the time your appeal request was received, and you are entitled to written notice of the decision on your appeal.

7. To assist your appeal, ERISA requires that plan administrators allow you to review important pension documents affecting your claim for benefits and to allow you to submit written material in support of your appeal.

The courts have held that you must exhaust your administrative remedies—that is, the appeal procedures before the plan administrators—before you can start a lawsuit for pension benefits. Those internal remedies can be skipped only if it would be futile to resort to them or if you have been wrongfully denied meaningful access to them.[16]

Can my creditors get to my pension benefits?

No. Pension plans must provide that benefits under the plan may not be assigned or transferred. You may make a *voluntary revocable* assignment of up to 10 percent of any benefits you are receiving, but a garnishment or levy is not considered a voluntary assignment. You may use vested benefits as collateral for reasonable loans from the plan, as long as fiduciary provisions of the plan are not violated.

Can I continue to receive my pension if I go back to work after retirement?

Generally, yes. You will not lose vested pension rights if you go back to work. But your pension plan may provide that, if you return to work for your employer, your benefit payments attributable to your employer's contributions can be suspended for the period of your reemployment. Similarly, if you retired under a multi-employer plan, benefit payments can be suspended during the period you are employed in the same industry, trade, craft, or geographical area.[17]

Can I receive both Social Security and a pension?

Yes, but some pension plans, called integrated plans, provide that pension benefits will be reduced if a recipient of pension benefits is also entitled to receive Social Security benefits. ERISA permits this, but forbids a pension plan from reducing pension benefits because of cost-of-living increases in Social Security.[18]

Do I lose my pension if my plan terminates?

Not necessarily. Both ERISA [19] and the Internal Revenue Code[20] provide some protections when a plan terminates.

Before ERISA, many workers lost their pensions because an employer went out of business or decided to discontinue its pension plan. Although ERISA does not require that an employer have a pension plan or that it continue to operate a plan already established, it does provide partial protection for employees whose pension plan is terminated. The principal protection offered by ERISA is an insurance program that guarantees the payment of some pension benefits to certain retirees if their pension plan is terminated.

The program works as follows. A Pension Benefit Guaranty Corporation (PBGC) was established by ERISA, and defined-benefit pension plans are required to pay insurance premiums to PBGC. In return for these premiums, PBGC guarantees that participants of defined-benefit plans will be paid at least some of their pension benefits if their plan folds or is terminated.[21]

Note, however, that the protection offered by this scheme is partial. Only participants in defined-benefit plans are protected by PBGC insurance. (If your plan is a defined-contribution plan, your vested interest is protected by your individual account in the pension trust.) Moreover, only vested benefits are guaranteed. Thus, participants in a defined-benefit plan whose benefits had not vested when the plan terminated are not protected. And even those with vested benefits are not guaranteed that they will receive all of their benefits. The PBGC guarantees payment of retirement benefits only up to certain limits set by law. Moreover, many pension plans pay death, medical, and disability benefits in addition to normal retirement benefits. PBGC guarantees only basic retirement benefits, so you may lose some of your benefits if your plan is terminated.

ERISA also protects employees against the termination of

their pension plan by stiffening the funding requirements for pension plans. Few pension plans have enough money on hand to pay all vested benefits. That is why the insurance/ guaranty provisions just discussed were enacted. These provisions are supplemented by requirements that employers contribute more money to pension plans, so there will be more funds available to pay beneficiaries in case the plan is terminated.

In addition to ERISA, the Internal Revenue Code provides that, upon complete or partial termination of any tax-qualified retirement plan, all accrued benefits are fully and immediately vested, to the extent then funded.[24] The benefits earned by the employees, whether or not vested, become vested by virtue of the termination. The assets are distributed to retirees and plan participants in an order of priority established by ERISA. If there are sufficient assets to pay all the earned benefits, they will be paid, because all accrued (earned) benefits became "vested" at termination. Those accrued benefits that became vested only by virtue of the plan termination are not, however, insured by the PBGC; if the plan does not have sufficient assets, some benefits will not be paid.

What happens to my vested benefits if I leave my job before retirement?

ERISA allows the plan to pay a lump sum for the entire amount of your vested benefits, even without your consent, if only a relatively small amount is involved (no more than $1750).[23] A higher "cashout" can be made with your consent if you leave employment under the plan.

You should realize that all or part of such a lump-sum distribution may be subject to income tax. You can deduct from the taxable distribution any contributions you made to the plan; and if part of the distribution is in the form of company securities, you can deduct any unrealized appreciation in the value of the securities.[24] The rest of the distribution is taxable.

You can avoid current taxes, however, by depositing the funds into an Individual Retirement Account (IRA), even if you are not otherwise eligible for an IRA. This "rollover" IRA must be set up within 60 days after you receive the distribution. (IRAs are discussed in greater detail later in this chapter.) You can also avoid current taxes on a lump-sum distribution by transferring the funds directly to your new employer's pension plan if the plan is "tax-qualified" and the plan permits the transfer. In addition, if you put funds into a rollover IRA, you can later transfer those funds into your new employer's plan if the plan is tax-qualified and the plan permits it.

Can my spouse continue to receive pension benefits after my death?

Yes, unless you elect otherwise.

Before ERISA, many plans had no provisions for continuing any part of the retiree's pension to the surviving spouse after the retiree's death. Other plans did allow a retiree to provide the surviving spouse with a portion of the retiree's pension if the retiree elected to have the amount of his (or her) pension benefit reduced. This is called a joint-and-survivor annuity.

Often, however, the employee neglected to sign the papers needed to provide the joint-and-survivor annuity for the surviving spouse. Under ERISA, a joint-and-survivor annuity automatically goes into effect when you retire or reach the normal retirement age, unless you specifically reject it in writing. If you do nothing, your spouse gets a survivor's benefit upon your death; if you reject the survivorship option in writing, your surviving spouse gets nothing upon your death. This survivor's benefit might not be payable, however, if you and your surviving spouse were married less than a year at the time of death.

The foregoing statements assume that you were retired, or had reached normal retirement age, at the time of death. If you die before retirement, your plan *may* require that your surviving spouse will receive an "early survivor annuity" only if the following three conditions are met: (1) your plan allows early retirement; (2) you reached the early retirement age, or ten years before the plan's normal retirement age, whichever is later; and (3) you signed a form agreeing to a reduced early retirement pension benefit in order to provide an early survivor annuity if you died before retirement. Under nearly all plans, your spouse will receive no survivor's benefits if you die before age 55.

Generally, the amount of your monthly pension benefit will be reduced if a survivor annuity is provided for your spouse. The amount of the reduction depends on the plan provisions and the difference in ages between you and your spouse. The survivor annuity must be at least half of the amount of the joint annuity that is payable to you and your spouse while you are both living. For example, if you would receive $200 a month without providing the survivor annuity, you might receive $160 a month under a joint-and-survivor annuity, and your spouse might receive $80 a month after your death.

ERISA does not require (though it does allow) pension plans to obtain approval of your spouse before you can reject the joint-and-survivor option or to notify your spouse that you rejected that option. ERISA prohibits plans from terminating or reducing payments to your surviving spouse due to remarriage. Plans may not limit payment of the survivor annuity to surviving female spouses, nor may plans condition payments on whether the surviving spouse was dependent for support on the employee.

Some pension plans provide life insurance protection so that if you die before reaching the normal retirement age, your spouse (or other beneficiary) will receive not only your vested accrued benefits under the plan but also life insurance proceeds.

If I get divorced, does my spouse have a right to share in my pension benefits?

Maybe. The courts have been split on this issue, but the trend seems to favor allowing one spouse to claim an interest in pension or retirement benefits of the other.[25] A major factor in determining whether benefits will be divided is whether the divorce action arises in a community property state or a common-law property state. Community property states consider all property accumulated by the spouses after the time of marriage to belong to both spouses. There are nine community property jurisdictions[26] and they tend to be more liberal in awarding benefits to the spouse as jointly owned and earned property.[27] Fewer common-law jurisdictions have awarded the spouse an interest in a pension or retirement fund; these are typically states that provide for "equitable distribution" of property in a divorce.[28]

Another major factor considered by the court is whether the pension has vested at the time of the divorce proceedings. If the pension has vested, the problem is simplified, because the court will recognize the pension as property. If it is not vested, there is a problem, because courts traditionally do not consider pension benefits that have not vested as definable property that can be divided.[29]

Can a pension plan discriminate on the basis of sex?

No. The federal courts have consistently held that Title VII of the Civil Rights Act of 1964 applies to retirement funds.[30] The relevant provisions of Title VII[31] make it an unlawful employment practice for an employer to discriminate against an employee on the basis of sex.

It is well known that, on the average, women outlive men. As a result of this, the average female employee will be eligible for pension benefits for more years than her male counterpart. Because of this disparity, some employers established retirement funds that distinguished between male and female employee beneficiaries, either paying the women smaller monthly pension benefits or making women contribute more to the pension fund during their working years. The United States Supreme Court ruled that these differences are illegal under Title VII.[32]

Title VII has also affected pension plans in which the employer has different retirement ages for men and women. In one case[33] a woman could retire at age 60 with full pension benefits if she had worked 20 years, while a man could not retire with full benefits until he was 65 and had worked a minimum of 25 years. The court found that the pension plan violated Title VII because it differentiated between men and women solely on the basis of sex.

Can I be forced to retire at age 65?

Generally, no. Under the federal Age Discrimination in Employment Act,[34] as amended in 1978, you generally cannot be forced to retire until age 70. The main exceptions are (1) an employee working for an employer with fewer than 20 employees; and (2) an employee who for the two years before employment was employed in an executive or policy-making position, and who is entitled to an annual benefit of at least $27,000 (exclusive of Social Security) from the employer's pension plan. A few states, including Alaska, California, Connecticut, Montana, and North Carolina, prohibit mandatory retirement at *any* age in private employment. For more discussion of mandatory retirement and other age discrimination issues, see Chapter 9.

What standards of conduct govern the investment of pension plan assets?

Before ERISA, a major problem faced by participants and beneficiaries of pension plans was the irresponsible way in which the assets of the plans were managed. Pension plan trustees, managers, and others sometimes used fund assets for their own benefit, and sometimes invested fund assets in real estate deals and high-risk schemes that went broke.

Under ERISA, plan trustees and others who exercise control over the management of a plan or the disposition of its assets or who render investment advice for a fee are required to discharge their duties solely in the interest of plan participants and beneficiaries. They are also required to use care, skill, and prudence in managing the plan's assets, and they must minimize the risk of losses to the fund by diversifying their investment of fund assets.[35]

ERISA also prohibits these persons from engaging in a wide range of practices harmful to the fund, such as lending the fund's money to friends, borrowing money from the fund for their personal use, selling their own property to the fund, and buying property from the fund. In addition, a plan may not have more than 10 percent of the fair market value of its assets invested in the employer's stock or real property.[36]

Can I sue plan administrators for violation of ERISA?

Yes. ERISA substantially strengthens the ability of plan participants, beneficiaries, and the government to sue persons operating pension plans. Under ERISA, participants and beneficiaries may bring lawsuits against plans and those who manage them to enforce rights created by ERISA and by their pension plan.[37] The actions available include the following:

1. Participants and beneficiaries may sue plan administrators who don't comply with proper requests for information, such as a request for plan documents or for a statement of vested benefits upon termination. Administrators may be personally liable to the participant or beneficiary for up to $100 per day from the date of the failure or refusal. Any person who fails to furnish information or to maintain records in accordance with the requirements of the law may be liable for a civil penalty of $10 for each employee with respect to whom the failure occurs. And there may be criminal liability for willful violations of disclosure requirements.

2. Participants and beneficiaries may sue to recover bene-

fits due, to enforce existing rights, or to clarify rights to future benefits under the terms of the plan.

3. Suit may be brought against persons who have any discretionary control over the management of a plan for breach of their duties under ERISA and the plan. These people will be personally liable for restoration of any losses that result from a breach of their duties.

4. Participants may sue to prevent any act that violates any provision of the new law or to enforce any provision of the law or the plan.

5. Participants also may ask the Secretary of Labor to exercise his authority to enforce the participation, vesting, or funding provisions of ERISA. And the Secretary also may sue to prevent improper practices or to enforce ERISA or plan provisions.

6. Under ERISA, courts may allow reasonable attorneys' fees and costs of the action to either party. This provision may encourage plan participants to bring lawsuits to vindicate their rights by making it economically possible to obtain a lawyer to bring these suits. But if you bring a frivolous suit, you may be required to pay your opponent's legal fees.

Can I establish my own pension plan?

Yes, and you probably should. You can establish an individual retirement account (IRA) to save money for your retirement. As explained below, you can take a tax deduction for the amount you deposit into an IRA (within certain limits), and the income earned in an IRA is not taxed until you retire. Under the Economic Recovery Tax Act of 1981 (ERTA),[38] you can establish an IRA even if you are already covered by a pension plan where you work.

How does an IRA work?

Each year you can put up to $2000 of your earned income (wages, salaries, and professional fees, but not dividends or interest) into an IRA. If your spouse is employed, he or she can set up an IRA too, subject to the same limits.

If your spouse is not employed, you can contribute to a "spousal IRA" on behalf of your spouse. Separate accounts will be established for you and your spouse. You cannot deposit more than $2250 per year into your IRA and the spousal IRA combined; but you can divide the contributions to the two accounts any way you want, so long as no more than $2000 is put into either account in a year.

You can deduct contributions to an IRA from your gross income on your income tax return so that you get the benefit of the tax deduction whether or not you itemize deductions. In addition, the income earned on your IRA is not taxed currently. It accumulates tax free until you begin taking the money out of the IRA upon retirement or disability. Thus you can defer taxes not only on your contributions but also on all earnings and gains in the account until you start withdrawals. Upon retirement or disability you may be in a lower tax bracket, and you may be able to use the retirement income tax credit and to take a double personal exemption (at age 65). To qualify for the IRA tax deduction you must establish your plan and make your contribution by the federal tax filing date (usually April 15 of the next year), or by any extended due date. Of course, the sooner you make your contribution, the sooner your funds start accumulating on a tax-deferred basis.

You do not have to contribute to your IRA every year—you can stop and start your contributions. And your contributions need not be in single large payments—you can make many payments during the year; in fact, many employers have payroll deduction plans for IRA contributions.

You can begin making withdrawals from your IRA without penalty when you reach 59½ years of age, and you must begin withdrawals when you reach 70½. Also, you can begin withdrawals before 59½ if you become disabled. If you withdraw any funds before 59½ or disability, you will be charged a 10 percent penalty tax, as well as the regular income tax on the amount withdrawn. You cannot borrow from your IRA or use it as collateral for a loan; if you do, not only will you suffer the tax penalty, but your IRA will be disqualified.

To open an IRA you must have a qualified custodian or trustee—such as a bank, broker, or other financial institution—to manage the account. In all other respects, you control the money in your IRA. You can choose among many savings and investment strategies. You can put the money into bank accounts, bank certificates, money market funds, mutual funds, bonds, common stocks, and even real estate (except your home). You can buy an annuity from an insurance company.

For more information about IRAs you can contact the Internal Revenue Service, or practically any bank, broker, or other financial institution.

Can my employer sponsor an IRA for me?

Yes. There are several ways your employer can sponsor an IRA for you.

1. Your employer can set up a group IRA plan. This may include some employees and exclude others. Your employer's contribution is limited to the lesser of 100 percent or $2000 of your annual pay. If your employer contributes less than the maximum allowed, you can contribute the difference. You are allowed to deduct both your contributions and your employer's contributions on your income tax return.

2. Your employer can set up a Simplified Employee Pension (SEP) plan. Under an SEP your employer can make much larger contributions—up to the lesser of 15 percent or $15,000 of your annual pay. An SEP differs from a group IRA in that an SEP plan must cover *all* employees over the age of 25 who have performed services for the employer during any three of the five calendar years immediately preceding the contribution and who earn at least $200 in the year of contribution. An SEP plan can be set up even when your employer has another pension or profit-sharing plan. Under an SEP, your employer must contribute at least the same percentage of your salary as the employer contributes out of earnings for himself or herself. Your employer must contribute at least 7.5 percent of your pay if, in determining his or her personal SEP contribution, your employer uses income above $100,000. Contributions can be based on the first $200,000 in annual pay.

3. Your employer may be able to set up a Keogh plan. These are limited to self-employed individuals, partnerships, unincorporated companies, and their employees. Keoghs are subject to strict requirements to protect employees of the self-employed, including the requirement that all eligible employees be covered.

You can set up a separate IRA even though you are participating in an SEP or Keogh plan, but not if you are participating in a group IRA. Under both SEPs and Group IRAs you own all the funds contributed in your name immediately—there is no vesting period. Even if you are fired the day after a contribution was made, the money is yours.

NOTES

1. A money purchase plan operates on contributions from your employer based on your earnings. Your employer must contribute to
the plan even if it shows no profit for the year. Upon retirement, you
receive the amount of money contributed to your account.

   In a profit-sharing plan your employer makes contributions only
out of profits. You receive your benefits at retirement, after a specified number of years, or upon the occurrence of a specific event.
Your employer can establish either a discretionary contribution formula or a fixed formula. Under a discretionary plan, your employer
is under no obligation to make contributions no matter how high his
annual profits; under a fixed formula, the employer must contribute
if the profits exceed a certain level.

   A cash or deferred profit-sharing plan is one in which you have the
option either to receive employer contributions in cash or to have
them contributed to a qualified profit-sharing or stock bonus plan.

   A stock bonus plan pays benefits with stock in the company. While
the employer has the option to distribute cash instead of stock, you
have the right to demand a distribution of employer securities. 26
U.S.C. §401 (a) (23).

   An employee stock ownership plan (ESOP) is a qualified plan
whose funds are invested in company stock. The employer contributes into the fund on the basis of your earnings. The funds are held
in trust for you, and vested benefits are distributed upon separation
or retirement. Benefit payments can be made in the form of stock or,
upon demand, in cash.

2. In a seasonal industry in which the customary period of employment
is less than 1000 hours in a calendar year, the Secretary of Labor sets
the time needed to qualify as a year of service. In the maritime
industry, 125 days constitute a year of service.

3. 26 U.S.C. §410(a) (3) (C).

4. 29 U.S.C. §1002(23).

5. 29 U.S.C. §§1053 *et seq*.

6. 29 U.S.C. §1053(a).

7. 29 U.S.C. §1053(a) (1).

8. 29 U.S.C. §1053(a) (3) (A).

9. 26 U.S.C. §401(d) (7).

10. 29 U.S.C. §1053(a) (2) (A).

11. 29 U.S.C. §1053(a) (2) (B).

12. 29 U.S.C. §1053(a) (2) (C) (i).

13. 29 U.S.C. §1056(a).

14. *Id*.

15. 29 U.S.C. §1133; 29 C.F.R. §2560.

16. *Amato v. Bernard*, 618 F.2d 559 (9th Cir. 1980); *Weeks v. Coca-Cola
Bottling Co. of Ark.*, 491 F. Supp. 1312 (E.D. Ark. 1980).

17. 26 U.S.C. §411(a) (3) (B); 29 C.F.R. §2530.203–3(b) (1).

18. 29 U.S.C. §1056(b); 26 U.S.C. §401(a) (15).

19. 29 U.S.C. §§1301 *et seq.*

20. 26 U.S.C. §§402 *et seq.*

21. For further information on plan termination insurance, you may get in touch with PBGC, 2020 K St., NW, Washington, DC 20006, Attention: Office of Communications; (202) 254–4817, for the "PBGC Fact Sheet."

22. A plan may be considered partly terminated if a corporation terminates all employees of a particular plan or division. In cases of this type, the benefits earned by that group of employees must be separated from the rest of the plan, to the extent of the plan assets attributable to their participation.

23. 29 U.S.C. §1054(d) (1).

24. 26 U.S.C. §402(e) (4) (D).

25. Foster & Freed, Spousal Rights in Retirement and Pension Benefits, 16 J. Family Law §187 (1977–78).

26. Ariz., Calif., Ida., La., Nev., N.M., P.R., Tex., and Wash.

27. *In re Marriage of Fitman,* 10 Cal. 3d 349, 530 P.2d 589, 118 Cal. Rptr. 621 (1975); *Guy v. Guy,* 98 Idaho 205, 560 P.2d 876 (1977); *Swope v. Mitchell,* 324 S.2d 461 (La. App. 1975); *Otto v. Otto,* 80 N.M. 331, 455 P.2d 642 (1969); *Cearley v. Cearley,* 544 S.W.2d 661 (Tex. 1976); *Payne v. Payne,* 82 Wash.2d 573, 512 P.2d 736 (1973).

28. *Pinkowski v. Pinkowski,* 67 Wis.2d 176, 226 N.W.2d 518 (1975); *Pellegrino v. Pellegrino,* 134 N.J. Super. 512, 342 A.2d 226 (1975); *Howard v. Howard,* 196 Neb. 351, 242 N.W.2d 884 (1976); *In re Marriage of Power,* 527 S.W.2d 949 (Mo. Ct. Rep. 1975); *Arnow v. Arnow,* 3 Fam. L. Rep. 2364 (Fla. 1977); *In re Ellis Marriage,* 538 P.2d 1347 (Colo Ct.App. 1975).

29. *In re Marriage of Brown,* 15 Cal.3d 838, 544 P.2d 561, 126 Cal. Rptr. 633 (1976); *Cearley v. Cearley,* 544 S.W.2d 661 (Tex. 1976).

30. *Burtmess v. Drewrys, U.S.A., Inc.,* 444 F.2d 1186 (7th Cir.), *cert. denied,* 404 U.S. 939 (1971).

31. 42 U.S.C. §2000e(2)(a)(1).

32. *Los Angeles Dep't of Water & Power v. Manhart,* 435 U.S. 702 (1978).

33. *Rosen v. Public Service Electric & Gas Co.,* 477 F.2d 90 (3d Cir. 1973).

34. 29 U.S.C. §§621 *et seq.*

35. 29 U.S.C. §1104(a) (B).

36. 29 U.S.C. §§1106, 1107.

37. 29 U.S.C. §1132; *see also* 29 U.S.C. §§1059(b), 1109(a), and 1131. Your right to sue pension plan administrators under the Labor-Management Relations Act (§301 and 302) have largely been eclipsed by ERISA, but you may still wish to sue under the LMRA. *See, e.g., Leonardis v. Local 282 Pension Trust Fund,* 391 F. Supp. 554 (E.D.N.Y. 1975).

38. 26 U.S.C. §408.

XVII

Workers' Compensation

Workers' compensation* is a general term for a form of income insurance that compensates workers and their families for wages lost and medical expenses incurred due to injury, disease, or death arising out of and in the course of employment. Every state has a workers' compensation statute. Although the statutes differ in many important respects, they have many similar features, such as standard benefits based on a percentage of lost wages and payment of benefits without regard to whether the employer was at fault.

This chapter gives a broad overview of the usual features of workers' compensation statutes, while highlighting some of the significant differences.[1] No attempt is made to describe the law of any particular state. Instead, you can consult the chart in Appendix 7 of this book, which sets forth some significant provisions of each state's statute. The chart is for illustrative purposes only, and you should not rely on the specific information in it; these statutes contain many details and exceptions, and they are frequently changed to keep up with economic developments and the cost of living.

What is the purpose of workers' compensation?

The main purpose is to provide certain and expeditious financial assistance to workers who lose wages due to injury on the job. In theory, the injured worker receives adequate assistance, but in practice the benefits are often meager.

Before workers' compensation laws were adopted, workers injured on the job had little recourse. Every year thousands

---

*The phrase "workers' compensation," which has been adopted recently by some states, is used in this book rather than the traditional phrase "workmen's compensation."

of workers were injured or killed in industrial accidents without receiving any compensation. The common-law system then in effect was often inequitable and was always uncertain, expensive, and time-consuming. The injured worker could recover damages from his employer only if he could prove that the employer had been negligent or at fault and that the worker's injury was the direct result of that conduct. When neither the employer nor the worker was at fault, or when the worker was at fault, the worker could recover nothing. Furthermore, the employer who was at fault could often avoid liability if the worker or a fellow worker were contributorily negligent. Sometimes the worker was denied compensation because he was deemed to have assumed the risk of being injured on the job. Even if the injured worker could prove that the injury was caused solely by the employer's fault, he usually had to sue his employer to recover damages. Expensive and time-consuming litigation was undesirable for both the worker and the employer, and generally provided inadequate relief for the worker, especially after attorneys' fees and court costs were paid.

As a result of these and other factors, injured workers seldom received significant compensation for lost wages and frequently became public charges. The burden of providing for those who could not care for themselves because of work-related injuries fell primarily on the worker and his family, and on society in general. Under workers' compensation, part of the burden is shifted to the employer, which can pass along the cost to its customers.

Between 1910 and 1921 almost every state adopted a workers' compensation statute to remedy many of the problems with the common-law system; as of 1963 every state had adopted such a statute. As a form of economic insurance, workers' compensation guarantees that every worker who is injured on the job promptly receives a weekly income, based on past earnings, to help replace the wages lost due to the injury or disease.

Are all workers covered by workers' compensation?

No. In some states (Colorado, Louisiana, New Jersey, Pennsylvania, South Carolina, and Texas), workers' compensation coverage is elective. Even in states in which coverage is compulsory, it may apply only to certain employers or industries.

Under compulsory coverage, all workers are automatically covered unless they are specifically exempted. Compulsory coverage often applies only to workers whose employers have more than a specified number of workers, and sometimes applies only to workers in specified jobs (such as hazardous or dangerous jobs). Also, certain workers—such as household and domestic servants, agricultural laborers, and casual employees—are typically excluded from compulsory coverage. Workers for charitable organizations are also often excluded.

Under elective coverage, the employer (and sometimes the employee) must elect coverage, unless the job is specifically included. Generally, an employer may elect to cover an employee (such as a household servant or agricultural laborer) who is exempt from compulsory coverage. To elect coverage, an employer generally must do certain acts in a prescribed manner to make the election effective. For example, the electing employer usually must give notice of election to the employee.

Whether compulsory or elective, only employees are covered; a bona fide employer-employee relationship must exist. An independent contractor is not covered. Usually a partner or volunteer is not covered. In some states, a corporate officer, director, or shareholder who has complete control and supervision of his job is not covered.

Almost every state has a statutory provision providing that for workers' compensation purposes a general contractor is considered the employer of employees of its subcontractors and is thereby liable for compensation benefits to injured employees of the subcontractor. Such "statutory employer" provisions protect employees of subcontractors that are uninsured (as where the subcontractor has less than the required number of employees or has failed to obtain the required coverage). Usually a general contractor becomes the statutory employer only if the work being done by the subcontractor at the time of the injury was work that ordinarily or appropriately would be performed by the general contractor's own employees.

If you are not covered by workers' compensation, your remedy against your employer is based on the common law; that is, you can sue your employer.

What are the typical features of a workers' compensation statute?

The typical workers' compensation law has seven characteristics:

1. You must be an employee.

2. You are automatically covered and can receive compensation for injuries arising out of and in the course of employment.

3. Negligence and fault are irrelevant to the determination of benefits.

4. The right to receive workers' compensation is an exclusive remedy; in return for the guaranteed compensation, you relinquish your common-law right to sue your employer for negligence.

5. Although you generally may not sue your employer, you still retain, in many states, the right to sue negligent third parties.

6. The usual rules of procedure and evidence are relaxed to facilitate the full implementation of the workers' compensation statute.

7. The employer alone bears the expense of providing workers' compensation coverage.

What benefits are included in the typical workers' compensation statute?

The most important benefits include:

- weekly disability income, based on your previous earning history; this disability income is generally between one-half and two-thirds of your average weekly wages;
- "scheduled" benefits for the loss or incapacity of a body member or organ, such as a leg, hand, or eye;
- hospital, surgical, nursing, and medical expenses, which may include rehabilitation expenses;
- burial expenses and death benefits to the family and dependents of a worker who dies from a work accident.

Each of these benefits is described more fully later.

Does workers' compensation cover all injuries or diseases?

No. Only injuries or diseases "arising out of and in the course of employment" are covered. In other words, a disability that is not causally related to the job is not covered by workers' compensation.

Generally, the phrase "arising out of and in the course of employment" is construed very broadly. If you can show that your injury was a result of being present at the job—that is, but for being at work, you would not have been injured—

compensation will be awarded. Even when the risk that
caused the injury is remote from the job itself and the
chain of causation is attenuated, the courts have awarded
compensation.

If you are injured going to or from work, the pivotal
question is whether you were within the "zone of danger"
associated with the job site. Compensation may be awarded if
the risk that caused the injury was an integral condition of the
job site that had to be confronted when going to or from
work. Injuries that occur away from the job site are usually
not compensable, though there are exceptions.

A problem in proving causation arises when you had a
pre-existing illness that was the cause of injury or death. You
generally have the burden of proving that the pre-existing
illness was aggravated by the conditions at the job. If you
cannot prove this, benefits may be denied.

Even if a disability is not covered by workers' compensation,
it might be covered by other disability income insurance.
Many employees—particularly those in unions—are covered
by private disability income insurance. In fact, several states,
including California, Hawaii, New Jersey, New York, and
Rhode Island, require employers to provide temporary disability income insurance coverage to all workers who are
covered by workers' compensation. Furthermore, if you have
a serious disability you may qualify for disability benefits
under Social Security (see Chapter 18).

Does workers' compensation cover all injuries on the job?
Yes, except for injuries caused by your own willful misconduct. Generally, you are entitled to compensation even if
your injury was caused by your own negligent or reckless
conduct; fault is immaterial.

Nevertheless, you may forfeit your right to compensation if
your misconduct involved prohibited overstepping of the
boundaries defining your job. Such prohibited acts could
place a resulting injury outside the "course of employment."
Examples: using company property for personal purposes
contrary to clearly stated company policy; doing acts expressly prohibited by company rules; and doing work that
your employer has specifically stated to be outside the scope
of your job. In addition, some workers' compensation statutes
provide that your compensation will be forfeited or reduced
for injuries caused by your deliberate or intentional violation

of known regulations designed to prevent employee injuries, or your knowing refusal to use safety devices or to observe safety rules.

Generally, you do not automatically forfeit compensation by being intoxicated at the time of injury, unless you were too intoxicated to perform your job; in that event, you in effect abandoned your employment and therefore were not injured ":n the course of employment." If you were sober enough to perform your job when you were injured, your right to compensation generally depends on the extent to which your intoxication caused your injury. Thirty-nine states have laws specifically governing the effect of intoxication on a workers' compensation claim: in some states (e.g., Texas), your intoxication would disqualify you completely, even if it did not contribute to causing the injury; in other states (e.g., New York), your intoxication would disqualify you only if it was the sole cause of your injury; other states fall between these extremes. In three states intoxication may result in reduction of compensation rather than forfeiture.

Am I entitled to disability compensation for all injuries at work?

No. Only "compensable disabilities" are eligible for compensation. The concept of a compensable disability is made up of two parts. First, there must be a medical disability or a physical impairment that affects your ability to work. Second, the disability or impairment must have rendered you unable to work; this is evidenced by proof that you have, in fact, not earned any wages.

Are occupational diseases covered by workers' compensation?

Unlike most injuries, occupational diseases may arise or become apparent many weeks, months, or even years after the injurious incident. In addition, the presence of carcinogens or other harmful environmental factors in the workplace can aggravate conditions generally considered natural diseases. As a result of these factors, many states have enacted statutes to deal with the unique problems of compensating victims of occupational diseases. If you are suffering from a disease that you may have gotten from or because of your job, you should get competent legal counsel to look at the workers' compensation statute in your state.

Under most workers compensation statutes, the statute of limitations begins to run when the disease produces a disability (i.e., when you are forced to resign) and you know or should know that you have an occupationally induced illness.

How is the amount of my disability income benefit determined?

To determine the amount of your disability income benefit, your "earning capacity" must be ascertained. Disability income benefits are intended to help replace earnings lost due to disability. The amount that you could be earning on the open market if you were not disabled is called your earning capacity. Sometimes, as with minors or college students, earning capacity may be much higher than actual earnings. Among the many complex variables to be considered in determining earning capacity are age, education, experience, job history, and, of course, actual pre-injury earnings.

If you were fully employed for an extended period of time (typically, one year) before the injury, your actual pre-injury earnings furnish the basis for determining your earning capacity. Sometimes your earning capacity may be much greater than your pre-injury earnings. Suppose, for example, you were disabled after working full-time for only one month; your actual earnings for the prior year would not reflect your real earning capacity. In that situation, your earning capacity may be based on the earnings of others engaged in similar full-time work over an extended period. Similarly, if you worked only intermittently, seasonally, or part-time, your actual earnings may not reflect your earning capacity; then your earning capacity may be based on your previous earning history and on the earnings of others engaged in similar work. If you normally worked full-time, however, your part-time earnings may be converted to a full-time basis in determining your earning capacity.

In addition to earning capacity, the amount of your disability income benefit depends on the duration and extent of your disability. The following four categories, which are used by all states, reflect the effect of your disability on your earning capacity:

Temporary total disability: You are totally unable to work while healing, but you will go back to work eventually.

Temporary partial disability: You are able to do some work while healing, though maybe not your regular job.

Permanent total disability: You are permanently unable to do the job or type of job you had before the injury.

Permanent partial disability: You can do part of the job you used to do or can do another lower-paying job.

What is included in determining my wages?

For determining benefits, your wages generally include more than your regular cash salary. Tips and gratuities that you and your employer consider compensation for work are also considered wages, as are bonuses, food, board, lodging, and all other incidental payments. If overtime is a usual and customary characteristic of the job, then it too is included in the wage determination.

If I am a skilled worker and I cannot perform my job after my injury, can I get total and permanent compensation?

Maybe. If you are a skilled worker and you cannot perform your previous job due to injury, you might be deemed totally and permanently disabled. On the other hand, a common laborer can be considered totally and permanently disabled only if the injury prevents her or him from performing any type of comparable labor.

What if I have a pre-existing condition that aggravates the injury?

You can still get workers' compensation. Some states apportion the amount of benefits based on the pre-existing condition and the aggravation of the injury. Generally, an employer takes a worker "as is"; the risk of employing a person with a pre-existing disease or infirmity is assumed by the employer. On the other hand, some states encourage employers to hire handicapped workers through a "second injury" rule. In that situation, if a worker has a pre-existing handicap, the employer's responsibility for workers' compensation benefits may be limited to a maximum period, say, two years.

What are "scheduled" benefits?

If you lose a body member or organ, or the use of a body member or organ, you will receive a scheduled benefit. This is a set amount of money paid (based on your wage level) for a certain number of weeks prescribed by statute—depending on what the loss was—without regard to wage loss during that period. In other words, you can work (even make more money than before) and still receive scheduled benefits.

Can I get disability benefits in addition to scheduled benefits?

Sometimes. Generally, scheduled benefits are in lieu of disability benefits. But you may receive disability benefits, even though you are receiving scheduled benefits for the partial or total loss of a member, if the injury has extended beyond the particular member, resulting in a loss of earning capacity.

Can I receive disability benefits for one injury and scheduled benefits for another?

Generally, yes, even if the injuries arise from the same incident. Separate injuries arising from the same incident are individually compensable. If they are really one injury, then a separate basis of compensation will not be allowed.

Can I recover for pain and suffering?

No. The only time you can recover for this is when the pain impairs your ability to earn a living.

What expenses does workers' compensation cover?

All states require employers to pay the medical expenses for injuries arising out of employment. This is often the most important workers' compensation benefit for the worker. Each state sets its own maximum limits for medical benefits, including the maximum dollar amount for which an employer can be liable. Every state authorizes payment for artificial limbs and the like.

Notwithstanding any maximum dollar amount for medical benefits, additional benefits may be available for physical rehabilitation of the worker. Virtually every state provides some rehabilitation benefits after a determination has been made that rehabilitation would be "feasible," "desirable," or "necessary" for the worker. Some states provide a maintenance allowance during the rehabilitation period. In addition to such state benefits for physical rehabilitation, injured workers often qualify for vocational rehabilitation under various federal and state programs.

What benefits are payable if I am killed on the job?

Your dependents are generally entitled to compensation for the loss of support due to a job-related death. The amount of dependency benefits is based on the type of dependent.

Presumptive dependents are persons presumed by law to be supported by you; these are usually your surviving spouse and minor children. This presumption of dependency may or may not be conclusive in obtaining total or partial benefits, depending on the state. Someone who is not a presumptive dependent may still be entitled to benefits as an *actual* dependent, upon proving that you were supporting him or her in whole or in part; this could be a relative (parent, brother, sister, etc.), and in some states, a lover or anyone else.

The amount of benefits payable to a presumptive or actual dependent depends on, among other things, whether the dependent was a total or partial dependent. A *total* dependent is someone who you totally supported and who has no other means of support; presumptive dependents are presumed to be total dependents. A *partial* dependent is someone who has sources of support other than you, but those sources are insufficient to maintain the standard of living to which the dependent has become accustomed as a result of your support.

Can I or my dependents receive a lump-sum compensation payment?

Generally, no. The usual compensation claim is paid in weekly periodic payments. The workers' compensation board or agency may, however, approve a lump-sum award if urgent reasons or unusual circumstances justify it. The applicant has the burden to prove that a lump-sum award would be in his or her best interests.

Can my employer and I compromise my claim?

Yes. Compromise agreements are encouraged to facilitate the friendly resolution of workers' compensation claims. Any voluntary agreement, however, must be in accord with the workers' compensation statute and must be approved by the proper authority. Thus, the agreement cannot be contrary to the law or tainted by fraud, mistake, or other improper conduct. The agreement cannot force you to surrender any legal rights. An agreement to pay less than the statutory minimum cannot be enforced.

How do I start my workers' compensation claim?

You must give notice of the injury to your employer as

soon as possible. The notice may be written or oral, so long as it complies with the requirements of the state. At a minimum, the notice must be sufficient to put your employer on notice that an investigation will occur and that a claim will be filed with the workers' compensation board.

A notice must be filed notifying all involved parties that a claim exists. The claim will usually be heard by a hearing officer, who may be a referee, arbitrator, or commissioner. To facilitate the resolution of these claims, the workers' compensation agencies have their own rules of procedure and evidence, which stress simplicity and informality. Nonetheless, all parties must be given a chance to be heard.

If you are unhappy with the decision of the hearing officer, you can appeal your claim to a full tribunal. As with the initial hearing, the rules of procedure and evidence are relaxed. In addition, the full tribunal can review the entire record, not just the portions of the decision that you feel were decided unfairly. If you are still dissatisfied with the findings of the full tribunal, you can appeal to the state courts. The usual role of the courts is to review the issues of law as applied to the facts. The court will review the decision of the administrative body and determine whether its decision was justified. In some states, the court has the power to re-examine the factual issues in considering your appeal.

Is there a time limit for filing a claim for workers' compensation?

Yes. Every state has a statute of limitations on the filing of workers' compensation claims, but they vary greatly. In some states, the statute of limitations starts to run when you are injured. In other states, the statute starts to run when you realize that you are in fact injured. With reference to occupational diseases, the statute generally starts to run when you know or should know that you have a disease and that it was connected with your job. In addition, the statute of limitations may be tolled during any period that you receive benefits before filing a claim.

If the statute of limitations has run, can I still pursue my workers' compensation claim?

Maybe. For example, the lateness of your claim might be excused if you thought your injury was minor or trivial, if your injury was latent, if there was a misrepresentation or mistake of fact, or if you were threatened in order to get you not to file a claim.

Can I reopen my claim once it has been closed?

Yes. The administrator of workers' compensation has the discretionary authority to reopen your case if your condition changes significantly, or if fraud, mistake, or abuse of discretion occurred in handling your claim.

Are workers' compensation benefits subject to taxes or to creditors' claims?

Workers' compensation benefits are not subject to income or payroll taxes. Also, in most states, such benefits are exempt from the claims of your creditors and from levy for the recovery of debts, and generally they may not be assigned or transferred; these exemptions might not apply, however, to unpaid taxes, attorneys' fees, alimony, or child support.

What happens if my employer does not provide workers' compensation coverage?

As discussed later, you generally cannot sue your employer for damages if you receive workers' compensation benefits. But if you are not covered by workers' compensation, you have the common-law right, like anyone else, to sue for damages caused by your employer's negligence. In such a lawsuit your employer is precluded from asserting the affirmative defenses (i.e., assumption of risk, contributory negligence, and fellow servant negligence) that historically prevented most workers from recovering against their employers for on-the-job injuries. In addition to potential civil liability from such a lawsuit, an employer in a mandatory coverage state who fails to provide required coverage may be liable for criminal penalties.

Can I sue my employer even though I receive workers' compensation benefits?

Generally, no. One of the precepts of the workers' compensation system is that the standard benefits for the injured worker are the worker's exclusive claim against the employer; that is, the employer that provides workers' compensation coverage to its workers is immune from civil lawsuits by its workers for damages.

Nonetheless, you may not be without remedy.[2] Most jurisdictions permit suit against an employer for injuries or death caused by the employer's intentional misconduct, such as an assault on a worker. In addition, a few jurisdictions permit suit for injuries or death caused by an employer's willful, wanton, or reckless conduct.[3] Several states[4] allow increased workers' compensation awards if injury or death is caused by failure to provide safety devices, to obey safety regulations, or to comply with duties imposed by statute or regulation; and two states allow increased awards for serious and willful misconduct of the employer.[5]

Generally, you retain the right to sue negligent third parties. For example, if you were injured by a malfunctioning machine at work and you were covered by your state's workers' compensation law, you would receive a set weekly income, but you could not sue your employer. Nevertheless, in most states, you could still sue the manufacturer of the machine on a negligence, strict liability, or product liability theory of recovery. If you recover damages from a third party, your employer's workers' compensation insurance carrier generally has a lien against that recovery to the extent of all wages and medical expenses for which it has paid.

Under what is known as the "dual capacity" theory, you might be able to sue your employer, not in its capacity as employer, but in some other capacity. For example, the employer may happen to be the manufacturer of a tool that injures one of its employees; the employee can sue, not as an employee, but as a user of the product. The dual capacity theory has been adopted in several states[6] and rejected in several others.[7]

Can I be discharged or disciplined for filing a workers' compensation claim?

In many states, yes. A few state workers' compensation statutes (e.g., California, Maine, Missouri, New York, Oregon, and Texas) generally prohibit retaliation against a worker for filing a claim and permit an aggrieved worker to sue for damages, such as back pay.[8] In a few other states, the courts have recently allowed workers to sue because of retaliation, even though the statutes do not authorize such suits, holding in effect that such suits should be allowed as a matter of public policy because injured workers should not be afraid to exercise their statutory right to compensation.[9] (For a full discussion of the recent trend toward recognizing such causes of action for "abusive" or "wrongful" discharge, see Chapter 3.) Except for these few statutory and judicial restrictions on retaliation, you are not protected against discipline or discharge for filing a claim. It is expected, however, that more legislatures and courts will act in the near future to remedy this problem.

Who pays for workers' compensation?

Employers. No state allows an employer to deduct the cost of workers' compensation coverage from your wages.

An employer may provide workers' compensation coverage in three ways. It may buy a private workers' compensation and employer liability policy from a commercial insurance carrier; it may buy coverage through a state workers' compensation fund; or it may set aside reserves sufficient to cover the risks involved. Most benefits are financed by the first two methods.

Are there any other compensation systems for injured workers?

Yes. The best known is the federal Longshoremen's and Harbor Workers' Compensation Act.[10] It provides compensation for the disability or death of an employee resulting from a work-related injury that occurs upon the "navigable waters of the United States"; this coverage has been expanded to include "any adjoining pier, wharf, dry dock, terminal, building way, marine railway, or other adjoining area customarily used by an employer in loading, unloading, repairing, or building a vessel."

Whether you are covered under the Act depends on two tests: (1) the situs test, under which the injury must have occurred upon navigable waters, as described above; and (2) the status test, under which the definition of a covered employee is "limited to a person engaged in maritime employment, including any longshoreman or other person engaged in longshoring operations, and any harborworker including a ship repairman, shipbuilder, and shipbreaker."[11]

The Act specifically excludes from coverage (1) a "master or member" or any person engaged by the master to unload or repair any vessel under eighteen tons net; and (2) officers or employees of the United States, any agency thereof, or of any state, foreign government, or political subdivision thereof. In addition, no compensation is payable where any injury resulted solely from the employee's intoxication or the willful intent of the employee to injure or kill himself or herself, or another.[12]

NOTES

1. For more details you should consult a treatise on the subject. The best known are: Larson, Workmen's Compensation Law; Schneider's Workmen's Compensation; and Blair's Reference Guide to Workmen's Compensation.
2. *See generally* Larson, 2A Workmen's Compensation Law, §69.10.
3. *See* Tex. Civ. Stat. art. 8306, §6; see also *Blankenship v. Cincinnati Milacron Chemicals*, 69 Ohio 2d 602 (1982); *Johns-Mansville Products Corp. v. Contra Costa Superior Court*, 27 Cal. 3d 456 (1980); *Mandolidis v. Elkins Industries*, 246 S.E.2d 907 (W.Va. 1978); cf. *Martinowski v. Carborundum Co./Electro-Mineral Division, et al.*, 108 Misc.2d 184, 437 N.Y.S.2d 237 (Sup. Ct. Niag. Co. 1981).
4. Ky. Rev. Stat. §342.165; Mo. Ann. Stat. §287.120(4); N.M. Stat. Ann. §52-1-10; N.C. Gen. Stat. §97–12; S.C. Code §42–9–70; Utah Code Ann. §35–1–12; Wis. Stat. Ann. §102.57.
5. Cal. Labor Code §4553; Mass. Ann. Laws chap. 152, §28.
6. *See, e.g., Bell v. Industrial Vangas, Inc.*, 30 Cal. 3d 268 (1981).
7. *Atchison v. Archer-Daniels-Midland Co.*, 360 So. 2d 559 (La. App. 1978), *cert. denied*, 362 So. 2d 1389; *DePada v. Spaulding Fibre Co.*, Inc., 119 N.H. 89, 397 A. 2d 1048 (1979); *Needham v. Fred's Frozen Foods, Inc.*, 171 Ind. App. 671, 359 N.E. 2d 544 (1977).
8. Cal. Lab. Code §132(a); Me. Rev. Stat. tit. 39 §111; Mo. Rev. Stat. §287.780; N.Y. Work. Comp. Law §120; Ore. Rev. Stat. §659.410; Tex. Ann., Stat. §8307c.
9. *E.g., Frampton v. Central Indiana Gas. Co.*, 297 N.E.2d 425 (Ind. 1973); *Kelsay v. Motorola, Inc.*, 384 N.E.2d 353 (Ill. Dec. 1978); *Murphy v. City of Topeka-Shawnee Co. Dep't of Labor Services*, 6 Kan. App.2d 489, 630 P.2d 186 (1981); *Lally v. Copygraphics*, 173 N.J. Super. 162, 413 A.2d 960 (1980). *Cf. Daniel v. Magma Copper Co.*, 127 Ariz. 320, 620 P.2d 699 (App. 1980).
10. 33 U.S.C. §903.
11. Larson, 4 Workmen's Compensation Law §89.00.
12. 33 U.S.C. §903(a) (1) and (2) (b).

XVIII

Social Security

Social Security is the popular name for the Old Age, Survivors, and Disability Insurance program (OASDI),[1] which was created in 1935 as part of the Social Security Act.[2] Under this program, benefits are paid to workers and their dependents and to the survivors of deceased workers. Social Security was designed to protect workers and their dependents from the loss of income due to the worker's old age, death, or disability. The three types of benefits are old age and disability benefits, which are payable to the worker; benefits for the dependents of a retired or disabled worker; and benefits for the surviving family of a deceased worker, including a lump-sum death benefit.

Social Security is administered entirely by the Social Security Administration (SSA), a federal agency. Note that workers' compensation is run entirely by the state, and that unemployment insurance is handled jointly by federal and state governments.

This chapter briefly discusses coverage and eligibility for each type of Social Security benefit and the procedures for obtaining benefits. The Social Security program—including coverage, eligibility, and benefits—is under active review by the federal government, so some details discussed in this chapter (especially regarding retirement ages) are subject to change.

Who is eligible for Social Security benefits?

Social Security is a form of income insurance, not welfare. Eligibility and benefits are based on a worker's work experience and earnings, not on need. The benefit received is based on the worker's average monthly earnings in covered employment.

The details of Social Security eligibility are complex, but there are two basic requirements. First, a family member must have worked in employment that is "covered" by the Social Security system.[3] Second, that person must have worked long enough in covered employment to have become "fully insured."[4]

What is covered employment?

Nearly all work (including self-employment and part-time work) counts toward establishing eligibility for Social Security benefits. Nine out of ten workers in the United States are covered by Social Security.

Most workers in jobs not covered by Social Security realize it and are covered by another retirement system; these include federal civilian employees and employees of some state or local governments.[5] Some workers may not realize, however, that they are not covered by Social Security. An employee of a non-profit organization, for example, is not covered unless the organization has elected to be covered by Social Security.[6] Even workers employed in jobs that are covered may be ineligible for Social Security benefits because their employers failed to comply with reporting requirements or did not pay Social Security taxes for them. The responsibility for withholding Social Security tax and paying the tax lies with the employer.

Unlike some income insurance programs (e.g., workers' compensation), domestic workers and farmworkers are covered by Social Security. Domestic workers—such as housekeepers, cooks, and gardeners—have been covered since 1951.[7] A domestic worker earns Social Security credit for each calendar quarter in which he or she earns cash wages of at least $50 from a single employer.[8] Farm workers are covered if they earn $150 or more in cash during a year from any one employer, or if they work for one employer for 20 or more days during a year and are paid in cash for work that is computed on the basis of time rather than piecework.[9]

How does a person become "fully insured"?

Fully insured status, the second requirement for Social Security eligibility, is acquired by working in covered employment for a sufficient number of calendar quarters. The number of quarters of coverage necessary to be eligible for benefits depends on the type of benefit involved. Generally, survivor benefits require the fewest quarters of coverage (as few as 6) and retirement benefits, the most (eventually, up to 40 quarters).

How do I compute how many quarters of coverage I have acquired?

The method of computing a person's eligibility for Social Security benefits has changed a number of times since the law was enacted in 1935.[10] Generally, between 1936 and 1977 a worker was credited with a "quarter of coverage" for each "calendar quarter" during which he or she earned *cash wages* of $50 or more. A "calendar quarter" is a three-month period beginning on January 1, April 1, July 1, or October 1.

In 1978 the method of computing quarters of coverage was changed. Under the new method the government announces each year the amount of earnings that will result in a credit for one quarter of coverage. A worker is credited with one quarter of coverage for each multiple of the amount set by the government, up to a maximum of four quarters per year. In 1978, for example, a worker was credited with one quarter of coverage for each $250 earned during the year, up to four quarters. The quarterly earning requirements thereafter have been $260 in 1979, $290 in 1980, $310 in 1981, $340 in 1982, and $370 in 1983.

Are quarters of coverage computed differently for self-employed persons?

Yes. Before 1978, self-employed persons received four quarters of coverage for each year in which they earned $400 or more. For 1978 and later years, the quarters of coverage are computed under the same method used for all other workers, except that the person must earn at least $400 in a year to be credited with any quarters of coverage for that year.

How many quarters of coverage do I need to be eligible for retirement benefits?

The number of quarters of coverage you need to be eligible to receive retirement benefits is listed in the table.

If you reach 62 in	Years you need	Quarters of coverage
1981	7½	30
1983	8	32
1987	9	36
1991 or later	10	40

Who is eligible to receive retirement benefits?

You are eligible for retirement benefits if you have reached 62, are fully insured (i.e., have accumulated the required number of quarters of coverage),and have retired from work. If you delay your retirement beyond age 62, you receive credit toward future benefits. In other words, the longer you delay your retirement, the greater your retirement benefit will be.

Are members of my family eligible to receive my Social Security benefits?

Yes. You, your spouse, and your children may be eligible for benefits.

The Social Security Law has specific provisions for spouse's benefits.[11] Under these provisions, your spouse is allowed to receive benefits based on your work record if your spouse's benefits, based on your spouse's work record, would amount to less than one-half your benefit. The monthly benefit for your spouse is one-half your monthly benefit.[12] You should consult your Social Security office for help in determining whether you should base your benefit on your work record or your spouse's.

Your spouse is entitled to benefits based on your work record if your spouse is at least 62 years of age. If you have been divorced, your former spouse is entitled to benefits based on your work record if your former spouse is at least 62, if you and your former spouse were married for at least ten years before divorcing, and if your former spouse is unmarried at the time of application for benefits.[13]

In 1977 the U.S. Supreme Court held that eligibility for the retirement benefits of a spouse could not be based on the sex of the applicant; subsequently, the statute and the regulations were changed to reflect that holding.[14] Before, a wife could receive retirement benefits based on her husband's work record, but not vice versa. Now, a husband is entitled to receive benefits on the basis of his wife's work record, and all eligibility conditions have been made sex-neutral.

Under what conditions are children eligible for benefits?

A child who is unmarried, under 18 (or under 19 and a full-time high-school student), and dependent upon a retired worker is eligible for benefits.[15] The term "child" includes adopted children, stepchildren, and under some circumstances, grandchildren.[16] The child's monthly benefit is equal to half the insured person's primary insurance amount if he or she is alive, and three-quarters if he or she has died.[17]

Can I work and still receive Social Security retirement benefits?

Yes. You are permitted to earn a limited amount of money and still continue to receive Social Security retirement benefits. If you earn more than this limited amount, your benefit will be reduced by $1 for every $2 earned over the limit.[18]

In 1983 the allowable annual limits were: under age 65, $4920; ages 65, $6600; age 70 and over, unlimited. These limits change periodically, and there are exceptions to these limits; you should consult your Social Security office for current information. Proposals have been made to eliminate the limits.

Dividends from stock and mutual funds, interest from savings accounts, gains from sales of securities, and pension and annuity payments are excluded in computing your income for these purposes.[19]

Who can receive disability benefits?

You are eligible for disability income benefits if you are disabled, are fully insured, and have accumulated 20 quarters of coverage in the last 40 quarters before becoming disabled.[20] The provisions discussed earlier governing the eligibility of your spouse and children to receive your retirement benefits also govern their eligibility to receive your disability benefits.[21]

How can I prove that I am disabled?

The Social Security Act defines disability as the "inability to engage in any substantial gainful activity by reason of medically determinable physical or mental impairment which can be expected to result in death or which has lasted or can be expected to last for a continuous period of not less than 12 months."[22] Establishing that you are disabled within the meaning of that provision will be the most difficult problem you face in applying for disability benefits. You have the burden of demonstrating to the SSA that you are disabled.[23] The existence of a disabling, medically determinable physical or mental impairment can be proved in several ways.

Some diseases (e.g., rheumatoid arthritis in major parts, advanced tuberculosis, acute epilepsy) are considered so serious as to be automatically "disabling." The SSA has complied a list of diseases considered to be disabling called the "list of impairments."[24] If you can establish that you suffer from a listed impairment, you will automatically be found disabled. You also can be found disabled if you can demonstrate that the disease that you have is the medical equivalent of a disease on the list of impairments. If your medical findings indicate that your condition is equal, in terms of severity and duration, to a listed impairment, you will be presumed disabled.[25]

If you are not presumed disabled, you can be found disabled if your physical or mental impairment is so severe that you cannot do your previous work and cannot (considering your age, education, and work experience) engage in *any other kind of substantial gainful work*. This means any form of labor that exists anywhere in the national economy, regardless of whether that work exists near where you live, or whether a specific job vacancy exists, or whether you would actually be hired if you applied for work.[26]

In trying to prove that you are disabled, you should assemble detailed evidence of your medical problems, age, education, and work history, and then submit this information to the SSA. A statement from your doctor is particularly important. It should outline your medical condition in detail and explain why your doctor believes that your condition prevents you from engaging in any substantial gainful employment; a short statement that he thinks you are disabled, without explaining why, will not be enough. If you have been treated by several doctors, obtain a statement from each. In addition to doctors' statements, you can submit statements from family and friends to verify, for example, that you are frequently tired and in pain and are therefore unable to work.

If you prove that you are unable to engage in your previous occupation, the SSA will try to show that you are able to perform some type of "work that exists in the national economy."[27] A "vocational expert" may testify at your hearing that jobs exist that a person of your age, experience, and medical condition can do.[28] Because the rules governing disability benefits are complex, the assistance of a lawyer or other representative experienced in Social Security cases often is essential. Obtain help before you apply for disability benefits, and do not hesitate to appeal an initial determination by the SSA that you are ineligible—such decisions often are overturned.

Who is eligible for survivors' benefits?

Survivors' benefits are payable to the spouse of the deceased worker or to the worker's parents and children.[29] The survivors' benefits provisions allow monthly cash benefits and a lump-sum death payment payable upon the death of the worker.[30]

When is a widow/widower entitled to survivors' benefits?

A surviving spouse who is 60 or older, or is between 50 and 60 and is disabled, will receive monthly survivors' benefits if the spouse was fully insured at death.[31] "Fully insured" for these purposes means the worker worked 6 out of the last 13 quarters, including the quarter in which death occurred. A surviving divorced spouse who meets these requirements and is now unmarried, and who was married to the deceased worker for at least 10 years, is also eligible for survivors' benefits. To be considered a surviving spouse by the SSA, you must have been married to the deceased worker for at least nine months, or have borne him a child, or have adopted his or her child.[32] A widow may also be eligible for mothers' insurance benefits if her husband died fully or currently insured, and if she is currently unmarried and is caring for the deceased husband's child.[33]

Can I and my family rely on social security for support upon retirement, disability, or death?

No, not entirely. The Social Security law was intended to provide workers and their dependents with some financial support in the event of retirement, disability, or death. The program was not intended to be a publicly funded equivalent of privately funded insurance and retirement plans; Social Security benefit levels provide merely a subsistence income.

You should, therefore, investigate pension plans associated with your employment and consider establishing an IRA or Keogh account. (For a full discussion of these subjects, see Chapter 16.) You should also consider disability income insurance to provide for you and your family if you become disabled, and life insurance to provide for your family after you die. These types of plans and coverage may be provided through your employer or your union, or may be developed by you.

How do I apply for Social Security benefits?

You must fill out an application for the Social Security Administration with proof of the necessary information, such as your age and identity. You can visit or write the nearest Social Security office; a list of these offices is contained in Appendix 8.

Appendix 9 contains a chart that describes what types of evidence you must submit to receive various Social Security benefits. For an extensive discussion on what constitutes evidence for proof, see *The Rights of Older Persons* by Robert N. Brown, another book in the ACLU series.

How long will it take the Social Security Administration to act on an application for benefits?

It depends on the kind of benefits sought and how quickly evidence supporting your claim can be obtained. Claims for retirement or survivors' benefits are generally processed more quickly than claims for disability benefits, which require more complicated proof. Generally, you can expect to receive a check for retirement or survivors' benefits within 60 to 90 days after you complete your application. Disability applications take much longer—often six months or more. To facilitate processing your claims, you should promptly supply all information that is requested.

The SSA may make advance payments on your benefits when there is evidence that you are entitled to benefits, even if more evidence may be needed to make a final decision.[34]

What if the SSA rejects my claim?

The SSA sometimes makes mistakes in deciding applications for Social Security benefits. This is especially true of applications for disability benefits; nearly half the original denials that are appealed are reversed on appeal. Although fewer mistakes are made in applications for retirement and survivors' benefits, mistakes *are* made and you should file an appeal if you believe your claim was wrongly denied.

Unless you appeal, the decision denying your benefits becomes "final."[35] If you later decide that the denial was erroneous, and re-apply for benefits, the SSA may point to the earlier denial and refuse to reopen your case.[36]

You can, however, request that the earlier decision be reopened. You have a right to have the decision reopened if you request it within 12 months of the decision. If you wait longer than 12 months, you must show "good cause" to have the case reopened, and the decision whether to reopen is solely within the discretion of the SSA and cannot be reviewed by a court.[37]

Can I appeal if the SSA stops sending me checks or reduces the amount of my checks?

Yes. You have an absolute right to request a reconsideration and a hearing, and if necessary, to challenge any reduction or suspension of your benefit.[38]

How do I appeal?

You begin your appeal by notifying the SSA that you disagree with its decision. You can call or visit a SSA office to discuss your situation. You may be able to resolve the problem in these informal discussions. If not, you must file a formal request for an appeal. This request should be in writing, either on a form provided by the SSA or by a letter you write yourself. You must file this appeal within 60 days after you received notice from the SSA of its unfavorable decision.

The SSA appeals process has several stages, the first of which is called "reconsideration." During this stage, the SSA's original decision (called an initial determination) is reconsidered or reviewed. You are entitled to submit further evidence in support of your claim during reconsideration, but you are not given an opportunity to appear personally or to call witnesses to support your claim.[39] If the SSA notifies you that it has reconsidered your claim and has upheld its initial determination, you have 60 days in which to request a formal hearing.[40] Again, your request should be in writing, either on an SSA form or in a letter.

What can I expect at my appeal hearing?

The hearing will be conducted by an administrative law

judge employed by the SSA's Bureau of Hearings and Appeals; these judges are not involved in the daily administration of Social Security. The only information the judge will have about your claim is that which is contained in your Social Security file, i.e., your application, evidence in support of your claim, and the SSA's reasons for denying your claim. Sometimes, the judge is the only person at an appeal hearing other than the claimant. Social Security hearings can be complicated, so you should have a lawyer to represent you. If you cannot afford to hire a private attorney, you should contact your local Legal Services office.

At the hearing, you have a right to (1) appear in person and to have a legal representative present;[41] (2) present evidence and make arguments in support of your position; (3) cross-examine witnesses who testify against you; and (4) request the opportunity to submit a post-hearing memorandum in support of your claim. In addition, you have the right to ask the judge, at least 5 days before the hearing, to issue subpoenas for evidence you need to support your claim.[42]

At the hearing, you should submit all the evidence you have assembled in support of your claim. On a disability claim, for example, you should bring your doctor to testify, or a letter from your doctor describing your condition and stating that it prevents you from engaging in any substantial gainful employment. Also, you should bring a friend or relative to the hearing who can testify about how your condition affects your daily life. For example, if your condition prevents you from lifting heavy objects or walking up stairs, bring someone to your hearing who can corroborate your testimony that you are unable to do these things. This type of testimony is very important, as it will help to give the judge a complete picture of the extent and nature of your disability.

Sometimes, the SSA will send a "vocational expert" to a hearing on disability benefits. The vocational expert, who is supposed to give an objective assessment of your ability to work, is paid by the SSA and will testify in support of the SSA's decision and against you. You or your representative should vigorously cross-examine this expert. Although vocational experts are not medical doctors, they sometimes make statements about a claimant's physical abilities. Since vocational experts lack medical training, these types of statements may be without sound medical basis. You should bring this act to the attention of the judge by asking the vocational expert about his or her training and the exact bases for any conclusions about your capacity to work.

What if I lose my appeal?

To request a review of the judge's decision by the SSA's Appeal Council, you must file a written request within 60 days after you receive it.[43] You may send any additional evidence to the Appeals Council that you wish considered in connection with the review.

The Appeals Council may elect not to review your case. If more evidence is needed to fully evaluate your claim, the Council may remand it back to the hearing judge to take more evidence. In any event, you will receive written notification of the Appeals Council's decision.

If the Appeals Council declines to review your case or upholds the SSA's denial of benefits, your only remedy is to sue the SSA in federal court. Such an action must be filed within 60 days after the Appeals Council decision.[44] If you have not already done so, you should, at this stage, seek the advice of a private attorney knowledgeable about Social Security, or a Legal Services attorney. Although you can bring this lawsuit without the aid of counsel, it is not advisable to do so.

Do I have a right to have the information in my social security file kept secret?

Yes, for the most part. In general, it is illegal for an SSA employee to disclose information from an SSA file to the public. Some exceptions do exist. For example, information can be given to other government agencies for legitimate governmental purposes, and your Social Security number and information about your Social Security coverage sometimes can be given to your past and present employers.[45]

NOTES

1. 42 U.S.C. §§401 *et seq*. The 1935 law provided only for retirement benefits; survivorship benefits were added in 1939, and disability benefits were added later.
2. 42 U.S.C. §§301 *et seq*. The Social Security Act, as amended, presently covers many other programs, in addition to OASDI, including grants to states for unemployment compensation administration;

grants to states for aid to dependent children, maternal and child welfare, and services to the aged, blind, and disabled; and health insurance for the aged.

3. 42 U.S.C. §410.
4. 42 U.S.C. §§414, 423(c); 20 C.F.R. §404.101–120.
5. 42 U.S.C. §418.
6. 42 U.S.C. §410(a) (8) (B); 20 C.F.R. §404.1026.
7. 65 Stat. 121 (1951).
8. 20 C.F.R. §404.1058.
9. 42 U.S.C. §410(f); 20 C.F.R. §1057.
10. *See* [1981] 1 Unempl. Ins. Rep. (CCH) ¶12,109.
11. 42 U.S.C. §401(b) (1), (c) (1).
12. 20 C.F.R. §404.333.
13. 42 U.S.C. §401(b) (1) and (c) (1).
14. *Califano v. Goldfarb*, 430 U.S. 199 (1977); 42 U.S.C. (c) (1); 20 C.F.R. §404.330 (1981).
15. 42 U.S.C. §402(d) (1).
16. 20 C.F.R. §404.354.
17. 20 C.F.R. §404.353(a).
18. 42 U.S,C. §403(d); 20 C.F.R. §404.434(b).
19. 26 U.S.C. §3121.
20. 42 U.S.C. §§423(a), 416(i).
21. 42 U.S.C. §402 *et seq*.
22. 42 U.S.C. §423(d) (1) (A).
23. 42 U.S.C. §423(d) (5); 20 C.F.R. §1512.
24. 20 C.F.R. §§404.1501 *et seq*., Appendix 1.
25. 20 C.F.R. §404.1526.
26. 42 U.S.C. §423(2) (A).
27. *Johnson v. Finch*, 310 F. Supp. 1235, *aff'd*, 437 F.2d 1321 (10th Cir. 1971).
28. 20 C.F.R. §404.1567(e).
29. 42 U.S.C. §402(e)–(h).
30. 42 U.S.C. §402(i); 20 C.F.R. §404.390–.394.
31. 42 U.S.C. §402(e) (1) (B).
32. 42 U.S.C. §416(c).
33. 42 U.S.C. §402(g) (1).
34. 42 U.S.C. §405(q) (1) (3); 20 C.F.R. §404.1810.
35. 20 C.F.R. §404.905.
36. 20 C.F.R. §404.909 (1981).
37. 20 C.F.R. §404.911; *Califano v. Sanders*, 430 U.S. 99 (1977).
38. 20 C.F.R. §§404.907, 404.930.
39. 20 C.F.R. §404.918.
40. 20 C.F.R. §416.1425.
41. 20 C.F.R. §416.1449.
42. 20 C.F.R. §416.1450(d).
43. 20 C.F.R. §416.1468(a).
44. 20 C.F.R. §416.1481.
45. 42 U.S.C. §1306; 20 C.F.R. §§401.300 *et seq*.

XIX

Unemployment Insurance

Unemployment insurance protects you if you become unemployed through no fault of your own. To partly offset the resulting wage loss, you receive a weekly benefit based on your regular pay.

State and federal governments recognize that unemployment and its attendant problems are often caused not by your actions but by forces beyond your control. These forces include the vagaries of the economy, natural disasters, and other situations that may cause you to leave work involuntarily. It is considered in the best interest of the state's citizens, including employers and workers, to provide benefits to the unemployed so they are not forced to use up their savings, go deep into debt, or move out of the state.

The state and federal governments have therefore established programs under which you are partly insured against loss of regular wages that occurs through no fault of your own. Benefits are paid to help keep you and your family going while you look for a new job or wait to resume an old job.

What kinds of unemployment benefits are there?

The main source of benefits is the federal-state unemployment insurance (UI) program. Under federal guidelines, every state—plus the District of Columbia, Puerto Rico, and the Virgin Islands—has such a program. The benefits under these state programs typically run for about 26 weeks, though they may be extended in certain circumstances, as discussed later.

The UI system is a coordinated program of the federal and state governments. It was established in 1935 under Title IX of the Social Security Act,[1] and was incorporated in 1954 into the Internal Revenue Code as the Federal Unemployment

Tax Act (FUTA).[2] State UI benefits are paid by each state's employment security agency from funds held in the Unemployment Trust Fund of the United States.[3] These funds come from employer contributions under FUTA to the trust fund. FUTA sets basic UI standards, but each state sets the specific rules for its program and administers the payment of benefits. Within the basic federal standards, state UI programs differ greatly, e.g., in eligibility rules, benefit amounts, and application procedures.

The state UI programs are the principal topic of this chapter. Due to the great differences in these programs, however, the discussion is necessarily general. Some details of these programs, as of January 1983, are set forth in Appendix 10. For more specific and up-to-date information, consult the local office of the employment security agency for your state.

In addition to state UI benefits, you may qualify for benefits under the federal Trade Adjustment Assistance (TAA) program if your job is eliminated by imported products.[4] Industries that have in the past been subject to TAA coverage include steel, automobiles, coal, textiles, shoes, and electronics. Qualifying workers may get benefits comparable to regular UI benefits for up to 12 months after exhausting regular UI benefits. In addition, the TAA program provides for training in new skills and for relocation assistance, plus up to six more months of benefits during training.

If your job is lost or interrupted as a direct result of a major disaster, you may qualify for benefits under the Disaster Unemployment Assistance (DUA) program.[5] Application for DUA benefits must be made within 30 days after the state employment security agency announces the availability of DUA. Weekly DUA benefits, which are comparable to regular UI benefits, begin a week after the disaster, and end about a year later, or earlier if it is determined that unemployment in the area is no longer attributable to the disaster. In addition to weekly benefits, DUA provides re-employment assistance services.

In addition to these government unemployment benefits, some unionized industries, such as steel and automobiles, have supplemental unemployment benefits (known as SUB). The employers contribute a set amount to an SUB fund for every hour worked. The benefits are paid to laid-off workers to supplement regular UI benefits.

How much is the weekly benefit?

Your weekly UI benefit amount is based in part on how much you earned when you were working. Each state has its own formula for this computation, and it is often complicated. Most states first determine your "high-quarterly wages" (that is, your wages for the quarter in which you earned the most) and then take a certain fraction of that, say 1/26; the result is your weekly benefit. Some states use average weekly wages rather than high-quarterly wages. A few states use annual wages. Under most formulas the computed weekly benefit will be about half of your average weekly earnings during the relevant period.

The weekly benefit determined by these computations is not necessarily what you will actually receive. Some states add a few dollars to the weekly benefit for each dependent. Every state has minimum and maximum benefits. As of January 1983 the minimums range from $7 to $57 and the maximums, from $84 to $258. In addition, many states limit the weekly benefit to a certain percentage (from 50 to 70 percent) of the state's average weekly wage.

Can I collect unemployment insurance benefits in addition to benefits from a pension plan, workers' compensation, or Social Security?

Generally, no. Most states eliminate or reduce UI benefits for any week in which you receive certain "disqualifying income." Typically, this includes dismissal pay, retirement pay, workers' compensation for temporary partial disability, and old-age benefits under the Social Security Act. Most states do not totally disqualify you if the disqualifying income you receive is less than the UI benefits due you. Rather, you receive the amount of the UI benefit reduced by the disqualifying income.

What happens if I earn some money while drawing unemployment insurance benefits?

This will not necessarily disqualify you from benefits. A small part of these earnings may be disregarded. Some states disregard a specific weekly amount, say $5 or $10. Others disregard a fraction of your weekly benefit amount, ranging from 1/5 to 1/2. Usually, any earnings in excess of the disregarded amount are deducted from your weekly benefit amount.

How long can I collect benefits?

The regular maximum duration in most jurisdictions is 26 weeks, with a few longer[6] and one shorter.[7] This regular maximum applies to all totally unemployed workers. In addition, some states set a maximum duration equal to the number of weeks you worked, or a maximum amount equal to the amount you earned during the preceding year.[8] If you barely qualified for benefits or if you are receiving the minimum benefit, you may have a maximum benefit duration of, say, 15 weeks instead of 26. If you receive *partial* benefits (because you are partly employed), you may get benefits for more than the usual maximum duration—the smaller benefit is spaced over a larger number of weeks.

When unemployment in the state reaches specified levels, a few states extend the benefit period: California and Hawaii by 50 percent; Alaska and Connecticut by 13 weeks; and Puerto Rico by 32 weeks in certain industries, occupations, or establishments. Furthermore, under the Federal-State Extended Compensation Program,[9] benefits may be extended during periods of high unemployment in the state, the nation, or both, by 50 percent, up to 13 weeks. In addition, Congress occasionally passes other temporary extended benefits programs; you can check with the local employment security office to find out whether such a program is in effect.

Are all workers covered by unemployment insurance?

No. Generally, to be covered by UI, you must have been an employee of a covered employer and been engaged in non-exempt employment:

1. You are covered only if you are considered the employee of someone else. Basically, you are considered an employee if you are subject to the control and direction of the person for whom you perform services.[10] An independent contractor, who is free of control and direction over the way he does a job, is not an employee.[11] And, of course, a self-employed person is not an employee. Corporate officers, commission drivers, and traveling salesmen may be considered employees.[12]

2. In most states you are covered only if your employer pays wages to one or more employees either (a) during more than a certain number of weeks (typically 20) in the current or preceding year, or (b) in excess of a certain amount (usually $250 to $300) in a quarter. In a few jurisdictions (Alaska,

District of Columbia, Hawaii, Maryland, Pennsylvania, Puerto Rico, Rhode Island, Virgin Islands, and Washington), you are covered without regard to the size of your employer.

3. Certain kinds of employment are specifically exempted from mandatory UI coverage.[13] These include employees of certain non-profit institutions, student nurses and interns, newsboys, casual laborers, certain government employees, some salesmen and brokers, minors working for parents, and parents working for children. Farm workers are now covered if they work for a large employer—one who, in the current or preceding year, has paid $20,000 or more per quarter in wages or has employed ten or more employees on 20 or more days in a quarter. Domestic workers are now covered if their employer paid at least $1000 in a recent quarter for such services.[14] Sometimes an employer may elect to cover exempt employees voluntarily.

If you meet these three tests, you are covered by UI and you may be eligible for benefits.

Who is eligible for unemployment insurance benefits?

Basically, you will get UI benefits if you were a covered employee and then, through no fault of your own, you became and remained unemployed. Specifically, you are eligible for UI benefits if you meet each of the following five conditions:[15] (1) you had "qualifying employment"; (2) you are "ready, willing, and able" to work; (3) you register for work with the state employment security office; (4) you file for benefits; and (5) the waiting period for benefits has elapsed.

Even if you meet these eligibility conditions, you may be disqualified for benefits if at least one of the following applies:[16] (1) you refuse suitable employment; (2) you were discharged for misconduct; (3) you quit your job without good cause; (4) your unemployment was caused by a labor dispute; or (5) you earn more than a specified amount of money.

What is "qualifying employment"?

To get UI benefits, you must have a minimum amount of employment within the year preceding your claim; this is called qualifying employment. Each state has minimum work or wage requirements: you must have recently worked a specified number of weeks, earned a specified amount of wages, or both. Some states use a formula incorporating one or more of these factors.[17] For example, in Colorado you must have worked in at least 40 of the 52 weeks before filing; in Nebraska, you must have earned at least $600 in the preceding year, including $200 in each of two quarters; and in New Jersey, you must have worked in at least 20 of the previous 52 weeks at $30 or more a week, or have earned more than $2200.

You can combine time worked and wages earned in more than one state to qualify for UI benefits or to increase the amount of such benefits.[18]

What does the "ready, willing, and able" requirement mean?

UI benefits are only for persons who are actively in the job market. If you are not able or ready to take a job, or not prepared to take one immediately, you will not be paid benefits until you satisfy the state UI office that you are again ready, willing, and able to work and are diligently seeking work. If you are retired or on vacation, you cannot collect UI benefits. If you are sick and cannot work, you cannot collect; but you may be eligible for disability benefits.

You should keep a written record of the name and address of each employer to whom you have applied for work (including the name of the person with whom you spoke, if possible), the date of the application, and the results. Each time you report to your local UI office, you must present this record, and you must sign a sworn form stating any job offers you received and any days you were not ready, willing, and able to work (you can't collect for those days). You are expected to look for a job on your own, though the local employment security office should help you. How you do this depends on your situation. In addition to registering with the local employment security office, you can check with a union, visit employers, comb newspaper want ads, check the Yellow Pages, or follow leads from relatives or acquaintances.

You can be disqualified from benefits if your job search efforts are deemed inadequate. Under an extended benefits program (described earlier), you may be disqualified if you do not make a "systematic and sustained" search for work;[19] this standard requires a more diligent search for work than is required for regular UI benefits. You can also be disqualified if you refuse a referral or an offer for suitable work without good cause. The period of disqualification runs from the time of the refusal until you have requalified.

The "ready, willing, and able" standard is defined differently in various states. In some states you must be able and available to perform work that you are qualified to perform by past experience or training, or that is generally similar to work for which you previously received wages; and you must be available for this work on a full-time basis at a locality in which you previously worked or in which this work is available. Other states require that you be able and available to work at your usual or customary trade, occupation, profession, or business for which you are qualified by past experience or training. Some states provide that you must be able and available for "suitable work"; what constitutes suitable work is discussed later.

What registration is required?

All states require an UI claimant to register for work with the local office of the state employment agency and thereafter to report to that office periodically, usually every week. If you fail to answer a notice from the agency regarding a possible job opening, you may be found in violation of the reporting requirement. Failure to register or report as required is grounds for denial or termination of benefits, unless there is "good cause" for the failure. Good cause may include circumstances beyond your control, inadequate or misleading statements by the employment office, coercion by the employer, or the employer's failure to inform you of your rights and obligations. A job interview is good cause for not reporting.[20]

If you cannot report on the assigned day, you should report as soon as possible and not wait until your next reporting day; otherwise, you risk losing benefits for the period you did not report.

The employment office may waive the registration and reporting requirements in exceptional circumstances. These circumstances may include your partial employment, return to full employment, unemployment due to a labor dispute, pursuit of vocational training, or living in an area that has no suitable work for you.

How do I file for benefits?

To file your claim, you must go in person to the local office of the state employment security agency, unless you get special permission to file by mail. You are ineligible for any benefits until you file a claim. You cannot get credit for any time you are out of work before you file the claim. Thus you should file your claim as soon as you become unemployed if you believe you may be entitled to benefits. Don't delay filing just because you don't have all the records you might need. File right away, and then get the records.

Take with you your Social Security card and any records, such as payroll slips and a dismissal notice, that will help you establish eligibility. The UI office will generally want to know, for the last year, who your employers were, how much you earned, where you worked, your employer's address, and any employer and employee identification numbers. The UI office will verify this information with the employers. Be sure to provide accurate information. You can be penalized for making misrepresentations, such as giving a false reason why you left your last job.

How long is the waiting period?

In most states you become eligible for benefits only after you have been unemployed for a week. In some of those states you will be compensated for that waiting period if you remain unemployed for a certain period of time: Louisiana (6 weeks), Minnesota (4), Missouri (9), New Jersey (3), Ohio (3), Pennsylvania (4), and Texas (4). A few states have no waiting period: Alabama, Connecticut, Delaware, Iowa, Kentucky, Maryland, Michigan, Nevada, New Hampshire, Virginia, and Wisconsin. Processing and verifying your claim may take several weeks, so expect some delay in getting your first benefit payment. You will get all the benefits that are due you.

What is "suitable employment" and how does refusal of such employment affect my claim?

Generally, even if you have met the foregoing eligibility requirements you will be disqualified for benefits if you refuse, without good cause, to apply for or accept suitable employment. The disqualification may last for the duration of your unemployment, or it may be for only a few weeks.

You cannot be disqualified for refusing to accept new work under any of the following conditions:[21] (1) the position offered is vacant due directly to a strike, lockout, or other labor dispute at the proposed place of employment; (2) the wages, hours, or other conditions of the work offered are substantially less favorable to you than those prevailing for similar work in the locality; or (3) acceptance of the job would require you either to join a company union or to resign from or refrain from joining a union.

You generally will not be disqualified for refusing to accept a job that is more hazardous than you are used to or that will adversely affect your health. Your physical condition (age, strengths, illnesses, etc.) may render a particular job unsuitable for you, though it may be suitable for someone else. Generally, a job will be considered unsuitable if you have no experience in that job. But the longer you remain unemployed, the more likely such a job will be considered suitable.

A job may be unsuitable because transportation to it is unduly expensive or difficult, or because the job is distant from your home. Long or unusual hours may render a job unsuitable if they might affect your health or domestic stability.

The extended benefits program (described earlier) imposes a broader interpretation of what constitutes "suitable work" than the regular benefits program. Basically, under the extended benefits program you must accept any job otherwise acceptable that pays more than the amount of your extended UI benefits together with any supplemental unemployment benefits (SUB).[22]

Can I get benefits if I quit my job or was fired?

It depends on the reasons. You will be denied benefits if you quit your last job without good cause or if you were fired from your last job for unreasonable or unjustifiable conduct or for other misconduct. Also, depending on the law in your particular state, you may be denied benefits if you quit your last job due to marriage or to join your spouse in another area, or if you lost your job because of a labor dispute. These disqualifying factors are discussed below.

If I am disqualified, am I permanently barred from getting UI benefits?

No. Disqualification from benefits is based on your *last* job. If, for example, you were fired for misconduct or you quit without good cause, you can requalify for benefits by obtaining "qualifying employment" (that is, a certain number of days or amount of earnings, or both). The amount of work needed to requalify is much less than the amount needed to establish eligibility. For example, in New York, you can requalify by working at least three days in each of four weeks or by earning at least $200. If the later job ends through no fault of your own, you can receive UI benefits without regard to the reason you lost your previous job. These requalification rules may not apply, however, if you were disqualified for misconduct connected with the job, for fraud in connection with a claim for UI benefits, or for receipt of disqualifying income.[23]

If you were disqualified by an inadequate search for work or by being unavailable for work, you can requalify simply by remedying the disqualifying factor, such as by widening your job search or by becoming available for work again. You should requalify as soon as you can, even if you have appealed the initial disqualification.

What constitutes "misconduct" as a ground for disqualifying me from receiving benefits?

Generally, you are disqualified from UI benefits if you were discharged for misconduct. The definition of misconduct varies from state to state, but some basic principles apply.

The concept of misconduct is aimed at disqualifying the claimant whose voluntary and intentional behavior brought about the discharge. The misconduct must indicate an intentional disregard for the employer's business. It need not violate the law or a moral code. Many courts and administrative agencies follow the decision of the Wisconsin Supreme Court in *Boynton Cab Co. v. Neubeck*,[24] in which the court said:

> . . . the intended meaning of the term "misconduct" . . . is limited to conduct evincing such wilful or wanton disregard of an employer's interests as is found in deliberate violations or disregard of standards of behavior which the employer has the right to expect of his employee, or in carelessness or negligence of such degree or recurrence as to manifest equal culpability, wrongful intent or evil design, or to show an intentional and substantial disregard of the employer's interests or of the employee's duties and obligations to his employer. On the other hand, mere inefficiency, unsatisfactory conduct, failure in good performance as the result of inability or incapacity, inadvertencies or ordinary negligence in isolated instances, or good faith errors in judgment or discretion are not to be deemed "misconduct" within the meaning of the statute.

Most states require that disqualification for UI benefits can occur only when the misconduct for which the employee was discharged was connected with the job. In those states, conduct off the premises of employment or after working hours usually cannot be grounds for disqualification. Some of those states, however, allow disqualification if the claimant was discharged due to conviction for a crime that makes continued employment a detriment to the employer.

An isolated violation of a company rule is generally not considered misconduct, unless the violation had particularly serious consequences. But repeated violations of an employer's rule, particularly after warnings, is considered to be evidence of misconduct in most states. Thus, being absent or late for work frequently would be considered misconduct, while isolated instances of either generally would not.

Mere inefficiency or the commission of an error in judgment, while grounds for discharge, are generally not disqualifying as misconduct. Rather, poor performance is grounds for disqualification only if it is a result of gross negligence or if it reflects an intentional disregard for the interests of the employer. Intoxication is generally not grounds for disqualification if the claimant is an alcoholic and thus the intoxication is a function of that disease rather than a result of the employee's free choice.

What constitutes good cause for quitting a job?

Generally, you cannot qualify for UI benefits if you quit your job voluntarily. On the other hand, if you quit voluntarily, but with "good cause," many states will allow you to get UI benefits. Basically, you are considered to have quit for good cause when you were virtually compelled to leave the job. The definition of good cause varies among the states. Some states include in their definition only factors relating to employment, while others have a more expansive definition that includes personal reasons. Personal reasons held to constitute good cause for quitting include moving with a spouse who has been transferred, caring for a sick relative in another state, and taking a higher-paying job that fails to materialize.[25] On the other hand, some states deny UI benefits if you quit due to your marriage or to following your spouse to another place.[26]

The U.S. Supreme Court has held that you cannot be denied UI benefits if you quit work due to your religious beliefs. In *Thomas v. Review Board of Indiana Employment*

Security Division,[27] the employee, a Jehovah's Witness, had been transferred to a job producing turrets for military tanks. He asked for other work on the ground that his religious beliefs would not allow him to produce weapons. When his requests were denied, he quit. The state denied his application for UI benefits because he did not have "good cause" to quit. The Supreme Court held that denying UI benefits in that situation would violate the employee's First Amendment right to the free exercise of religion.

If you quit because the work harms or threatens your health (for example, the hours of employment are so long that they threaten your health), you will be deemed to have quit for good cause. There is disagreement among the states on whether forced retirement is a basis for good cause; in most states, an employee who is forced to retire can receive UI benefits if otherwise eligible.[28]

Can I collect benefits if I go out on strike?

Generally, no. If you go out on strike, you cannot collect UI benefits, except that in New York, Rhode Island, and the Virgin Islands striking workers can collect UI benefits after a limited period of disqualification. The states generally disqualify you while you are on strike because you left work voluntarily, and because they do not want to prolong labor disputes by subsidizing strikers. But if you are permanently replaced during a strike, then the employer-employee relationship has ended involuntarily, and you can collect UI benefits.

You may be disqualified as a striker even if you are not actively or deliberately on strike. Generally, if you are out of work due to a labor dispute, you will be denied UI benefits if you are participating in financing, or directly interested in the dispute.[29] In most states, this includes workers who don't cross picket lines and workers who don't even want to be on strike, but who will be affected by the outcome of the labor dispute. In sum, if you voluntarily go on strike or if you are in a position to gain or lose from the outcome, you will be considered to be "participating in" the labor dispute and will be barred from collecting UI benefits. In some states UI benefits may be suspended for a period of time even if you are not "participating in" the labor dispute.

Can I collect benefits if I move to another state?

Yes. Under the Interstate Reciprocal Benefit Payment Plan,[30] in which all states participate, you can file for UI benefits in a state other than the one in which you worked. In that event, the state in which you file acts as the agent state in your claim against the liable state in which you accumulated benefits. The UI laws of the liable state govern your eligibility and the amount and duration of benefits. The agent state will help the liable state gather information about your eligibility, availability, and capability for work. Also, if you are deemed eligible for UI benefits by the liable state, you must register for work with the UI office in the agent state, and you are subject to the reporting requirements there.

Can a woman be denied benefits because of pregnancy?

No. The Unemployment Compensation Amendments of 1976 (which took effect in 1978)[31] expressly prohibit a state from denying UI benefits solely on the basis of pregnancy or termination of pregnancy. Pregnant claimants are eligible for benefits according to the same rules and standards that apply to other claimants.[32]

What happens if I get a job?

You are required to report it immediately to the UI office.

Can an alien receive benefits?

An otherwise eligible claimant can receive UI benefits without regard to alienage, except that an illegal alien cannot receive benefits.

Can the state stop paying benefits without first granting me a hearing?

Yes. In 1976 the U.S. Supreme Court ruled that recipients of certain disability benefits were not entitled, as a matter of due process, to a hearing before the termination of their benefits.[33] The same principle applies to UI benefits. Nevertheless, you are still entitled to a prompt post-termination hearing.

What can I do if my benefits are denied or terminated?

If you are denied UI benefits or if your benefits are terminated, you are entitled to a hearing before an administrative hearing officer. You should request such a hearing in writing; your local office may provide a form. You may be deemed to waive your right to a hearing if you do not request it promptly.

The hearings are usually informal; formal rules of procedure and evidence are generally not applicable. At the hearing, you and your employer may give testimony and may present witnesses and documentary evidence. You may be represented by counsel. If you are unhappy with the decision of the hearing officer, you can appeal to the board or other tribunal set up for that purpose by your state. If you are still dissatisfied with the results, you can appeal to the state courts.

During the pendency of any appeal of denial or termination of benefits, you should continue reporting to your local UI office. This will establish your continuing eligibility if you receive a favorable decision on appeal.

Where does the money come from to pay for UI benefits?

It comes from taxes, or "contributions," imposed by the federal and state governments on employers. (Alabama, Alaska, and New Jersey require employees to share in the cost.) The tax is a certain percentage of the employer's covered payroll. Basically, the covered payroll is the first $7000 of each employee's taxable wages.[34] Generally, the taxable wages include regular and overtime pay, bonuses, commissions, room and board, sick pay, and vacation pay, but not reimbursed expenses, insurance premiums, pension plan contributions, and other payments. Your employer cannot deduct anything from your wages to pay the UI tax, even if you agree to it. (In Alabama, Alaska, and New Jersey, of course, your employer can deduct your part of the UI tax from your pay.)

An employer is faced with two kinds of UI tax—one to the federal government, and another to each state in which it operates. The federal tax rate is 3.4 percent of the employer's covered payroll. Most employers, however, don't pay that much to the federal government because they are entitled to a credit of up to 2.7 percent for state UI taxes and for the "experience rating" adjustments described below. Thus the minimum or net federal tax rate is 0.7 percent, assuming maximum credit.[35]

State UI tax rates vary greatly. Generally, each state has a minimum rate and a maximum rate. As a percentage of the employer's covered payroll, the minimum rates range from zero to 3.7 percent and the maximum rates range from 2.95 percent to 10.0 percent (see Appendix 10.) The rate an employer pays depends on its experience rating. An employer that generates a lot of unemployed workers will have a much higher tax rate than an employer that has a very stable workforce. The experience rating system encourages stable employment and shifts some of the cost of UI programs onto the businesses that generate more unemployment.

Generally, all UI benefits are funded by state UI taxes. The federal UI taxes do not finance the payment of benefits; they go toward the costs of administering the federal and state programs.

The money for the Disaster Unemployment Assistance (DUA) program mentioned earlier does not come from payroll taxes; the funds are appropriated by Congress to the Federal Disaster Unemployment Assistance Administration (FDUA) of the Department of Housing and Urban Development.[36] The FDUA reimburses each state for the DUA benefits it pays out.

NOTES

1. 49 Stat. 640 (1935).
2. 26 U.S.C. §§3301 *et seq*.
3. 42 U.S.C. §1104(g).
4. 19 U.S.C. §§2271 *et seq*.
5. Disaster Relief Act of 1974, 42 U.S.C. §5177.
6. D.C. (34), La. (28), Mass. (30), Pa. (30), Utah (36), Wash. (30), W.Va. (28), and Wis. (34).
7. P.R. (20).
8. D.C., Mass., Penn., Utah, Wash., Wis., W.Va. From: "All State Coverage and Benefits Chart," [1981] 1B Unempl. Ins. Rep. (CCH) ¶2001.
9. Federal-State Extended Unemployment Compensation Act of 1970, 26 U.S.C. §3304 note.
10. *See, e.g., Claim of Watz*, 60 A.D.2d 259, 400 N.Y.S.2d 889, *aff'd*, 46 N.Y.2d 876 (1977).
11. *See, e.g., Cool v. Ross*, 57 A.D.2d 450, 396 N.Y.S.2d 76, *aff'd*, 44 N.Y.2d 750 (1977).
12. *E.g.*, N.Y. Labor Law §512(b) (2).
13. *See, e.g.*, N.Y. Labor Law §§511, 563, 564.
14. *E.g., Van Waes & Associates Realty, Inc. v. Ross*, 76 A.D.2d 1016, 429 N.Y.S.2d 673 (3d Dep't 1980).
15. [1976] 1B Unempl. Ins. Rep. (CCH) ¶¶1945–1960.
16. *Id.*, ¶¶1965–1995.
17. *See* "All-State Coverage and Benefits Chart," [1981] 1B Unempl. Ins. Rep. (CCH) ¶3001.

18. Interstate Arrangement for Combining Employment and Wages, 20
    C.F.R. Part 616.
19. [1981–1982 Transfer Binder] Unempl. Ins. Rep. (CCH) ¶21,626.
20. *See Zielenski v. Board of Review, Div. of Employment Security*, 85
    N.J. Super. 46, 203 A.2d 635 (App.Div. 1964).
21. 26 U.S.C. §3304(a) (5).
22. [1981–1982 Transfer Binder] Unempl. Ins. Rep. (CCH) ¶21,626.
23. 26 U.S.C. §3304(a) (10).
24. 237 Wis. 249, 296 N.W. 636, 640 (1941).
25. *See, e.g., Andersen v. Ind. Comm.*, 167 Colo. 281, 447 P.2d 221
    (Sup.Ct. 1968).
26. *See, e.g.*, N.Y. Labor Law §593(1) (b).
27. 450 U.S. 707 (1981).
28. *See Warner Co. v. Unemp. Comp. Bd. of Review.*, 396 Pa. 545, 153
    A.2d 906 (1959); *Campbell Soup Co. v. Bd. of Review, Div of
    Employment Security*, 13 N.J. 431, 100 A.2d 287 (1953); *E.S.C. v.
    Magma Copper Co.*, 90 Ariz. 104, 366 P.2d 84 (1961). *See also Duval
    Corp. v. E.S.C.*, 83 N.M. 447, 493 P.2d 413 (1972); *Reynolds Metals
    Co. v. Thorne*, 8 Ala. 78, 133 So.2d 709 (Ct.App. 1961). For further
    discussion, see [1977] 1B Unempl. Ins. Rep. (CCH) ¶1975.
29. *See Apperley v. General Motors Corp.*, 20 Mich. App. 374, 174
    N.W.2d 3 (Ct.App. 1969); *Harding Glass Co. v. Crutcher*, 244 Ark.
    618, 426 S.W.2d 403 (1968).
30. *See* 26 U.S.C. §3304(a) (9).
31. 26 U.S.C. §3304(a) (12).
32. *See Gols v. Ross*, 59 A.D.2d 994, 399 N.Y.S.2d 337 (3d Dep't
    1977).
33. *Mathews v. Eldridge*, 424 U.S. 319 (1976).
34. In 1983 contributions were required on wages up to $7000 in all
    states except Del., Ala., D.C., $7500; Ken., V.I., W.Va., $8000;
    Mont., $8,200; N.J., $8800; Minn., $9000; R.I., $9200; Iowa, $9400;
    N.D., $10,150; Nev., $10,200; Wash., $11,400; Ore., $12,000; Haw.,
    $13,800; Ida., $14,400; Utah, $14,800; Alas., $20,200; P.R., all wages.
35. 26 U.S.C. §§3301 *et seq.*
36. 42 U.S.C. §§5142 *et seq.*

Appendices

Appendix 1
(to Chapter III)

Federal Anti-Reprisal Statutes

The following statutes contain provisions prohibiting reprisals against employees for reporting violations of, or asserting rights under, those statutes:

Age Discrimination in Employment Act of 1967, 29 U.S.C. §623.

Asbestos School Hazard Detection & Control Act, 20 U.S.C. §3608.

Civil Rights Act of 1964, Title VII, 42 U.S.C. §2000e–3.

Civil Rights of Institutionalized Persons Act, 42 U.S.C. §1997(d).

Civil Service Reform Act of 1978, 5 U.S.C. §§2301, 2302, 7102, 7116.

Clean Air Act Amendments of 1977, 42 U.S.C. §§7401, 7622.

Comprehensive Environmental Response, Comp. & Liability Act of 1980, 42 U.S.C. §9610.

Conspiracy to Obstruct Justice Act, 15 U.S.C. §1985(2).

Consumer Credit Protection Act of 1968, 15 U.S.C. §1674.

Employee Retirement Income Security Act of 1974 (Pension Reform Act), 29 U.S.C. §§1140, 1141.

Energy Reorganization Act Amendment of 1978, 42 U.S.C. §5851.

Fair Labor Standards Act, 29 U.S.C. §215.

Federal Mine Safety and Health Act Amendment of 1977, 30 U.S.C. §§815, 820(b).

Federal Railroad Safety Act Amendment, 45 U.S.C. §441.

Federal Water Pollution Control Act of 1972, 33 U.S.C. §1367.

International Safe Container Act of 1977, 46 U.S.C. §1506.

Jury Duty Act, 28 U.S.C. §1875.

Longshoremen's and Harbor Workers' Compensation Act of 1972, 33 U.S.C. §948(a).

Migrant and Seasonal Agricultural Worker Protection Act of 1983, 29 U.S.C. §1855.

National Labor Relations Act, 29 U.S.C. §158.

Occupational Safety and Health Act of 1970, 29 U.S.C. §660.

Railroad Employers Act of 1908, 45 U.S.C. §60.

Safe Drinking Water Act of 1974, 42 U.S.C. §300j–9.

Solid Waste Disposal Act of 1976, 42 U.S.C. §6972.

Surface Mining Control & Reclamation Act of 1977, 30 U.S.C. §§1201, 1293.

Toxic Substances Control Act of 1976, 15 U.S.C. §2622.

Appendix 2
(to Chapter V)

Legal Resources for Victims of Employment Discrimination

Lawyers in Private Practice

Equal employment law is very technical and changes frequently. It is therefore important that you find an attorney who is experienced in this area. Most EEOC offices have lists of private attorneys who work in the civil rights field. Also, civil liberties and civil rights organizations in your area may be able to refer you to an experienced private attorney.

Legal Services Organizations

If you are poor or unemployed you may be eligible for free legal assistance from a local legal services organization supported by federal and local funding. These organizations, usually referred to as Legal Aid Societies or Legal Services Organizations, employ lawyers who provide legal assistance to poor people in all areas of law, including discrimination law. These organizations exist in nearly every city and county in the country.

To find your nearest legal services organization you should look through the phone book or call a local government official for advice. If you have difficulty finding the appropriate local organizations, there are several national organizations you might want to contact.

National Legal Aid and Defender Association
1625 K Street, NW, 8th Floor
Washington, DC 20006
  (202) 452–0620

Most legal services lawyers or their organizations are members of the NLADA. The NLADA may be able to refer you to the appropriate legal services office in your area.

Legal Services Corporation
733 15th St., NW
Washington, DC 20005
    (202) 272–4000

The Legal Services Corporation is an independent agency that provides federal funding to most legal services organizations. It should be able to refer you to an appropriate legal services office in your area.

National Civil Liberties and Civil Rights Organizations

Several national civil liberties and civil rights organizations have state and local offices (usually called chapters or affiliates) throughout the United States. Generally, the national offices will not be able to assist you directly, but will refer you to one of their local offices, which may assist you.

The local offices of the following major organizations are listed in your telephone directory. If you cannot find them, you should write to the national offices for referrals.

American Civil Liberties Union
132 W. 43d St.
New York, NY 10036
    (212) 944–9800

The ACLU specializes in free-speech law but is also involved in discrimination law. There are state affiliates and local chapters of the ACLU in nearly every state.

Mexican Legal Defense and Education Fund
28 Geary St.
San Francisco, CA 94108
    (415) 981–5800

MALDEF specializes in discrimination law and represents almost exclusively Mexican-Americans. Its offices are located primarily in the Midwest, the Southwest, and the West.

National Association for the Advancement of
   Colored People
186 Remsen St.
Brooklyn, NY 11201
   (212) 858-0800

The NAACP, the oldest and largest of the civil rights
organizations, specializes in racial discrimination law on behalf of blacks. It has state and local chapters throughout the
United States.

National Urban League
425 13th Street, NW
Washington, DC 20004
   (202) 393–4332

Like the NAACP, the National Urban League specializes
in racial discrimination law on behalf of blacks, and has offices
throughout the United States.

Puerto Rican Legal Defense Fund
95 Madison Ave.
New York, NY 10016
   (212) 532–8470

The PRLDF specializes in discrimination law and particularly in bilingual education law. It maintains several offices,
primarily in the Northeast.

Regional, Local, and Specialized Civil Liberties and Civil Rights Organizations

There is a large number of regional, local, and specialized
civil liberties and civil rights organizations across the United
States. Many of them are very small and operate primarily or
solely through volunteer help. Others employ staff attorneys.

ACLU Southern Regional Office
52 Fairlie Street
Atlanta, GA 30303
   (404) 523–2721

The ACLU Southern Regional Office specializes in voter discrimination law and jury discrimination law in the South.

> Center for Constitutional Rights
> 853 Broadway
> New York, NY 10003
>   (212) 674–3303

The Center for Constitutional Rights focuses on many constitutional issues, including discrimination issues.

> Center for Law and Social Policy
> 1751 N St., NW
> Washington, DC 20036
>   (202) 872–0670

The Center for Law and Social Policy is involved in civil liberties, civil rights issues, and occupational health and safety issues.

> Lawyers Committee for Civil Rights Under Law
> 733 15th St., NW
> Washington, DC 20005
>   (202) 628–6700

The Lawyers Committee concentrates on all aspects of racial discrimination law, primarily on behalf of blacks. It maintains a number of regional and local offices, and it often uses the volunteer services of lawyers in private law firms.

> NAACP Legal Defense Fund
> 10 Columbus Circle
> New York, NY 10019
>   (212) 586–8397

The Legal Defense Fund, an organization entirely separate from the NAACP (except for the shared name), has the largest national legal staff of any civil rights organization. It concentrates on all aspects of racial discrimination law and represents blacks almost exclusively. Although the Legal Defense Fund has no local offices, it maintains a close relationship with hundreds of lawyers, many of whom are black, and most of whom are in small private law firms located primarily in the South that specialize in civil rights law.

National Conference of Black Lawyers
126 W. 119th St.
New York, NY 10026
   (212) 866–3501

NCBL, an organization of black lawyers, focuses on all aspects of discrimination law through its national network of black lawyers.

National Lawyers Guild
853 Broadway
New York, NY 10003
   (212) 260–1360

The Guild, a membership organization of civil rights lawyers, focuses upon unpopular legal causes, including the rights of minorities. It maintains offices in most major cities.

Native American Rights Fund
1506 Broadway
Boulder, CO 80302
   (303) 447–8760

The Native American Rights Fund specializes in Native American issues and represents indigent Native Americans exclusively. It has several offices in the West and in the Southwest.

Southern Poverty Law Center
1001 S. Hull St.
Montgomery, AL 36101
   (205) 264–0286

The Southern Poverty Law Center specializes in the legal problems of the poor, and primarily represents poor blacks. It focuses its efforts throughout the South.

The following organizations provide assistance in the area of sexual harassment:

Women's Legal Defense Fund
2000 P St., NW
Washington, DC 20036
  (202) 887-0364

Working Women's Institute
593 Park Ave.
New York, NY 10021
  (212) 838-4420

The Institute also has a Legal Back-up Center which can provide help in litigating cases of sexual harassment.

Alliance Against Sexual Coercion
P.O. Box 1
Cambridge, MA 02139
  (617) 547-1176

AFSCME
1625 L St., NW
Washington, DC

Write for information about what unions can do to help women workers.

Appendix 3
(to Chapter XIX)

States with Laws on Age Discrimination in Employment

All but ten states have laws prohibiting age discrimination in employment. Because the federal ADEA requires you to use any available state remedy, you must know whether your state prohibits age discrimination in employment and what remedies are provided. The following is a list of states with some provisions on age discrimination; states not listed have no laws on age discrimination in employment. Check with the state agency listed for details on the law in your state.

State	Enforcement agency
Alaska	Commission for Human Rights
California	Dept. of Industrial Relations
Colorado	none
Connecticut	Commission on Human Rights and Opportunities
Delaware	Dept. of Labor
District of Columbia	Commission on Human Rights
Florida	Commission on Human Relations (Civil Service Commission for public employees)
Georgia	none
Hawaii	Dept. of Labor and Industrial Relations
Idaho	Commissioner of Labor
Illinois	none
Iowa	Civil Rights Commission
Kentucky	Commission on Human Rights
Louisana	none
Maine	Human Rights Commission
Maryland	Commission on Human Rights
Massachusetts	Commission Against Discrimination

Michigan	Civil Rights Commission
Minnesota	Dept. of Human Rights
Montana	Commission on Human Rights
Nebraska	Equal Opportunity Commission
Nevada	Equal Rights Commission
New Hampshire	Commission for Human Rights
New Jersey	Div. on Civil Rights
New Mexico	Human Rights Commission
New York	Div. of Human Rights
North Carolina	Human Relations Commission
North Dakota	none
Ohio	Dept. of Industrial Relations
Oklahoma	none
Oregon	Bureau of Labor
Pennsylvania	Human Relations Commission
Rhode Island	Dept. of Labor
South Carolina	Human Affairs Commission (public employees only)
Texas	none (public employees only)
Utah	Industrial Commission
Washington	Human Rights Commission
Wisconsin	Dept. of Industry, Labor, and Human Relations

Appendix 4
(to Chapter XV)

Wage-Hour Administration Offices

Office of the Wage-Hour Adminstrator
14th and Constitution Ave., NW
Washington, D.C. 20210

Regional Offices
Atlanta Region (AL, FL, GA, KT, MS, NC, SC, TN): 1371
Peachtree St., NE Atlanta, GA 30367 (404–881–4801)
>   Area Offices: Atlanta, Birmingham, Charlotte, Columbia,
>   Fort Lauderdale, Jackson, Jacksonville,
>   Knoxville, Louisville, Miami, Montgom-
>   ery, Nashville, Raleigh, Savannah, Tampa

Boston Region (CN, ME, MA, NH, RI, VT): JFK Federal
Bldg., Government Center, Room 1612C, Boston, MA 02203
(617–223–5565)
>   Area Offices: Boston, Hartford, Portland, Providence

Chicago Region (IL, IN, MI, MN, OH, WI): 230 South
Dearborn St., Chicago, IL 60604 (312–353–7250)
>   Area Offices: Chicago (North), Chicago (South), Cin-
>   cinnati, Cleveland, Columbus, Detroit,
>   Grand Rapids, Indianapolis, Madison,
>   Milwaukee, Minneapolis, South Bend,
>   Springfield

Dallas Region (AR, LA, NM, OK, TX): 555 Griffin Square
Bldg., Yound and Griffin Sts., Dallas, TX 75202 (214–767–6891)
>   Area Offices: Albuquerque, Corpus Christi, Dallas,
>   Fort Worth, Houston, Little Rock, New
>   Orleans, San Antonio, Tulsa

Denver Region (CO, MT, ND, UT, WY): 1961 Stout St.,
Denver, CO 80202 (303–327–4613)
>   Area Offices: Denver, Salt Lake City

Kansas City Region (IO, KA, MO, NE): 911 Walnut St., Kansas City, MO 64106 (816–374–5381)

Area Offices: Des Moines, Kansas City, Omaha, St. Louis

New York Region (CZ, NJ, NY, PR, VI): 1515 Broadway, New York, New York 10036 (212–944–3348)

Area Offices: Albany, Bronx, Brooklyn, Buffalo, Caribbean, Hato Rey, Hempstead, Newark, New York, Trenton

Philadelphia Region (DE, DC, MD, PA, VA, WV): Gateway Bldg., 3535 Market St., Philadelphia, PA 19104 (215–596–1194)

Area Offices: Baltimore, Charleston, Harrisburg, Hyattsville, Philadelphia, Pittsburgh, Richmond

San Francisco Region (AZ, CA, HA, NV): 450 Golden Gate Ave., San Francisco, CA 94102 (415–556–3592)

Area Offices: Glendale, Honolulu, Los Angeles, Phoenix, Sacramento, San Francisco, Santa Ana

Seattle Region (AS, ID, OR, WA): 909 First Ave., Seattle, WA 98104 (206–442–1916)

Area Offices: Portland, Seattle

Appendix 5
(to Chapter XVI)

Government Publications on Pensions

Listed below are Department of Labor publications on the Employee Retirement Income Security Act. They may be obtained from the area offices listed in Appendix 8 or from Pension and Welfare Benefit Programs, Labor-Management Services Administration, Room N4659, U.S. Department of Labor, 3d St. and Constitution Ave., NW, Washington, DC 20216.

What You Should Know About the Pension and Welfare Law. A 76-page comprehensive booklet explaining the rights of participants in pension and welfare plans and opportunities under ERISA for self-employed individuals and for employed individuals without pension coverage on their jobs.

Know Your Pension Plan. A 16-page booklet explaining various aspects of pension plans to help workers understand their plans and including a checklist for the provisions of a plan.

How to File a Claim for Your Benefit. An easy-to-read booklet outlining the steps necessary for filing a claim and what participants can do if a claim for benefits has been denied.

Often-Asked Questions About the Employee Retirement Income Security Act of 1974. An easy-to-use booklet that answers the questions pension plan participants ask most often about ERISA.

Coverage Under the Employee Retirement Income Security Act. A 12-page booklet listing the types of welfare and pension plans and types of benefits covered by ERISA.

Reporting and Disclosure: Employee Retirement Income Security Act of 1974. A 16-page booklet explaining ERISA's reporting and disclosure provisions and how they affect workers and their beneficiaries, employers, and plan administrators.

Fiduciary Standards: Employee Retirement Income Security Act of 1974. An 11-page booklet outlining the fiduciary provisions of ERISA.

Appendix 6
(to Chapter 16)
Labor-Management Services
Administration: Area Offices

Atlanta, GA 30309
1365 Peachtree St., NE
(404) 881–4090

Boston, MA 02108
110 Tremont St.
(617) 223–6736

Buffalo, NY 14202
111 W. Huron St.
(716) 846–4861

Chicago, IL 60604
175 W. Jackson Blvd.
(312) 353–7264

Cleveland, OH 44199
1240 E. 9th St.
(216) 522–3855

Dallas, TX 75202
555 Griffin Sq. Bldg.
(214) 767–6831

Denver, CO 80294
1961 Stout St.
(303) 837–5061

Detroit, MI 48226
231 W. Lafayette St.
(313) 226–6200

Hato Rey, PR 00918
Carlos Chardon St.
(809) 753–4441

Honolulu, HI 96850
300 Ala Moana
(808) 546–8984

Kansas City, MO 64106
911 Walnut St.
(816) 374–5261

Los Angeles, CA 90012
300 N. Los Angeles St.
(213) 688–4975

Miami, FL 33169
111 N.W. 183d St.
(305) 350–4611

Minneapolis, MN 55401
100 N. 6th St.
(612) 725–2292

Nashville, TN 37203
1808 W. End Bldg.
(615) 251–5906

Newark, NJ 07102
744 Broad St.
(201) 645–3712

New Orleans, LA 70130
600 South St.
(504) 589–6173

St. Louis, MO 63101
210 N. 12th Blvd.
(314) 425–4691

New York, NY 10007
26 Federal Plaza
(212) 264–1980

San Francisco, CA 94105
211 Main St.
(415) 556–2030

Philadelphia, PA 19106
601 Market St.
(215) 597–4961

Seattle, WA 98174
909 1st Ave.
(206) 442–5216

Pittsburgh, PA 15222
1000 Liberty Ave.
(412) 644–2925

Washington, DC 20036
1111 20th St., NW
(202) 254–6510

Appendix 7
(to Chapter 17)

**Significant Provisions of State
Workers' Compensation Laws**

	Occupational Diseases	Agricultural Workers	Domestic Workers	Permanent Total Benefits
ALABAMA Div. of Workmen's Compensation Dept. of Industrial Relations Industrial Relations Building Montgomery 36130 1(205)832-3626	1. Not included in definition 2. Yes 3. Full 4. Must occur soon after 5. Pneumoconiosis, black lung	No; employer may choose selective coverage	Not permitted to be covered	1. 66⅔% 2. $60 to 25% a.w.w. 3. $161 to 66⅔% a.w.w. 4. Duration of disability
ALASKA Workmen's Compensation Division Dept. of Labor P.O. Box 1149 Juneau 99821 1(907)465-2700	1. Yes 2. No 3. Full, not peculiar to occupation 4. None 5. None	Yes, except part-time workers	Yes (babysitters and cleaning persons)	1. 66⅔% 2. $65 or average wage if less 3. $858 to 133% of a.w.w. 4. Duration
ARIZONA Workmen's Compensation Division Industrial Commission 1601 W. Jefferson St. Phoenix 85007 1(602)271-4411	1. No 2. Yes 3. Peculiar to occupation 4. None 5. None	Yes	No	1. 66⅔% 2. Not prescribed by statute 3. $203.86 4. Life
ARKANSAS Workmen's Compensation Commission Justice Building State Capital Grounds Little Rock 72201 1(501)372-3980	1. Yes 2. Yes 3. Peculiar to occupation 4. Disablement or injury must occur within 1 yr. of last exposure[1]	No; employees may elect coverage	No	1. 66⅔% 2. $15 3. $140 4. Duration of disability

Permanent Partial Benefits	Schedule Benefits		Waiting Period	Rehabilitation Statutes	Death Benefits
	Wks	Maximum			
1. 66⅔%	1. 222	$35,742	3 days;	Employers liable	1. 50%
2. $60 to	2. 170	27,370	temporary	for reasonable	2. 66⅔%
25% a.w.w.	3. 200	32,200	total only	costs of	3. $60 to
3. $161 to	4. 139	22,349		vocational	25%
66⅔% a.w.w.	5. 124	79,964		rehab. services;	4. $161
4. 300 wks.	6. 53	8,533		refusal to	to 66⅔%
				accept services	a.w.w.
				means no	5. 500 wks.
				compensation	
1. 66⅔%	Law provides	$43,680	3 days;	Maximum	1. 66⅔%
2. $65 or	for mone-	33,600	retroactive if	$100 a month	2. 66⅔%
average	tary	40,320	disability	for perma-	3. $45 to
wage if less	limitation	28,700	over 28 days	nently disabled;	$75 (accord-
3. $858 to	but no	22,400		total maxi-	ing to no.
133% of	weekly limit	7,280		mum $5,000 for	of dep.)
a.w.w.				additional	4. $858
4. During				compensation	to 200% of
disability					a.w.w.
					5. Widowhood;
					children until
					19 or married
1. 55%	1. 260	$43,725	7 days;	Industrial	1. 35%
2. not	2. 217	36,438	retroactive	Commission	2. 66⅔%
prescribed	3. 217	36,438	if disability	authorized to	3. none
by statute	4. 173	29,150	over 2	provide awards	4. $107.03
3. $168.19	5. 130	21,863	wks.	as are necessary	to $203.81
4. During	6. 87	14,575		for vocational	5. Widow-
disability				rehab.	hood; chil-
					dren until 18
					or married
1. 66⅔%	1. 200	$28,800	7 days;	Maximum	1. 35%
2. $15	2. 150	21,000	retroactive if	$400 for training	2. 66⅔%
3. $140	3. 175	24,500	disability	of workers	3. $15
4. 450 wks	4. 125	17,500	over 2 wks.	with silicosis or	4. $140
	5. 100	14,000		asbestosis;	5. Widow-
	6. 40	5,600		workers with	hood; chil-
				permanent	dren until
				disability, reason-	18 or married
				able expenses	
				for 60 wks.	

	Occupational Diseases	Agricultural Workers	Domestic Workers	Permanent Total Benefits
CALIFORNIA Administrative Div. Div. of Industrial Accidents Dept. of Industrial Relations State Bldg. Annex 455 Golden Gate Ave. San Francisco 94102 1(415)557-3356	1. Yes 2. No exclusions 3. Full 4. None 5. Silicosis from underground mine	Yes	Yes (minimum required 52 hrs. or $100 in last 90 days)	1. 66⅔% 2. $49 3. $175 4. Life
COLORADO Workmen's Compensation Benefit Selection Dept. of Labor & Employment 200 E. 9th Ave. Denver 80203 1(303)837-1100	1. Yes (excludes heart attack) 2. Yes 3. Full 4. None 5. If injury begins 5 yrs. after job, presumed not job related	Yes	Yes, for any domestic workers whose employer spends over $2,000 a yr. in wages	1. 66⅔% 2. No statutory minimum 3. $261.80 to 80% of a.w.w. 4. Life
CONNECTICUT Workmen's Compensation Commission 115 Main St. Bridgeport 06604 1(203)889-3821	1. Yes 2. Yes 3. Only peculiar to occupation 4. None 5. Certain occupations	Yes	Yes (domestic workers employed more than 26 hrs. per wk. by one)	1. 66⅔% 2. $20[3] 3. $310 to 66% of a.w.w. 4. Duration of disability
DELAWARE Dept. of Labor 801 West St. Wilmington 19899 1(302)571-2710	1. Yes 2. No exclusion 3. Full 4. None 5. None	Yes, if employer insures payment for such workers	Yes (household workers who earn $1300 in 3-month period)	1. 66⅔% 2. $58.40 to 22⅘% of a.w.w. as actual wage if less 3. $175.28 to 66⅔% of a.w.w 4. Duration

Permanent Partial Benefits	Schedule Benefits		Waiting Period	Rehabilitation Statutes	Death Benefits
	Wks	Maximum			
1. 66⅔% 2. $30 3. $70 4. 619 wks.	Ratings vary for injury, age, and occupation		3 days; temporary total disabilities only	Living expenses paid while in a rehab. program	1. 2. 3. $49 4. $175 5. Up to $50,000 ($55,000 with children)
1. 66⅔% 2. No statutory minimum 3. $84 4. During disability	1. 208 2. 104 3. 208 4. 104 5. 139 6. 35	$17,472 8,736 17,472 8,736 11,676 2,940	3 days; retroactive if injury over 2 wks.	Vocational rehab. 26 wks; can be extended another 26 wks. (tuition, fees, transportation)	1. 66⅔% 2. 66⅔% 3. $65.45 4. $261.80 to 80% of a.w.w. 5. Widowhood; children until 18 or married
1. 66⅔% 2. $20 3. $285 to 66⅔% 4. 780 wks.	1. 312 2. 252 3. 238 4. 188 5. 235 6. 52	$88,920 71,820 67,830 53,580 66,975 14,820	3 days; retroactive if injury over 7 days	Maximum $40 a week payable in addition to compensation during rehab.	1. 66⅔% 2. 66⅔% 3. $20 4. $285 to 66⅔% 5. Widowhood; children for 780 wks.
1. 66⅔% 2. $58.40 or actual wage if less 3. $175.28 4. 300 wks	1. 250 2. 220 3. 250 4. 160 5. 200 6. 75	$43,820 38,562 43,820 28,045 35,056 13,146	3 days; no waiting period if amputation or hospitalized; 7 days retroactive	In discretion of Industrial Accident Board (inc. board, lodging, travel)	1. 66⅔% 2. 80% 3. $58.40 to 22⅔% of a.w.w. 4. $175.28 to $210.23 5. Widowhood; children until 18[4]

	Occupational Diseases	Agricultural Workers	Domestic Workers	Permanent Total Benefits
DISTRICT OF COLUMBIA Office of Worker's Compensation Programs District Office No. 40 U.S. Dept. of Labor Rm. 802 177 K St., NW Washington 20211 1(202)254-3470	1. Yes 2. No 3. Full 4. None 5. None	No coverage	Yes	1. 66⅔% 2. $114.06 to 50% of a.w.w. 3. $496.70 to 200% of a.w.w. 4. Duration
FLORIDA Bureau of Workmen's Compensation Div. of Labor Ashley Bldg. Tallahassee 32301 1(904)488-7396	1. No[6] 2. Yes 3. Full 4. Death must follow within 350 wks. of last exposure 5. None	All except certain employees[7]	Not covered	1. 60% 2. $20 or actual wage if less 3. $228 to 66⅔% of a.w.w. 4. Duration
GEORGIA Board of Workmen's Compensation 499 Labor Bldg. 254 Washington St. Atlanta 30334 1(404)656-2900	1. No 2. Yes 3. Full coverage 4. Silicosis, asbestosis, 3 yrs.; other diseases, 1 yr.; death, 7 yrs. 5. None	Not covered	Not covered	1. 66⅔% 2. $25 or actual wage if less 3. $115 4. Duration
HAWAII Dept. of Labor and Industrial Relations 825 Mililani St. Honolulu 96813 1(808)548-3150	1. No 2. No exclusions 3. Full coverage 4. No provision 5. No provision	Covered	Workers employed for family or household whose wages are $225 during calendar yr.	1. 66⅔% 2. $59 to 25% of a.w.w. 3. $235 to 100% of a.w.w. 4. Duration

Permanent Partial Benefits	Schedule Benefits		Waiting Period	Rehabilitation Statutes	Death Benefits
---	Wks	Maximum	---	---	---
1. 66⅔% 2. $144.06 to 50% of a.w.w. 3. $456.24 to 200% of a.w.w. 4. Duration	1. 312 2. 244 3. 288 4. 205 5. 160 6. 52	$142,346 111,323 131,397 93,529 72,998 23,724	3 days; retroactive if injury over 14 days	Max. $25 a week payable for maintenance of disabled in addition to compensation	1. 50% 2. 66⅔% 3. $114.06 to 50% of a.w.w. 4. None 5. Widowhood;[5] children until 18
1. 60% 2. $25 or actual wage if less 3. $228 to 66⅔% of a.w.w. 4. 350 wks.	Benefits are calculated on basis of wage-loss formula		7 days; retroactive after more than 14 days	Div. of Labor & Employment Opportunity directed to assist permanently disabled workers	1. 45% 2. 60% 3. $20 or actual wage if less 4. $228 to 100% of a.w.w. 5. Widowhood; children until 18[8]
1. 66⅔% 2. $25 or actual wage if less 3. $115 4. Duration	1. 255 2. 160 3. 225 4. 135 5. 125 6. 60	$25,875 18,400 25,815 15,525 14,375 6,900	7 days; retroactive if over 28 days	Rehab. services $5,000 (52 wks. incl. board, lodging, travel); can be extended	1. 66⅔% 2. 66⅔% 3. $25 or actual wage 4. $115 5. 400 wks.
1. 66⅔% 2. $59 to 25% of applicable min. 3. $235 to 100% 4. Varies	1. 312 2. 244 3. 288 4. 205 5. 160 6. 52	$73,320 57,340 67,680 48,175 37,600 12,220	2 days; retroactive if over 5 days	Max. $5,000 for permanently disabled	1. 50% 2. 66⅔% 3. $59 to 25% of applicable min. 4. $176 to $235 5. Widowhood; children until 18 yrs.

	Occupational Diseases	Agricultural Workers	Domestic Workers	Permanent Total Benefits
IDAHO Industrial Commission Statehouse Boise 83720 1(208)384-2193	1. No 2. No 3. Characteristic & peculiar to occupation 4. [10] 5. None	No compulsory or elective coverage	Not covered	1. 60% 2. $99 to 45% of a.w.w. 3. $132 to 90% of a.w.w. 4. 52 wks. then 60% of a.w.w.
ILLINOIS Industrial Commission 160 N. LaSalle St. Chicago 60601 1(312)435-6555	1. No 2. No exclusions 3. Full 4. Certain limitations 5. Black Lung	All except those working for employer who employs less than 500 man-hrs. per 3 mos.	Workers employed 40 hrs. a wk. for 13 wks. are covered	1. 66⅔% 2. $147.82 to 50% of a.w.w. 3. $394.19 to 133½% of a.w.w. 4. Life
INDIANA Industrial Board 601 State Office Bldg. 100 N. Senate Ave. Indianapolis 46204 1(317)633-6452	1. No 2. Yes 3. Full 4. Disability or death must result within a certain amount of time 5. Pneumonconiosis	No compulsory or elective coverage	Not covered	1. 66⅔% 2. $50 or average wage if less 3. $140 4. 500 wks. thereafter payments may be made indefinitely

Permanent Partial Benefits	Wks	Schedule Benefits Maximum	Waiting Period	Rehabilitation Statutes	Death Benefits
1. 55% 2. Same as max. 3. $121 to 55% of a.w.w. 4. Varies in proportion to whole man	1. 300 2. 270 3. 200 4. 140 5. 175	$36,300 32,670 24,200 16,940 21,175	5 days; retroactive if over 2 wks.	Rehab. Div. of Industrial Commission provides physical and vocational rehab. (job placement, board, lodging, transportation)	1. 45% 2. 60% 3. No min. 4. $99– $132 to 45–60% of a.w.w. 5. 500 wks.
1. 66⅔% 2. $80.90– $96.90 (or employee's wage if less) 3. $282.25 to 100% of a.w.w. 4. During disability	1. 300 2. 190 3. 275 4. 155 5. 160 6. 50	$118,257 74,896 108,402 61,099 63,079 19,710	3 days; for temporary total only; retroactive if over 14 days	Employers pay for treatment, nutrition, training for mental, physical, & vocational rehab.	1. 66⅔% 2. 66⅔% 3. $147.82 to 50% of a.w.w. 4. $394.19 to 133⅓% of a.w.w. 5. Widow-hood; children until 18[11]
1. 60% 2. No statutory minimum 3. $75 4. 500 wks.	1. 250 2. 200 3. 225 4. 175 5. 175 6. 75	$18,750 15,000 16,875 13,125 13,125 56,250	7 days; retroactive if over 21 days	Ind. Rehab. Services Board has jurisdiction to provide services to handicapped	1. 66⅔% 2. 66⅔% 3. $50 or average wage if less 4. $150 5. 500 wks.

	Occupational Diseases	Agricultural Workers	Domestic Workers	Permanent Total Benefits
IOWA Industrial Commissioner Workmen's Compensation Services State Capitol Complex Des Moines 50319 1(515)281-5935	1. No 2. Yes 3. Full 4. Certain time limits 5. 12	Covered if employer wage payments were 1,000 or over (1 yr.)	Covered earnings of $200 in last 15 wks.	1. 80% 2. $36 or actual wage if less 3. $501 to 200% of a.w.w. 4. Duration
KANSAS Director Division of Worker's Compensation 535 Kansas Ave. 6th floor Topeka 66612 1(913)296-7474	1. No 2. Yes 3. Full 4. Silicosis, 1 yr., and death after 3 yrs.; other diseases, 1 yr. from last exposure 5. None	No statutory coverage	If employer had a payroll of average $10,000 for employees	1. 66⅔% 2. $25 3. $187 to 75% of a.w.w.[13] 4. Duration
KENTUCKY Director Div. of Workmen's Compensation Dept. of Labor Capital Plaza Tower Frankfort 40601 1(502)564-5550	1. No 2. No 3. Full 4. None 5. Pneumoconiosis, 10-yr. exposure; special black-lung statute	No statutory coverage	Employed 40 hrs. a wk. in a house	1. 66⅔% 2. $46.65 to 20% of a.w.w. 3. $233.26 to 100% of a.w.w. 4. Life

Permanent Partial Benefits	Schedule Benefits		Waiting Period	Rehabilitation Statutes	Death Benefits
	Wks	Maximum			
1. 80%	1. 250	$115,250	3 days; retroactive if injury over 14 days	Max. $20 a wk. plus other comp. for 13 wks; can be extended	1. 80%
2. $36 or actual wage is less	2. 190	$ 87,590			2. 80%
	3. 220	$101,420			3. $36 or actual wage
3. $461 to 122% of a.w.w.	4. 150	$ 69,150			4. $501 to 200% of a.w.w.
	5. 140	$ 64,540			
4. Proportional to injury	6. 56	23,050			5. Widowhood; children until 18[11]
1. 66⅔%	1. 210	$39,270	7 days; retroactive after 21 days illness	26 wks. medical, physical, & vocational services; can be extended 26 wks.; total $12,000 (board, lodging, travel)	1. 66⅔%
2. Not stated	2. 150	28,050			2. 66⅔%
	3. 200	37,400			3. $25
3. $187 to 66⅔% of a.w.w.	4. 125	23,375			4. $187 to 66⅔%
	5. 120	22,440			5. Widowhood; children until 18[5]
4. 415 wks. total maximum of $50,000	6. 30	5,610			
1. 66⅔%	Determined as percentage of permanent total disability.		7 days; retroactive if injury over 2 wks.	Vocational rehab. services 26 wks. (reasonable costs of board, lodging, travel can be extended)	1. 50%
2. No statutory minimum					2. 75%
3. $174.95 to 60% of a.w.w.					3. $46.65 to 20% of a.w.w.
4. During disability					4. $174.95 to 75% of a.w.w.
					5. Widowhood; children until 18[5]

	Occupational Diseases	Agricultural Workers	Domestic Workers	Permanent Total Benefits
LOUISIANA Dept of Labor 1045 State Land & Natural Resources Bldg. P.O. Box 44063 Baton Rouge 70804 1(504)389-5313	1. No 2. No 3. Full 4. None 5. Unfavorable un- less worked for 12 months	Covered	Not covered	1. 66⅔% 2. $49 to 20% of a.w.w. 3. $367.25 to 66⅔% of a.w.w. 4. Duration
MAINE Chairman Industrial Accident Commission State Office Bldg. Augusta 04330 1(207)623-4511	1. No 2. No 3. Full 4. Disability must occur within set time of last exposure 5. Silicosis, 2 yrs. out of 15	Not covered	Not covered	1. 66⅔% 2. $25 3. $367.25 to 166⅔% of a.w.w. 4. Duration of disability
MARYLAND Chairman Workmen's Compen- sation Commission 108 E. Lexington St. Baltimore 21202 1(301)383-4775	1. No 2. No 3. Full 4. Disability or death must occur within certain time after exposure 5. Silicosis, asbestos	Covered if 3 or more full-time employees or payroll of $15,000	Covered if employee made $250 in any calendar quarter	1. 66⅔% 2. $25 or a.w.w. if less 3. $248 to 100% of a.w.w. 4. Duration

Permanent Partial Benefits	Wks	Schedule Benefits Maximum	Waiting Period	Rehabilitation Statutes	Death Benefits
1. 66⅔% 2. $49 to 20% of a.w.w. 3. $164 to 66⅔% of a.w.w. 4. 450 wks.	1. 200 2. 150 3. 175 4. 125 5. 100 6. 50	$32,800 24,600 28,700 20,500 16,400 —	7 days; retroactive if over 6 wks.	No provisions in workmen's compensation law	1. 32½% 2. 65% 3. $49 to 20% of a.w.w. 4. $164 to 66⅔% of a.w.w. 5. Widowhood; children until 18[5]
1. 66⅔% 2. No statutory minimum 3. $332.16 to 133% of a.w.w. 4. Duration of disability	1. 200 2. 165 3. 200 4. 165 5. 100 6. 50	$73,450 60,596 73,450 60,596 36,725 18,363	3 days; retroactive if illness over 14 days	Maximum $35 a wk. for 52 wks.; can be extended (plus travel, sustenance, post-secondary education)	1. 66⅔% 2. 66⅔%[14] 3. $25 4. $367.25 to 200% of a.w.w. 5. Widowhood; children until 18[5]
1. 66⅔% 2. $50 or actual wage if less 3. $166 to 166⅔% of a.w.w. or $83 to 33⅓% of a.w.w. (non-serious) 4. Duration	1. 300 2. 250 3. 300 4. 250 5. 250 6. 125	$66,132 55,055 66,132 55,055 55,055 10,375	3 days; retroactive if injury over 14 days	Benefits up to $40 a wk. (if required to live away from home) & transportation	1. 66⅔% 2. 66⅔% 3. $25 or average wage if less 4. $248 to 100% of a.w.w. 5. Widowhood[15]; children until 18[5]

	Occupational Diseases	Agricultural Workers	Domestic Workers	Permanent Total Benefits
MASSACHUSETTS Chairman Industrial Accident Board 100 Cambridge St. Boston 02202 1(617)724-3400	1. Yes 2. Yes 3. Full 4. None 5. None	Covered	Seasonal casual (less than 16 hrs. a wk.) are elective. All others covered	1. 66⅔% 2. $40 3. $269.93 to 100% of s.a.w.w. 4. Duration
MICHIGAN Director Bureau of Worker's Compensation Dept. of Labor 309 N. Washington Ave. Lansing 48933 1(517)373-3480	1. Yes 2. Yes 3. Full 4. None 5. None	Covered	Covered unless employed less than 35 hrs. a wk. for 13 wks.	1. 66⅔% 2. $144–$159 + extra for dependent 3. $181–$210 4. Duration
MINNESOTA Administrator Div. of Workmen's Compensation Dept. of Labor and Industry Space Center, 5th fl. 444 Lafayette St. St. Paul 55101 1(612)296-2258	1. Yes 2. No exclusions 3. Full 4. None 5. None	Covered, if they don't work for family farm	Covered, if earns more than $500 in 3 mo. period from single household	1. 66⅔% 2. $122 to 50% of a.w.w. (or employee's actual wage if less) 3. $267 to 100% of a.w.w. 4. Duration

| Permanent Partial Benefits | Schedule Benefits | | Waiting Period | Rehabilitation Statutes | Death Benefits |
	Wks	Maximum			
1. 100%	Fixed	$6,750	5 days;	In addition to	1.
2. No statutory minimum	sums allowable in	5,250	retroactive	other compensations, rehab.	2.
3. $245.48	addition	6,000	after 6	offered in form of	3. None
4. During disability	to other	4,500	days	travel, room, &	4. $110
	compensation	6,000		board	+ $6 for
		4,500			each additional child
					5. 400 wks.;[16] children until 18[5]
1. 66⅔%	1. 269	$48,689	7 days;	Services up to	1. 66⅔%
2. No statutory minimum	2. 215	38,915	retroactive if	52 wks.; can be	2. 66⅔%
3. $181	3. 215	38,915	over 2	extended 52	3. $144–
–$210 (+	4. 162	29,322	wks.	wks.	$156
extra for	5. 162	29,322			4. $181–$204
dependent)					5. 500 wks.;
4. During					children
disability					until 21[5]
1. 66⅔%	1. 270	$65,880	3 days;	Employers	1. 50%
2. No statutory minimum	2. 220	53,680	temporary	liable for any	2. 66⅔%
3. $244 to	3. 220	53,680	total only;	expense	3. No
100% of	4. 165	40,260	retroactive	reasonable &	statutory
a.w.w.	5. 160	39,040	after 10	necessary;	minimum
4. 350	6. 85	20,740	days	liable for 156	4. $244 to
wks.				wks. additional	100% of
				compensation	a.w.w.
				during retraining	5. Widowhood;[15] children until 18[5]

	Occupational Diseases	Agricultural Workers	Domestic Workers	Permanent Total Benefits
MISSISSIPPI Chairman Workmen's Compen- sation Commission 1404 Walter Sillers State Office Bldg. P.O. Box 987 Jackson 39205 1(601)354-7496	1. No 2. No 3. Full (direct casual relation between disease & illness necessary) 4. None 5. None	No coverage	No coverage	1. 66⅔% 2. $25 3. $112 4. 450 wks.; total $40,950
MISSOURI Director Division of Workmen's Compensation P.O Box 58 Jefferson City 65101 1(314)751-4231	1. No 2. Yes 3. Full 4. None 5. None	Covered, if employer elects by purchase of valid com- pensation insurance policy	Not covered	1. 66⅔% 2. No statutory minimum 3. $174 4. Duration
MONTANA Administrator Div. of Labor & Industry 815 Front St. Helena 59601 1(406)449-2047	1. No 2. No 3. Full 4. Silicosis 5. Black lung	Covered	No coverage	1. 66⅔% 2. No statutory minimum 3. $219 to 100% of a.w.w. 4. Disability
NEBRASKA Presiding Judge Workmen's Compen- sation Court State Capitol Lincoln 68509 1(402)471-2658	1. Yes 2. Yes 3. Full 4. None 5. None	No coverage	No coverage	1. 66⅔% 2. $49 or actual wage if less 3. $180 4. Duration

Permanent Partial Benefits		Schedule Benefits		Waiting Period	Rehabilitation Statutes	Death Benefits
	Wks	Maximum				
1. 66⅔% 2. $25 3. $112 4. 450 wks.; total $40,950	1. 200 2. 150 3. 175 4. 125 5. 100 6. 40	$22,400 16,800 19,600 14,000 11,200 4,480		5 days; retroactive if illness over 14 days	Max. $10 a wk. for not more than 52 wks.	1. 35% 2. 66⅔% 3. $25 4. $112 5. 450 wks.; total $40,950
1. 66⅔% 2. None 3. $95.54 4. 400 wks.	1. 232 2. 175 3. 215 4. 150 5. 140 6. 44	$24,381 18,392 21,755 15,764 13,376 4,204		3 days; retroactive after 4 wks. disability	Max. $35 for 20 wks.; in unusual situation, can be extended	1. 66⅔% 2. 66⅔% 3. None 4. $150 5. Widowhood;[15] children until 18[5]
1. 66⅔% 2. No statutory minimum 3. $109.50 to 50% of a.w.w. 4. 500 wks.	1. 280 2. 200 3. 300 4. 180 5. 165 6. 40	$30,660 21,900 32,850 19,710 18,068 4,380		5 days; retroactive after 5 days disability	A Max. $50 payable for maintenance while receiving rehab.	1. 66⅔% 2. 66⅔% 3. $99 to 50% of a.w.w. 4. $219 to 100% of a.w.w. 5. Widowhood;[15] children until 18[5]
1. 66⅔% 2. $40 or actual wage if less 3. $180 4. 300 wks.	1. 225 2. 175 3. 215 4. 150 5. 125 6. 50	$40,500 31,500 38,700 27,000 22,500 9,000		7 days; retroactive if disability over 6 wks.	Vocational rehab. fund provides payment for all or part of rehab. services without limit	1. 66⅔% 2. 75% 3. $49 or actual wage if less 4. $180 5. Widowhood;[15] children until 18[5]

	Occupational Diseases	Agricultural Workers	Domestic Workers	Permanent Total Benefits
NEVADA Chairman Industrial Commission 515 E. Musser St. Carson City 89701 1(702)855-5284	1. No 2. No 3. Full 4. 12 mos. from date of last exposure; silicosis, exposure 3 yrs. out of 10 5. None	No coverage	No coverage	1. 66⅔% 2. Same as maximum 3. $270.20 to 150% of a.w.w. 4. Life
NEW HAMPSHIRE Claim Supervisor Workmen's Compensation Division Dep't of Labor 1 Pillsbury St. Concord 03301 1(602)271-3176	1. Yes 2. No specific exclusions 3. Full coverage 4. None 5. Heart and lung for firefighters	Covered	Covered to the extent covered by federal Social Security Act	1. $92 to 66⅔% of a.w.w. 2. $30 or actual wage if less 3. $234 to 100% of a.w.w. 4. Duration
NEW JERSEY Director Div. of Workmen's Compensation Dept. of Labor & Industry Bldg. John Fitch Plaza Trenton 08625 1(609)292-2414	1. No 2. No 3. Full 4. None 5. None	Covered	All	1. 66⅔% 2. $53 3. $199 to 75% of s.a.w.w. 4. 450 wks. (can be extended)

Permanent Partial Benefits	Schedule Benefits		Waiting Period	Rehabilitation Statutes	Death Benefits
	Wks	Maximum			
1. Varies with percentage of disability 2. No statutory minimum 3. Varies with percentage of disability 4. 241 wks.	Payment depends on the amount of disability and claimant's a.w.w.		5 days; retroactive if disability over 5 days	The Industrial Commission provides rehab counseling & training	1. 66⅔% 2. 66⅔% 3. No statutory minimum 4. $270.20 to 150% of a.w.w. 5. Widowhood;[15] children until 18[5]
1. $92 to 66⅔% of a.w.w. 2. $30 or a.w.w. if less 3. $234 to 100% of a.w.w. 4. During disability	1. 214 2. 175 3. 214 4. 151 5. 126 6. 52	$50,076 40,950 50,076 35,334 29,484 12,168	3 days; retroactive if disability over 7 days	Rehab. services are good for one year— Employer pays for board, travel, lodging, books, & tools	1. Per wage and compensation schedule 2. Same as above 3. $30 or average wage if less 4. $234 to 100% of a.w.w. 5. 400 wks. (children until 18)[5]
1. Based on wage & compensation schedule 2. $35 3. $199 4. 550 wks.	1. 330 2. 245 3. 315 4. 230 5. 225 6. 60	$62,634 37,902 59,787 31,694 23,850 2,820	7 days; retroactive if disability over 7 days	Rehab. Commission can order rehab. services	1. 50% 2. 70% 3. $53 4. $199 to 75% of a.w.w. 5. Widowhood;[17] children until 18[5]

	Occupational Diseases	Agricultural Workers	Domestic Workers	Permanent Total Benefits
NEW MEXICO Labor Commissioner Labor & Industrial Commission Rm. 129, Villagra Bldg. Santa Fe 87503 1(505)827-2721	1. No 2. No 3. Full 4. Silicosis, exposure 1,250 shifts and disablement within 2 yrs.; other time limits too 5. None	No coverage	No coverage	1. 66⅔% 2. $36 or actual wage if less 3. $221.50 to 100% of state average weekly wage 4. 600 wks.
NEW YORK Chairman Workmen's Compensation Board 2 World Trade Ctr. New York 10047 1(212)488-4141	1. Yes 2. No exclusions 3. Full 4. Silicosis, exposure for 6 mos. 5. 60 days of exposure to dust in state is considered injurious	Covered, if wage payments of farmer exceeds $1,200 for yr.	Covered, if employed 40 hours per wk.	1. 66⅔% 2. $30 or actual wage if less 3. $215 4. Duration
NORTH CAROLINA North Carolina Industrial Commission 4000 Old Wake Forest Rd. Raleigh 27661 1(919)733-3201	1. No 2. Yes 3. Full 4. Silicosis, 21 yrs. in state, 10 yrs. from last exposure 5. None	Not covered	Not covered	1. 66⅔% 2. $30 3. $210 to 100% of a.w.w. 4. Duration of disability

Permanent Partial Benefits	Wks	Schedule Benefits Maximum	Waiting Period	Rehabilitation Statutes	Death Benefits
1. 66⅔% 2. $36 or actual wage if less 3. $221.50 to 100% of a.w.w. 4. 600 wks.	1. 200 2. 125 3. 200 4. 115 5. 130 6. 40	$44,300 27,688 44,300 25,473 28,795 8,860	7 days; retroactive if disability over 4 wks.	Receive maintenance and other expenses up to $1,000 plus other compensation	1. 66⅔% 2. 66⅔% 3. No statutory minimum 4. $221.50 to 100% of a.w.w. 5. Widowhood; children until 18[5]
1. 66⅔% 2. $30 or actual wage if less 3. $105 4. During disability	1. 312 2. 244 3. 288 4. 205 5. 160 6. 60	$32,760 25,620 30,240 21,525 16,800 6,300	7 days; retroactive if disability more than 14 days	$30 a wk. max. for maintenance; additional compensation available for rehab.	1. 66⅔% 2. 66⅔% 3. $30 4. $215 5. Widowhood; children until 18[5]
1. 66⅔% 2. $30, schedule; no run for non-schedule 3. $210 to 100% of a.w.w. 4. 300 wks.	1. 240 2. 200 3. 200 4. 144 5. 120 6. 70	$50,400 42,000 42,000 30,200 25,200 14,700	7 days; retroactive if disability more than 28 days	Rehab. compensation at discretion of Industrial Commissioner	1. 66⅔% 2. 66⅔% 3. $20 4. $210 to 100% of a.w.w. 5. Widowhood; children until 18[5]

	Occupational Diseases	Agricultural Workers	Domestic Workers	Permanent Total Benefits
NORTH DAKOTA Chairman Workmen's Compensation Bureau Russel Bldg. Highway 83 N. Bismarck 58505 1(701)224-2700	1. Yes 2. Yes 3. Full 4. None 5. Firemen & police officers (certain diseases)	Not covered	Not covered	1. 66⅔% 2. $140 to 60% of s.a.w.w., (or employee's wage if less) 3. $233 to 100% of s.a.w.w. (+ $5 for each dependent) 4. Duration
OHIO Administrator Bureau of Workmen's Compensation Ohio Dept. Bldg. 65 S. Front St. Columbus 43215 1(614)466-2950	1. No 2. Yes 3. Full 4. Must be contracted within 12 mos. previous to disablement. Certain diseases for firemen & police; limits for silicosis 5. None	Covered	Covered, if earned more than $160 in one calendar quarter	1. 66⅔% 2. $137.50 to 50% of a.w.w. 3. $275 to 100% of a.w.w. 4. Life
OKLAHOMA Chairman State Industrial Commission 2101 N. Lincoln Jim Thorpe Bldg. Oklahoma City 73105 1(405)521-3661	1. Yes 2. Yes 3. Full 4. None 5. None	Covered, if employer had payroll of $25,000 in calendar yr.	Covered, if employer had payroll of $10,000 for such workers in calendar yr. (less than 2 employees are exempt)	1. 66⅔% 2. $30 or actual wage if less 3. 66⅔% of s.a.w.w. 4. Duration

340

Permanent Partial Benefits	Schedule Benefits		Waiting Period	Rehabilitation Statutes	Death Benefits
	Wks	Maximum			
1.	1. 250	$10,000	5 days; retroactive if disability more than 5 days	Rehab. services unit coordinates medical, economic, & social benefits— paid in lieu of compensation	1. 66⅔%
2. $40	2. 250	10,000			2. 66⅔%
3. $40	3. 234	9,360			3. $10
4. 500 wks.	4. 150	6,000			4. $210 to 100% of s.a.w.w.
	5. 150	6,000			5. Widowhood;[18] children until 18[5]
	6. 50	2,000			
1. 66⅔%	1. 225	$30,938	7 days; retroactive if disability over 3 wks.	Max. $84 a wk. for 1 yr. Industrial commission pays costs of artificial appliances	1. 66⅔%
2. $68.75 to 25% of a.w.w., schedule; no minimum for non-schedule	2. 175	24,063			2. 66⅔%
	3. 200	27,500			3. $137.50 to 50% of a.w.w.
3. $137.50 to 50% of a.w.w.[19]	4. 150	20,625			4. $275 to 100% of a.w.w.
	5. 125	17,188			5. Widowhood;[20] children until 18[5]
4. [19]	6. 25	3,438			
1. 66⅔%	1. 250	$22,500	3 days; retroactive if disability over 5 days	Services for 52 wks.; can be extended 52 wks. (Books, lodging, transportation, equipment)	1. $50
2. $30	2. 200	18,000			2. $75
3. $90	3. 250	22,500			3. None
4. 500 wks.	4. 200	18,000			4. $155 to 66⅔% of s.a.w.w.
	5. 200	18,000			5. Widowhood;[15] children until 18[5]
	6. 100	9,000			

	Occupational Diseases	Agricultural Workers	Domestic Workers	Permanent Total Benefits
OREGON Chairman Workmen's Compensation Bldg. Labor & Industrial Bldg., Rm. 201 Salem 97301 1(503)378-3311	1. No 2. Yes 3. Full 4. None 5. Lung, cardiovascular for firemen	Covered	Covered	1. 66⅔% 2. $50 or 90% of actual wage, whichever is less 3. $286.88 to 100% of a.w.w. (+ $5 for each dependent) 4. Duration
PENNSYLVANIA Director Workmen's Compensation Bureau Dept. of Labor & Industry Labor & Industry Bldg. Harrisburg 17120 1(717)787-4335	1. Yes 2. No 3. Full 4. Disability or death must occur within 300 wks. of last exposure 5. If illness from hazard in occupation	Covered, if employee paid $150 or employed 20 days	Not covered	1. 66⅔% 2. $131 to 50% of s.a.w.w. 3. $262 to 100% of s.a.w.w. 4. Duration
PUERTO RICO Chairman Industrial Commission G.P.O. 4466 San Juan 00936 1(809)783-4455	No information	Covered (same as other workers)	Not covered	1. 66⅔% 2. $12.50 3. $31.25 4. Duration

Permanent Partial Benefits	Schedule Benefits		Waiting Period	Rehabilitation Statutes	Death Benefits
	Wks	Maximum			
1. 66⅔% 2. $100 or 90% of actual wage, but not less than $25 3. $286.88 to 80% of a.w.w. 4. Varies in proportion to scheduled injuries	$100 for each degree of injury for scheduled injuries in monthly payments	$19,200 15,000 15,000 13,500 10,000 6,000	3 days; retroactive if disabled more than 14 days	Expends such funds as necessary for rehab.	1. 2. 3. Same as maximum 4. $134.44 to $286.88 5. Widow-hood; children until 18[5]
1. 66⅔% 2. None 3. $262 to 100% of a.w.w. 4. 500 wks.	1. 410 2. 335 3. 410 4. 250 5. 275 6. 60	$107,420 87,770 107,420 65,500 72,050 15,720	7 days; no waiting period for scheduled injuries; retroactive after 14 days	Employers liable for all rehab. services. Dept. of Labor furnishes counseling and rehab. services	1. 51% 2. 66⅔% 3. $135 to 50% of s.a.w.w. 4. $262 to 100% of s.a.w.w. 5. Widow-hood;[15] children until 18[5]
1. 66⅔% 2. $10 3. $45 4. 450 wks.	1. 300 2. 200 3. 300 4. 175 5. — 6. 60	$10,000 9,000 10,000 7,875 — 2,700	3 days; retroactive if disability over 7 days	Manager of State Insurance Fund authorized to refer claimant for rehab. services, not to exceed 26 wks.	1. 50% 2. $5 3. $12.50 4. $31.25 5. Widow-hood; children until 18[5]

	Occupational Diseases	Agricultural Workers	Domestic Workers	Permanent Total Benefits
RHODE ISLAND Administrator Division of Workmen's Compensation Dept. of Labor 235 Promenade St. Providence 02908 1(402)277-2722	1. Yes 2. No 3. Full 4. None 5. None	Not covered	Not covered	1. 66⅔% 2. 3. $238 to 100% of a.w.w. (+ $6 for each dependent) 4. Duration
SOUTH CAROLINA Director Industrial Commission 1800 St. Julian Pl. Middleburg Office Park Columbia 29204 1(803)758-7108	1. No 2. Yes 3. Full 4. Pulmonary diseases, inhale for 1 yr. and suffer total disability 5. Firefighters (heart or respiration)	Not covered	Covered, if employer had annual payroll of over $3,000	1. 66⅔% 2. $25 3. $216 to 100% of a.w.w. 4. 500 wks.
SOUTH DAKOTA Director Div. of Labor & Management Dept. of Labor Foss Bldg., Rm. 425 Pierre 57501 1(605)224-3681	1. No 2. Yes 3. Full 4. None 5. None	Covered, if working with threshing machinery, corn huskers, or other mechanized farming equipment	Covered, if employed 24 hrs. a wk. for more than 6 wks. in 13 wk. period	1. 66⅔% 2. $96 to ½ of maximum a.w.w. (or average wage if less) 3. $191 to 94% of s.a.w.w. 4. Duration

| Permanent Partial Benefits | Schedule Benefits | | Waiting Period | Rehabilitation Statutes | Death Benefits |
	Wks	Maximum			
1. 66⅔% 2. $30, schedule 3. $217 to 100% of a.w.w. (non-schedule) 4. Duration	1. 312 2. 244 3. 312 4. 205 5. 160 6. 60	$14,040 10,980 14,040 9,225 7,200 2,700	3 days; temporary total only; retroactive if disability over 2 wks.	Curative center is open to help injured workers	1. 66⅔% 2. 66⅔% 3. — 4. $217 to 100% of a.w.w. (+ $6 for each dependent) 5. Widowhood;[15] children until 18[5]
1. 66⅔% 2. $25, (schedule; no statutory minimum for non-schedule) 3. $216 to 100% of a.w.w. 4. 340 wks. up to $40,000	1. 220 2. 165 3. 195 4. 140 5. 110 6. 80	$47,520 35,640 42,120 30,240 23,760 17,280	7 days; retroactive after 14 days	Disabled employees may receive vocational rehab. from State Vocational Rehab. Dept.	1. 66⅔% 2. 66⅔% 3. $25 4. $216 to 100% of a.w.w. 5. 500 wks.; children until 18[5]
1. 66⅔%, schedule; 50%, non-schedule 2. $96 to ½ of maximum a.w.w. (no statutory minimum for non-schedule) 3. $126 to 94% of s.a.w.w. 4. During disability	1. 200 2. 150 3. 160 4. 125 5. 150 6. 50	$38,200 28,650 30,560 23,875 28,650 9,550	7 days; retroactive after 7 days disability	Employees entitled to additional compensation based on percentage of s.a.w.w.	1. 66⅔% 2. 66⅔% 3. $96 or average wage if less 4. $191 + $50 mo. per child 5. Widowhood;[15] children until 18[5]

	Occupational Diseases	Agricultural Workers	Domestic Workers	Permanent Total Benefits
TENNESSEE Director Workmen's Compensation Dept. of Labor 501 Union Bldg. Nashville 37219 1(615)741-2395	1. Yes 2. No 3. Full 4. None 5. Black lung	Not covered	Not covered	1. 66⅔% 2. $15 3. $126 4. 550 wks., but after 400 wks. max. reduced to $15
TEXAS Chairman Industrial Accident Board Box 12757, Capitol Station Austin 78711 1(512)475-3126	1. Yes 2. Yes 3. Full 4. None 5. None	No coverage	No coverage	1. 66⅔% 2. $25 3. $154 4. 401 wks.
UTAH Workmen's Compensation Industrial Commission 350 E. 500th S. Salt Lake 84111 1(801)533-6411	1. No 2. Yes 3. Full 4. Various provisions (see statute) 5. Black lung	All except certain employees who made less than $2,500 and certain others	Covered, if work 40 hrs. a wk. for some employer	1. 66⅔% 2. $45–$85 3. $218 to 85% of s.a.w.w. 4. 171 wks.; can be extended if unable to work

Permanent Partial Benefits	Wks	Schedule Benefits Maximum	Waiting Period	Rehabilitation Statutes	Death Benefits
1. 66⅔% 2. $15 3. $119 4. 400 wks., max. of $40,000	1. 200 2. 150 3. 200 4. 125 5. 100 6. —	$25,200 18,900 25,200 15,750 12,600 —	7 days; retroactive after 14 days disability	Commission of Insurance is authorized to refer people to State Dept. of Education	1. 50% 2. 66⅔% 3. $15 4. $26 5. Widowhood;[20] children until 18[5]
1. 66⅔% 2. $25, schedule 3. $133 4. 300 wks.	1. 200 2. 150 3. 200 4. 125 5. 100 6. —	$26,600 19,950 26,600 16,625 13,300 —	7 days; retroactive after 14 days	Industrial Accident Board can authorize rehab. for vocational training	1. 66⅔% 2. 66⅔% 3. $25 4. $133 5. Widowhood; children until 18[5]
1. 66⅔% 2. $45–$70 (not more than a.w.w.) 3. $171 to 66⅔% of s.a.w.w. 4. 312 wks.	1. 187 2. 168 3. 125 4. 88 5. 120 6. —	$31,977 28,728 21,375 15,048 20,520 —	3 days; temporary total only; retroactive after 14 days disability	Max. $1,000 for certain disabilities; if no rehab. possible, 85% of s.a.w.w. for life	1. 66⅔% 2. 66⅔% 3. $45–$70 4. $218 to 85% of s.a.w.w. 5. 312 wks.[21]

	Occupational Diseases	Agricultural Workers	Domestic Workers	Permanent Total Benefits
VERMONT Commissioner Dept. of Labor & Industry State Office Bldg. Montpelier 05602 1(802)828-2286	1. No 2. Yes 3. Full 4. Disablement, 5 yrs.; death, 12 yrs. 5. Policemen & firemen (heart)	All, unless employer payroll less than $2,000	No coverage	1. 66⅔% 2. $113 to 50% of s.a.w.w. 3. $225 to 100% of s.a.w.w. (+ $5 for each dependent under 21) 4. 330 wks.
VIRGINIA Chairman Industrial Commission Blanton Bldg. P.O Box 1794 Richmond 23214 1(804)786-3642	1. No 2. Yes 3. Full 4. Pneumoconiosis, 90 work shifts 5. Black lung	Covered, if employer has $15,500 payroll or employs 4 full-time workers	No coverage	1. 66⅔% 2. $57.75 to 25% of s.a.w.w. or e.a.w.w. if less 3. $231 to 100% of s.a.w.w. 4. Duration
WASHINGTON Director Dept. of Labor & Industry General Administration Bldg. Olympia 98504 1(206)753-6341	1. No 2. No 3. Full 4. None 5. None	Covered unless employee earns less than $150 per calendar year	Covered, if regularly employed for over 40 hrs. a wk.	1. 60%– 75% 2. $46.69– $81.23 3. $223.34 to 75% of s.a.w.w. 4. Duration

Permanent Partial Benefits	Wks	Schedule Benefits Maximum	Waiting Period	Rehabilitation Statutes	Death Benefits
1. 66⅔% 2. $113 to 50% of s.a.w.w. 3. $225 to 100% of s.a.w.w. 4. 300 wks.	1. 215 2. 175 3. 215 4. 175 5. 125 6. 52	$48,375 39,375 48,375 39,375 28,125 11,700	3 days; temporary total only; retroactive after 7 days	Rehab. good for 1 yr.; employer pays for room & board, travel, books, etc.	1. 66⅔% 2. 76⅔% 3. $113 to 50% of s.a.w.w. 4. $225 to 100% of s.a.w.w. 5. Widowhood; children until 18[5]
1. 66⅔% 2. $57.75 to 25% of s.a.w.w. or e.a.w.w. if less 3. $213 to 100% of s.a.w.w. 4. 500 wks.	1. 200 2. 150 3. 175 4. 125 5. 100 6. 50	$46,200 34,650 40,425 28,875 23,100 11,550	7 days; retroactive if disability over 3 wks.	All reasonable and necessary rehab. services (paid for by the employer)	1. 66⅔% 2. 66⅔% 3. $57.75 to 25% of s.a.w.w. or employee's wage if less 4. $231 to 100% of s.a.w.w. 5. Widowhood; children until 18[5]
None	Fixed Sums	$36,000 32,400 36,000 25,200 14,400 4,800	3 days; retroactive after 14 days	Supervisor of Industrial Insurance can authorize program of vocational rehab. for 52 wks.	1. 60% 2. 70% 3. $42.60– $74.31 4. $223.34 to 75% of s.a.w.w. 5. Widowhood; children until 18[5]

	Occupational Diseases	Agricultural Workers	Domestic Workers	Permanent Total Benefits
WEST VIRGINIA Workmen's Compensation Fund 112 California Ave. Charleston 25305 1(304)348-2580	1. Yes 2. Yes 3. Full 4. Pneumoconiosis, 2 continuous yrs. 5. Pneumoconiosis, exposure 10 of previous 15 yrs.	Covered if employer has 6 or more employees	Not covered	1. 70% 2. $92.02 to 33⅓% of s.a.w.w. 3. $276.26 to 100% of s.a.w.w. 4. Life
WISCONSIN Administrator Workmen's Compensation Div. Dept. of Industry, Labor, & Human Relations 201 E. Washington Ave. P.O. Box 7901 Madison 53701 1(608)266-1340	1. Yes 2. No 3. Full 4. Silicosis, must be exposed at least 90 days 5. None	Covered, if at least 6 employees for 20 or more days	Not covered	1. 66⅔% 2. $20 3. $269 to 100% of s.a.w.w. 4. Life
WYOMING Director Workmen's Compensation Dept. 2305 Carey Ave. Cheyenne 82002 1(307)777-7441	1. Yes 2. Yes 3. Full 4. None 5. None	Covered, if engaged in property farming for 6 mos.	Not covered	1. 2. No minimum 3. $274.15 to 66⅔% of s.a.w.w. 4. Duration, up to $30,000

| Permanent Partial Benefits | Schedule Benefits | | Waiting Period | Rehabilitation Statutes | Death Benefits |
	Wks	Maximum			
1. 70% 2. $92.09 to 33% of s.a.w.w. 3. $184.17 to 66⅔% of s.a.w.w. 4. 336 wks.	Varies with extent of injury		3 days; retroactive after 17 days	Max. $10,000 may be granted for physical & vocational rehab.	1. 70% 2. 70% 3. $92.09 to 33⅓% of s.a.w.w. 4. $276.26 to 100% of s.a.w.w. 5. Widowhood; children until 18[5]
1. 66⅔% 2. $20 3. $90 4. 1,000 wks.	1. 500 2. 400 3. 500 4. 250 5. 275 6. 55	$35,000 28,000 35,000 17,500 19,250 3,850	3 days; retroactive after 7 days	40 wks. maintenance plus traveling costs	1. 66⅔% 2. $20 3. No minimum 4. $269 to 100% of s.a.w.w. 5. 300 wks. (can be extended)
1. 2. 3. $268.02 to 66⅔% of a.w.w. 4. In proportion to scheduled injuries	1. 150 2. 122 3. 135 4. 100 5. 94 6. 40	$40,203 32,698 36,183 26,802 25,194 10,721	3 days; temporary total disability only; retroactive after 8 days	No specific provisions, but artificial devices and treatment are provided	1. 2. 3. No minimum 4. $268.02 to 66⅔% of a.w.w. 5. 231 wks.

Occupational diseases:

1. Occupational diseases included in definition of personal injury in order to allow recovery of workmen's compensation?

2. Ordinary diseases of life excluded?

3. Occupational disease gets full coverage, or excludes diseases not "peculiar to trade," etc.?

4. Time from job exposure to date of illness?

5. Presumptions of types of illness?

Permanent total benefits:

1. Maximum percentage of employee's wages.

2. Minimum payments per week.

3. Maximum payments per week.

4. Maximum period of time.

Permanent partial benefits:

1. Maximum percentage of employee's wages or wage loss.

2. Minimum payments per week.

3. Maximum payments per week.

4. Maximum period for non-scheduled injuries.

Scheduled benefits:

1. Arm.

2. Hand.

3. Leg.

4. Foot.

5. Eye.

6. Ear.

Death benefits:

1. Maximum percentage of employee's wages for spouse only.

2. Maximum percentage of employee's wages for spouse plus children.

3. Minimum payments per week.

4. Maximum payments per week.

5. Maximum period of time for spouse or for children.

A.w.w. = average weekly wage. N.a.w.w. = national average weekly wage. S.a.w.w. = state average weekly wage.

1. Three years for silicosis, asbestosis; radiation, none. For death following continuous disability for which compensation has been paid or awarded, death must occur within 7 years after last exposure.

2. In the absence of evidence, silicosis or asbestosis presumed not to be from occupation unless during 10-year period. Exposed to dust 5 years, of which 2 years in state.

3. According to number of dependents: $10 for each dependent child under 18.

4. May be continued beyond

352

age 18 if physically or mentally incapable of support. In addition payments may be continued up until age 25 for full-time students.

5. If child is a student, can receive benefits until he or she is 23.

6. Disablement or death from an occupational disease treated as an accidental injury.

7. Except those performing agricultural labor on a farm in the employ of a bona fide farmer or association of farmers, employing 5 or 10 regular employees at one time for seasonal employment in less than 30 days, provided such seasonal employment does not exceed 45 days in the same calendar year.

8. Can be extended to 22 if child is a full-time student.

9. In proportion to scheduled injuries; in other words, it varies.

10. Death or disablement must result within 4 years in case of silicosis or 1 year in case of other occupational diseases after last exposure.

11. Can be extended until 25 if child is a full-time student.

12. In absence of conclusive evidence, disability or death from pneumoconiosis

shall be presumed not to be due to the occupation unless during the 10-year period preceding disablement the employee had been exposed to 5 years of dust particles of which 2 had been in this state.

13. Based on employee's gross weekly wage.

14. Maximum wages determined by employee's gross wages.

15. Lump sum of 2 years' benefits payable upon remarriage.

16. Benefits continue for widows.

17. There will be a deduction from death benefits to widow for any money she earns after 450 weeks.

18. Benefits payable only if widow was living with or dependent on decedent.

19. Can elect plan A, 66 2/3% of earning capacity, maximum of 100% of s.a.w.w. not to exceed $12,500; or plan B, based on permanent disability, maximum of 200 weeks of disability to 90% and at 56 or 66 2/3% of e.a.w.w.

20. Only if incapable of self-support or dependent.

21. Upon remarriage, a lump sum of 52 weeks or remainder of award, whichever is first. Also after 312 weeks compensation can be extended if there is dependency.

Appendix 8
(to Chapter 18)
Administration on Aging:
Regional Offices

Region I
(CT, ME, MA, NH, RI, VT)
J. F. Kennedy Federal Bldg.
Government Center, Rm. 2007
Boston, MA 02203
  (617) 223–6885

Region II
(NJ, NY, PR, VI)
26 Federal Plaza, Rm. 4106
Broadway and Lafayette Sts.
New York City, NY 10007
  (212) 264–4952, 4513

Region III
(DE, DC, MD, PA, VA, WV)
P.O. Box 13716
3535 Market St. 5th fl.
Philadelphia, PA 19101
  (215) 596–6891

Region IV
(AL, FL, GA, KY, MS, NC,
  SC, TN)
50 7th St., NE
  Rm. 326
Atlanta, GA 30323
  (404) 526–2042

Region V
(IL, IN, MI, MN, OH, WI)
300 S. Wacker Dr., 15th fl.
Chicago, IL 60606
  (312) 353–4904

Region VI
(AR, LA, NM, OK, TX)
Fidelity Union Tower Bldg.
  Room 500
1507 Pacific Ave.
Dallas, TX 75201
  (214) 749–7286

Region VII
(IA, KS, MO, NE)
610 E. 12th St.
Kansas City, MO 64106
  (816) 374–2955

Region VIII
(CO, MT, ND, SD, UT, WY)
Federal Office Bldg.
19th and Stout Sts.
  7th fl.
Denver, CO 80202
  (303) 837–2951

Region IX
(AZ, CA, HI, NV, AS, GU, TT)
50 UN Plaza, Rm. 206
San Francisco, CA 94102
  (415) 556–6003

Region X
(AK, ID, OR, WA)
Arcade Plaza Bldg. 622
1321 2d Ave.
Seattle, WA 98101
  (206) 442–5341

Appendix 9
(to Chapter 18)
Evidence to Be Submitted by
Social Security Claimants

	Age	Marriage	Divorce	Parent-child	Dependency or support	School attendance	Child in care	Death of worker
Insured person	X							
Spouse (62 or over)	X	X						
Spouse under 62 (with child in care)	X			X			X	
Divorced Spouse (62 or over)	X	X	X					
Child	X			X	X	X		X (survivor claims)
Surviving spouse (60 or over, 50 or over if disabled)	X	X						X
Surviving divorced spouse (60 or over, 50 or over if disabled)	X	X	X					X
Surviving spouse or surviving divorced spouse under 60 (with child in care)		X	X	X			X	X
Parent	X			X	X			X
Surviving spouse (lump sum)	X							X
Equitably entitled person (lump sum)								X
Funeral home (lump sum)								X

Appendix 10
(to Chapter 19)
Significant Provisions of State Unemployment Insurance Laws (January 2, 1983)

U.S. Department of Labor, Employment and Training Administration, Unemployment Insurance Service

Prepared for ready reference; consult the state law and state employment security agency for authoritative information.

State	Qualifying wage or employment (number × wba or as indicated)[1]	Waiting weeks[2]	Computation of wba (fraction of high-quarter wages (hqw) or as indicated)[1,3]	Weekly benefits allowed (wba) for total unemployment[4]	
				Min.	Max.
AL	1-1/2 × hqw; ≤ $522.01	0	1/24	$15	$90
AK	$1000; wages in 2 quarters	1	3.4-1.0% of annual wages + $24 per dependent (dep.) up to $72	34-58	156-228
AZ	1-1/2 × hqw; $1000 in HQ	1	1/25	40	115
AR	(30 × hqw) ÷ 26; wages in 2 quarters	1	1/26 up to 66-2/3% of state aww[14]	31	136
CA	8 wks. employment at $20 + BP wages of $900 or total BP wages of $1200	1	1/24-1/33	30	166
CO	40	1	60% of 1/13 of claimant's hqw up to 50% of state aww	25	190
CT	40	0	1/26, up to 60% of state aww + $10 per dep. up to 1/2 wba	15-22	156-206
DE	36	0	1/104, up to 66-2/3% of state aww[14]	20	150
DC	1-1/2 × hqw; ≤ $450; $300 in 1 quarter	1	1/23 up to 66-2/3% of state aww + $1 per dep. up to $3	13-14	206[4]
FL	20 wks. employment at average of $20 or more	1	1/2 claimant's aww	10	125
GA	1-1/2 × hqw	1[2]	1/25 + $1	27	115
HI	30; 14 wks. employment	1	1/25 up to 66-2/3% of state aww	5	178

Earnings disregarded[5]	Proportion of base period wages[6]	Benefit weeks for total unemployment[7]		Size of firm (1 worker in specified time and/or size of payroll)[16]	1982 rates (% of wages)[9]	
		Min.[8]	Max.		Min.	Max.
$6	1/3	11+	26	20 wks.	0.5[9]	4.0[9]
3/4 wages over $50	Weighted schedule of bpw in relation to hqw	16	26	Any time	1.0[9]	4.86[9]
$15	1/3	12+	26	20 wks.	0.10	2.90
2/5	1/3	10	26	10 days	0.7[9]	6.1[9]
Lesser of $25 and 25% of wages	1/2	12+ to 15[7]	26[7]	over $100 in any quarter	0.9[9]	4.2
1/4 wba	1/3	7+ to 13	26	13 wks. or $500 in CQ	0.0	4.5
1/3 wages	Uniform	26[7]	26[7]	20 wks.	1.5[9]	6.0[9]
Greater of $10 or 30% of wba	1/2	18	26	20 wks.	1.6[9]	8.5[9]
1/5 wages	1/2	17+	34	Any time	1.0[9]	5.4[9]
$5	1/2 wks. employment	10	26	20 wks.	0.1	4.5
$8	1/4	4	26	20 wks.	0.06	5.38
$2	Uniform	26[7]	26[7]	Any time	0.6[9]	4.5[9]

State	Qualifying wage or employment (number × wba or as indicated)[1]	Waiting weeks[2]	Computation of wba (fraction of high-quarter wages (hqw) or as indicated)[1,3]	Weekly benefits allowed (wba) for total unemployment[4]	
				Min.	Max.
ID	1-1/4 × hqw; ≤ $910.01 in 1 quarter; wages in 2 quarters	1	1/26 up to 60% of state aww	36	159
IL	$1600; $440 outside HQ	1	1/2 claimant aww up to 50% of state aww[13]	51	168-224
IN	1-1/4 × hqw; ≤ $1500; $900 in last 2 quarters	1	4.3% of hqw credits[3]	40	84-141
IA	1-1/4 × hqw; $200 in qtr other than HQ	0	[3,13]	17-21	158-190
KS	30; wages in 2 quarters	1	4.25% of hqw up to 60% of state aww	40	163
KY	1-1/2 × hqw; 8 × wba in last 2 quarters; $750 in 1 quarter and $750 in other quarters	0	1.185% of BP wages up to 55% of state aww	22	140
LA	30	1[10]	1/20-1/25[14]	10	205
ME	(2 × annual aww in each of 2 qtrs.) + (7 × annual aww in BP)	1	1/22 up to 52% of state aww +$5 per dep. to 1/2 wba	22-27	124-186
MD	1-1/2 × hqw; $576.01 in 1 quarter; wages in 2 quarters	0	1/24 + $3 per dep. up to $12	25-28	153[4]
MA	30; ≤ $1200	1	1/19-1/26 up to 57.5% of state aww + $6 per dep. up to 1/2 wba[3]	12-18 14-21	156-234 172-258

Earnings disregarded[5]	Proportion of base period wages[6]	Benefit weeks for total unemployment[7] Min.[8]	Max.	COVERAGE Size of firm (1 worker in specified time and/or size of payroll)[16]	TAXES 1982 rates (% of wages)[9] Min.	Max.
1/2 wba	Weighted schedule of bpw in relation to hqw	10[7]	26[7]	20 wks. or $300 in any quarter	0.9[9]	4.0[9]
1/2 wba	Uniform	26	26	20 wks.	0.6[9]	5.7[9]
20% of wba from other than BP employer	1/4	9+	26	20 wks.	0.3	3.0
1/4 wba	1/3	15	26	20 wks.	0.0[9]	6.0[9]
$8	1/3	10	26	20 wks.	0.06	4.30
1/5 wages	1/3	22	26	20 wks.	1.0[9]	10.0[9]
1/2 wba	2/5	12	28	20 wks.	0.10	3.39
$10	1/3	7+ to 22	26	20 wks.	2.4	5.0
$10	Uniform	26[7]	26[7]	Any time	0.1	5.0
40% (not less than $10 nor more than $30)	36%	9+ to 30	30	13 wks.	2.9	6.7

State	Qualifying wage or employment (number × wba or as indicated)[1]	Waiting weeks[2]	Computation of wba (fraction of high-quarter wages (hqw) or as indicated)[1,3]	Weekly benefits allowed (wba) for total unemployment[4]	
				Min.	Max.
MI	18 wks. employment at 20 × state min. hourly wage	0	70% of claimant's after-tax earnings up to a maximum of 58% of state aww.	41-44[4]	197
MN	15 wks employment at $30 or more	1[10]	[13]	30	191
MS	40; $480 in 1 quarter; wages in 2 quarters	1	1/26	30	105
MO	30 × wba; $300 in 1 quarter; wages in 2 quarters	1[10]	4.5%	15	105
MT	20 wks. employment at $50 or more	1	1/2 wks. of claimant's a.w.w. up to 60% of state a.w.w.	39	158
NE	$600; $200 in each of 2 quarters	1	1/17-1/24	12	106
NV	1-1/2 × hqw	0	1/25, up to 50% of state aww	16	149
NH	$1700; $800 in each of 2 quarters	0	1.8-1.2% of annual wages	26	132
NJ	20 wks. employment at $30 or more; or $2200	1[10]	66-2/3% of claimant's aww up to 50% of state aww	20	158
NM	1-1/4 × hqw	1	1/26; not less than 10% nor more than 50% of state aww	29	142
NY	20 wks. employment at average of $40 or more[11]	1[12]	67-50% of claimant's aww	25	125
NC	1-1/2 × hqw; ≤ 6 × state aww	1	1/26 up to 66-2/3% of state aww	15	166

| | Duration in 52-week period | | | COVERAGE | TAXES | |
| Earnings disregarded[5] | Proportion of base period wages[6] | Benefit weeks for total unemployment[7] | | Size of firm (1 worker in specified time and/or size of payroll)[16] | 1982 rates (% of wages)[9] | |
		Min.[8]	Max.		Min.	Max.
Up to 1/2 wba[5]	3/4 wks. employment	13+	26	20 wks. or $1000 in CY	1.0	9.0
$25	7/10 wks. employment	11	26	20 wks.	1.0[9]	7.5[9]
$5	1/3	13+	26	20 wks.	2.4	4.0
$10	1/3	10+	26	20 wks.	0.8[9]	5.2[9]
1/2 wages in excess of 1/4 wba	Weighted schedule of bpw in relation to hqw	8	26	Over $500 in current or preceding yr.	1.5[9]	4.4[9]
1/2 wba	1/3	17	26	20 wks.	0.1	3.7
1/4 wages	1/3	11	26	$225 in any quarter	0.3[9]	3.6[9]
1/5 wba	Uniform	26	26	20 wks.	0.05	6.5
Greater of $5 or 1/5 wba	3/4 wks. employment	15	26	$1000 in any yr.	1.2[9]	6.2[9]
1/5 wba	3/5	19	26	20 wks. or $450 in any quarter	0.6[9]	4.0[9]
[12]	Uniform	26	26	$300 in any quarter	1.5	5.2
10% aww in HQ	1/3 bpw	13	26	20 wks.	0.1	5.7

State	Qualifying wage or employment (number × wba or as indicated)[1]	Waiting weeks[2]	Computation of wba (fraction of high-quarter wages (hqw) or as indicated)[1,3]	Weekly benefits allowed (wba) for total unemployment[4]	
				Min.	Max.
ND	40 × min. wba; wages in 2 quarters	1	1/26 up to 67% of state aww	47	175
OH	20 wks. employment at $20 or more	1[10]	1/2 claimant's aww + d.a. of $1-92 based on claimant's aww and number of deps. [3,17]	10	158-250
OK	1-1/2 × hqw; ≤ $1000 in BP; $7000	1	1/25 up to 66-2/3% of state aww	16	197
OR	18 wks.; < $1000 in BP	1	1.25% of bpw up to 60% of state aww	44	175
PA	37+ to 40; $800 in HQ and $1320 in BP; at least 20% of bpw outside HQ	1[10]	1/23-1/25 up to 66-2/3% of state aww + $5 for 1 dep.; $3 for 2d	$35-40	205-213
PR	40 × wba ≤ $280; $75 in 1 quarter; wages in 2 quarters	1	1/11-1/26; up to 50% of state aww	7	84
RI	20 wks. employment at $67 or more; or $4020	1	55% of claimant's aww up to 60% of state aww, + $5 per dep. up to $20	37-42	154-174
SC	1-1/2 × hqw; ≤ $900; $540 in 1 quarter	1	1/26 up to 66-2/3% of state aww	21	118
SD	$728 in HQ; 30 × wba outside HQ	1	1/26 up to 62% of state aww	28	129
TN	40; $494.01 in 1 quarter	1	1/25-1/31	20	110

Earnings disregarded[5]	Proportion of base period wages[6]	Benefit weeks for total unemployment[7] Min.[8]	Max.	Size of firm (1 worker in specified time and/or size of payroll)[16]	1982 rates (% of wages)[9] Min.	Max.
1/2 wba	Weighted schedule of bpw in relation to hqw	12	26	20 wks.	0.5[9]	5.0[9]
1/5 wba	20 × wba + wba for each credit wk. in excess of 20	20	26	20 wks.	1.1	4.8
$7	1/3	20+	26	20 wks.	0.1	3.1
1/3 wba	1/3	8+[7]	26[7]	18 wks. or $225 in any quarter	2.0[9]	3.8[9]
Greater of $6 or 40% wba	At least 18 credit wks. for min., 24 for max.	26	30	Any time	2.5[9]	6.6[9]
wba	Uniform	20[7]	20[7]	Any time	2.95[9]	2.95[9]
$5	3/5 wks. employment	12	26	Any time	2.8[9]	6.0[9]
1/4 wba	1/3	14	26	20 wks.	1.3	4.10
1/4 wages up to 1/2 wba	1/3	18+	26	20 wks.	0.2	7.7
$30	1/3	13	26	20 wks.	0.65	7.0

State	Qualifying wage or employment (number × wba or as indicated)[1]	Waiting weeks[2]	Computation of wba (fraction of high-quarter wages (hqw) or as indicated)[1,3]	Weekly benefits allowed (wba) for total unemployment[4]	
				Min.	Max.
TX	1-1/2 × hqw; ≤ $500 or 2/3 FICA tax base	1[10]	1/25[17]	27	168
UT	20 wks. employment at $50 or more; ≤ $1,200	1	1/26 up to 65% of state aww	10	166
VT	20 wks. employment at $35 or more	1	1/2 claimant's aww for highest 20 weeks up to 60% of state aww	18	146
VA	50; wages in 2 quarters	0	1/25	44	138
VI	26+ to 30; ≤ $99 in 1 quarter and wages in 2 quarters	1	1/23-1/25	15	124
WA	680 hrs.	1	1/25 of average of 2 hqw up to 55% of state aww	49	178
WV	$1150 and wages in 2 quarters	1	1.5-1.0% of annual wages up to 70% of state aww	18	211
WI	15 wks. employment; average of $70.01 or more with 1 employer	0	50% of claimant's aww up to 66-2/3% of state aww	37	196
WY	1-6/10 × hqw; ≤ $600 in 1 quarter	1	1/25 up to 55% of state aww	24	180

		COVERAGE		TAXES	
	Duration in 52-week period				
Earnings disregarded[5]	Proportion of base period wages[6]	Benefit weeks for total unemployment[7]		Size of firm (1 worker in specified time and/or size of payroll)[16]	1982 rates (% of wages)[9]	
		Min.[8]	Max.		Min.	Max.
Greater of $5 or 1/4 wba	27%	14 +	26	20 wks.	0.1	4.0
3/10 wba than regular employer	Weighted schedule of bpw in relation to hqw	10-22	26	$140 in CQ in current or preceding CY	1.3[9]	2.8[9]
$15 + $3 for each dep. up to 5	Uniform	26	26	20 wks.	1.7	6.0
Greater of 1/3 wba or $10	1/3	12	26	20 wks.	0.8	6.9
1/4 wages in excess of $5	Uniform	26	26	Any time	3.7[9]	3.7[9]
$5 + 1/4 wages	1/3	16 + to 30[7]	30[7]	Any time	3.0[9]	3.0[9]
$25	Uniform	28	28	20 wks.	2.5[9]	8.5[9]
Up to 1/2 wba[5]	8/10 wks. employment	1-12 +	34	20 wks.	0.5	7.4
Greater of $15 or 25% wba	3/10	12-26	26	$500 in current or preceding CY	0.38	3.08

[1]Weekly benefit amount abbreviated in columns and footnotes as wba; base period, BP: base-period wages, bpw; high quarter, HQ; high-quarter wages, hqw; average weekly wage, aww; benefit year, BY; calendar quarter, CQ: calendar year, CY; dependent, dep.; dependents allowances, da.; minimum, min.; maximum, max.

[2]Unless otherwise noted, waiting period same for total or partial unemployment. Waiting period may be suspended if Governor declares State of emergency following disaster, *N.Y.* In *Ga.* no waiting week if claimant unemployed not through own fault.

[3]When States use weighted high-quarter, annual-wage, or average weekly-wage formula, approximate fractions or percentages figured at midpoint of lowest and highest normal wage brackets. When da provided, fraction applies to basic wba. In States noted variable amounts above max. basic benefits limited to claimants with specified number of dep. and earnings in excess of amounts applicable to max. basic wba. In *Ind.* da. paid only to claimants with earnings in excess of that needed to qualify for basic wba and who have 1-4 deps. In *Iowa, Mich.* and *Ohio* claimants may be eligible for augmented amount at all benefit levels but benefit amounts above basic max. available only to claimants in dependency classes whose hqw or aww are higher than that required for max. basic benefit.

In *Mass.* for claimant with aww in excess of $66 wba computed at 1/52 of 2 highest quarters of earnings or 1/26 of highest quarter if claimant had no more than 2 quarters work.

[4]When 2 amounts given, higher includes da. Higher for min. wba includes max. allowance for one dep.; *Mich.* higher amount if more than 1 dependent exemption allowed. In *D.C.* and *Md.*, same max. with or without dep.

[5]In computing wba for partial unemployment, in States noted full wba paid if earnings are less than 1/2 wba; 1/2 wba if earnings are 1/2 wba but less than wba.

[6]States noted have weighted schedule with percent of benefits based on bottom of lowest and highest wage brackets.

[7]Benefits extended under State program when unemployment in State reaches specified levels: *Calif., Hawaii,* by 50%; *Conn., Idaho* (until Dec. 31, 1982), *Md.* (until June 4, 1983), *Oreg.* (until Oct. 2, 1982), *Wash.* (until Feb. 26, 1983), by 13 weeks. In *P.R.* benefits extended by 32 weeks in certain industries, occupations or establishments when special unemployment situation exists. Benefits also may be extended during periods of high unemployment by 50%, up to 13 weeks, under Federal-State Extended Compensation Program.

[8]For claimants with min. qualifying wages and min. wba. When two amounts shown, range of duration applies to claimants with min. qualifying wages in BP; longer duration applies with min. wba; shorter duration applies with max. possible concentration of wages in HQ; therefore highest wba possible for such BP earnings. *Wis.* determines entitlement separately for each employer. Lower end of range applies to claimants with only 1 week of work at qualifying wage; upper end to claimants with 15 weeks or more of such wages.

[9]Represents min.-max. rates assigned employers in CY 1982. *Ala., Alaska, N.J.* require employee taxes. Contributions for 1982 required on wages up to $6,000 in all States except *Ala., Del., Mo.,* and *Pa.,* $6,600; *Ark.,* $6,900; *Conn.* and *Ill.* $7,000; *D.C.,* $7,500; *Ky., Mont., V.I.,* and *W. Va.,* $8,000; *N.J.,* $8,200; *Minn.,* $8,300; *N. Mex.,* $8,500; *R.I.,* $8,600; *Iowa,* $8,700; *N. Dak.* $9,240; *Nev.,* $9,300; *Wash.,* $10,800; *Oreg.,* $11,000; *Utah,* $12,000; *Hawaii,* $13,100; *Idaho,* $13,200; *Alaska,* $14,600; *P.R.,* all wages.

[10]Waiting period compensable if claimant unemployed at least 6 weeks and not disqualified, *La.;* after 9 consecutive weeks benefits paid, *Mo.;* when benefits are payable for third week following

waiting period, *N.J.;* after benefits paid 4 weeks, *Pa., Tex.,* after any 4 weeks in BY, *Minn.;* after 3d week of total unemployment, *Ohio.*

[11]Or 15 weeks in last year and 40 weeks in last 2 years of aww of $40 or more, *N.Y.*

[12]For *N.Y.,* waiting period is 4 effective days accumulated in 1-4 weeks; partial benefits 1/4 wba for each 1 to 3 effective days. Effective days: fourth and each subsequent day of total unemployment in week for which not more than $125 is paid.

[13]To 60% State aww if claimant has nonworking spouse; 66-2/3% if he had dep. child, *Ill.;* 1/19-1/23 up to 58% of State aww for claimants with dep., *Iowa.;* 60% of first $85, 40% of next $85, 50% of balance. Max. set at 66-2/3%, *Minn.*

[14]Up to 66-2/3% of State aww, *La.* 1/52 up to 66-2/3% and max. wba frozen until January 1984, *Ark.,* 63% until 1983, *Del.*

[16]$1,500 in any CQ in current or preceding CY unless otherwise specified.

[17]Max. amount adjusted annually: by same percentage increase as occurs in State aww (*Ohio*) by $7 for each $10 increase in average weekly wage of manufacturing production workers (*Texas*).

AMERICAN CIVIL LIBERTIES UNION HANDBOOKS